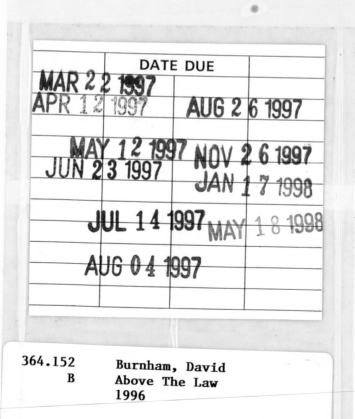

ALSO BY DAVID BURNHAM

A Law Unto Itself: Power, Politics and the IRS

The Rise of the Computer State

DAVID BURNHAM

ABOVE THE LAW

Secret Deals, Political Fixes and Other Misadventures of the U.S. Department of Justice

A LISA DREW BOOK

SCRIBNER *New York London Toronto Sydney Tokyo Singapore*

SCRIBNER
1230 Avenue of the Americas
New York, NY 10020

SCRIBNER and design are trademarks of Simon & Schuster Inc.

Designed by Jennifer Dossin

Manufactured in the United States of America

10 9 8 7 6 5 4 3 2 1

Library of Congress Cataloging-in-Publication Data
Burnham, David, date.
Above the law : secret deals, political fixes and other misadventures of the
U.S. Department of Justice / David Burnham.
p.   cm.
Includes bibliographical references and index.
1. United States. Dept. of Justice. 2. Misconduct in office—United States.
3. Political corruption—United States. I. Title.
KF5107.B87   1996   95-34544
364.1'32'0973—dc20   CIP

ISBN 0-684-80699-1

Acknowledgments

The debts accumulated in writing this book are enormous. It thus is a genuine pleasure to thank various individuals and institutions for their generous assistance.

Susan Long, a professor at the Syracuse University's School of Management, gave vast quantities of her wisdom, time and energy. David Banisar, a policy analyst at the Electronic Privacy Information Center, also was extraordinarily helpful, assisting in the search for literally hundreds of critically important documents with a seemingly endless supply of intelligence, enthusiasm and good cheer. In the early stages of my research, Rich Lucas pitched in with much invaluable research at the Library of Congress.

Large and small favors were granted by Linda Amster, *New York Times*; Judi Bari, environmentalist; Jerry Berman, Electronic Frontier Foundation; Mark Bohannon, Democratic National Committee; Stanley M. Brand, Washington attorney; Malcolm Byrne, National Security Archive; Julia Cass, coauthor of *Black in Selma*; Joseph Charney, assistant district attorney, Los Angeles County; J. L. Chestnut, civil rights lawyer, Selma, Alabama; Mae and Robert Churchill, friends, counselors, innkeepers and mad news clippers; Dayna Cunningham, lawyer, Legal Defense Fund, NAACP; Dennis Cunningham, San Francisco lawyer; Ira DeMent, former U.S. attorney in Montgomery, Alabama; James Dempsey, Subcommittee on Civil and Constitutional Rights, House Judiciary Subcommittee; Joan Deppa, journalism professor, Newhouse School of Public Communications, Syracuse University; Whitfield Diffie, Sun Microsystems; Lowell Dodge, Justice Department Division, GAO; Thomas Edsall, *Washington Post* reporter; John T. Elliff, Senate Intelligence Committee; Edward J. Epstein, writer; Mary Fricker, *Santa Rosa Press Democrat*; Arthur Gelb, New York Times Company Foundation; Ross Gelbspan, *Boston Globe*; Robert Gelman, Information Subcommittee, House Government Operations Committee; Bennett L. Gershman, Pace University Law School; Don Goldberg, House Government Operations Committee; Sharon Greene, chief Washington librarian for the American Bar Association; Wade Greene, Rockefeller Family Associates; Rockefeller Foundation's Bellagio Study and Research Center; Mary Stake Hawker, Deer Creek Foundation; Seymour Hersch, reporter; Philip B. Heymann, Harvard Law School; Richard Horne, lawyer in Mobile, Alabama; Janina Jarulzelski, Oversight Subcommittee, House Committee on Energy and Commerce; Arnold Kalman, Philadelphia attorney; Yale Kamisar, University of Michigan Law School; W. A. Kimbrough, Jr., former U.S. attorney, Mobile, Alabama; Joseph Krovisky, Justice Department; Kenneth C. Laudon, New York University; Katherine Leroy, Subcommittee on Civil and Constitutional Rights, House Judiciary Committee; Ted Leventhal, journalist; Michael Levine, former DEA agent; Miranda Maroney, administrator, Transactional Records Access Clearinghouse; David W. Marston, Philadelphia attorney; Morton Mintz, former reporter, *Washington Post*; Jim Mulvaney, *Newsday* reporter; Victor S. Navasky, editor; Peter Neumann, Stanford Research Institute; Otto G. Obermaier, U.S. attorney, Southern District of New York; Ron Ostrow, reporter, *Los Angeles Times*; Michael Rand, Bureau of Justice Statistics; Harold Relyea, Government Division, Congressional Research Service, Library of Congress; Mary Ronan, National Archives; Donald Ross, Rockefeller Family Fund; Marc Rotenberg, Electronic Privacy Information Center; David Rubin, dean of the Newhouse School of Public Communications, Syracuse University; Greg Rushford, *Legal Times*; Cathy Seddon, Information Subcommittee, House Government Operations Committee; Phil Shipman, Senate Judiciary Committee; William M. Simpich, San Francisco lawyer; Patrick Sloyan, *Newsday* reporter; David Sobel, Electronic Privacy Information Center; Peter Stockton, Oversight Subcommittee, House Committee on Energy and Commerce; Harry Subin, New York University Law School; Stuart Taylor, *Legal Times*; Athan Theoharis, Marquette University; Alice Travis, Democratic National Committee; Kent Walker, Justice Department; Barclay Walsh, *New York Times*; Ben Ware, vice chancellor, Syracuse University; Kendall Weaver, AP Bureau Chief, Montgomery, Alabama; Henry Weinstein, *Los Angeles Times*, federal court reporter; Neil J. Welch, retired FBI official; Glynn Wilson, Alabama freelance reporter.

Clarissa Wittenberg and Jim Lardner have generously extended their editorial talents, moral support and friendship to my efforts to understand the Justice Department and its place in American society. They have saved me from bad judgments, lack of clarity, gross errors and clumsy writing. They of course bear no responsibility for those occasions when I ignored their counsel.

From the very beginning, my editor, Lisa Drew, was a highly informed, thoughtful and enthusiastic supporter. As the researching and editing process went forward, she offered the guidance that is essential to such a sweeping project. As she has done in the past, Robin Straus, my close friend, mentor and agent, was insightful, helpful and supportive, even in my more grumpy periods. Jane Herman provided careful and consistent copyediting. Kate Boyle and Marysue Rucci shepherded me through the editing and production process with great skill and finesse.

My wife, Joanne Omang, who was working on her own book at the same time that I was struggling with mine, was her extraordinarily loving, unflappable, patient, brilliant and supportive self. To her, to my two dear daughters, Sarah and Molly, and to all the other helpers—named and unnamed—this book is dedicated.

Contents

ABOVE THE LAW

1

Law, Order and Politics: The Working of the United States Justice Department

W hen the Federal Bureau of Investigation (FBI) arrested four Arab immigrants for bombing New York's World Trade Center, the FBI agents acted in the name of their parent organization, the United States Justice Department.

When government antitrust lawyers filed suit against AT&T charging that America's most powerful monopoly was illegally retarding the development of a revolutionary new age in communications, they did so in the name of the United States Justice Department.

When the Drug Enforcement Administration (DEA) forcibly abducted deposed dictator Manuel Noriega from Panama to face federal drug trafficking charges in Florida after his capture by U.S. military units, the DEA agents acted under the name of their parent organization, the United States Justice Department.

When four hundred deputy U.S. marshals confronted a violent mob of Mississippians in an ultimately successful effort to carry out the court-ordered admission of James Meredith to the University of Mississippi, they did so as an arm of the United States Justice Department.

When the Immigration and Naturalization Service (INS) rounded up scores of illegal Chinese aliens after their freighter went aground on a beach near New York City, the INS agents acted in the name of their parent organization, the United States Justice Department.

When the solicitor general of the United States, in an appearance before the United States Supreme Court, argued that the nation's Constitution required congressional districts of substantially equal population, he did so as a senior official in the United States Justice Department.

When Al Capone was incarcerated in Alcatraz Prison, America's most notorious gangster experienced life in one of the toughest environments in the United States. The escape-proof prison, located on an island in San Francisco Bay, was operated by the Bureau of Prisons, an arm of the United States Justice Department.

When the nation became obsessed with communism immediately after World War II, the principal operator of the government's massive and freewheeling effort to discharge allegedly disloyal federal employees was the United States Justice Department.

When evidence emerged suggesting that the Defense Department's nuclear weapons facility near Denver was violating the nation's environmental laws, the U.S. attorney for Colorado became the lead player in directing the federal investigation of the corporation that managed the facility.

Thus, in an amazingly helter-skelter way, the Justice Department and its component parts—the solicitor general, the ninety-three U.S. attorneys, the FBI, the antitrust division, the DEA, the INS, the U.S. Marshals and the Bureau of Prisons—have become a significant force in almost every aspect of American life, directly and indirectly influencing the way we work, the way we communicate, the way we learn, the way we govern ourselves and even the way we play.

The broad impact of the Justice Department is not perceived or understood for several reasons. A powerful contrary notion—the idea that the department is just a small bunch of good guy cops going after a lot of bad guy criminals—has been fostered by a compliant media which for many years has lived off staged events, official press releases and the not-for-attribution whispers of ambitious prosecutors. A videotape sequence of agents smashing down the front door of a major cocaine dealer is the lifeblood of television, almost as addictive as the drug itself. A carefully leaked story that the FBI is investigating eight members of

Congress for corruption makes the front pages of three major New York and Philadelphia newspapers on the very same day.

The unquenchable thirst for good visuals, hot scoops and a simple story line means the media frequently miss or ignore the quiet but momentous events that often occupy the Justice Department. Of course the reporters and television cameras were present in Little Rock, Arkansas, when the 101st Airborne Division arrived to enforce the federal court order integrating the schools. But the long series of intense White House meetings between Attorney General Herbert Brownell, Jr., and President Dwight D. Eisenhower that led up to Ike's historic decision were largely ignored.[1] Nor did reporters pay a great deal of attention when Stuart M. Gerson, an assistant attorney general in the Bush administration, filed a forty-seven-page memorandum opposing the request that the federal court require the president to obtain a declaration of war from Congress before he ordered American troops to attack Iraqi forces in Kuwait.[2]

The pervasive ignorance about the Justice Department's underlying powers and day-to-day operations, however, cannot be blamed only on the media. Frequently, information about momentous actions and decisions of the Justice Department never sees the light of day because of the agency's strenuous and effective efforts to keep secret the darker aspects of its business.

On August 3, 1948, for example, apparently without informing anyone outside of the Justice Department and only a very few within, Attorney General J. Howard McGrath and FBI Director J. Edgar Hoover agreed upon a plan by which President Harry Truman could suspend many of the key safeguards of the Constitution. Under the top-secret agreement, code-named "Security Portfolio," the bureau was authorized, in the event of an ill-defined emergency, to summarily arrest up to 20,000 persons and place them in national security detention camps. A watch list of those who would be detained—along with detailed information about what they looked like, where they lived and their place of employment—was developed by the FBI. The decision as to who was placed on the watch list was left to the FBI and included many whose only crime was to openly criticize some aspect of American life. The McGrath-Hoover detention plan did not require the FBI to obtain individual arrest warrants and it would have denied detainees the right to appeal their arrest in federal court.[3]

Two years later, Congress approved the Internal Security Act of 1950, one section of which officially authorized an emergency detention program. The new legislation, however, presented the attorney general and FBI director with a problem. Because the program authorized by Congress did not suspend the Constitution—detainees, for example, could appeal their incarceration in federal court—it placed the department's secret detention program, which offered no such right, in violation of the law.

This incongruity worried Hoover, a canny bureaucrat who almost always sought and obtained higher approval for his questionable activities. For two years, while the FBI continued to secretly establish the detention camps and work out detailed seizure plans for thousands of individuals, Hoover kept badgering President Truman's attorney general for private relief. His request: McGrath's official permission for the FBI to ignore the 1950 law and carry on with the more ferocious 1948 program.[4]

On November 25, 1952, the attorney general, a heavy-drinking former chairman of the Democratic National Committee, caved in to Hoover. "Pursuant to the questions which you have raised in the latter memorandum, I wish to assure you that it is the Department's intention in the event of an emergency to proceed under the program as outlined in the Department's Portfolio invoking the standards now used," McGrath wrote in a brief note.[5]

This remarkable letter, in which the nation's senior law enforcement official formally advised the nation's top cop to go on breaking the law, remained secret for more than twenty years.

A second example of the Justice Department's considerable skill at hiding some of its important business from the public occurred about ten years later. At some point in the second half of 1961, Attorney General Robert F. Kennedy was told that, in the last years of the Eisenhower administration, the CIA had hired Sam Giancana, a senior member of the Mafia, to engage in certain "clandestine efforts," sometimes referred to as "dirty business," against Fidel Castro.

The subsequent Senate investigation into the Giancana affair, and several other American attempts to assassinate world leaders, found evidence that Kennedy, after being informed that the CIA had hired an organized crime boss to assassinate Castro, had complained about the agency's failure to consult him about the arrangement but did not seem to question its basic propriety. In addition, the committee was unable to find evidence that either Kennedy or Hoover, after learning about the plot, "ever inquired into the nature of the CIA operation" with Giancana, or that the attorney general instructed the CIA not to engage in assassination plots in the future. Considering Kennedy's intense public commitment to the federal government's all-out attack on organized crime, the attorney general's apparent lack of curiosity about the CIA-Giancana connection was surprising, perhaps even suggestive. The 1974 Senate investigation, however, further discovered that, between May 1961 and May 1962, Robert Kennedy attended a series of White House meetings that did in fact lead to the development of another "contingency plan in connection with the possible removal of Castro from the Cuban scene."[6]

After an extensive investigation of the meetings, the Senate committee said the records it had obtained did not make clear precisely how the officials who took part in these secret sessions were using the word "removal." From the context, however, the committee decided that the assassination of the Cuban leader may well have been the objective.

This conclusion is consistent with the committee's finding that several more efforts to assassinate Castro did in fact go forward during the Kennedy years. By a bizarre coincidence, for example, one of the last U.S. attempts to assassinate the Cuban leader occurred at about midday on November 22, 1963—the same hour and day that John F. Kennedy was gunned down in Dallas. During this particular effort against Castro, which was never consummated, a CIA officer gave a Cuban agent a CIA-designed poison-pen device that was to be used to murder the Cuban leader. Attorney General Kennedy's extensive, but finally murky, involvement in clandestine efforts to get rid of Castro remained secret for more than a decade.

On November 21, 1986, Attorney General Edwin Meese ordered a secret "inquiry" into the Reagan administration's sale of arms to Iran, which had just been revealed by a Lebanese newspaper. Three years later, during a related criminal trial, Meese acknowledged that, as a personal friend and political adviser to the president, the initial purpose of his 1986 probe was to head off a political firestorm that "could very well cause the possible toppling of the President himself."

"And your focus was really not the focus of an attorney general wearing the attorney general's hat but it was basically to try to gather information to protect the President as best you could and deal with this enormous political problem brewing in Congress, correct?" Meese was asked.

"Yes," he replied.[7]

To achieve the narrow goal of protecting his boss from an impeachment investigation by the House of Representatives, the chief law enforcement officer of the United States acted in a most unprofessional way. Instead of selecting seasoned criminal investigators or experts in the legal aspects of covert operations to make his emergency inquiry of the arms sales, Meese chose a small number of personal staff members and political appointees. In picking the members of this team, Meese rejected the formal request of the assistant attorney general in charge of the department's Criminal Division that the FBI be brought into the investigation.[8]

Meese also failed to immediately seal important files of the National Security Council (NSC) when his special team arrived at the White House. According to one critical analysis, this failure meant that many of the central documents in the case were altered or destroyed, "almost guaranteeing that we will never know the complete truth about what transpired." Further undermining the credibility of the investigation, the critics said, was the fact that Meese's team disregarded "standard investigative procedures such as taking notes in key interviews."[9]

By the time the disturbing defects of Meese's secret little "inquiry" became known, important parts of the record had disappeared and the Reagan administration, close to the end of its second term, was no longer in danger of disintegrating.

The power of the attorney general and the United States Justice Department to influence the lives of individual Americans and the course of American history in both open and secret ways is clear. This book is the story of the misuse of that power. It describes situations when—through political calculation, malice, incompetence or neglect—the official agents of this increasingly powerful institution have done harm.

One of the mysteries of modern life is why—while the people working within large organizations often try to do good—the systems they serve often do not. The answer to this apparent conundrum may be more obvious than it seems. Most individuals have an internal moral compass, an ethical guidance system that imposes on them responsibilities and obligations to family, friends and neighbors. By definition, however, large organizations do not have such a compass and seem to demand a blind loyalty that frequently works to subvert the idealism of their employees. As the world continues to create larger, more powerful and less accountable organizations, the task of nurturing the humanity of those who work for dominant organizations like the Justice Department may be one of the most difficult challenges of our age.

However, it is equally obvious that over the years, thousands of principled men and women have sought to exercise the powers of the Justice Department in idealistic and constructive ways to deter or incapacitate society's outlaws. Ruthless criminals have been sent to prison. Dangerous spies have been uncovered. Exploitative corporations have been forced to live by society's laws and regulations. Organized efforts designed to deny black Americans their right to vote have been dismantled. It is thus easy to identify countless individual examples in which the Justice Department has met, and even exceeded, the expectations of the American people. That story is an important one that any objective critic must affirm. This book examines the darker side.

WHO'S IN CHARGE HERE?

The grand pooh-bah of this incredible mélange of investigative, prosecutive, policy-making and advisory powers, at least according to the official organizational charts, is the attorney general of the United States. As I write, the position is held by a Harvard-trained Miami lawyer named Janet Reno. Like every one of the seventy-six men who preceded her, Reno was appointed by the president, confirmed by the Senate and serves as a member of the cabinet.

In many other ways, however, Attorney General Reno is an oddity. Unlike the men George Washington and Ronald Reagan selected as their first attorneys general, for example, Reno did not come to President Bill Clinton's attention because she had previously been his personal lawyer, the one responsible for protecting the family fortune. That, of course, was the most significant characteristic of Washington's Edmund Randolph and Reagan's William French Smith.

Reno also had never been the head of the Democratic Party in her state, the national chairman of her president's political party or her president's campaign manager, nor was she an obvious candidate for high elective office herself, all attributes of a surprisingly large number of attorneys general.

It was Levi Lincoln, a Massachusetts lawyer President Thomas Jefferson selected to be attorney general in 1801, who was the first out-and-out political leader to hold the job. Many others followed. President Woodrow Wilson's best-remembered attorney general, A. Mitchell Palmer, was an influential Pennsylvania Democrat, a former member of the Democratic National Committee, former senior member of the House of Representatives and a leading candidate to be the Democratic Party's next nominee for president at the time of his appointment. Warren Harding's attorney general, Harry M. Daugherty, arguably the biggest crook ever to hold the office, had been Harding's campaign manager before his appointment. Franklin Roosevelt's first attorney general, Homer S. Cummings, was a Connecticut politician who previously had headed the Democratic National Committee. Two of Truman's attorneys general, J. Howard McGrath and J. P. McGranery, were cut from the same cloth. Herbert Brownell, Jr., Eisenhower's first attorney general, was a New York politician who directed Dewey's two failed attempts to become president but hit the jackpot as Ike's de facto campaign manager. Robert Kennedy and John N. Mitchell were the campaign directors and senior political strategists for the men who appointed them, John Kennedy and Richard Nixon. The man Nixon chose as attorney general when Mitchell stepped down to direct Nixon's ill-fated second campaign was Richard G. Kleindienst. Kleindienst's achievements included a year or so as the 1968 director of field operations for Nixon's campaign committee and as the general counsel of the Republican National Committee and, before that, a stint with the presidential campaign organization of Barry Goldwater. Griffin B. Bell, an experienced corporate lawyer, was the chairman of JFK's campaign in

Georgia, a federal judge and a family friend before Jimmy Carter selected him to be attorney general. Edwin Meese III, Reagan's second attorney general, got his start in public life as a hard-charging local
prosecutor during the turbulent free speech disputes at the University
of California at Berkeley. He then became a leading conservative figure,
first as an assistant to Governor Reagan in Sacramento and then to
President Reagan in Washington.

It is hard to overstate the casually cynical way so many presidents
have gone about the job of selecting their attorneys general. One interesting example of how little presidential concern is generally invested
in assuring the quality of the person often called "the nation's number
one law enforcement officer" involved Franklin Roosevelt.

Shortly before New Year's Day of 1939, FDR asked Robert H. Jackson
to join him for lunch at the White House. Jackson, a distinguished and
competent lawyer then serving as the solicitor general, was the obvious
candidate to replace Homer Cummings, FDR's first attorney general,
who had recently announced his plans to retire after six years in office.

During the lunch, Jackson later recalled, Roosevelt told him that he truly
was the person he wanted to nominate as attorney general. "But here's my
problem. Frank Murphy has been beaten for governor of Michigan.
Frank hasn't got one nickel to rub against another. He's got to have a job
on the federal payroll. Having been governor of Michigan, and having been
in the Philippines as high commissioner, I can't offer him anything less
than a cabinet position. It's the only vacancy I've got. I don't think
Frank ought to be attorney general. It isn't his forte, but temporarily I don't
know of anything to do but appoint him and take care of him."[10]

Jackson later wrote that he told FDR he understood the president's
dilemma and would be willing to stay on as solicitor general. So, early
in 1940, Frank Murphy became attorney general, a position he held
until FDR found him another job about a year later, when Jackson took
on the overall command of the Justice Department.

In backhanded ways, even the Justice Department sometimes has
obliquely acknowledged the seedy character of several of its maximum
leaders. Consider, for example, the two long rows of portraits that hang
along the echoing hallway outside the spacious fifth-floor office of the
attorney general. These are the attorneys general of the United States.
A few faces, however, are missing in action. The mystery of their ab-
duction was solved a few years ago when an enterprising *Washington
Post* reporter noticed "The Hall of Shame," a short hallway located in a
seldom visited area on the building's seventh floor. Hanging there in
not-so-splendid obscurity were John Mitchell, Richard Kleindienst,
Harry Daugherty and Ramsey Clark. The first three, of course, were
perfectly understandable: They had all been charged with committing
criminal acts while in office.

But why Clark? Although he had indeed been viewed as an outspoken liberal while serving as Lyndon Johnson's attorney general, did the profoundly conservative civil servants of the Justice Department really think liberalism was a sufficiently serious offense to warrant Clark's exile? Maybe not. His crime, it seems, was an artistic one. Apparently, Clark had been banished to the seventh floor because of his decision to hire an artist who had painted his official portrait in a mildly unorthodox impressionistic style. (Edwin Meese, one of Ronald Reagan's more controversial attorneys general, had not been banished to the seventh floor despite his having been investigated by three special prosecutors and the conclusion of one of them that he had violated a number of criminal statutes.[11] Meese, it should be recalled, was never actually indicted.)

The involvement of so many attorneys general in the rough and tumble of national politics is not, by itself, improper. And the performance of distinguished attorneys general like Theodore Roosevelt's Charles J. Bonaparte, Franklin Roosevelt's Francis Biddle and Jerry Ford's Edward H. Levi proves that even with its built-in conflicts, the job can be handled in an honorable fashion. But the powerful intensity and nonstop nature of the political connections makes it reasonable to ask how frequently self-serving partisan considerations come into play at the Justice Department; the extent to which improper considerations have influenced law enforcement actions—who gets investigated and who gets charged—and the advice given to a succession of presidents on sensitive policy issues.

Given the fact that so many attorneys general actually have directed the political campaigns of the men who appointed them, it is hardly surprising that some enforcement actions are judged in political, sometimes partisan, terms. While such considerations are difficult to prove and almost always denied, concrete evidence of such calculations does exist. During an examination of Attorney General Robert Kennedy's Justice Department papers at the Kennedy Library in Boston, for example, I found copies of political polls conducted by Louis Harris, Oliver Quayle and several other pollsters in 1961, 1962 and 1963. One of the polls sought to assess the views of Democratic voters in Maryland, including how they felt about "Negro Opportunity in Maryland," "Negro Equality in U.S.," "President's Civil Rights Program" and the conflicting rights of property owners and Negroes in public accommodation disputes.

This particular poll, which Attorney General Kennedy probably had before him in late 1963 as he was making enforcement decisions regarding the nation's civil rights laws, carried an unsigned handwritten notation that Joseph Tydings—a liberal Maryland senator of the day—"is anxious to keep this confidential."[12]

A key point of representative democracy at the federal level, of course, is to make the government, including the Justice Department, responsive to the will of a majority of the voters that elected the president. It remains unsettling, however, to know that Kennedy—the chief law enforcement officer of the United States—was scanning the latest political polls while deciding how the department would handle various civil rights challenges. Was the attorney general making his decisions on the basis of his assessment of the legal issues or because the polls showed that 44 percent of the Democratic voters felt Negroes should be given a better opportunity to participate in American life; 37 percent said there should be no change; 12 percent were unsure and 7 percent said they should have less opportunity?

The concern about the extent to which improper political considerations manifest themselves within the Justice Department is reinforced by the curious fact that the department employs far more political appointees, in relation to its size, than do nine other major civilian agencies of the federal government. Considered together, for example, the agencies within the Justice Department have eleven times more political appointees at the managerial level than the Veterans Administration, four times more than Treasury and three times more than Health and Human Services.[13]

The relatively high-profile position of the politicos in the department does not fully demonstrate just how political the agency has been at various times in its history. Consider, for example, that up until the end of World War II every individual FBI agent served at the pleasure of J. Edgar Hoover. This meant that during the first years of the bureau agents who displeased the director for any reason at all were subject to summary dismissal. Such dismissals, of course, tended to reduce the likelihood of agency whistle-blowers challenging the bureau regarding its partisan or otherwise improper activities. While this unique power has been gradually reduced by such changes as the special rights granted to returning veterans, agents have always been subject to frequent transfers, some of them punitive in nature. To this day the considerable authority of the FBI contrasts with the situation at the IRS, where the tax agency's criminal investigators are represented by a union and enjoy normal civil service protections.

Yet another factor contributing to the blatantly partisan cast of many department decisions is the process by which U.S. attorneys—the senior federal law enforcement official in each of the ninety-three districts—get their jobs. According to the Constitution, U.S. attorneys are appointed by the president with the advice and consent of the Senate. In fact, as will be explored in greater detail in a later chapter, it is the other way around. Almost always, U.S. attorneys are selected by the senator or other senior elected official in each state who belongs to the party in control of the White House, and that candidate is then confirmed by the president. This means that the federal prosecutor in each district is usually more responsive to the focused political needs of the appointing senator than to the orders of the attorney general.

Americans, of course, like to believe that law enforcement decisions are made by television-land law enforcement professionals, not political operatives. Throughout the long history of the Justice Department, however, most U.S. attorneys and attorneys general have either been young lawyers who see these attention-gathering jobs as the perfect springboard to higher political office, or older men who are buddies of the president. Recent examples of the former are Rudolph Giuliani in New York, James Thompson in Illinois, William F. Weld in Massachusetts and Richard Thornburgh in Pennsylvania. When it comes to the challenging job of running the Justice Department, professional competence has seldom been a concern of either party.

THE MUSCLE OF THE FEDS

Apprehension about the arbitrary power of the government to prosecute its people is not new. More than seven hundred years ago, for example, under pressure from his barons, King John of England signed the Magna Carta, one of the key documents of constitutional history. "No free man shall be taken or imprisoned or dispossessed, or outlawed, or banished, or in any way destroyed, nor will we go upon him, nor send upon him, except by the legal judgement of his peers or by the law of the land." Paragraph 39 of the Magna Carta was the simple but far-reaching promise of the king to live by the law.

Such promises of even-handed justice, of course, are much easier to make than to keep, a point noted several centuries later by H. L. Mencken, the outspoken American writer, editor and scholar. "I marvel that no candidate for a doctorate has ever written a realistic history of the American Department of Justice, ironically so called. It has been engaged in sharp practices since the earliest days and remains a fecund source of oppression and corruption today. It is hard to recall an administration in which it was not the center of grave scandal."[14]

While Robert H. Jackson, FDR's third attorney general, was more cautious than Mencken in his judgment, he, too, saw that the prosecutor could be a source of mischief. In a frequently quoted, but still pertinent, talk to a group of Justice Department officials in 1940, Jackson outlined the dangers:

> The prosecutor has more control over life, liberty and reputation than any other person in America. He can have citi-

zens investigated and, if he is that kind of person, he can have this done to the tune of public statements and veiled or unveiled intimations. Or the prosecutor can choose a more subtle course and simply have a citizen's friends interviewed. The prosecutor can order arrests, present cases to the grand jury in secret session, and on the basis of his one-sided presentation of the facts, can cause the citizen to be indicted and held for trial. He may dismiss the case before trial, in which case the defense never has a chance to be heard. Or he may go on with a public trial. If he obtains a conviction, the prosecutor can still make recommendations as to sentence, as to whether the prisoner should get probation or a suspended sentence. . . .[15]

The final report of the Watergate special prosecutor on the abuses of federal powers leading to the resignation of President Richard Nixon also spoke about the inherent capacity for prosecutorial harm. "Although matters that reach the court obviously invoke court control over a prosecutor's public conduct," the report observed, "the discretionary process of initiating and conducting investigations bears great potential for hidden actions that are unfair, arbitrary, dishonest, or subjectively biased."[16]

Bennett L. Gershman is a contemporary student of prosecutorial power. From his current position as a professor at the Pace University School of Law in White Plains, New York, he has been studying prosecutors and their professional lapses for more than fifteen years. Before joining the academic world, Gershman was a full-time professional prosecutor, first in the office of Frank S. Hogan, the Manhattan district attorney, and then with Maurice Nadjari, a special state prosecutor appointed to combat corruption within the criminal justice system of New York City. "The prosecutor's power to institute criminal charges is the broadest and least regulated power in American criminal law," Gershman said recently.[17]

Few law enforcement officials, judges, lawyers, legal scholars and others experienced in the day-to-day operations of America's criminal justice system would quarrel with the assessment of Jackson, the Watergate special prosecutor or Gershman. In fact, considering only the powers that today are expressly granted the Justice Department by law, a persuasive argument can be made that Attorney General Reno and her lieutenants exercise more unfettered control over the American people than the officials of any other agency in the United States government.

IN THE BEGINNING

Ⅰt was not always this way. In its infancy, the office of attorney general was of relatively little importance. Yet even in its earliest enfeebled years the office was confronted by a serious and apparently unanticipated problem. From the very beginning, by lawful mandate, unlike the president or any of his other cabinet members, the attorney general was burdened with an inherent conflict of interest that has been a difficult challenge for every person who has held the position in modern history.

The Constitution of the United States, adopted by the required number of ratifying states in 1789, established the broad outlines of the federal government: an executive branch headed by the president, a national legislature and the judiciary. Shortly thereafter, in its first session, the new Congress began its work by approving separate laws creating three specific departments within the executive branch that would operate under the command of the just-elected president. On July 27, August 7 and September 2, 1789, the separate bills establishing the departments of Foreign Affairs (the State Department), Treasury and War (the Defense Department), respectively, were signed into law by President Washington. According to a provision in the Constitution, each of these departments was to be headed by an official who would be appointed by the president and confirmed by the Senate.

Then, on September 24, 1789, Washington signed a fourth law, this one dealing with the basic structure of the new government, the "Act to Establish the Judicial Courts." The law, first of all, authorized the creation of the Supreme Court, the circuit and district courts and, curiously, the positions of federal prosecutor and marshal, one for each of the nation's thirteen judicial districts. The very last sentence of the Judiciary Act established the position and described the duties of the attorney general.[18]

As required by the Constitution, the attorney general, like the secretaries of state, war and treasury, was beholden to the chief executive because it was the president who appointed him, and now her, to the position. Despite this basic similarity in the offices, however, there was one critical difference.

This difference begins with the confusing fact that the provision of law creating the office of attorney general was located in the statute creating the judicial, rather than the executive, branch of government. But the key details of the difference were spelled out in four laws that describe the specific duties and responsibilities of the attorney general and the three other members of the original cabinet.

The July 27 law creating the position of secretary of state required the holder of this position to perform "such duties as shall, from time to time, be enjoined on or entrusted to him by the President of the United States" relating to dealings with foreign states and princes. The secretary of war, whose position was established by the August 7 law, was to carry out various military duties "as the President of the United States shall from time to time, order or instruct."

The September 2 law concerning the treasury secretary was a bit less precise: It called upon him to carry out a number of specific functions connected with the management of the revenue and public debt and to undertake "services relative to the finances, as he shall be directed to perform." Any possible doubts about who would be doing the directing was resolved in another section of the law describing the line of succession within the Treasury Department in the event that the secretary "shall be removed from office by the President of the United States. . . ."

The brief statutory provision creating the position of attorney general was very different. "And there shall be appointed a meet person, learned in the law, to act as attorney-general for the United States, who shall be sworn and affirmed to a faithful execution of his office; whose duties it shall be to prosecute and conduct all suits in the Supreme Court in which the United States shall be concerned, and to give his advice and opinion of law when required by the President of the United States, or when requested by the heads of any of the departments, and shall receive such compensation for his services as shall, by law, be provided."[19]

That's it. Unlike the three secretaries, the early attorneys general were not administrators with a department to run and a single, clear, legally mandated loyalty to the president. Instead, the law said, the attorney general had different kinds of duties: advise the president on the nuances of law and represent the government in the Supreme Court. Thus, from the very beginning, the attorney general was an unusual hybrid with inherently conflicting loyalties. As an officer of the court, the goal was justice. As an adviser to the president, the goal was to advance the interests of the president.

At first, this conflict was mostly theoretical, because the 1789 Judiciary Act did not give the attorney general any executive powers, not even the authority to supervise the thirteen federal prosecutors and the cases they were bringing in the different districts. For the first two decades, in fact, the attorneys general kept no records of their advisory opinions, partly because they served on a part-time basis without the help of a single assistant.

The conflict became more acute in 1870, when, after many decades of debate, Congress approved a law creating the Justice Department, an agency within the executive branch. While the 1870 statute explicitly authorized the attorney general to supervise and control the new department and the already existing federal prosecutors and marshals who became a part of it, the 1789 provision, which obliged the attorney general to also serve as an officer of the court, was left unchanged.

Daniel J. Meador, an assistant attorney general during the Carter years and now a professor at the University of Virginia Law School, has given considerable thought to this predicament—one faced by no other member of the president's cabinet. In a 1980 analysis of the attorney general, the Justice Department and the White House, Meador noted that the attorney general has over the years been referred to as a "quasi-judicial" officer. He also cited the 1854 opinion of Attorney General Caleb Cushing that the attorney general's job was to give legal advice to his client—the president and the government—and at the same time to serve as "a public officer, acting judicially, under all the solemn responsibilities of conscience and of legal obligation."[20]

Whitney North Seymour, Jr., a U.S. attorney in the Southern District of New York from 1970 to 1974, also commented on the problematic statute that requires the attorney general to serve two distinct and sometimes conflicted masters—the president and the law. To the president, he is a political and personal adviser. But for the public, Seymour argued, the law also imposes the duty of providing "nonpartisan, even-handed Justice." Time and time again, he wrote, "these two functions collide with each other head on."

Thus, from the earliest days of the nation's history, the attorney general has been in an uncomfortable, frequently impossible position. As an officer of the court, the attorney general seeks justice. As a cabinet member and adviser to the president, the attorney general seeks to protect the White House from its "enemies" no matter how honorable they may be.

But with the 1870 decision making the attorney general the commander of what has developed into a formidable investigative force, the challenge became even more difficult. Rather than possessing two sometimes conflicting faces, as suggested by Meador and Seymour, the modern attorney general exhibits three.

THE GROWTH OF THE LAW

In the first years, the legal jurisdiction of the attorney general was as restricted as his administrative fiat, essentially limited to a tiny handful of laws involving truly national issues like treason, piracy and counterfeiting. Almost all criminal enforcement activities were controlled by local authorities, such as the elected county sheriff.

But starting with the populist movement that gathered steam in the last few decades of the nineteenth century and the progressive era that swept the nation in the first years of the twentieth, Congress began to expand the legal responsibilities of the federal government and the Justice Department. There was the Interstate Commerce Act of 1887, which attempted to control the railroads; the Sherman Antitrust Act of 1890, which held that combinations of business that restrained trade were illegal; the Food and Drug and Meat Inspection acts of 1906; and the White Slave Traffic Act of 1910, prohibiting the transport of women across state lines for immoral purposes. The rapidly growing place of the federal government in American life was pushed along, of course, by ambitious politicians like President Theodore Roosevelt.[21]

Then came laws prohibiting the interstate transportation of stolen cars and stolen securities and, in the wake of the heavily publicized Lindbergh kidnapping case of 1932, a law giving the FBI broad authority to investigate such crimes. With Franklin Roosevelt's New Deal, Harry Truman's Fair Deal, the Kennedy brothers' New Frontier and Lyndon Johnson's Great Society, the federal jurisdiction continued to expand.

Fueled partly by the existence of problems that ignored state boundaries and partly by the political requirement that Congress and the White House appear concerned about crime, the growth in the statutory authority of the national government has been phenomenal. There is no limit, it seems, to America's faith in the law, and to the nation's moralistic and somewhat naive belief that there are virtually no problems that cannot be resolved by the passage of a criminal statute. One aspect of this faith, of course, may be the visceral understanding that the adoption of a criminal prohibition makes the public feel good without the necessity of raising their taxes.

As a result, by 1992, there were over 3,000 separate federal offenses listed on the books. These ranged from statutes dealing with the serious matters presented by big-time bank swindlers, sleazy purveyors of tainted food and drugs and spies to more trivial business problems such as the one addressed in Title 18, Chapter 89, Section 1821 of the Federal Criminal Code: a law authorizing federal imprisonment of up to one year for any person convicted of the interstate transportation of dentures which were manufactured without a prescription from a licensed dentist.[22]

Yet even the dizzying increase in the number of specific federal offenses substantially underestimates the growth in the statutory authority of the national government. This is because the Justice Department, with the approval of the courts, has steadily expanded the categories of cases it can bring under long-standing laws originally used for far more restrictive purposes. Perhaps the most astonishing such metamorphosis involves the federal mail fraud statute, a vaguely worded law originally approved by Congress in 1872. Under the creative Justice Department lawyering of the last few years, this century-old statute has been molded to prosecute and convict the owners of a Long Island pet cemetery who did not cremate the deceased dogs and cats in the dignified way they had promised, a Virginia physician who solved the infertility problems of a number of women by impregnating them with his own semen, a group of college athletes who allegedly defrauded several universities by entering into financial agreements in violation of the rules of the National Collegiate Athletic Association and even a former governor of Illinois who allegedly had deprived the state's voters of "honest and faithful service" when he accepted through the mail some stock from a horse racing company.[23]

The rapid growth in the legal responsibilities and activities of the Justice Department has been reflected, of course, in a steady expansion of the agency's staff and budget. At first, as already noted, the attorney general had no staff. Shortly after the beginning of the twentieth century, approximately thirty years after the creation of the Justice Depart-

GROWTH IN FEDERAL PROSECUTORS
1980–1992
(per million population)

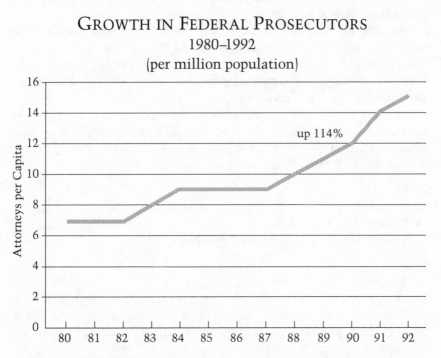

Although Presidents Reagan and Bush both argued for a smaller and less intrusive federal government, their views apparently did not apply to the Justice Department: During their time in office the number of federal prosecutors more than doubled. As a result of the serious budget problems of the Clinton years, this expansion has come to an end. (TRAC ANALYSIS OF JUSTICE DEPARTMENT AND CENSUS BUREAU DATA)

ment, the attorney general was, at least in theory, responsible for the work of 260 employees in Washington and another 1,300 around the country. Last year, the department had approximately 100,000 employees, a sixty-six-fold increase in departmental employees since 1904.

The Justice Department's lawyers, investigators, economists, computer scientists, engineers, psychologists, prison guards, clerks and specialists (in DNA analysis, the thought processes of serial murderers and the placement of hidden recording devices) are members of a federal army who have come to occupy a position in our country that even a few decades ago would have been unimaginable.

The cost of maintaining this army—paying its salaries and benefits, providing the necessary offices and purchasing the elaborate computers and other necessities of the trade—came to about $11 billion in 1993. For that $11 billion—which included $2 billion for the FBI, $700 million for the DEA, $1 billion for INS, $2 billion for the Bureau of Prisons and $1.8 billion for the lawyers working in the Justice Department proper and the offices of the ninety-three U.S. attorneys—the public gets a good deal of activity.

The FBI, for example, among other accomplishments during fiscal year 1993, reported it had investigated 64,871 violent crime matters, 47,418 white-collar crime matters and 5,824 civil rights matters. The DEA said it had made 21,799 drug arrests. The INS reported it had apprehended 1,197,000 individuals.

The Justice Department as a whole reported it had collected $151 million in criminal fines—all but $5.6 million of it through the seizure of tainted property—and $440 million in civil penalties and forfeitures. The Bureau of Prisons detained 65,000 men and women.

A WEEK IN THE LIFE
OF THE JUSTICE DEPARTMENT

All these numbers, however, are curiously unsatisfying. Glance back at them and you will see why: Despite the appearance of solid fact, none of them provide a context against which the daily choices of federal prosecutors can be judged.

Federal laws, scores of court decisions, administrative rules and a long historical tradition give federal prosecutors unrivaled control over all criminal and civil enforcement efforts at the federal level. While the agencies can open preliminary investigations pretty much at will, Justice Department lawyers and the ninety-three U.S. attorneys exercise a virtually unchecked authority in deciding which of the agency investigations will move forward: who will be called before a grand jury, what questions they will be asked and who will be publicly charged. In recent years, as Congress passed laws reducing the authority of judges to decide individual prison terms, the prosecutors also have taken over de facto control of federal sentencing.

Obtaining an overall view of the work performed by an agency as large and as complicated as the Justice Department is not easy. The FBI, DEA and INS, for example, while eating up about one quarter of the department's annual budget, are very secretive about their investigative actions, many of which are never made public. A federal investigation, even those that never result in prosecution, can be a massive event in an individual's life. Later chapters will focus on selected aspects of these investigative agencies.

But getting a handle on the department's prosecuting side also is challenging. According to the department, for example, formalized complaints—what the Justice Department calls "matters"—can be referred to federal prosecutors by something like two hundred federal agencies as well as state and local organizations. In dealing with this highly varied mass of incoming matters, the prosecutors can choose from dozens of possible options. Some matters are immediately dropped; others are declined after weeks or months or years of consideration. In addition, because of the way the laws are written, a person believed to have committed a single criminal act usually can be charged under a variety of statutes, depending upon special circumstances and the whim of the individual prosecutor. It is this power to select the law under which an individual will be charged, and thus the potential penalty, that in the end gives the prosecutors near total control over federal sentencing decisions.

In an effort to make the pattern of these extremely complicated processes more comprehensible, I propose that instead of looking at the Justice Department's workload for one whole year, we focus our view on a single week. My chosen week, which statistical analysis indicates is quite typical, begins on Sunday, May 2, and ends on Saturday, May 8, 1993.[24]

But in undertaking this examination, where in the legal process should the accounting begin? Should we first focus on "matters," all the suspicious situations the agencies refer to the Justice Department? Or should we instead start by looking at "cases," those situations where the department decides to bring a formal charge against an individual? Although there is merit in either of these approaches, I have decided upon a third strategy: an examination of all the criminal and civil "matters" and "cases" that the department in one way or another disposed of during our test week.

All together, during this particular seven-day period, data tapes obtained from the Executive Office of United States Attorneys show that Justice Department lawyers working in Washington and the assistant U.S. attorneys around the country disposed of a grand total of 5,725 matters and cases. These included 3,101 civil actions, 2,191 criminal and 433 that were declined after an hour or less of consideration.

This means that if all ninety-three U.S. attorneys' offices were equally busy—which they of course are not—each would have closed, in one way or another, about sixty-one matters that week.

On just the criminal side, the FBI was the source for about one third of the department's business. Most of the balance of the criminal matters came from the Drug Enforcement Administration; the Bureau of Alcohol, Tobacco and Firearms; the Customs Bureau; the Immigration and Naturalization Service, the Postal Service and the Internal Revenue Service.

The single largest clump of the Justice Department's criminal business—slightly more than one out of four—involved drugs. Two other areas of major federal concern were guns and immigration. Added together, these three categories made up 695 of the 2,191 criminal matters and cases that were disposed of during the first week in May, just under one third of the total.

As already noted, Congress over the years has passed literally thousands of laws making a huge variety of other kinds of specific acts a possible criminal offense. This fact means that a strong majority of all the matters and cases dealt with by the Justice Department that week involved a truly dazzling array of allegations.

Between May 2 and May 8, 1993, for example, the federal government disposed of one matter involving computer fraud, a second concerning corruption charges against a single federal law enforcement official, a third relating to the smuggling of cigarettes and a fourth connected with labor racketeering—the use of union power for personal gain. Also disposed of that week were matters and cases involving three persons the government believed had violated the nation's copyright laws, two people who were thought to have breached consumer product safety statutes and six individuals investigated for disobeying the nation's customs laws.

It is widely assumed that the Justice Department channels a substantial part of its resources into enforcing federal regulatory laws, an activity which by definition cannot usually be assumed by state and local prosecutors. For the last thirty years, in fact, this basic belief about the federal government has fueled an intense lobbying effort by business organizations such as the Chamber of Commerce and the National Association of Manufacturers to reduce federal enforcement when it comes to the corporations. The core of this campaign—first successfully articulated by Ronald Reagan, then a middle-aged actor on the corporate payroll of General Electric—was a heartfelt denunciation of the federal government's unnecessary and heavy-handed regulation of business.

When it comes to the Justice Department, however, the evidence shows the Reagan complaint echoed recently by the Republican Congress wasn't true when Reagan was working for General Electric, it wasn't true when he was president and it isn't true today. Of all the matters and cases disposed of in the 1993 test period, only eighteen of them, less than one percent of that week's total, involved possible violations of environmental, consumer protection or occupational safety and health laws.

When it comes to prosecuting criminals, the phrase "disposed of" suggests only one outcome: conviction. But in the lingo of the Justice Department, the phrase has many possible meanings. Of the eighteen environmental, consumer and safety matters processed during the test week, for example, six involved alleged criminal violations against employees. These six matters were "disposed of" in the sense that the U.S. attorneys declined to prosecute a single one of them, thus totally ignoring the formal recommendations of the Mine Safety and Health Administration.

The eighteen matters also included two situations involving criminal allegations where consumers were believed to be at risk. One of these was declined by the Justice Department before it got to court, the other was dismissed by a federal judge at the request of the Justice Department.

The last ten of the eighteen matters and cases disposed of that week concerned the environment; situations where the FBI, the EPA and a handful of other agencies had obtained evidence indicating that corporations and others had violated the law in a criminal way while dealing with their hazardous and toxic waste products.

Half of the ten were declined by the Justice Department. One was disposed of by a court of appeals. The remaining four—slightly less than one quarter of all the health, safety and environmental matters disposed of during the week all over the nation—resulted in findings of guilt. Yet not one individual involved in these four cases was sentenced to prison.

The Justice Department's data show that the department's handling of this group of regulatory matters during the test week was noticeably less harsh than its handling of most other categories of crime. In immigration cases, for example, instead of most of the matters being dismissed and none of the individuals going to prison, four out of five were found guilty and two out of three were sent to prison. In drug cases, half were found guilty and two out of five went to prison. Of all the 2,191 individual criminal matters and cases dealt with in that first full week of May 1993, almost half, 46 percent, resulted in a finding of guilt, while only about one third, 32 percent, ended up being sentenced to prison.

THE CIVIL SIDE

Although it is often forgotten by the public and press, the Justice Department has civil, as well as criminal, enforcement responsibilities. One distinction between the two is that individuals found guilty of a crime can be sent to prison while those found liable in a civil proceeding cannot. Another distinction is that while a criminal conviction always carries with it an implicit finding of moral fault, civil findings usually are more neutral.

As noted earlier, during the first week in May, the Justice Department disposed of 3,101 civil matters and cases, considerably more than the 2,191 on the criminal side of the ledger.

Criminal and civil matters, however, are not really comparable. One key difference relates to the fact that in criminal matters the government is always the plaintiff, the agency that represents society as a whole in the prosecution of an individual or organization that has been accused of committing a crime. In criminal cases, the prosecutor always represents the victim.

In civil matters, on the other hand, the government can be either the plaintiff or the defendant. One example of the former is when the Justice Department sues a school board for violating the civil rights laws or a corporation for failing to meet its tax liabilities. In the latter case, the Justice Department defends a government agency, and sometimes a specific official, who has been sued by a private party or, more rarely, by another agency. In some circumstances, the department also moves to defend a particular law that is under attack by a regulated company that thinks the law is too strong or by a public interest group that believes it too weak.

In civil actions where the government is the plaintiff, the prosecutor is not actively concerned with capturing and punishing the offenders. Rather, the primary goal is to seek financial or other redress.

During our sample week, the Justice Department was the plaintiff in 20 percent of the civil matters disposed of and the defendant in 63 percent. The balance of civil matters fell into a number of special categories.

The top agency involved was the IRS, followed by the Defense Department, the Farmers Home Administration, the Social Security Agency, the FBI and the DEA. There were 118 DEA cases disposed of that week—4 percent of the total—in which the government was seeking to seize the assets of drug suspects.

INACTION GALORE

A complete inventory of every criminal and civil enforcement action of the United States Justice Department—a comprehensive listing of every single person or corporation it sued, arrested, indicted or imprisoned—does not begin to provide a full accounting of the department's significant role in American life.

This is partly because such a list, by definition, fails to include all the criminal investigations that the prosecutors chose *not to make* and all the persons and corporations the prosecutors chose *not to charge*. It also does not consider all the cases that result in findings of *not guilty*.

When the FBI arrested four Arab men for bombing the World Trade Center in New York City and federal prosecutors subsequently persuaded a jury to convict them on every single charge, the stories about the government's successful handling of the matter were, of course, big news all over the country. As a result, the nation was generally reassured about the dedication and effectiveness of the Justice Department.

But when the Justice Department fails to act, when serious public problems are systematically ignored or powerful corporations escape prosecution, the inaction rarely is commented upon. This is partly because, for obvious reasons, the Justice Department works much harder at publicizing those occasions when it is locking up the bad guys than those situations when, for one reason or another, it is not. Surprising as it may seem, the actions not taken by the department are more frequent and, at least in some instances, more significant than the actions taken.

The sheer volume of matters that federal prosecutors decide to pass up would come as a surprise to most Americans. During all of 1993, for example, federal investigative agencies presented U.S. attorneys slightly less than 100,000 matters which they felt warranted criminal prosecution. In that same year, the Justice Department filed only 37,000 cases. In other words, the prosecutors chose to act on only two out of five of all the situations in which the agencies had decided a federal crime had been committed. (If those situations are added when the Justice Department declines to act after less than an hour of consideration, the prosecutors bring charges in only one out of three of the referrals they receive.)

First off, it must be immediately and emphatically emphasized that a substantial number of the 63,000 matters that the federal prosecutors did not prosecute that year probably deserved to be rejected. According to a department list of seventeen official explanations why matters can be declined, an assistant U.S. attorney has many valid reasons for killing a case, all of which demand serious consideration: perhaps no federal law was violated, or there was a lack of criminal intent, or the evidence was weak, or there was a witness problem or, given the press of more important cases, there simply wasn't time to prosecute. The assistant can also choose not to prosecute because the suspect is already facing criminal charges or the matter has been sent to state authorities or the problem has been resolved by a civil or administrative process.

On the other hand, federal prosecutors sometimes look the other way because of direct, improper and politically motivated interference. About twenty years ago, for example, President Richard Nixon called up his attorney general and told him that he would fire the assistant attorney general for antitrust matters unless a department investigation of ITT was immediately abandoned. Although Nixon's intervention was regarded as a rare event, such presidential abuse is probably a lot more common than most Americans suppose. Almost a hundred years ago, for example, when a high official in the Republican Party complained to President Theodore Roosevelt about an investigation of price-fixing by a particular corporation, the president immediately instructed his attorney general to hold up on the probe until after the election.

But because the White House has only so much time and only so many political chits to give away, and because the Justice Department and the ninety-three U.S. attorneys each year process tens of thousands of cases, interference from the president or his staff on behalf of special friends and supporters is by necessity a rare event.

Yet that fact does not mean that the department's control over who does and does not get prosecuted is a process that should be overlooked. The inactions of prosecutors that result from their unconscious class biases or political pressure from a politically powerful institution in an individual district can cause just as much damage as the inactions that grow out of secret pressures from the White House.

In this regard, despite all the excellent reasons the Justice Department prosecutors may offer for not going ahead on a particular case, the dissimilar death rates observed for the different broad categories of federal crime raise good and interesting questions about what is going on. So, like the epidemiologist who seeks understanding of a particular health problem by analyzing the medical records of both those who became ill and those who did not, let's explore some of the patterns of nonprosecution at the federal level of government.

First, we already know that in recent years federal prosecutors rejected about three out of five of all the criminal matters recommended to them by the agencies. The records indicate, however, that when it comes to which categories of matters develop into criminal charges, the Justice Department is not exactly an equal opportunity prosecutor.

In 1993, for example, according to the data from the sample week, federal prosecutors brought criminal charges in 61 percent of all the drug matters brought to them by the DEA, the FBI and a handful of other agencies. At the same time, the prosecutors moved in the same way on only 47 percent of the regulatory matters brought to them by the FBI, the FDA, the EPA and other such organizations.

This difference might be explained in part by the fact that regulatory statutes are more complex than the drug laws, and that business offenders can afford better lawyers. Yet one must also take into account the economic, racial and class biases of the young lawyers making most of the decisions, and the long-established political connections of at least some of the businesses that have been accused of violating federal law.

Sometimes, the unannounced judgment calls of prosecutors become more apparent when tracked over time. From 1980 to 1993, for example, the proportion of all federal cases in which the lead charge involved drugs almost tripled, jumping to 27 percent in 1993 compared with 10 percent of the total in 1980. During the same period, regulatory prosecutions underwent a substantial decline, dropping to 3 percent in 1993 compared with 8 percent in 1980.

We already know that 46 percent of all the 2,191 criminal matters disposed of during the first week of May 1993 were by findings of guilt. But the data show that the likelihood of such a finding was highly varied, ranging from a low of 2 percent for those charged with violating civil rights laws to a high of 86 percent for individuals charged under the immigration statutes.

Finally, we also know that federal prison was the outcome in 32 percent of all the matters dealt with in the sample week. Once again, however, there were sharp variations in likelihood of going to prison, depending upon the original charge. A prison sentence resulted from 62 percent of the immigration cases that were disposed of that week. At the other end of the prison scale was official corruption, 10 percent; organized crime, 6 percent; and civil rights, 2 percent.

Because the data show that the Justice Department's efforts to enforce selected regulatory laws were decreasing while drug prosecutions were increasing, one might assume the changes simply reflected the openly acknowledged policies of the Reagan, Bush and Clinton administrations to emphasize narcotics enforcement over other kinds of criminal problems.

But the displacement explanation—that one bucket in a well has to go up when the other comes down—is much too simple. Even within the context of limited resources, it is not necessarily true that regulatory enforcement must go down because narcotics enforcement is going up. Changes in enforcement policy also reflect the conscious choices of hundreds of like-minded officials. This can be deduced from how the department dealt with one of the most politically sensitive enforce-

8 ABOVE THE LAW

ment issues to confront federal prosecutors: the savings and loan scandals that occurred during President Reagan's second term and President Bush's four years in office. After initially fumbling the ball, and under heavy criticism from the Democratic Congress, the prosecutors in power realized that something had to be done about bank fraud. Yet during that same period when the overall proportion of regulatory prosecutions was declining and narcotics prosecutions were climbing, the percentage of white-collar crime prosecutions, which included the savings and loan matters, did not decline.

A second illustrative example of how prosecutors shape their workload involves federal regulatory cases. During the 1980–93 period, when the absolute number of the nation's federal prosecutors was more than doubling, the number of regulatory actions steadily declined. If the prosecutors had not made a deliberate decision to ignore such crime when they could, if the government's enforcement policy had not been altered, the absolute number of regulatory crimes necessarily would have increased along with the growing number of available prosecutors.

ORGANIZATIONAL CRIME

The matter-by-matter, case-by-case information logged into the Justice Department's computers demonstrates that in an absolute sense only a tiny fraction of the business disposed of by federal prosecutors during our sample week—less than one percent of the total—involved allegations of occupational health, consumer safety and environmental crimes. The data further demonstrate that slightly less than one fourth of these eighteen matters were prosecuted and that none of the four defendants ultimately found guilty were sent to prison.

In one way, this record speaks for itself. It is obvious, for example, that despite genuine public concern about environmental, consumer and occupational health hazards—manifested by congressional approval of dozens of national laws during the last two decades—that federal prosecutors made a unilateral decision to set their own priorities. In the simplest terms: Immigration and drug cases, with a high proportion of disenfranchised defendants, were emphasized. Complex cases aimed at well-defended corporations or high-paid executives were downplayed.

In some other ways, however, the record requires further explanation. Bad as the Justice Department's record looks on its own, how does it look when examined in relation to the world in which we all live?

In 1989, there were 21,500 homicides in the United States. During that same year, 5,700 workers died from work-related injuries and an additional 50,000 to 70,000 are estimated to have died prematurely as a result of on-the-job exposure to benzene, arsenic, asbestos, coal dust, vinyl chloride, dioxin and other toxins.[25]

These figures are drawn from a 1991 analytic report published in the *Journal of the American Medical Association*. The two physicians who wrote this study, Philip J. Landrigan and Dean B. Baker, noted that in addition to those known to have died as a result of injuries at work, and those estimated to have died as a result of workplace exposures, another 10 million workers each year suffer traumatic, nonfatal, on-the-job injuries as a result of collapsing trench walls, chemical explosions and other such events.

The numbers given by Landrigan and Baker are considered quite reliable. Because of the large number of assumptions that must be made, however, estimating the number of Americans who are either killed or injured because of faulty consumer goods or who die prematurely because of various forms of air and water pollution is much more speculative.

Despite the serious problems, many experts agree that the annual death toll from the sale and use of defective automobiles, appliances, medical devices, unsafe food and drugs and other consumer products, and the deaths and disease from pollution involves thousands, perhaps even hundreds of thousands, of Americans.

In summary—and now limiting our consideration only to deaths connected to the workplace—the best estimates indicate that almost three times more Americans are dying from their jobs than are dying at the hands of a murderer.

Some of these workplace deaths were true accidents, a bolt of lightning or some other freakish act of God. Others certainly involved occasions when the workers failed to follow established procedures. But the record shows that a significant but unknown proportion of these deaths were the result of deliberate and knowing decisions by managers to put the lives of their employees at high risk.

A well-established tactic for corporate managers who wished to avoid the expense of protecting their employees was to deliberately withhold their knowledge of hazards from the employees. One of the best-documented cases involved the Johns-Manville Company, which for about thirty years maintained a policy of not informing its workers that they were developing asbestosis—an untreatable and often fatal disease caused by breathing asbestos fibers.

The policy was memorialized in an incredible memorandum about asbestosis written by a Johns-Manville medical director. "They [the workers] have not been told of the diagnosis," he wrote, "for it is felt that as long as the man feels well and is happy at home and work, and his physical condition remains good, nothing should be said. . . . [I]t is felt that he should not be told of his condition so that he can live and work at peace *and the company can benefit from his many years of experience*"[26] (emphasis added).

Another well-known case of deliberate corporate endangerment occurred on April 27, 1978, when fifty-one workers were killed in Willow Island, West Virginia, when the cooling tower of the generating plant that was under construction suddenly collapsed. A later investigation by the Occupational Safety and Health Administration (OSHA) concluded that "the disaster was the direct result of illegal corner-cutting on the part of Research-Cottrel Inc., the New Jersey firm that was building the tower."[27]

Although OSHA recommended that criminal charges be brought against the company, the U.S. attorney in the area refused to prosecute. As a result, Research-Cottrel was only required to pay an $85,100 administrative penalty, $1,668.63 per dead worker.[28]

Under principles of American law, four elements are required for an event to be considered a crime in a formal sense. First, there almost always has to be an overt act or deed. Talking about doing a bad thing almost never is a crime. Second, the overt act in question must be prohibited by a law. Third, the person committing the overt act usually must have intended to do it. This is why a person who accidentally kills another in a car crash may be charged with manslaughter rather than murder. Finally, because of our belief that humans possess free will, the person charged in most cases must have the capacity to have committed the act. Although the law on this point has been changing in recent years, a truly insane person who is unable to distinguish between right and wrong has long been viewed as not having the capacity to commit a crime.

Given this framework, it is easy to understand how an armed adult male who kills a storekeeper during the course of a robbery is charged with homicide. At the same time, however, it is hard to comprehend why corporate executives such as the knowing medical director at Johns-Manville or the managers at Research-Cottrel are not also so charged.

That question, of course, has many answers. With fingerprints and DNA typing and surveillance cameras, it is often easy to identify the robber who kills a storekeeper. In a large corporation, however, identifying a responsible individual is usually much harder. Sometimes, in fact, it appears that one of the purposes of large bureaucracies is to obscure individual responsibility.

Another important factor that makes corporate crime control difficult is that the business world, over the years, has spent millions of dollars in a generally successful lobbying campaign to dilute the clarity and effectiveness of the laws that would hold corporate officials accountable for their harmful acts.

The same lobbyists also have continually sought to reduce the yearly appropriations for agencies such as OSHA and the EPA, which are often responsible for at least the first stages of investigating tragic events such as the 1978 deaths at the Willow Island cooling tower. Incomplete or incompetent investigations are a real hurdle to later prosecutions. At the same time, these lobbyists and their allies have worked to elect presidents like Richard Nixon and Ronald Reagan, who appointed administrators openly hostile to prosecuting the corporate officials responsible for the unnecessary deaths of workers, consumers and the public at large.

As the Justice Department records from the spring of 1993 suggest, the U.S. attorneys who decide which matters will go forward and which will be dismissed are still very much a part of the informal national apparatus that has effectively guaranteed that serious corporate crimes will be essentially ignored when it comes to criminal prosecutions. To fully understand just how successful this effort has been, it is necessary to back away and look at the larger picture.

Until about twenty-five years ago, the task of reducing the safety and health hazards faced each day by the American worker was left to state agencies, which many years of experience had shown were largely ineffective. But then, in an effort to win the backing of AFL-CIO president George Meany and the votes of blue-collar workers, the Nixon administration threw its support behind a bill to make worker safety a federal responsibility. With the somewhat unexpected blessing of the Republican president, the Democratic-controlled Congress swiftly approved the Occupational Safety and Health Act of 1970.

This ambitious, perhaps even naive, law centers on the proposition that every American is entitled to work under the safest possible conditions. It further holds that employers who fail to take appropriate steps toward achieving such conditions—not taking time, for example, to shore up the dangerous walls of earthen trenches—should be penalized. In most such situations, the Labor Department was authorized to impose civil fines.

But Congress believed there was one category of abuse where the possibility of a civil fine would not be a sufficient deterrent. So it added a provision that in those cases where a worker was killed, and it could be shown that the employer had willfully violated federal safety standards, the government could bring criminal charges. As already mentioned, the basic differences between a civil and a criminal charge is that when found guilty of the second, a jury has decided the individual deserves formal censure and as a result can be sentenced to prison. A criminal conviction is thus viewed as serving as a deterrent to others who might be tempted to commit the same act.

The new law and the federal enforcement agency that was created by

it—the Occupational Safety and Health Administration (OSHA)—have
been controversial from the start, subject to persistent attack by almost
every business organization in the country. Despite these attacks,
OSHA began to undertake the complex process of adopting national
safety standards and sending inspectors into the field to look for violations of them. As a result, tens of thousands of employers have been required to pay civil fines, usually small ones, because they exposed their
workers to unnecessary hazards.

While the civil enforcement of the Occupational Safety and Health
Act has been extremely spotty in relation to the underlying problem,
when compared with the criminal enforcement effort it seems ferocious.

Since the passage of the 1970 law, 200,000 Americans have died
while working. While some of these deaths were accidents, credible evidence shows that a substantial number were not. As a result of the investigations of all these deaths, according to a 1992 study, the Labor
Department referred a grand total of eighty-eight criminal cases to the
United States Department of Justice, the federal prosecutors agreed to
bring criminal charges in twenty-five of the matters, and only one business executive was sent to prison. The time served was forty-five days.[29]

This record speaks for itself: 200,000 deaths, 25 Justice Department
prosecutions, one 45-day jail sentence. Without giving any credence to
the possibility of knowing conspiracies, it is clear that hundreds of responsible federal officials under five separate political administrations—beginning with Nixon and ending with Clinton—have somehow
carried out an unstated, perhaps even unconscious, government policy
of great consequence: In direct violation of the 1970 law, corporate executives who knowingly exposed their workers to conditions that
caused their deaths have almost always been protected from the unpleasant mess of criminal charges. The Justice Department and the
ninety-plus U.S. attorneys were lead players in this tragedy.

2

Beyond
the Fringe

T he judge presiding in the federal courtroom in Denver was not amused. "Well, Mr. Anderson, let me try to express my concern a little more specifically," District Court Judge Jim R. Carrigan began. "Your duty as an attorney, representing the United States of America, and the Environmental Protection Agency, is to get as thorough a cleanup within the applicable statutes as you can."

"That's correct," replied David Anderson, a lawyer with the Justice Department's Environment and Natural Resources Division.

"And your duty to the Army, your other client," Judge Carrigan continued, "is to not spend any more of its money [on the cleanup] than is necessary. Would you agree?"

Suddenly, no longer in accord with the judge, Anderson flatly rejected Carrigan's suggestion that as a lawyer in the Environment and
Natural Resources Division of the Justice Department his obligations
to the EPA conflicted with his duties to the army. Focusing in on the
specifics of the case, and not directly responding to the judge's conflict
of interest question, Anderson added the extraneous point that he "had
never heard from the Army that they wish to keep their costs at a minimum. I have never received that direction."

Carrigan, however, remained doubtful. If the army was unconcerned
about the cleanup costs, he asked Anderson, "why haven't they cleaned
it up before then? Why are they waiting for a court order to go ahead?"[1]

About a week later, at another hearing, Judge Carrigan brought up the
same point with one of Anderson's bosses. "All right, Mr. Flint," the judge
said. "You understand that attorneys in your office have taken the position that a particular attorney can represent both the Environmental
Protection Agency and the United States Army in this litigation? To
me, the interests of the two agencies are just contrary. I'm a simple
small-town farm boy, practiced in a town of 7,500 people, and it seemed
to me, in the old days, you couldn't represent people who were on opposite sides of a lawsuit if you were one attorney."

But Assistant Attorney General Myles Flint, like Anderson, was not
prepared to accept the judge's view of the situation. "It is the position of
the Department of Justice of the United States that there is no conflict
of interest here, either factually or legally," Flint replied.[2]

The immediate matter at stake in the dispute between Flint, Anderson and Judge Carrigan was of considerable consequence. How could a
single Justice Department lawyer represent two federal agencies—one
the polluter, the other the pollution fighter—in working out the procedural details involved in the cleanup of a massive cesspool of toxic
wastes that another court would later describe as "one of the worst hazardous waste pollution sites" in the country?[3]

The army had constructed the Rocky Mountain Arsenal, a twenty-
seven-square-mile area in the suburbs to the northeast of Denver, in the
middle of World War II to manufacture and assemble chemical warfare
agents and incendiary munitions. Over the years, portions of the
arsenal were leased to private companies, including the Shell Oil
Company, for the manufacture of pesticides and herbicides. In 1956, the
army built what it called Basin F, a 92.7-acre artificial lake with a
capacity to store up to 243 million gallons of liquid hazardous waste.
Although Basin F was lined with a three-eighths-inch-thick asphaltic
membrane, it apparently began leaking almost immediately. In 1983,
the army told the EPA that some of the hazardous wastes had seeped
into the groundwater.

In November 1986 and October 1987, the state of Colorado sued the army, seeking a number of remedies for what it alleged were violations of Colorado's environmental laws. Colorado's suit was based on two important provisions of the Resource Conservation and Recovery Act of 1976. One of these provisions authorized the EPA to extend certain hazardous waste enforcement responsibilities to the states. The second waived the immunity of the federal government from civil suits brought by state and local agencies seeking to enforce their own hazardous waste laws.

After a good deal of legal maneuvering, Justice Department lawyers, arguing for the army, informed Colorado that the United States had not waived its immunity from being sued because the cleanup of Basin F was not governed by the Resource Conservation Act of 1976 but by a different law. Had the Justice Department prevailed with this argument, the state of Colorado would have been blocked from supervising the cleanup of Basin F.

From the very beginning of the long dispute, however, Judge Carrigan had indicated that in his view the individual Justice Department lawyers in his courtroom who claimed to speak for both the army and the EPA had a conflict of interest and that this conflict meant the people of Colorado were not being adequately represented. On June 24, 1988, as a result of his concern, Carrigan ordered both the state and the Justice Department to file briefs on the conflict question.

As it did in its oral arguments, the Justice Department asserted there was no conflict. Even on those occasions when a single Justice Department attorney was in court representing both sides, the department said, that attorney actually was speaking for the president who, in the end, was responsible for all parts of the executive branch. Colorado, on the other hand, argued that on its face the representation of the army and the EPA by the same Justice Department attorneys violated the code of professional responsibilities. In addition, the state said there was concrete evidence that during the development of the Justice Department's ultimate position regarding Basin F, "EPA officials were not consulted or involved in constructing the initial draft of the brief and were provided less than 72 hours to review it."

In early 1989, Carrigan ruled against the Justice Department and the army and in favor of the state. "The same Justice Department attorneys have repeatedly claimed to represent both the Army and the EPA in this action, even though the Army is the defendant and the EPA acts for the United States as the plaintiff," Carrigan wrote. "Since it is the EPA's job to clean up as quickly and thoroughly as possible, and since the Army's obvious financial interest is to spend as little money and effort as possible on the cleanup, I cannot imagine how one attorney can vigorously and wholeheartedly advocate both positions."

Were he to grant the Justice Department's request and remove Colorado from the process, the judge continued, "the Army's cleanup efforts would go unchecked by any parties whose interests are in a sense adverse to those of the Army," and there would be "no vigorous independent advocate for the public interest."[4]

Judge Carrigan's challenge to the Justice Department, later upheld by the Tenth Circuit Court of Appeals, naturally focused on the single case before him and the question of how the Justice Department's lawyers appearing in his court could represent both sides of the multimillion-dollar dispute. In many ways, however, the Basin F case dramatically illustrates the core contradiction that makes the Justice Department such a difficult place to work. Because that contradiction was, and is, as visible as a thunder storm in the summer sky, Flint and Anderson and all the other government lawyers were forced to resort to shouting foolish denials.

But from the moment George Washington's first attorney general took office to the long tedious battle about the Basin F cleanup, the gnawing difficult question has remained: Who do the attorney general, and all the Justice Department attorneys, represent? How, at the same time, is it possible for them to serve the immediate political interests of the president and, as officers of the court, the long-term well-being of the American people? It is a true conundrum.

OVER THE EDGE

A s is noted throughout this book, many of the broad policy determinations and specific decisions of the Justice Department, its ninety-three U.S. attorneys, the FBI, the Drug Enforcement Administration (DEA) and the Immigration and Naturalization Service (INS) are permeated with profound contradictions and politics in a way that is only barely understood by the public. As is also noted, these difficult challenges are, up to a point, an inherent part of representative democracy.

Within the framework of our Constitution and laws, the Justice Department has been asked to try to represent the sometimes conflicting interests of the public and the government. An elected president does indeed have the right and obligation to influence, within the boundaries of the law, the policies and strategies of the executive branch of government that he commands. Furthermore, a Justice Department that sought to enforce the law in a rigid and mechanical fashion in a nation as large and varied as the United States would be a genuine horror.

But there are conflicts and there are conflicts. And there are actions that are acceptable and actions that are not. This chapter presents a gallery of Justice Department happenings where the responsible actors—presidents and their staff assistants, attorneys general and their political advisers, U.S. attorneys and their assistants—have been unable or unwilling to discriminate between what was proper and what was not. Some of these bizarre occurrences, like the Justice Department lawyers who insist they can appropriately represent both sides in a legal dispute, go to the heart of the internal contradictions of the structure of the government. Other events are included here because of their blatant and wrongful impact on the political process of the United States. Additional situations, however, have been granted a place in this gallery of abuses not so much because of their tangible *impact* on the body politic, but because of *who* the players were, *how* the games were played and *what* the selected situations disclose about the dynamics of the largely invisible political environment in which the Justice Department has always functioned.

Some of the excesses meet all of these criteria: They were in fact significant events, the officials who ordered them were surprising, given their public commitment to conflicting goals, and they help us understand some of the hidden currents in the political ocean in which the Justice Department swims. Other matters in this collection meet only some of the criteria. The secret intelligence and counterintelligence activities of both the Nixon and Johnson administrations, for example, impacted in a tangible way on the course of American history. But because President Nixon and Attorney General Mitchell never put much emphasis on due process or civil liberties, their abuse of the Justice Department is in some ways less shocking than the offenses of other administrations who claimed to be more principled. This chapter, then, seeks to explore the details of some of those situations—great and small, premeditated and accidental, static and continuing—where the Justice Department went beyond the fringe.

ALL THE WAY WITH LBJ: CORRUPTING THE FBI AND AMERICAN POLITICS

T he note had a chummy tone, one buddy to another, unusual considering it had been sent to a powerful White House figure by a middle-level federal official who had always displayed a keen appreciation for the nuances of Washington protocol. Although the one-page letter was responding to the White House official's congratulations for a job well done, in this case a secret project that the bureaucrat and his agency had undertaken for the president, it began with a teasing salutation, "Dear 'Bishop.' "

After thanking the "bishop" for his "very thoughtful and generous" comments, the bureaucrat turned chatty. "Please be assured that it was a pleasure and a privilege to be of assistance to the President and all the boys that were with me felt honored in being selected for the assignment," he wrote. "I think everything worked out well, and I'm certainly glad that we were able to come through with vital tidbits from time to time which were of assistance to you and Walter. You know you only have to call on us when a similar situation arises."[5]

The author of the September 1964 letter, the self-styled provider of "vital tidbits," was Cartha D. "Deke" DeLoach, a shrewd, ambitious, sometimes ingratiating, frequently bullying, FBI executive with no shortage of political savvy. The recipient was Bill Moyers, then a brilliant and very young special assistant to Lyndon Baines Johnson. The gifted Moyers had begun his working life as a minister, hence the bantering reference to his status in the hierarchy of the church.

Although DeLoach's confidential note to Moyers contained few specifics, the "assignment" it referred to surely must be considered one of the most brazen examples of the unlawful and improper political misuse of the FBI by a president of the United States.

As is frequently the case in large government agencies, the evidence indicates that this particular outrage had not originated with the troops. Had DeLoach been challenged at the time, like many of history's long line of functionaries, he probably would have claimed he was only following orders. And in fact, the actual source of the offense appears to have been President Johnson and two of his closest assistants, Walter Jenkins and Bill Moyers.

Johnson, like many of the U.S. presidents before him, was a proud, ambitious and ruthless man. He had come to the White House through gruesome misfortune, and now was possessed by a passionate desire to prove himself to the world in a national election, to win the support of an overwhelming majority of the American people even if that achievement required secret FBI wiretaps, improper FBI efforts to interfere in the constitutionally protected political activities at the Atlantic City convention, searches of FBI files for embarrassing information on Barry Goldwater's staff and other such abuses.

Exhaustive searches of the records of the White House and the FBI have failed to locate a presidential memo in which LBJ listed the specific political tasks that he wanted the bureau to undertake for him at the 1964 Democratic convention and how he wanted these tasks to be achieved. But what the FBI did was to create a clandestine investigative unit which used a wide range of sophisticated techniques—legal, quasi-legal and illegal—to enhance Johnson's control of the delegates who were gathering in Atlantic City to nominate him as the Democratic Party's candidate for president.

The central focus of Johnson's concern appears to have been Dr. Martin Luther King, Jr., and a handful of Mississippi civil rights activists who planned to challenge some of the Democratic regulars at the session. Although LBJ's nomination at the forthcoming convention was an absolute certainty, the president apparently felt compelled to achieve the control that only an all-knowing, all-controlling God could have. With the help of DeLoach and Moyers and Jenkins, Johnson was remarkably successful in achieving at least the outward appearance of his ambitious goal.

WHAT DO WE KNOW
AND WHEN DID WE LEARN IT?

Eleven years later, in the wake of Nixon's Watergate scandals, a mildly skittish investigation by Senate Democrats found very little written evidence of this long-secret example of Johnson's passionate need to dominate the political perceptions of the American people. The few surviving letters and memoranda, however, provide compelling evidence about just how easy it had been for the Johnson team to persuade the nation's number one law enforcement agency to become an active partner in the president's political campaign. The documents also illuminate the extremely fragile nature of all representative democracies and the vulnerability of political debate to clandestine manipulation.

LBJ's secret political hit squad was substantial: twenty-seven FBI agents, one radio repairman and two stenographers. Its full name, "Special Squad," disclosed nothing about its actual purpose. The Special Squad functioned for only one week, from August 22 to August 28, 1964, and focused entirely on that summer's Democratic convention in Atlantic City, New Jersey. As indicated by the letter to Moyers, the unit was headed by DeLoach, an FBI executive so close to Johnson that the president, many months before, had ordered White House technicians to install a special telephone line that ran directly from the White House to the bedroom DeLoach shared with his wife.

The documents do not provide ironclad proof as to the patrimony of the Special Squad. But DeLoach himself, on the day after the squad was disbanded, wrote an internal memorandum asserting that the unit had been sent to Atlantic City "at the direction of the president."[6]

Other actors may also have played a role in the squad's creation.

More than ten years after it came into existence, an FBI study discovered that a few weeks before the squad began operating in Atlantic City, Walter Jenkins, a special assistant to the president, and John Doar, a highly respected figure in the Justice Department's Civil Rights Division, had made separate requests to the FBI for any information the bureau might have about the Mississippi Freedom Democratic Party and forty persons the MFDP was sending to Atlantic City. Because the FBI's preconvention search uncovered no information about the irritating splinter party, it is possible that the requests from Doar and Jenkins contributed to the agency's decision to create the special squad in Atlantic City. Given the intimate nature of Johnson's relations with De-Loach, however, it seems most likely that the unit was established as a result of an oral request from LBJ.[7]

The 1975 FBI account of the Special Squad noted that several of its members tried to persuade bureau investigators that the unit's primary function was to assure the safety of President Johnson. Yet even while making such a defense, one of the agents added that "it was obvious that DeLoach wanted to impress Jenkins and Moyers with the Bureau's ability to develop information that would be of interest to them."[8]

But partly because the record showed so few contacts between the squad and the Secret Service—the agency which carries the legal responsibility for protecting the president—the author of the FBI followup report, one H. N. Bassett, seemed skeptical about these assertions. Strengthening his doubt, it appears, was Bassett's discovery that twenty of the twenty-five reports prepared by the squad for Jenkins and Moyers "do not appear to relate directly with possible civil unrest, demonstrations or with the protection of the President."[9]

Knowing what we now do about the FBI's undercover political operations during the forty-year period from the late 1930s to the mid-1970s, the various tactics of the Atlantic City squad are not all that surprising. Well before the 1964 convention, for example, the unit contacted an unknown number of individuals who worked for the targeted organizations and persuaded them to provide the FBI with tips about any actions the organizations were planning to take during the convention. Presumably these informants were paid for their services.

A second, long-favored FBI intelligence-gathering tactic involved the misuse of press credentials. In Atlantic City, the FBI induced the National Broadcasting Company (NBC) to lend it press passes so that several agents could pretend to be working reporters. Partly because of the authenticity of their credentials, the fake reporters were able to win the confidence of the dissidents, and thus obtained informed and authoritative tips about the planned activities of the groups.

Finally, with the help of a large number of improper electronic listening devices, the Special Squad developed a massive record of almost everything that was said in the offices and hotel suites of most of the civil rights activists whose political ventures worried the president.

Both the tactics and the out-and-out political purpose of the squad were clearly suggested in an eight-page followup memorandum that De-Loach drafted the day after the Democratic convention ended. Because the purpose of the memo was to persuade J. Edgar Hoover to write letters of commendation to the members of the squad, DeLoach may have been engaging in some self-serving puffery. The fact remains, however, that almost all of his claims were later confirmed by post-Watergate investigations.

"By means of informant coverage, by use of various confidential techniques, by infiltration of key groups through use of undercover agents, and through the utilization of agents using appropriate cover as reporters, we were able to keep the White House fully apprised of all major developments during the convention's course," the senior FBI executive said. One FBI "reporter" was so successful, DeLoach continued, that he was able to persuade an unnamed civil rights leader to give him " 'off-the-record information' for background purposes, which he requested our 'reporter' not to print." In FBI parlance, the phrase "confidential techniques" usually referred to telephone wiretaps and electronic bugs.

But DeLoach and his gang of thirty did not limit their activities simply to collecting political intelligence for President Johnson. In addition to serving as LBJ's eyes and ears, the squad members undertook partisan political actions that would have been inappropriate for a presidential campaign committee, let alone the nation's premier law enforcement agency. In the terms of the spy world, the line between intelligence gathering and counterintelligence was not maintained. In a section of his report beginning with the heading "Daily Counter Measures by Special Squad," the FBI official proudly described several situations where his agents had become directly involved in the political process by secretly intervening to head off political demonstrations and other planned actions which might have proven embarrassing to the president. On the Sunday before the convention, for example, DeLoach reported that the squad had learned that civil rights activists had brought to Atlantic City the burned-out skeleton of a car—possibly the one in which the three civil rights workers were driving shortly before they were murdered in Philadelphia, Mississippi. The activists apparently planned to use the wrecked car as the symbolic focus for a demonstration which at least implied criticism of the Johnson administration. The FBI official said the squad quickly located the truck carrying the vehicle on a street in Atlantic City and then, through contacts with the local police, took an unspecified action that "thwarted the racial group's plans to parade this burned out car through Atlantic City streets."

On a second occasion, DeLoach said, the squad learned that one of the civil rights organizations was attempting to promote "a stall-in to block access to the Convention Hall." The official indicated that because the key planner of this effort was also an FBI informant, the squad would be able "to completely thwart" the proposed action.

The fallout, actually the lack of fallout, from the dirty work of the Special Squad is instructive. While holding vague, conspiratorial suspicions about LBJ and the FBI, the civil rights activists never fully appreciated the extent to which the bureau had succeeded in penetrating their ranks through the use of illegal listening devices and informants, or why so many of their political plans went astray. For his deft handling of the assignment, Hoover gave DeLoach a meritorious service award. The White House, having learned the political usefulness of FBI assistance in Atlantic City, soon picked up on DeLoach's offer to call on him for additional help. On October 28, 1964, for example, after undertaking a search of its files, the FBI provided the presidential staff with name-check information on fifteen persons working for Senator Barry Goldwater, Johnson's opponent in the presidential campaign. Although there is no record proving that the Johnson team used the FBI information in the campaign, some of it was judged to be negative.[10]

On another occasion, the Johnson administration asked the FBI to determine whether any members of the Communist Party or other subversive groups were providing information to Senator William Fulbright and other Senate critics of the Vietnam War in connection with a televised hearing about the war. While the bureau was either unable or unwilling to undertake such a sensitive investigation, it side-stepped the appearance of default by sending Marvin Watson, another White House aide, a detailed analysis of the parallels that existed between the senatorial statements and the documented "publications or statements of Communist leaders."[11]

Almost a decade after the Johnson excesses of the summer and fall of 1964, as the nation confronted the Watergate scandals of Richard Nixon, Bill Moyers chose to speak out about the perverse pressures of the White House. His forum was an investigative report on national public television.

"Was Watergate a string of deplorable incidents by a handful of men or an attitude toward power and law that could recur?" he asked. "Were the men linked to it acting out of character with the times or responding to something intrinsic in American life today? This report is a personal attempt to explore those questions, to get to the roots of the Watergate morality."[12]

The historians, political scientists and columnists who Moyers invited to explore the lessons of Watergate with him—men like Henry Steele Commager, James David Barber, Richard L. Strout and George

Will—all argued that the Nixon excesses were the product of larger historical forces, not merely the work of a few rotten apples. Commager, for example, focused on the Cold War pressures that had contributed to an imperial presidency. Will, on the other hand, emphasized the continuing habit of the American political system to elevate second-rate men to the White House.

Moyers, in his own comments during the program, adopted these broader explanations for Watergate, properly resisting the temptation to view Richard Nixon and John Mitchell as uniquely evil. Moyers, however, did not offer the viewers a candid confession of his own sins.

Instead, in a passing admission that our knowledge of the FBI's Atlantic City squad now makes understandable, Moyers said that sometime in the early sixties he had "discovered that in our infirmity, we were all susceptible." Perhaps the preacher turned White House staff member turned television essayist chose to remain silent about his own intimate involvement in the corrupting of the FBI out of a sense of loyalty to his former boss. Whatever the explanation for the silence, it would appear likely his association with the FBI was an embarrassment he did not care to confront.

More recently, when questioned about the incident, Moyers has adopted a different strategy. On the one hand, without further research at the Johnson Library, he said he doesn't trust his memory to respond accurately to questions about those distant days. On the other hand, despite his inability to remember important details, he was sure that the primary assignment of the Special Squad was the physical protection of LBJ.[13]

Partly because the Atlantic City follies of 1964 remained hidden from the public for more than a decade and partly because the investigators and the subjects of the investigation were from the same party, Lyndon Johnson, Bill Moyers and Walter Jenkins never had to answer for the arrogant misuse of their lawful powers. On August 20, 1974, however, after an extensive investigation and a lengthy series of hearings, the House Judiciary Committee voted to impeach Richard Nixon. The second paragraph of Article II of the impeachment resolution summarized one of the reasons why the House committee had concluded that Nixon's actions warranted his "removal from office."

The president, the resolution said, "misused the Federal Bureau of Investigation, the Secret Service and other executive personnel, in violation or disregard of the constitutional rights of citizens, by directing or authorizing such agencies to conduct or continue electronic surveillance or other investigations unrelated to national security, the enforcement of laws, or any other lawful function of his office[.]"[14] The same words, of course, could have been correctly applied to Lyndon Johnson.

THE DEPARTMENT OF POLITICAL JUSTICE:
THE WAR ON INFLATION

In late July 1919, Homer Cummings, then the chairman of the Democratic National Committee, returned to Washington from a trip around the country and warned President Wilson that the American people were demanding government action to bring down the cost of living. During the second quarter of that year, prices had begun to skyrocket and the Republicans in Congress launched a full-fledged attack on the Democratic administration for its inaction.

A vacuum of power existed at the highest levels of the government, particularly on domestic issues, because Wilson had become obsessed by the peace treaty and then had suffered a disabling stroke. But the political warning from Cummings made a great deal of sense to the ambitious professional politician who was the nation's attorney general.

The name of A. Mitchell Palmer, an amiable Quaker from the Poconos region of Pennsylvania and longtime member of the House of Representatives, has gone down in history largely because immediately after World War I Palmer and a very young J. Edgar Hoover championed a brutal and largely unlawful war on alien radicals. (The story of the Palmer raids—the low point of which was the summary arrest of about 5,000 radical aliens in early 1920—is told in Chapter 9.)

Outrageous and ugly though the Palmer raids were, a second effort by the attorney general, this one to combat inflation, was in its own small way an even more unpleasant example of how easy it is for senior Justice Department officials to exercise the agency's vast public powers to suit their partisan purposes.

Palmer had been a Wilson supporter for many years, serving as his successful floor manager at the Democratic convention in 1912. But because of the opposition of some of Wilson's staff, this support didn't pay off until March 5, 1919, when the president chose him to be his attorney general.[15] The armistice agreement had been signed just four months before, on November 11, 1918, but the nation was still in an official state of war because of profound divisions over Wilson's peace plans.

In the summer of 1919, as discovered by the chairman of the Democratic National Committee, inflation was a very hot subject with the American people. The widespread public concern about the cost of living was important to Wilson because the administration needed every ounce of support it could muster for the president's idealistic plans to rebuild the family of nations. But inflation was of even more interest to Palmer, who then saw himself as the leading contender for the 1920 Democratic presidential nomination. Palmer wanted to prove to the nation that he was the kind of politician who could manage what was viewed by many as a national crisis.

On July 31, 1919, with Wilson's approval, the attorney general called eight high government officials, including the Secretaries of Treasury, Agriculture, Labor and Commerce, to a three-hour meeting in his fifth-floor Justice Department office. The goal was to work out a comprehensive government plan to fight inflation.[16]

A few days later, on August 5, 1919, Palmer emerged from a White House meeting with Wilson and announced to newsmen that "the Department of Justice will use all of its agents throughout the nation to hunt down the hoarders and profiteers in food." The full powers of the government, including the war power acts still on the federal books, would be mobilized.[17] Three days later, the president himself, in a speech to Congress, promised to do everything he could to bring down prices.

Shortly thereafter, in a bit of pure politically inspired showboating, Palmer shuffled the Justice Department–appropriated dollars to create one of the most curious appendages in the history of the agency: the Division of Women's Activities. The stated purpose of the new agency was to promote thrift, which it did in part by distributing complaint cards so that women shoppers around the nation could turn in merchants who charged excessive prices.

In a subsequent statement in the Justice Department's 1920 annual report, Attorney General Palmer explained that "the women of the country, in whose hands rests the power largely to control the cost of living through their purchases, have been organized to . . . hunt out profiteers and report violations of the Lever Act."[18]

The work of the Women's Division was coordinated in each state by a Justice Department employee. Directors were appointed in many counties, who in turn named chairpersons in the larger cities and towns. According to the division, it eventually distributed more than one million pamphlets, arranged for the publication of innumerable articles and answered thousands of requests for information.

The attorney general's deep concern about inflation, his willingness even to create an unheard-of Women's Division, might seem strange if we did not know his eye was on winning the Democratic nomination for president in 1920. It makes even more sense if we remember that the woman's vote, for the first time in American history, would become a crucial factor in the upcoming election.

"In 1916 women enjoyed the presidential vote in only twelve states. By May of 1919 this number had increased to twenty-nine, representing nearly two thirds of the electoral college. The proposed Nineteenth Amendment [giving women the vote] was submitted to the states in

June 1919. If it was ratified in time, 27 million women would be eligible
to vote in 1920; even without it, the number would reach nearly 17 million," observed Christopher N. May in his brilliant and detailed analysis of the period.[19] It was indeed ratified on August 26, 1920, just in time
for the November election. "There was good reason to believe that a
politician who appeared to be waging a fearless campaign against rising
prices would reap his reward at the polls," May added.[20]

A Senate subcommittee in the Republican-controlled Congress heard
testimony from one Olivia Brueggeman, the former executive secretary
of women's activities in Missouri. Brueggeman claimed that she and
two other officers used Justice Department travel vouchers to attend
the state's Democratic convention, where one of the women was a voting delegate. She also asserted that Justice Department officials in
Washington had pressed them to obtain more publicity for Palmer. Although Howard Figg, the man in charge of the Women's Division, dismissed Brueggeman's testimony, May found that most of her
statements were corroborated by other witnesses.

The attorney general's blatant little political game would have remained an amusing footnote in the history of the Justice Department
except, as is frequently the case with a powerful agency, there were
some real casualties. Fair-price committees, which had operated during
the war, were soon revived in three quarters of the states and began
working with the Justice Department to establish fair profit margins for
different segments of the economy. U.S. attorneys were instructed to
give the press complete details in all cases of profiteering and hoarding.
Federal agents began to seize privately held stockpiles of eggs, pork and
other commodities that the government believed were being kept off
the market to force an escalation in prices.

With the passage in October 1919 of new, and very vague, price-
fixing provisions, a special Justice Department unit known as the
"Flying Squad" was created, which began to bring charges against those
who received unjust or unreasonable prices for their goods. By late
December the Justice Department reported it had filed almost 180
criminal charges for profiteering and made 100 seizures of hoarded
commodities. One of those charged was Jess Willard, who five months
before had lost his heavyweight boxing title to Jack Dempsey. Willard
was accused of charging illegal prices for his firewood. A member of the
fair-price committee in Topeka, Kansas, had paid $3.50 for a cord of
wood on Willard's farm. This, the U.S. attorney said, was "double what
it should have been."[21]

One area that received special attention was clothing, where the law
frequently was enforced even in areas where the merchants had been
given no guidance as to what was an appropriate markup. On April 20,
1920, federal agents arrested Joseph Nichthauser, a Brooklyn clothier,

for charging $45 for a raincoat which he had purchased for $25 or $30. He was charged and released on $2,000 bail. The next day, Nichthauser, the father of three, took his life in what the *New York Times* described as the first suicide growing out of the government's war on profiteering.

As a result of focusing on the likes of Willard and Nichthauser, of course, the Justice Department had almost no time to indict large corporations. The failure to investigate the right targets came to bother some editorial writers. When the former boxer was indicted for selling overpriced firewood, for example, the *St. Louis Post-Dispatch* raised questions about why the department would angle for a minor figure like Willard when "there are oil whales to be harpooned."[22]

What made the program uniquely hateful was that less than two years after Palmer had launched it, the United States Supreme Court ruled—in a case brought against a St. Louis grocery for selling 100 pounds of sugar for $10.07—that the principal law authorizing the effort, the Lever Act, was unconstitutional because its strictures were so vague and uncertain that they violated the Bill of Rights. The law, the court said, was "void for repugnancy to the Constitution." In throwing out the case, the court said the Lever Act was totally arbitrary. Trying to enforce it would be just as unfair as trying to enforce a statute that "penalized and punished all acts detrimental to the public interest when unjust and unreasonable in the estimation of the court and the jury."[23]

Because the ruling nullified the law on the grounds that no one could understand its strictures, the Supreme Court did not bother to confront a second major constitutional problem relating to the statute. The legislation was originally approved by Congress when the United States and Germany were fighting and was thus "a war act." Attorney General Palmer, however, applied the law after the armistice had been signed in 1918. The original dubious use of the war legislation grew even more suspect after Congress added a key amendment to the Lever Act months after most of the American troops had returned from the fighting in Europe. All of these serious constitutional problems were known and discussed during the period Attorney General Palmer was leading the Justice Department into his high-profile war against price fixers. But Palmer, the presidential candidate, was not about to allow a few legal niceties to upset the campaign strategy which he hoped would carry him into the White House.

ALL WE DO IS ENFORCE THE LAW

T he shameless shenanigans of A. Mitchell Palmer are a particularly egregious example of how an ambitious attorney general can manipulate the powers of the Justice Department to meet his personal political needs. Given the place of the attorney general in the president's cabinet and the frequency with which attorneys general have been political cronies of the man in the White House, however, it surely will surprise no one that presidents also have secretly intervened in the Justice Department to protect their friends and allies.

In the boom years after World War II, a dramatic change came over the worn, old mill town of Reading, Pennsylvania. Located about sixty miles northwest of Philadelphia, and an easy drive from such population centers as New York City and Baltimore, Reading had developed into a unique center of organized vice. In the age before the establishment of legalized casinos in Atlantic City, Reading became a magnet for high rollers from all over the East Coast. By the early 1960s, the town boasted a $1.3-million-a-year numbers bank, more than two hundred pinball machines rigged to work as slot machines, a high-stakes dice game, five houses of prostitution employing ten or more women each and an illegal $4-million-a-year still, the largest such operation uncovered by federal agents since Prohibition.

Reading's illegal operations flourished in part because of the corrupt understanding that Abe Minker, once an immigrant fruit peddler, had reached with Mayor John C. Kubacki and Police Chief Charles S. Wade. The operations came to an end because Attorney General Robert Kennedy decided to let two young Justice Department lawyers— Thomas F. McBride and Henry S. Ruth—see what they could do to combat the organized crime and systemic corruption that was then in control of Reading. The two men were among the best the Justice Department had, attracted to federal service by the idealism of the Kennedy campaign.

It may have been the relative openness of the organized crime operations in Reading that irked Kennedy. Or perhaps the attorney general calculated that while mounting a successful campaign against the Cosa Nostra in New York, Chicago or Philadelphia would be an extremely difficult challenge, beating the mob in this small Pennsylvania city of only 90,000 residents was achievable. Whatever his reason, Kennedy's judgment about the vulnerability of organized crime in Reading turned out to be correct.

Despite the initial refusal of the FBI to have any part in the Reading investigation, and repeated obstacles thrown in their path by the federal judges whose loyalties tended toward the Democratic machine that had arranged their appointments, McBride and Ruth prevailed. Police Chief Wade was convicted of perjury. Facing a stiff prison sentence, Wade then agreed to testify against Mayor Kubacki and Abe Minker, who were found guilty of extortion. A reform mayor, Eugene Shirk, was elected. With the help of a new police commissioner, Reading's open gambling and prostitution operations were closed down.[24]

The Reading investigation had been enormously satisfying and, emboldened by their success in this relatively small pond, McBride and Ruth dreamed of uncovering even more challenging conspiracies. During the course of their systematic exploration of the Reading underworld, the two lawyers had picked up a steady stream of rumors that a substantial number of the state judges and magistrates in Philadelphia had connections to that city's organized crime.

"We decided to begin our investigation by pulling some tax returns," recalled Ruth in an interview. "But because we knew that most of the IRS employees had obtained their jobs through the Democratic machine, we were worried that news of the investigation would immediately become known to the subjects. So, in an attempt to get around this problem, we decided to use special agents from what the IRS then called its 'Intelligence Division.'

"The special agents began pulling the returns at 3 A.M., but despite our hopes of secrecy, within hours after we began going through the files, someone made a call to Representative William Green," Ruth continued. Green, the boss of the Democratic organization in Philadelphia, was also a key leader in Congress. "He immediately called Bobby, complaining that October—just before the election—was a terrible time to begin an investigation.

"Kennedy instantly called us," recalled Ruth. "He was furious. 'There are times to start an investigation and times not to start. Can't you wait until December?' "

McBride, a respected organized crime prosecutor who had originally earned his spurs fighting the Mafia in New York City under District Attorney Frank Hogan, has a slightly different memory of the affair. "Bill Green called the president, the president called the attorney general, the attorney general called Henry Peterson, my immediate boss, and Henry called me," he said. Peterson, McBride explained, was the one who told him about Green's direct complaint to the president.

Whatever the mechanism, the investigation was not to be. Robert Kennedy, who had come into office obsessed by organized crime and Jimmy Hoffa, had moved to either slow or stop an investigation of systemic corruption in the judicial system of one of America's largest and most corrupt cities at the private request of a powerful Philadelphia political boss. Shortly after the attorney general's call to the two young prosecutors, President Kennedy was assassinated. Although Robert Kennedy was to remain attorney general until February 1965, the Philadelphia investigation somehow faded from view.

YOU'RE FIRED

T here are, of course, far more draconian ways to deal with federal prosecutors whose actions upset the political understandings of the party that controls the Justice Department: You fire them. Although there are a handful of exceptions, virtually all executive branch officials appointed by the president are subject to dismissal by the president. This is at it should be. Because under the law the president is responsible for directing the executive agencies, he necessarily must have the authority to assure that the government's senior executives follow his lead. But this power obviously can be exercised in improper ways.

On December 15, 1971, for example, President Richard Nixon dispatched a brief note to Robert L. Meyer, the U.S. attorney in Los Angeles.[25] "Your letter of November 4, submitting your resignation as United States Attorney for the Central District of California, has come to my attention," it began. Meyer had been forced by the Justice Department to write the resignation letter. There is also evidence that Meyer's departure was the result of considerable discussion at the highest levels of the government, and not just a small matter that by some chance had come to the president's attention. "In accepting this resignation, effective January 1, 1972, as you have requested, I want to express my appreciation for your service to our government and to extend my best wishes for the holiday season." As already noted, Meyer's resignation was not voluntary. More important, the Nixon administration, far from appreciating Meyer's services, was furious with him for taking actions that had deeply offended a number of President Nixon's most passionate supporters.

The event that ultimately led to the end of Meyer's career in government had occurred a year and a half earlier on a hot summer night in a run-down section of downtown Los Angeles. It was shortly after 9:15 P.M., and six illegal aliens were getting ready to go to bed in the small skid-row apartment they shared on the second floor of an old brownstone apartment at 826 East 7th Street. One of the young aliens, Guillermo Beltran Sanchez, twenty-two, was using a needle to paint a tattooed flower on his ankle. A second, Guillardo Alcazar Sanchez, twenty-one, was at a mirror either shaving or combing his hair.[26]

Suddenly, according to the later testimony of Angel Michel Bartoleno, twenty-four, a third young man in the apartment, there came "very hard blows" on the outer door. Without any warning, he continued, several officers burst through the door, guns blazing. One young man died instantly, his body riddled with forty buckshot wounds.[27] Another ran to a back porch where he was shot by police officers waiting in the alley below.

It was immediately apparent that the raid had been drastically botched. The individual the officers were looking for was not in the apartment, and neighbors, shown his photograph, said he was unknown to them. No one in the apartment was armed and no weapons were found in the rooms. No one in the apartment spoke any English. Although a first-day story by the notoriously cautious *Los Angeles Times* called the killings a mistake, from that point on the word was qualified by quotation marks, a subtle newspaper method for indicating to the reader that the description is not necessarily to be taken at face value.[28]

Three days after the raid, seven police officers were charged with manslaughter and assault by the local district attorney. While not directly challenging the action, Deputy Police Chief Daryl Gates told the *L.A. Times* that policemen were humans subject to making the same kind of mistakes as other citizens and he was worried the charges could have "a devastating effect on morale."[29] A few months later the local charges were dismissed for technical reasons before they were presented to a jury.

From the very beginning, however, initially with the approval of Attorney General John Mitchell, U.S. Attorney Meyer had been investigating the case. On March 4, 1971, four of the policemen were charged by a federal grand jury of violating the civil rights of the dead Mexican aliens. The action brought cries of outrage from Los Angeles mayor Sam Yorty and the city's police chief at the time, Edward M. Davis. The federal investigation of the case had been "precipitous, provocative, political and in extremely bad faith and bad taste," Davis said. The indictments, he added, were "persecutions" brought by a "propagandized" grand jury by liberal Republicans "in a cheap attempt to get minority votes."[30] Yorty said the Nixon administration should fire Meyer, who he charged was using the indicted officers as "scapegoats for his political ambition."

On August 8, 1971, thirteen months after the killings, a federal jury of eight women and four men acquitted the officers on all charges. It was all over. Although Nixon and Mitchell had sought to maintain their rapport with moderate Republicans such as Robert Finch, a California liberal chosen to be the administration's first secretary of the Department of Health, Education and Welfare, the backbone of the president's support in the Los Angeles area was dyed-in-the-wool conservatives like Yorty and Davis.

Shortly after the acquittal, Meyer submitted his forced resignation, effective on January 1, 1972, and Nixon accepted it in mid-December. A few weeks later Meyer spoke out in an interview. The criticism of him as a "moderate" or "liberal" by Yorty, Davis and Los Angeles sheriff

Peter Pitchess, he said, had caused Nixon to fire him. The former prosecutor said his prosecution of the police officers was not his only philosophical difference with the Nixon administration. But the cases were
central to the dispute. "They were the fulcrum and the point of controversy," he said.[31]

MR. CLEAN?

It is not every day that the dirty laundry of an administration gets
hung out to dry in the clear bright sunshine as did President Nixon's decision to fire Meyer or Robert Kennedy's decision to hold up or kill the
investigation of organized corruption in Philadelphia. The small number of such events that tumble into public view, however, should not
lead to the conclusion that they rarely occur. In fact, given the deep secrecy that naturally surrounds private telephone calls to the president
or the attorney general—especially from members of Congress who
happen to belong to the same party—it is truly amazing how many
high-level political fixes in the Justice Department are reported at all.

Perhaps one of the best documented of these cases involves a president widely regarded as among the most honorable chief executives in
the recent history of the United States. For an FBI agent named Thomas
J. Morris, the high point of the case must have been when he found
himself in the White House Oval Office questioning his ultimate boss,
President Jimmy Carter.

Morris was investigating a serious matter: Should the Democratic-
controlled Justice Department bring charges of obstruction of justice
against Joshua Eilberg, a Democratic member of the House of Representatives, because of his efforts to persuade a Democratic president to fire
U.S. attorney David Marston, who was investigating the congressman?
About six weeks before, the same FBI agent had questioned Attorney
General Griffin Bell about the same situation.

Because FBI agents are seldom required to interrogate the president of
the United States, Morris probably was a bit nervous. As the White
House interview continued, however, Morris must have become truly dis-
tressed. The story President Carter was telling him about his political intervention in the Justice Department was substantially at odds with the
account of the attorney general.

The case had crashed into the nation's headlines on January 20, 1977,
when the Carter administration fired David Marston, a young, brash
and entirely too talkative federal prosecutor in Philadelphia, the Eastern District of Pennsylvania. During the eighteen months that preceded

his dismissal, Marston had become a minor folk hero in the district by investigating and indicting a number of Pennsylvania's notoriously corrupt politicians, Democrats and Republicans.

In one important way, Marston's dismissal had been a routine event. Marston was a Republican who had been appointed eighteen months before by Jerry Ford. Carter was a Democrat who like George Washington—and every president since—understood that the power to investigate and indict usually is far too sensitive a matter to leave in the hands of a prosecutor from the opposing party.

So Carter's decision to force the resignation of a particular U.S. attorney was in itself not of particular interest. Marston's booting becomes notable because of the vast gap it revealed between the high-flown rhetoric of the Carter administration and some of its practices.

Questions still remain about why it happened and how it happened. Was the firing, as the Carter supporters have since claimed, a simple patronage issue, the removal of an ill-equipped headline hunter to allow the appointment of a qualified Democrat? Or, as some of the evidence suggests, had the president bounced Marston because the young prosecutor's ongoing corruption investigations were seriously wounding the Democratic machine in Pennsylvania and threatened to end the political careers of two senior Democratic House members who were important to the Carter administration's legislative plans?

The allegation that led FBI Agent Morris to question Carter and Bell was not a trivial matter. Congressman Eilberg and several other powerful Democratic figures were suspected of taking cash bribes from their constituents in return for providing them a variety of government favors. In one of the more original schemes, ambitious parents of students with poor academic records were making substantial payoffs—up to $20,000—to get their undistinguished children accepted into the medical school of the University of Pennsylvania. During meetings and telephone calls with a number of federal officials, including one conversation with President Carter, Eilberg strongly urged the Democratic administration to appoint its own federal prosecutor in Philadelphia. The outstanding question: Did Eilberg's confidential pleadings amount to obstruction of justice?

In most circumstances, of course, the details of such high-level political interventions in the handling of a criminal case remain completely hidden from the public. In the Eilberg affair, however, the FBI's unusual obstruction of justice investigation led Special Agent Morris to question Carter, Bell and several other senior administration officials. Upon the completion of each interview, as required by bureau regulations, Morris routinely prepared a confidential summary of what the witness had told him.

Morris interviewed Bell in his large fifth-floor Justice Department of-

fice in mid-February of 1978, less than four months after the key events
in the case had occurred. Given the touchiness of the matter, Morris's
summary suggests that the attorney general was remarkably forthcoming.

On November 8 or 9, 1977, Bell said, "President Carter called him
concerning a conversation that the President had with Eilberg on November 4, 1977. President Carter told him [Bell] that Eilberg had called
him [Carter] telephonically, and complained that Marston was only
prosecuting Democrats," the agent wrote in the official account of the
interview.[32]

Bell explained that Carter had begun their brief conversation with a
general question about the Marston situation. The attorney general said
he had responded to this initial query by telling the president that he
was not satisfied with Marston's performance and intended to dismiss
him within the next six or seven weeks, certainly by the end of 1977.

The leader of the free world, on the other hand, apparently was not
satisfied with the attorney general's performance, at least when it came
to dumping the troublesome prosecutor. "President Carter asked him
[Bell] to try to speed up the replacement of Marston," Morris quoted
Bell as saying. "The President used a term like 'expedite,' although it
was Bell's recollection that this was not the exact word he used."

Bell further recalled telling the president that he had stopped taking
Eilberg's telephone calls. "[T]he president responded to this by saying
something to the effect that 'Yeah, that's why I've had to talk to him,' "
the attorney general told the FBI agent. At that point in the interview,
for the second time in the FBI agent's seven-page, single-spaced summary, the notes show that President Carter was fully aware of the political dimensions of the situation. "The President then related to him
[Bell] that, according to Eilberg, Marston, as a Republican, was engaged
in prosecuting only Democrats."

Morris interviewed President Carter about the Eilberg affair toward
the end of March, six weeks after his talk with Bell. Sitting in on the
meeting was White House attorney Robert Lipshutz. Although Morris's
summary shows that Carter confirmed he had indeed received a call
from the Democratic congressman, the president's memory of what Eilberg said to him and what he then said to his attorney general sharply
conflicted with the summary of Bell's account.

Eilberg had not seemed angry or upset during the call, the president
said. The congressman's central concern was that the administration's
long delay in finding a replacement for the position of U.S. attorney in
Philadelphia was creating dissension within the Democratic delegation
and that the matter should be resolved.

Carter further told Morris that Eilberg never mentioned Marston by
name and had limited his remarks to a very general discussion of the
position of U.S. attorney. The president, Morris wrote, said he "was not

aware at the time, nor was he made aware by Eilberg, that there was any criticism about how the United States Attorney in Philadelphia was conducting himself, nor was he made aware of any criticism concerning any of the other United States Attorneys in Pennsylvania. He did not recall that Eilberg said anything at all concerning Marston 'prosecuting Democrats.' "[33]

The FBI summaries of the interviews with Carter and Bell showed one other point of basic conflict. "President Carter relayed the substance of the Eilberg conversation to the Attorney General," Morris said. "He does not recall making specific reference to Marston by name."

So Carter and Bell, in their official statements to the FBI, had distinctly different memories about the Eilberg call to the president and precisely how the president had responded to it. Carter said the call was very general, that Marston's name was never mentioned, that Eilberg never complained that the U.S. attorney in Philadelphia was going after Democrats and that he had not mentioned Marston's name during his discussion with the attorney general. Bell, on the other hand, said President Carter mentioned Marston's name, that Carter told him he wanted the ouster of the federal prosecutor speeded up and that Carter had specifically quoted Eilberg as complaining that Marston was going after Democrats.

There are good reasons for the Carter administration to be touchy about the Marston affair. After all, in reaction to Watergate, Jimmy Carter had promised he would never tell the American people a lie, and announced a policy that neither he nor the White House would intervene in particular cases being considered by the Justice Department.

It may have been this sensitivity which led Bell, when he got around to publishing his Justice Department memoirs in 1982, to retell the story of Eilberg's call to Carter. Bell's second version of the Eilberg caper is of interest because it, almost in a single breath, confirms the event itself and contradicts an important aspect of what the attorney general had told Special Agent Morris about the event in 1978.

On November 4, 1977, Bell wrote, Eilberg "telephoned Carter and said Marston had to go. Eilberg gave no reason and the president didn't ask." Somehow, Bell's embarrassing recollection that the president had told him that Marston was "only prosecuting Democrats" had been forgotten. In this reshaped history of the event, Bell said the "president said there was pressure from the Democrats in Pennsylvania to replace Marston and asked why it had taken so long. I think Jimmy Carter talked to Eilberg because he badly wanted the congressman's support for pending energy legislation and because Eilberg was chairman of the House Judiciary Subcommittee on Immigration, Refugees and International Law, another area the President was trying to reform."[34]

The conflicting accounts of the president and the attorney general probably mean the precise details of the case will never be fully resolved. But there is no question that Eilberg believed himself the target of a Justice Department investigation, that he asked the president of the United States to appoint a Democratic replacement for the prosecutor who was directing the investigation, that the president relayed the message to the attorney general and that the offending prosecutor was removed.

Because Eilberg did not limit his lobbying to the president and the attorney general, however, Special Agent Morris obtained other testimony that tends to confirm the highly political character of the congressman's approach. On March 2, 1977, for example, Eilberg met with William B. Gray, at that time the director of the Executive Office of United States Attorneys, and Michael Egan, the associate attorney general responsible for overseeing the selection of all Justice Department appointees.

According to Morris's summary of his interview with Gray, Eilberg told the two men that Marston was a publicity seeker who was using his position as U.S. attorney to run for governor, and that he "has got to be, or who ought to be, gotten rid of before he indicts him [Eilberg] and every other Democrat in Philadelphia."[35]

The FBI summaries contain no indication that any of the five officials—from President Carter on down—ever expressed any interest in the substance of the corruption investigations that had brought on Eilberg's open complaints or even stopped to question the appropriateness of Eilberg's demands that Marston be replaced. In his official memoir, however, Bell sought to get in the last self-serving word. The scandals that had sent former attorney general John Mitchell to prison, he opined, left only one clear message: "That the attorney general be free from political influence is essential to public confidence in his office."[36] Too bad Carter and Bell didn't always act on this maxim.

DECENT PEOPLE

During the four years of the Bush administration, several Democratic-controlled committees of the House and an assortment of environmental groups mounted a series of attacks on the way the Justice Department was enforcing the environmental laws. One of the best documented of these assaults—described later in this book—involved the department's environmental crimes unit and its success in blocking several key prosecutions.

But it wasn't only those with obvious partisan or advocacy interests that questioned the Justice Department performance under Attorney General Richard Thornburgh and his successor, William P. Barr. One of the most unusual challenges came from an institution that normally remains firmly under the control of the Justice Department: a federal grand jury.

The case began, curiously enough, in Denver just a few months after Judge Carrigan had published his ruling on the handling of the pollution problem at the Rocky Mountain Arsenal's Basin F, when a team of seventy-five agents from the Federal Bureau of Investigation and the Environmental Protection Agency raided a second Defense Department facility in Colorado. The name of this other facility was the Rocky Flats Nuclear Weapons Plant and the date was June 6, 1989. Armed with a search warrant of more than a hundred pages, the agents eventually carted away millions of pages of documents.[37]

The target of the FBI-EPA raid was a 6,550-acre manufacturing facility that since 1952 had been producing small plutonium devices designed to trigger nuclear bombs when they reached their targets.[38] Owned by the Department of Energy, the plant at that time was operated by the Rockwell International Corporation. This was apparently the first time in American history that the facility of one federal agency was raided for purposes of criminal investigation by two other federal agencies.

Seven weeks later, at the request of Michael Norton, the U.S. attorney for Colorado, District Court Judge Sherman G. Finesilver impaneled a twenty-three-member special grand jury to consider the evidence of whether various environmental crimes had been committed at the government-owned plant. Norton had decided a special grand jury should be created so its members could devote all of its attention to the massive Rocky Flats investigation.

The grand jury commenced its work on August 1, 1989, and was released from service on March 24, 1992. During the two-and-a-half-year period it was in session, jury members typically met at the Federal Courthouse in Denver for about one week each month. Hundreds of thousands of documents were reviewed, more than one hundred officials testified.[39]

It turned out to be a contentious and difficult time for the jurors, who slowly came to realize that their view of conditions at Rocky Flats and who should be held accountable for them was very different than that of U.S. Attorney Norton and Justice Department officials in Washington. In the end, according to an authoritative account published in *Westward*, an aggressive Denver-area weekly, when Norton told the jurors he would not draft an indictment naming Rockwell and DoE officials, they drafted one on their own and adopted it unanimously. When Norton tried to discourage them from writing what is called a "presentment," a document that outlines criminal violations but does not bring specific charges, they drafted one anyway and unanimously approved it. When Norton asked them to adopt the indictment he desired, containing the charges which Rockwell ultimately pleaded guilty to, they refused.

In a near final draft of the indictment obtained by *Westward* reporter Bryan Abas, the jurors called Rocky Flats "an ongoing criminal enterprise" that was being allowed to operate in an illegal manner only because duplicitous government and corporate officials had engaged in "a campaign of distraction, deception and dishonesty."[40]

The jurors' conclusions about the underlying crimes at the nuclear facility were equally sweeping. "When agents of the Federal Bureau of Investigation and the Environmental Protection Agency raided the Rocky Flats plant on June 6, 1989, they found compelling evidence that hazardous and radioactive waste had been illegally stored, treated and disposed of in violation of the Resource Conservation and Recovery Act [RCRA]. The agents discovered that the Clean Water Act and other environmental statutes were being violated through a variety of continuing acts, including the illegal discharge of pollutants, hazardous materials and radioactive matter into local rivers. The agents also discovered a culture of criminal misconduct, in which corporate bonuses were obtained through illegal means."[41]

Because of the absolute secrecy that surrounds the workings of all grand juries, the profound conflict that had developed between the jurors and the prosecutor did not become public for many months. But because of another aspect of grand jury rules, the jurors in the end were officially powerless. Although the institution of the grand jury was originally established to serve as a citizen check on abusive prosecutors, grand juries today almost always act as rubber stamps. In point of fact, under current federal law, no grand jury, including Grand Jury 89-2, is authorized to indict anyone without the prosecutor's signature. And in this particular case, Mr. Norton seems to have lost his pen.

Two days after the dismissal of the grand jury Norton announced that he had entered into a plea bargain agreement with Rockwell in which the corporation agreed to plead guilty to five felony and five misdemeanor charges and to pay an $18.5 million fine. The grand jury, of course, had played no part in the agreement Norton had worked out with Rockwell. Significantly, the agreement did not include any criminal charges against the individual managers at either Rockwell or the Energy Department, and closed the door on further prosecution.

Because the public at that time did not know about the very different views of nineteen members of the grand jury, Norton and his Justice Department supervisors in Washington were able to hail the agreement as a significant victory for the government, emphasizing that it was the second largest fine in the history of environmental enforcement in the United States. (The largest fine was paid as a result of the Exxon Valdez spill in Alaska.) This claim, however, is less impressive than it sounds when the penalty is compared to the size of the corporation. During the year the $18.5 million fine was imposed, for example, it represented only four tenths of one percent of the $5.2 billion in business Rockwell did with the federal government. The fine also was minuscule in relation to the $1 billion it now appears taxpayers will pay to clean up the radioactive materials and other chemical wastes that now pollute the Rocky Flats area.

The rebellion of the special grand jury in Denver—and the reporting of this event by the press—infuriated the Justice Department. In the case of the grand jury, the FBI was ordered to investigate who had leaked the draft of its report to the reporters. U.S. Attorney Norton issued a rebuttal asserting that the grand jury had made accusations that were neither justified nor supported by any evidence. "Largely due to the United States' inability to use grand jury information to respond to or refute these falsities, the public perception is being created that the Government has behaved irresponsibly, which is patently false," Norton declared.

Also outraged was Barry Hartman, first the deputy and then the acting assistant attorney general for the department's Environment and Natural Resources Division at the time of the government's investigation of Rocky Flats and its settlement with Rockwell. "Plain nonsense," Hartman began, with the sweeping dismissal favored by all bureaucrats when presented with evidence of questionable activities.

But then, in a remarkably contradictory statement, the former senior Bush administration official proceeded to confess to a personal mind-set that appears to perfectly illuminate the Justice Department's approach to corporate crime in general and environmental crime in particular.

"Environmental crimes are not like organized crime or drugs," Hartman explained. "There, you have bad people doing bad things. With environmental crimes, you have decent people doing bad things. You have to look at it this way.

"Companies pollute legally and illegally," he continued. "You have to rely on the good sense of the prosecutor to determine when an individual should be indicted. It can't be taken lightly. It will have a major effect on people's lives, whether or not they are found guilty. They might lose their house, their car. It will change their lives. This has become a very scary proposition for the business community."[42]

Hartman's compassion for corporate America was truly touching. Unfortunately, however, an examination of the nation's environmental laws does not disclose a single provision that distinguishes between "bad people doing bad things" and "decent people doing bad things."

How did Hartman make this distinction while he was acting as one of the nation's senior lawyers? Did he consider the suspect's social class or race or position on the corporate ladder? With absolutely no guidance from the law, it must have been a difficult choice for him.

In a wonderfully scandalous way, Hartman seemed to confirm the worst suspicions of Grand Jury 89-2 and, at the same time, opened a small window onto a very large and outrageous fact about the United States Department of Justice. The world simply is not like we always have been told. In the application of federal law, nice people don't come in last.

The aborted grand jury investigation of Rocky Flats and Barry Hartman's bizarre mea culpa were, in their own right, beyond the fringe. But because these two related events are part of a much larger and seemingly persistent pattern of misuse of Justice Department powers to advance certain partisan, corporate and racial interests, the question must be asked whether what we see when we look beyond the fringe is the exception or the rule.

3

Seven Bad
Ways to Run
an Agency

Rachel Carson's *Silent Spring*, published in 1962, was certainly one of the most influential American books of the twentieth century. Her powerful analysis reshaped the world's thinking about the cataclysmic environmental dangers that she believed were threatening the future of human life.

Like *Uncle Tom's Cabin* during the tumultuous years shortly before the beginning of the Civil War, Carson's book demanded a national political response. And it was not long in coming. With the apparently enthusiastic backing of such unlikely figures as Richard Nixon, Congress approved a half dozen far-reaching pollution control laws during a brief flurry of action in the 1970s.

A basic principle behind these new laws was the notion that the hazards they sought to allay had become so grave that a nationally directed enforcement campaign was required to deal with them. Erratic regional efforts, directed by local agencies, would no longer do. Because the poisoned rivers and contaminated winds paid no mind to state borders, isolated areas where serious pollution problems would be ignored were now unacceptable. With the Clean Water Act, the Clean Air Act, the Toxic Substances Control Act, the Resources Conservation and Recovery Act, the Federal Insecticide, Fungicide and Rodenticide Act and many other laws, Congress created a federal enforcement apparatus under which the Justice Department was required to play a prominent and controlling role.

To a surprising extent, however, analysis of federal enforcement data and follow-up interviews with selected government officials strongly suggest that the Justice Department has largely ignored Congress's mandates. In fact, as will become devastatingly clear, the evidence demonstrates that the Justice Department is a chaotic, slipshod, almost medieval institution which has largely failed to coordinate federal enforcement and regulation efforts in this and many other significant areas.

Although it is entirely natural for Justice Department officials to defend their institution, especially during the years when they were running the show, attorneys general from both parties show surprising agreement when it comes to making one negative point about their agency. As mentioned briefly in a previous chapter, a surprising number agree that, as a class, U.S attorneys—the federal government's front-line prosecutors—are loose cannons. Ramsey Clark, Lyndon Johnson's attorney general, contended that U.S. attorneys are usually more responsive to the senators who obtained their appointment than to the attorney general, their nominal boss. "Without [the support of the] U.S. attorney, there will be no prosecution, and through him there can be malicious prosecution," Clark wrote.[1] "The offices of the U.S. attorneys are independent baronies," griped Griffin Bell, the attorney general during most of the Carter years.[2] "The Justice Department is hard to get a hold of, it's a whole bunch of little freewheeling satrapies," complained William Barr, an attorney general for George Bush.[3]

Given the national fixation on Washington, it is hard to comprehend just how much power is exercised by the independent U.S. attorneys and how little by what is often referred to as "main Justice." One measure of the relative strength of the two camps concerns who is bringing the cases. According to a 1994 analysis by the Executive Office of United States Attorneys, for example, 95 percent of all criminal cases and approximately 66 percent of all civil cases of the federal government are now brought by the U.S. attorneys.[4]

An old and important principle of American life, at all levels of government, is that significant laws should be consistently enforced. Of course we understand that some laws are trivial and will rarely be acted upon. There are, after all, only so many agents and so many hours in a day, and priorities must be set. Some of the enforcement needs, say, of the federal district of Montana are different from those of the federal district embracing Manhattan, the Bronx and several of New York City's suburban counties to the north.

But from the cop on the beat to the FBI agent in the suite, there is a need to apply society's important prohibitions in a firm and consistent manner, to see to it that similarly situated people are treated in similar ways. This is partly a matter of basic fairness. At least as important, however, is the fact that grossly uneven enforcement efforts do not command respect. When people come to feel that the chances of detection are slim and the possibility of prosecution erratic, the temptation to break the law grows stronger.

At the federal level, the attorney general is sworn to provide the American people with consistent and reasonable enforcement. This obligation goes back a long way, first being imposed in 1861 when Congress, early in the Civil War, passed a law requiring the attorney general to supervise the work of the U.S. attorneys. In 1870, in a partially related law that authorized the creation of the United States Justice Department, Congress required the attorney general, among other duties, "to make all necessary rules and regulations for the government of the said Justice Department and for the management and distribution of its business."[5] Almost a century later, President Lyndon Johnson issued a still-standing executive order that requires the attorney general to coordinate "the criminal law enforcement activities and crime prevention activities of all federal departments and agencies."[6]

To a degree that is almost incomprehensible, the attorneys general of the United States have been unable or unwilling to coordinate the operations of the Justice Department and, more broadly, all federal enforcement programs. Of course, there have been occasions—the savings and loan scandals of the mid-1980s is one example—when public concern about a specific issue led the department to lurch into a frenzied enforcement effort. But for most of its history, the department has drifted along without the guidance of coherent plans.

Yes, enforcement directives are periodically issued from Washington. Yes, the department has a system in which U.S. attorneys are requested to give some matters more attention than others. And certainly attorneys general have stepped in and exercised their authority in a given high-priority case, as when the Justice Department brass in Washington took over the prosecution of Panama's dictator Manuel Noriega from the U.S. attorney in Miami.

But all this is posturing, froth without substance. The attorney general is largely irrelevant when it comes to directing substantial chunks of the agency's enforcement activities. By giving constant speeches, issuing press releases, holding regular news conferences and frequently testifying before Congress, a long line of attorneys general have tricked the Washington press corps, members of the House and Senate and thus the rest of the country into believing that they run their agency. For a variety of fundamental personal, political and philosophical reasons, however, attorneys general and their top assistants historically have exercised surprisingly little direct influence over the day-to-day operations of the department's principal components.

In the summer of 1995, more than two years after Janet Reno became the attorney general, the General Accounting Office criticized the nonexistent management efforts of the Justice Department. "Over the last ten years," the GAO said, "Attorneys General did not issue prosecutorial priorities through any specific process." Rather, the report continued, the directors of this important agency relied upon press conferences, speeches and budget testimony—none of which are regularly distributed to the individual U.S. attorneys—to set their enforcement policies. While Ms. Reno did announce that violent crime and medical fraud were her two top matters of concern, the report said that as of February 1995 no procedures had been set in place to make sure her orders were being followed.[7]

One part of the problem is structural. While the attorney general is required by one group of laws to direct and coordinate the enforcement activities of U.S. attorneys, the FBI and the DEA, another law says that the president is the only person who can remove a U.S. attorney or the FBI director. The second part is political—political in the sense that, responding to wave after wave of public concern, the Justice Department now has established nine major enforcement areas that it says are top-priority business. The obvious problem: It is very hard to give anything top priority when everything has been so designated.

Nonfeasance is the failure to do what duty requires. In certain circumstances it is a crime. If nonfeasance happened to be one of those crimes that the Justice Department enforced, the living attorneys general could be among the first to be prosecuted, assuming the statute of limitations hadn't run out on some of the more senior members of this small club.

Were the Justice Department only a mom-and-pop grocery store in a small town somewhere in America, the failure of almost all attorneys general to make a serious attempt to understand and supervise the operations of their agency would be of little concern. Obviously, however, the Justice Department is a massive organization with many essential missions and, despite its chaotic character, a very real impact—direct and indirect—on the lives of every American.

"The lawyers who control this department don't like planning," said one Justice Department professional in a recent interview. "Since the earliest days, they have viewed almost any assessment of their performance as a personal threat."

As in the Sherlock Holmes story about the dog that failed to bark, the best proof of the department's profound resistance to evaluation is something that has never happened. To this day, more than a century after Congress passed the first law authorizing the attorney general to supervise the operations of the U.S. attorneys, the Justice Department has yet to seriously measure and compare the performance of its front-line troops who actually carry out much of the department's work. How is this possible?

It is true that the Justice Department has for many years collected raw data about matters referred to it and cases brought by it. Yet it is also true that the Justice Department has systematically ignored the collected data, never seeking to understand the larger patterns and trends. How could all those serious men, and one woman, year after year, pretend they were in charge of their department when in fact they had no knowledge of what their federal prosecutors—a major component of the department—were doing? How could so many attorneys general solemnly announce their national law enforcement priorities without ever checking to see whether the promises they were making were in fact being kept?

One answer, of course, is obvious. All attorneys general and most senior Justice Department officials are lawyers who through their training and experience tend to view the whole world as a long string of distinct "cases." From their perspective, almost any attempt to examine a problem by clustering similar cases or administrative actions for focused examination is inherently suspect. With uncanny regularity, Justice Department lawyers have rejected the use of epidemiological methods to identify the pathologies of their agency, arguing that such an approach is unworkable and even harmful. It is quite mad that those in charge of an agency which is processing more than 200,000 matters a year are trying to manage it largely on a case-by-case basis.

Other obscure forces are also at work. Robert Kastenmeier, for example, became the chairman of the House Judiciary Subcommittee on the Courts, Civil Liberties and the Administration of Justice in 1970. From this position, the Wisconsin Democrat devoted a great deal of his time to trying to fathom the inner operations of the Justice Department. "After many years, I slowly came to understand that our attorneys general don't want to know what the department is doing and, even on those occasions when they do, rarely have the necessary administrative skills and political authority to make it function according to their wishes," the retired congressman told me. "The real power in the Justice Department,

the FBI, the DEA and so on seems to lie out in the districts. An individual
U.S. attorney or an individual senior agent in charge of an FBI office can
pretty much pursue any goal that appeals to him."[8]

Edward H. Stephenson, Jr., an assistant director of Congress's General Accounting Office who devoted more than ten years of his professional career to analyzing the problems of the Justice Department,
made much the same point. "There is no strategic overall management
plan to direct law enforcement resources in the United States," he said.[9]

Not that the suggestion implicit in the comments of Kastenmeier
and Stephenson would be easy to achieve. Curiously, the only known attempt to require federal prosecutors to develop strategic enforcement
plans in a systematic way was initiated by President Reagan's laid-back
first attorney general, William French Smith. In 1981, Smith ordered
each of the U.S. attorneys to form a broadly based law enforcement
committee within their districts. One specific task assigned to these
committees was to develop separate crime fighting plans for all of the districts. Requiring the development of ninety-three individual plans, of
course, did not come close to meeting the attorney general's lawful
mandate to coordinate federal enforcement efforts. But it was a beginning.

The well-meaning but clumsy exercise soon sank under its own
weight. From an examination of the district plans submitted by a sample
of U.S. attorneys headquartered in five major U.S. cities, it is not hard to
understand why. Under the plan submitted by Dan K. Webb, the U.S. attorney for the Northern District of Illinois (Chicago), for example, the law
enforcement committee for that district attempted to identify the
"most significant current criminal problems" that confronted the office. The committee, it turned out, had a hard time making choices.

In the area of white-collar crime alone, the group identified eight
broad categories of events, all of which it felt were the "most significant." They were: (1) health and safety violations, (2) investment fraud,
(3) commodities fraud, (4) securities fraud, (5) advance fee schemes, (6)
professional or fiduciary violations, (7) antitrust violations including
price-fixing and bid-rigging and (8) energy-related fraud "including
theft, embezzlement and deception regarding energy products." The
Chicago-area committee also identified some other very large criminal
problems that required front-burner consideration. Among them were
such matters as organized crime, violent crime and drug crime.[10] So
much for establishing priorities.

In a letter accepting the planning document, Rudolph Giuliani, then
the associate attorney general, reached the interesting conclusion that
the prosecutor's blueprint provided "a sound and comprehensive foundation for federal law enforcement coordination in the Northern District of Illinois." Exactly how Webb's forty-seven-page laundry list of
must-do enforcement matters would achieve this goal was a mystery.

The failure of Webb to develop a comprehensive enforcement plan for his district illustrates the real difficulty of setting priorities in a world where years of inflated political promises have given the public unrealistic expectations of what law enforcement can achieve. The challenge becomes even more difficult at the national level. In fact, as we know, no attorney general has ever developed a set of realistic enforcement goals and a unified plan of action, let alone monitored the activities of the department's agencies to make sure that the plan was being followed.

The old laissez-faire system of Justice Department management, where attorneys general and their lieutenants have remained blissfully unaware of what their troops were doing, may be coming to an end. If this change actually should come to pass, however, the motivating force will not be the department's thoughtful decision that it was required, but a new law. On August 3, 1993, with the signing of the Government Performance and Result Act, Congress ordered every federal agency to begin developing a "strategic plan."

The Justice Department plan, an internal memorandum said, would cover five years, spell out the goals and objectives of the department's major functions and summarize the resources necessary to achieve these goals. "By March 31, 2000, the Department must submit to Congress an annual report on the actual performance of programs compared to the goals expressed in the performance plan. If the performance goals are not met, the report is to explain why and state plans to meet the goal."[11]

AN EVEN MORE SILENT SPRING — COURTESY OF THE U.S. JUSTICE DEPARTMENT

The Justice Department's failure to set true priorities extends to every area of the substantive law. But the default is especially noticeable when it comes to Rachel Carson's concern, the environment. Despite Congress's general and specific orders that the attorney general guide and coordinate a host of specific national enforcement programs to deal with various environmental problems, the nation's chief law enforcement officers have allowed the relevant laws to be executed in an extraordinarily uneven way. So uneven, in fact, as to suggest that the very idea of a coherent national effort to protect the environment is largely an illusion.

In addition to general statutes and executive orders dating back to 1861, the basic power of the attorney general to enforce the nation's environmental laws rests on the fact that only the Justice Department—in this case a relatively small group of lawyers in Washington and, more important, nearly 4,100 federal prosecutors working out of U.S. attorneys' offices all over the nation—has the legal authority to bring criminal and civil actions against the accused. While environmental agencies like the EPA, the Coast Guard and the Interior Department can impose certain kinds of administrative fines, it is the Justice Department alone that has the power to fire the big guns.

In some ways, of course, the very biggest stick in the war to save the environment is the criminal charge. The key fact about a criminal charge is that in certain circumstances, when brought against an individual, it can lead to time in prison. Corporate executives hate prison. The second important weapon in the Justice Department armory is the civil suit. Such suits, which generally are easier to bring than criminal charges, are called for when the government feels a large penalty is appropriate or it wants to obtain a court order requiring the defendant to undertake a major corrective action. Although the EPA and a dozen other agencies can undertake investigations and propose sanctions for polluters who break the law, the final controlling voice in the initiation of criminal and civil actions rests with federal prosecutors. The Justice Department thus is the ultimate gatekeeper.

All the government's enforcement actions—whether criminal, civil or administrative—are of course brought under laws that have been approved by Congress as a result of public concerns. Mobilizing the citizenry over these concerns are a variety of public interest groups such as the Sierra Club, the National Resources Defense Council and the National Audubon Society. The same constituent pressures have also prompted Congress to provide the hundreds of millions of dollars in funding required to hire tens of thousands of EPA experts, FBI agents, federal prosecutors, Interior Department inspectors and Agriculture Department investigators to enforce the environmental laws.

But an encyclopedic understanding of all the statutes and regulations, and a complete accounting of all the investigators and inspectors who have been hired to enforce them, leaves out the single most important piece of information: Which laws are being enforced, how frequently are they being enforced and where are they being enforced? Amazing as it may seem, no one—not the Justice Department, not the environmental groups, not the reporters, not the Congress—knows the answers to these questions, because no one has undertaken the necessary evaluation.

KEEPING THE GOLDEN STATE GOLDEN

Consider California, where four largely independent U.S. attorneys are the senior Justice Department representatives in the state. The main office of the U.S. attorney for the Southern District is located in San Diego. Los Angeles is headquarters for the Central District. The Northern District's principal office is located in San Francisco. Sacramento is home base for federal prosecutors in the state's Eastern District.

With thousands of miles of fragile coastline, millions of acres of irrigated farmland, hundreds of significant mining and drilling operations, a large number of gritty industrial areas and an environmentally alert population, one might well expect California to be a state where federal prosecutors would lead the nation in the aggressive enforcement of federal pollution control laws. This is not the case.

A little background information is required to understand why this is so and how we know it. For the last twenty years, U.S. attorneys around the country have been required to send Washington detailed information about those matters that were referred to them by such enforcement and regulatory agencies as the FBI, the DEA and the EPA, as well as reports on the actions they took as a result of these referrals. Every year, a massively simplified summary of the information coming from the ninety-three districts is published in a slim annual report by the Executive Office of United States Attorneys. But because there is a huge variation in the number of people living in each district and the number of federal prosecutors working in each district, the summary figures have almost no value as a tool for considering the performance of the individual offices. Knowing that a U.S. attorney in Florida brought 300 cases while a U.S. attorney in Oregon brought 150 means nothing until you factor in such information as how many people live in the district.

Starting about five years ago, the Transactional Records Access Clearinghouse (TRAC), whose establishment is discussed in the author's note at the rear of this book, initiated the first of a long series of unique studies about the daily operations of the federal government. The first step in these studies is to identify internal administrative files containing information such as the number of persons charged with a federal crime in each district. TRAC obtains these records, in computer form, under the Freedom of Information Act. To provide context to the Justice Department information, TRAC also obtains annual population counts for each district from the Census Bureau as well as detailed year-to-year staffing information from the Office of Personnel Management. With these and other denominators it then becomes possible, for the first time ever, to begin making legitimate comparisons of Justice Department enforcement actions on a year-to-year and district-to-district basis. What were the long-term enforcement trends for various kinds of offenses? How did the enforcement effort in one region or district compare with another? Did these differences make sense in terms of what was known about the underlying problems in each district?

As already suggested, the raw counts of criminal and civil matters in each district are not very helpful for comparative purposes because there is so much variation in the number of people living within district borders. California's Central District, the area around Los Angeles, for example, with almost 16 million residents, is the state's largest. California's Southern District, San Diego, with only 2.7 million, is the smallest.

When considering the actions that the federal government took to clean up pollution in a specific area, it obviously would be best to know the size of the pollution problem that it confronted. But because there is no reliable information about the extent of such problems in the different districts, we chose to begin with population. While certainly not a perfect alternative, this approach makes some sense because the amount of pollution in an area obviously has some connection with the number of people who live there.

The study of federal environmental activities in California was one of TRAC's first projects. During the 1980s, for example, TRAC's data showed that Californians represented more than 10 percent of the U.S. population, and that California was the home office for about 10 percent of the nation's federal prosecutors.

During those same years, however, the administrative records of the Justice Department indicated that environmental matters brought by the federal prosecutors in the state amounted to a bit less than 4 percent of the civil matters and about 7 percent of the criminal cases initiated throughout the country.[12] So California, in relation to its population and its cadre of federal prosecutors, was getting less federal environmental enforcement than other parts of the nation.

The aberrations that emerged within each of the state's four districts were even more pronounced. Between 1981 and 1990, federal prosecutors in San Diego brought fifteen such matters per 10 million population, Sacramento brought ten, Los Angeles seven and San Francisco a bit more than one.

In summary then, this is what was found: In relative terms, the U.S. attorneys in California had brought considerably fewer criminal and civil cases concerning the environment than had federal prosecutors in the rest of the country. The anomalies among the four federal districts within the state were far more extreme. Again in relation to population, the U.S. attorney and his assistants in the Southern District had initiated twelve times more enforcement cases per capita than their colleagues in the Northern District and twice as many as were brought in the Los Angeles area.

What was going on? Why was California getting the short end of the stick? Why, more particularly, were northern Californians being uniquely shortchanged?

Federal prosecutors, in a series of interviews conducted between 1991 and 1994, contended that the significant variations in enforcement rates made sense, and that they could largely be explained by the existing pollution problems of each district. "I can only attribute it to the nature of the caseload, to the nature of the industrial base and the population in the area," said Barry Hartman, then the deputy assistant attorney general in the Environment and Natural Resources Division of the Justice Department.[13]

That explanation, however, doesn't hold water. Because of the vast reach of federal environmental laws, the relatively small number of criminal and civil cases that the federal government is ever able to bring, and the large number of pollution problems throughout all of California, it is impossible to argue that the federal enforcement effort in the four districts was in any way related to the actual violations that were occurring in the districts.

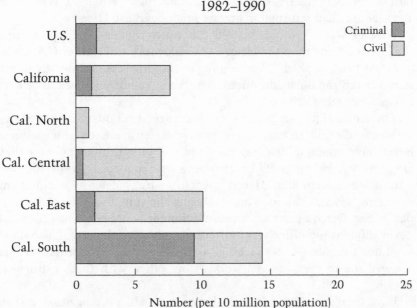

FEDERAL ENVIRONMENTAL PROSECUTIONS
1982–1990

U.S. attorneys use enormous discretion in how they enforce federal criminal and civil laws within their districts, in some cases perhaps electing not to deal with certain problems at all. (TRAC ANALYSIS OF JUSTICE DEPARTMENT AND CENSUS BUREAU DATA)

Here is one example. From 1981 to 1990, the federal prosecutors in the Northern District of California, an area with a population of 6.8 million, failed to bring a single criminal case under the nation's environmental laws—the Clean Air Act, the National Environmental Act, the Rivers and Harbors Act, the Water Pollution Control Act and an assortment of other statutes. Although we all know that the people of northern California are a very special and caring breed, can anyone believe that the lumber companies, the mining corporations, the oil drillers and the waste disposal specialists for a booming district with almost 7 million people never violated any environmental laws?

THE MODIFIED CHAOS THEORY

There appears to be a better, although startling, explanation. Peter Nunez was the U.S. attorney in San Diego during most of the 1980s. A generally respected federal prosecutor during that period, in 1989 he was selected by President Bush to come to Washington and be his assistant secretary of the treasury for law enforcement. When interviewed in 1993, Nunez had returned to private practice in San Diego.

Why, he was asked, was his office so much more active in protecting the environment than the offices of California's three other U.S. attorneys? At first he joked. "You're going to ruin my reputation with all my friends from the Bush administration. We were not supposed to be avid environmentalists."[14]

The amiable former prosecutor then turned serious. "United States attorneys do talk to each other from time to time, but they almost never have concrete discussions about the enforcement policies they are pursuing. Meetings of U.S. attorneys tend to focus on a specific case or how we can handle the latest hot issue—drugs, defense procurement problems, savings and loan fraud. During the time I was the U.S. attorney in San Diego I can't say the environment was a hot issue. In fact, I never thought my office was particularly active in the area. I also must say I don't remember ever seeing Justice Department information that allowed me to compare the work of my office with that of other offices."

Why then had Nunez's team been so much more aggressive than those of his colleagues? "I think it really was an accident, the inadvertent result of some steps I took for unrelated purposes," he said. "It certainly wasn't the result of any conscious policy on my part."

Nunez said that when he became a U.S. attorney in the spring of 1982, he was something of a professional prosecutor in the sense that he had served as an assistant U.S. attorney in the district for a number of years. "Mostly because of this previous experience, I had a very general feeling that we should make a somewhat greater effort in the white-collar-crime area," he explained.

"At about the same time I took over the office," Nunez continued, "I happened to persuade a good young assistant attorney from New Jersey named Steve Crandall to come to San Diego. Steve, it turned out, had done some environmental criminal cases back east and it was natural for him to keep going."

The opposite side of this particular coin, of course, was the total lack of any criminal enforcement actions by the office of the U.S. attorney in San Francisco. From late 1981 to the spring of 1990, this office was headed by a conservative supporter of Ronald Reagan, one Joseph Russoniello.

Now a partner in one of San Francisco's most distinguished law firms, Russoniello was not at all defensive about his nonexistent environmental record. While acknowledging that the residents of the northern California district were deeply concerned about the issue, he at first seemed to argue that their concern was misdirected. "Look out that window," he said, gesturing toward the panoramic view of San Francisco Bay that was visible from his elegant twentieth-floor office. "The place is immaculate." And on a beautiful crisp morning in November the bay indeed did appear unsullied.[15]

But sensing perhaps the fatuous nature of his opening defense, Russoniello quickly tried another rationalization. "Every one of the seven local district attorneys within the boundaries of the Northern District had environmental enforcement units that were scrabbling for good cases. The state also was aggressive in the area. Because of these efforts, the federal government didn't have to be the first in the tank—and we weren't."

Russoniello's second excuse, of course, ignored the inconvenient fact that determined county and state environmental efforts were also being mounted in the three other federal districts, all of which chose to play a considerably more active role.

Despite powerful evidence to the contrary, it is an important part of the belief system of most Americans that bureaucracies are directed by the principles of scientific management: clearly articulated objectives, defined tasks, formal systems of control.

When something goes wrong with your insurance company or the department of motor vehicles, we usually conclude that the management system has broken down, not that the company or department has no management system at all, which is the situation at the Justice Department. In the 1964 formulation attributed to the scholars Warren G. Bennis and P. L. Slater, the Justice Department is not a bureaucracy, but an "adhocracy." More than a decade later, a third scholar, Henry Mintzberg, developed a formal description of an adhocracy. Among the attributes identified by Mintzberg were: "coordination by direct supervision and standardization are discouraged," "the organization is decentralized 'selectively,' " "power over different decisions is diffused in uneven ways, subject to the availability of information and expertise needed to deal with the issue at hand."[16]

The Justice Department's nonexistent effort to develop a balanced, area-wide program to enforce the environmental statutes in California's four federal districts might stand as a perfect example of "adhocracy" at work. A series of laws going back more than a century require the attorney general to coordinate the work of U.S. attorneys and all federal enforcement efforts. Other laws mandated broad enforcement efforts in which islands of pollution would not be tolerated. The result: The responsible attorneys general develop no national programs, the responsible attorneys general make no effort to comprehend what the four U.S. attorneys are doing in the state and the scattered criminal and civil actions that in fact are taken appear to be random events.

IS ANYONE IN CHARGE HERE?

Given the requirements of law, given the get-tough, take-charge rhetoric of attorneys general, given an expectation of at least a modicum of competence, the random nature of this administrative process is hard to credit. Maybe the casual dopiness suggested by our examination of federal environmental efforts is the exception.

On the other hand, maybe it is not. As already noted, the Justice Department is a large complicated agency with a huge range of obligations. As a natural consequence, the different parts of the department—such as the U.S. attorneys, the FBI, the federal parole board—all have been given a good deal of power to set their own agendas. In this freewheeling environment, even a highly experienced manager with the best intentions would have trouble grabbing the department's reins.

Former attorneys general, when asked, always profess to have had a profound interest in managing the department they theoretically were appointed to lead. But it is clear from how they described their workday that almost all of their time was actually spent in attempting to get on top of the crisis of the moment.

"It is hard for me to break out how much of my time was allocated for this and how much for that," said William Barr, the Bush administration's second attorney general, about a year after leaving office. "To tell you the truth that time is pretty much a blur. One minute you're sitting there helping to plan a hostage rescue and the next minute someone comes in with a Supreme Court brief and says the Civil Division wants to say this and we want to say that and we need a decision immediately. Then someone else is standing there telling me that we're losing all our people on the southwest border because of the pay differential and we want to do this but we need your approval. The next minute someone calls up and says the legislation on Capitol Hill concerning the 'digital telephony' issue [wiretapping] is in trouble and that it is essential you call senator so-and-so and explain what our position is. Then you are told there are a group of widows of slain police officers out in the conference room and you go out and give a brief speech about law enforcement and sacrifice and so forth. It is just a blur. Every day."[17]

The machine-gun-like intensity of the attorney general's workday makes the development of thoughtful Justice Department policies difficult. But the hope that one of the government's most important functions will benefit from reasoned analysis is made even more unlikely by the simple fact that in recent years very few attorneys general, or their top assistants, have remained in office long enough to develop a good understanding of the very complicated department they are, at least in theory, attempting to direct.

"Turnover at the senior policy level [of the Justice Department] makes it difficult to maintain management direction and control initiatives," a thoughtful report by Congress's General Accounting Office concluded. To dramatize its concerns, the GAO calculated the time served by top department officials during a recent ten-year period. On average, for example, attorneys general remained in office for only 23.2 months, deputy attorneys general 13.5 months and associate attorneys general 18.6 months. "Several former Justice officials expressed their concerns over lack of continuity in Department management. One former official expressed the view that no management institutions survive from one administration to another as new managers are brought in and old policies are discarded," the GAO said.[18]

THE CRIME OF THE CENTURY

Because the Justice Department has never developed a way to hold itself accountable, and because the department is, as Attorney General Bell said, a collection of independent fiefdoms, the course of the agency can easily be influenced by invisible bureaucratic currents.

One classic example of the wonderfully nutty way a long line of attorneys general have failed to manage the department involves the Dyer Act, a 1919 statute making the interstate transportation of stolen cars a federal crime. This case is interesting because it illustrates two key facts. First, over the years, top Justice officials have seldom given much thought to the long-term consequences of various federal enforcement policies. Second, even when they have stopped to think, they seldom have had the power to change the policies they found wanting.

Although the legislative history of the Dyer Act shows that the sponsors of the law were primarily concerned with full-time commercial car thieves, the federal government soon turned its attention to the far easier task of prosecuting and imprisoning young men who were stealing cars on a casual, spur-of-the-moment basis. This choice was to become a matter of considerable consequence. By 1964, Dyer Act cases were consuming a substantial chunk of FBI investigative time. More important, Dyer Act cases represented the largest single category of all federal prosecutions in the United States and, as a natural result, fully one out of four of all those serving time in federal prison.

It must be remembered that every enforcement hour devoted to chasing young car thieves meant an enforcement hour subtracted from more serious matters.

The curiously intense federal war against the little guy had not been ordered by the attorney general or any other high-ranking Justice Department official. Instead, the full-bore campaign had been quietly launched by the FBI for reasons that had almost nothing to do with crime fighting. Harry I. Subin, now a professor at New York University Law School, uncovered the FBI's actual motives in a 1964 study he undertook for a tiny iconoclastic think tank that was then operating within the Justice Department.

Subin told the story in an internal analysis he sent to Attorney General Ramsey Clark the next year. "A small percentage of these cases involved car theft rings or individual commercial thefts," he found. "A great majority of them were thefts of automobiles by young persons for use in transportation or 'joy rides.' "[19]

The basic recommendation in Subin's forty-four-page report was hardly controversial: The federal government should leave the prosecution of joyriders to the states. But his analysis of why the Justice Department had gotten into the business in the first place was a different matter. In dry lawyerly language, Subin concluded that the whole federal auto-theft program was part of a fraudulent effort by Hoover's FBI to polish its image. "It is clear," he said, "that Dyer Act investigations are of primary importance in the Bureau's evaluation of its overall accomplishments."

The FBI's so-called evaluation of itself was a numbers game so absurd that it should have embarrassed even the most outrageous con man. In playing this particular game, the FBI had for many years assured the Justice Department, Congress and the press that the bureau, unlike most government agencies, actually was a moneymaking proposition. In other words, the FBI asserted, the bureau was spending substantially less money on salaries and expenses than it was collecting in fines and other such payments. In order to make this claim, each year Hoover included the alleged value of the automobiles recovered under the authority of the Dyer Act prosecutions as part of the total funds the bureau was saving the United States Treasury. He made this claim despite the fact that almost all of the recovered automobiles he was claiming as U.S. property belonged to individual citizens.

To document the scam, the Subin memo quoted the FBI section of the attorney general's 1963 Annual Report. " 'Fines, savings and recoveries resulting from FBI investigations totaled $186,225,348. . . . This sum amounted to a *return to the government* of $1.37 cents for every dollar in the FBI's appropriation' " (emphasis added).

Regarding that portion of the FBI's dazzling financial feat attributed to all the stolen cars that had been returned to their owners, the young lawyer limited himself to one dead-pan comment. "It is not clear why this sum is considered either a saving or recovery to the United States, if one excludes the unlikely possibility that the 19,192 recovered automobiles [that the FBI that year was claiming] all were Government-owned."[20]

Almost ten years earlier, in October 1956, Subin reported that the Eisenhower administration also had taken a crack at getting the FBI out of the auto theft business. But because of strong objections from Hoover, he explained, "nothing ever came of this proposed change."

Subin recently said that his 1965 recommendation to cut back sharply on Dyer Act prosecutions, like the effort under the Eisenhower administration, was quickly shot down, this time by Fred Vinson, then the assistant attorney general heading the Justice Department's Criminal Division. The see-no-evil, speak-no-evil order was delivered in a memo from Vinson to Attorney General Ramsey Clark. "Vinson's memorandum was to the effect that everything I said was very helpful, and provided the only data we had, but that nothing needed to be done," Subin wrote. "It is clear that no one wanted the Bureau to even see what I had written."[21]

Subin, who has been contemplating the criminal justice system and its problems for more than thirty years, added this commentary about the Justice Department of the mid-1960s that still rings true. "Aside from the fraud which the FBI was perpetrating with auto theft policy," he said, "the most interesting thing about the episode, as in so many others in the criminal area, was that the Department did not know what it was doing."[22]

As Subin was suggesting, this was not just one more funny story about the bad-old FBI. In one of the all-time classic the-tail-wags-the-dog situations, a minor aspect of the FBI's overall public relations program had profoundly distorted the federal government's basic criminal enforcement agenda for several decades. Equally important, for most of those years, the men who had been appointed to lead the Justice Department were so uninterested in its enforcement priorities that they had allowed a substantial part of the federal government's investigative, prosecutive and penal resources to be squandered on a trivial crime.

According to a later report by the General Accounting Office, the Justice Department did not get around to issuing guidelines that effectively ordered the FBI to stop presenting Dyer Act cases to federal prosecutors until June of 1970. For some reason, this particular guideline seemed actually to affect policy and the final act in this seemingly endless farce was quite brief. In 1967, auto theft cases made up 16 percent of all federal prosecutions. By 1975, they had dropped to only 3.9 percent of the total.[23]

WHO WAGES THE WAR ON CRIME?

Proper management obviously involves a lot more than making sure that your troops are firing at the right targets. A good manager must also try to anticipate where the forthcoming struggles are likely to erupt so the troops can be deployed along the battle line in the best possible location. This challenge exists for all managers regardless of whether they are directing the operations of a big-city hospital in New York, a small research company in California, a public school in Alabama or, need I say it, the United States Justice Department. Given the reality of limited resources, then, how well or poorly has the Justice Department done when it came to the important process of allocating federal prosecutors around the nation?

Management choices like these are never easy. In the case of the Justice Department, they are especially difficult, because there is so little accurate, consistent and up-to-date intelligence about the department's potential targets. Unlike the school superintendent who can usually predict the size of an incoming class by tracking changes in the area's birthrate and immigration patterns, it is much harder to anticipate the actions of militant third world organizations contemplating a terrorist act, organized drug gangs marketing their illegal contraband or slick operators systematically looting the Medicare and Medicaid programs.

But ignoring an essential responsibility simply because the task is difficult has always been a recipe for trouble. As in many other areas of the Justice Department, this has been the foolish choice of an impressive number of attorneys general. It should be understood that through much of its history, the department was a relatively small and slow-growing organization. This pattern came to an end about fifteen years ago. From 1980 to 1992, two Republican presidents and a mostly Democratic Congress agreed upon a phenomenal and largely unnoticed increase in federal prosecutors. Put in relative terms, the number of assistant U.S. attorneys grew ten times faster than the nation's population, climbing from 1,621 in 1980 to 3,883 in 1992. In 1980, there were seven prosecutors for every million people in the United States. By 1992 there were fifteen.[24]

During this thirteen-year period of extraordinary growth, five different attorneys general assumed the legal and political responsibility for directing the operations of the Justice Department. There are no indications that any of them ever explored the critical process by which the federal prosecutors, clearly one of the department's most valuable resources, were distributed among the ninety-three districts. This failure, while entirely consistent with the performance of those who had preceded them, contributed to one of the grand and continuing mysteries of the Justice Department: the crazy-quilt way federal prosecutors are deployed along the front lines of the federal government's war on crime.

Going back to the establishment of the Justice Department immediately after the Civil War, how to distribute prosecutors has been a process dominated by a constantly changing set of unarticulated political pressures originating mostly in personal friendships and connections. As long as the department remained an agency with relatively narrow responsibilities that were of minor concern to the general public, the failure to allocate resources in some vaguely rational way was of little consequence. But with the rapid growth in both the size and reach of federal agencies during the last few decades, the distribution of federal prosecutors has become an important matter, something that directly or indirectly affects all Americans. Despite this fact, the allocation of assistant U.S. attorneys among different cities and regions of the country today remains as irrational as it has always been. Here are a few examples.

Vermont, New Hampshire and the Northern District of New York are three federal districts located along the Canadian border in the northeastern corner of the United States. In addition to their geographic similarities, none of the districts is very populous and none boasts major urban centers where organized crime has made serious inroads. But for reasons the department is unable to explain, the three districts are totally different in one important measure: In 1992, Vermont was blessed with twenty-four assistant U.S. attorneys per million population (2.4 per 100,000), New Hampshire fourteen (1.4 per 100,000) and Northern New York eight (.8 per 100,000).

Heading west, to the mountain/central area of the United States, there are five federal districts that again appear to have a number of demographic, geographic and economic similarities. As we found in the Northeast, however, the 1992 allocation of federal prosecutors was highly erratic. Among the five, Wyoming came out on top with thirty assistant U.S. attorneys per million population. Then came South Dakota with twenty, North Dakota with sixteen, Montana with thirteen and Idaho and Utah, combined, with twelve. Why in the world would Montana, the land of the big sky, on a per capita basis have two and a half times more prosecutors than Utah, a district with that region's most populous city?

Now consider the 1992 staffing of the offices serving several of the nation's largest metropolitan areas: Southern New York (Manhattan) and Southern Florida (Miami) had forty-one per million, Eastern Pennsylvania (Philadelphia) twenty, Southern Texas (Houston) nineteen,

FEDERAL PROSECUTORS
Comparison of Staffing
in the Largest Metropolitan Areas

DISTRICT	ATTORNEYS PER CAPITA*
California, North	12
California, Central	13
Massachusetts	13
Michigan, East	13
Texas, North	15
Illinois, Northern	16
Texas, South	19
New York, East	20
Pennsylvania, East	20
Florida, South	41
New York, South	41
D.C.	212

*Per million population

The Justice Department's allocation of resources—in this case federal prosecutors—is often whimsical and highly political. Partly because federal prosecutors in Washington, D.C., handle local as well as federal crimes, the large number of attorneys in the nation's capital in relation to its population is misleading. (TRAC ANALYSIS OF JUSTICE DEPARTMENT AND CENSUS BUREAU DATA)

Northern Illinois (Chicago) sixteen, Central California (Los Angeles) thirteen and Northern California (San Francisco) twelve.

One can intuitively understand the reasoning behind the decision to assign a relatively large number of federal prosecutors in Manhattan and Miami. But what is the explanation for Philadelphia having so many more in relation to its population than Los Angeles?

Aggressive U.S. attorneys have been complaining to Washington about not having an adequate number of prosecutors for many decades. During those years, Washington typically responded by granting the squeakiest wheels a few more bodies. But it obviously was a sensitive, highly political, seat-of-the-pants and unpredictable process.

"We don't have a perfect way to decide staff questions," admitted Laurence S. McWhorter in a disarming 1990 interview. McWhorter then was the director of the Executive Office of the United States Attorneys. "Law is not a precise instrument and there is a lot of history involved. At some points the department has emphasized big cities. At other times, farm bankruptcies have been a concern. An important factor is what has occurred in the past, the tradition of each district."

At first, McWhorter actually sounded rather thoughtful, especially when he listed the factors the Justice Department considered when making personnel assignments, among them: criminal caseload, civil caseload, number of grand jury hours, trial activity and the "average assistant U.S. attorney workweek."

The Justice Department, it seemed, was assigning additional prosecutors on the basis of the work performed by each office. If the world were a perfect place, the idea of basing deployment decisions on workload would be entirely sensible.

In the real world, however, the number of staff each office has been allocated largely determines how many cases it will prosecute. And, within the broad boundaries set by staff size, each U.S. attorney exercises almost complete control over the work performed by the assistant U.S. attorneys in his or her office. In a 1993 study on how all the responsible federal agencies responded to the wave of bank and thrift fraud that swept the nation in the late 1980s, for example, the General Accounting Office noted that federal prosecutors operated "with much program autonomy. Because they are subject to removal only by the president and are geographically separated from national headquarters, the U.S. attorneys have significant discretion in setting prosecutorial policies and managing their offices."[25]

Although the 1993 study did not provide a concrete analysis of how the choices of individual prosecutors influenced criminal enforcement patterns in different districts, the GAO had, ten years before, examined the declination policies followed by a sample of seven U.S. attorneys for several categories of crime. The auditors found that while federal prosecutors in one district would not consider prosecuting a bank fraud or embezzlement case unless it involved more than $5,000, prosecutors in another district had adopted $500 as their cutoff point. For crimes involving thefts from interstate shipments, three of the sample offices refused to bring cases unless goods worth a minimum of $5,000 had been stolen, three had $1,000 limits and one would prosecute matters involving as little as $600.[26]

The point here is not to suggest that U.S. attorneys in different parts of the United States should have precisely the same standards. Given the vastly different levels of business activity on Wall Street in New York City and Main Street in Montpelier, Vermont, it makes sense that the federal prosecutors in the two locations adopt different guidelines.

But what is unacceptable, even a bit demented, was for Larry McWhorter and the Justice Department to cite workload statistics such as the number of grand jury hours as a fair way of deciding the relative size of each of the ninety-three offices. Because staff size and the unilateral decisions of U.S. attorneys directly impact on the number and kind of cases brought by each office, caseload data is what scientists call a dependent variable. Detailed information about the caseload might help individual U.S. attorneys keep track of what their prosecutors are doing. But as a yardstick for measuring the comparative needs of all the offices, it is almost totally worthless.

It is hard to believe that an important and massive agency like the Justice Department—then employing nearly 100,000 persons—could function on the basis of such foolish principles. It gets worse. For in addition to basing its allocation decisions on a series of murky and easy-to-manipulate factors, the Justice Department has for many years failed to utilize a readily available and obvious independent variable: the number of people living in each district. Given the vast differences in district populations—they range in size from 466,000 to 15.7 million people—the department's persistent reluctance to adopt population as the basic starting point for the allocation of its resources is mysterious.

During a 1990 interview, McWhorter provided a list of general variables that he said the agency had long used in the "multistep decision-making process" to determine staffing levels of the individual districts. McWhorter's list had fifteen variables, including the number of judges, average work week and number of client agents. Population wasn't one of them.

In March 1991, my research organization, TRAC, issued a report that, for the first time ever, examined the number of federal prosecutors working in each district on a per capita basis and questioned the whole Justice Department allocation process.

The Justice Department stuck by its guns. Planning experts in the agency, said Wyoming's U.S. attorney, Richard Stacey, "are aware of hundreds of nuances that the authors of this report don't know any-thing about. The planners do a very careful and painstaking job of allo-cating those resources to put the troops where they are needed."[27] It is worth noting that at the time he was vigorously defending the Justice Department's allocation process, Wyoming, never recognized as one of the nation's major crime centers, had far more assistant U.S. attorneys per capita than Boston, Chicago, Detroit, Houston, Los Angeles and San Francisco.

In late 1993, at the request of the House Subcommittee on Informa-tion, Justice, Transportation, and Agriculture, TRAC updated its data analysis of how the Justice Department allocated its prosecutors. On the basis of this study, the subcommittee held a hearing during which the Justice Department attempted to defend its procedures. The chair-man, a California Democrat named Gary Condit, was not impressed. "I don't want to harp on this population thing, but for the life of me, I can-not understand how you can have a larger population in inner cities and how you can't equate that and give it [population] at least some addi-tional weight. For you to dismiss population the way you do is astound-ing. It has been over a decade in California that the inner cities of Los Angeles, the inner cities of San Francisco, the inner cities of San Jose and Sacramento have had Asian gang problems, illegals, et cetera, et cetera, et cetera. You didn't have to wait around. It is happening today. It happened a year ago, ten years ago. Still, we seem to be getting less representation from you folks than other areas that have very very small populations. Do you understand how illogical your argument sounds?"[28]

At first, TRAC's analysis documenting the nonsensical way the de-partment was mobilizing its prosecutors appeared to win the day when a few months later Attorney General Janet Reno ordered her staff to develop "a principled and equitable model to allocate resources."[29]

The complicated task had already been taken on by Kent Walker, an assistant U.S. attorney who was on detail to Washington from his regu-lar post in San Francisco. After weeks of study, Walker concluded in a preliminary report to Reno that the existing system was seriously flawed. Department prosecutors were being sent to the wrong districts, he said, as a result of "political pressure" from "rural states with strong senators," from districts that had been "the focus of prior administra-tions' priorities" and from areas close to Washington "whose crime problems are better known to DOJ staff and who are in a better position to lobby for more resources."[30]

Walker proposed that the department adopt a system under which staffing would be based on a number of objective measures indicating the levels of federal crime in an area. To get at white-collar crime, for example, he suggested comparing such factors as the total business receipts, IRS collections, hospital beds, bank and savings and loan deposits and government employees in each district.

A few months later, after completing elaborate computer studies of the relative standings of the ninety-three districts under his new proposal, Walker recommended what would have been a drastic rearrangement of department staffing. Employees assigned to Manhattan, the Southern District of New York, for example, would have dropped from 414 to 298. The Northern District of West Virginia, another overstaffed district, would have lost exactly half of its personnel—thirty-six to eighteen. Under the model, other areas would have seen dramatic increases. One such boost would have gone to the Central District of California, Los Angeles, where its staff would have gone from 439 to 624.[31]

As this is written, Reno's well-intentioned effort appears to have been stopped in its tracks. According to U.S. attorneys from several areas in the nation, a barrage of complaints from powerful senators and federal prosecutors from the most overstaffed districts resulted in the immediate shelving of the project. "Patronage is serious business—the heart of the department—and Reno never had a chance," said one participant.[32]

TROUBLE IN BLUE GRASS COUNTRY

The bizarre failure of attorneys general to manage the resources and enforcement efforts of the Justice Department in some kind of vaguely sensible way is so sweeping that its impact on the lives and welfare of the public is hard to grasp. But there have been dozens of more focused Justice Department outrages that illustrate the same point in an easier to understand way.

On August 3, 1990, for example, a businessman named Charles Hayes came to the office of the U.S. attorney in Lexington, Kentucky, and removed two truckloads of aging government computers. For many years, Hayes had lived in São Paulo, Brazil, with his wife, Guiomar, where, according to his own words, it is just possible he was involved in some kind of mysterious undercover political operation.

In the hot summer of 1990, his life appeared to be far less glamorous. Hayes was the owner and operator of Challenger, LTD, a grandly named secondhand junk business; of Challenger Auto Sales, a used car lot; and the Granny Goodwitch Shop, a tobacco store—all located on the grounds of a defunct school in Nancy, Kentucky, near Lexington.

About a month before, the General Services Administration, the government's housekeeping agency, had informed Hayes that his sealed bid for the equipment, designated as Lot 097, had been successful. For a grand total of $45, Hayes was now the owner of obsolete word processing equipment consisting of thirteen terminals, two central memory units, two cartridge module drives and nine printers.

Although the Justice Department had certified that the old computer gear no longer contained any proprietary information, during the six-year period from 1983 to 1989 it had been used to prepare and store tens of thousands of pages of official documents and records generated by the twenty-five prosecutors responsible for enforcing federal law among the 1.8 million people living in the eastern half of Kentucky.

Shortly after Hayes left with his small haul, the department learned that a mistake had been made: The equipment it had just sold still contained a great deal of extremely sensitive information. Held within the electronic files, for example, were the names of all the confidential informants in the area who had helped the government make its criminal and civil cases, details concerning the status of ongoing criminal investigations, transcripts of secret grand jury proceedings, confidential information about individuals who had been placed in the witness protection program and personal facts about local Justice Department employees.

Although Hayes had only paid $45 for Lot 097, the failure of the government to properly clear the gear it had sold him eventually would bring him a great deal of grief. On August 17, a full two weeks after driving away from the U.S. attorney's office, Hayes got his first warning of the coming storm when he was visited by FBI Agent Terrence S. Moore.

According to the government's official version of events, the second-hand dealer was at first uncooperative, refusing to let Moore inspect the reels of tape and floppy disks that he had just acquired. Soon, however, Hayes relented and a government inspection team including the computer manager of the federal prosecutor's office, a technical expert from the vendor and two Secret Service agents were allowed to look over the equipment. The team determined that the two cartridge module drives, or CMDs, were missing. "When confronted with this discrepancy, the defendant claimed he had sold the CMDs and all the backup cartridges. When asked the names of the buyers of the information, the defendant refused to provide them at that time."[33]

The Justice Department was extremely worried about the gaping wound that it seemingly had inflicted upon itself. So worried, in fact, that unknown to Hayes at the time of the official inspection visit, the department had already initiated an indirect effort to penetrate the junkman's operation. On August 17, 20 and 24, an ostensible friend of Hayes named Ron Beckman, who had secretly agreed to serve as an undercover operative for the FBI, initiated three conversations with Hayes that were recorded by the bureau. Beckman's apparent goal was to find out whether some grand conspiracy was at work.

Although the transcripts of these talks are murky and the events they describe extremely confusing, it appears that Beckman may have been directed by the FBI to help the agents make a serious criminal case against Hayes by encouraging him to sell the information recorded on the computer equipment to a mysterious man who "was in the market for merchandise."[34]

Beckman also told Hayes that the potential customer had indicated to him that "if you've got enough there and it's good, he'd buy it all. Man said money was no problem."

It was all too exciting, and the possibility of making some real money from his $45 investment appears to have addled Hayes's syntax, if not his judgment. "We're talking big ones here, son, not one, not two either," he replied. "Big ones and I'm not talking about hundreds, either, [stuttering] thousands. I'm talking probably two billion, somewhere along there, two million clear cut."

A bit earlier in the conversation, while discussing some current and never explained threat to himself, Hayes dropped a cryptic hint about his earlier career in Brazil. "And fact about it, let me tell you something, somebody threaten me, that don't mean goddamn diddley shit. Hell, if I can take down a fucking Minister of Brazil, what is he [the unidentified threat in Kentucky], a pissant, a fucking attorney. Now come on, Ron, if I can move from underneath the secret police, goddamn, what does a fucking attorney mean to me."

Hayes's erratic behavior, and his reference to defeating the secret police in Brazil, must have caused a stir in the U.S. attorney's office in Lexington. But what made the team even more nervous was the presence of James R. Freeman, one of Hayes's part-time employees. Freeman was a computer techie who appeared to have sufficient skills to make copies of all the confidential information the Justice Department had so casually sold to Hayes. It appeared that the genie, quite literally, had escaped the bottle.

On August 31, despite the possibility that copies of the confidential information may have already been recorded, the government moved to recork the bottle. The operation began late Friday afternoon when James Underwood, the district's chief deputy marshal, arrived at Hayes's place of business with eight deputy marshals, a rented truck and an amended writ of possession that required immediate execution "due to the sensitivity of the information and the possibility that the information might be transferred to others."[35]

The securing of the heavy computer equipment, the exhaustive search of all the buildings for related tapes and papers and the loading of the material onto the truck, Underwood said later, took the marshals more than fourteen hours and was not completed until the early morning hours of Saturday.

On September 6, under the mandate of a temporary restraining order and accompanied by his attorney, Hayes was questioned about the whole situation by Jeffrey S. Gutman, a lawyer from the Justice Department's Civil Division in Washington. Although Gutman continued to insist that Hayes's "evasiveness, uncooperativeness and misleading, if not false, statements to government employees served to mask his efforts to market this proprietary information," the businessman insisted the government had got it all wrong.

Hayes told Gutman under oath that he had not viewed or copied any of the sensitive information in question and that, to the best of his knowledge, neither had any of his associates. He insisted that outside of some kidding remarks with his wife and friends, including the undercover FBI operator Beckman, he had never offered to sell any of the material.[36]

On October 29, 1991, District Court Judge Eugene R. Siler issued sweeping third-party injunctions permanently ordering Hayes and his friends from ever "possessing, retrieving, copying, duplicating, disseminating, disposing, transferring, selling, discussing or publishing, orally or in any other manner, any information or data which was stored in any part of the computer equipment or related items" that had been given them by the U.S. attorney in August.[37]

Looked at from one perspective, this was what most reporters would call a nonstory because, from their point of view, nothing had happened: The secret files, it appeared, had not been compromised. Looked at from another perspective, however, the department's clumsy sale of the information-laden computer equipment was extremely significant.

First of all, the Kentucky caper was not an isolated event. According to the General Accounting Office, even as the computer security fiasco in Lexington was unfolding, another U.S. attorney's office warned that it, too, may have compromised sensitive information the same way. The location of this second office was never disclosed. A little less than a year later, however, Milton J. Socolar, special assistant to the comptroller general, in an unclassified version of a secret report to Congress, indicated that the Justice Department's failure was not limited to just one or two offices. "Our review showed similar patterns of neglect and inattention nationwide," Socolar testified.[38]

Although the Justice Department clearly had no interest in advertising the fact, even it realized that the Hayes case had spotlighted a grave internal flaw: The agency's basic security procedures were a joke. But given the vast amounts of confidential information in the department's files, the joke wasn't very funny.

Over the next six months, in yet another of those classic close-the-barn-door cases, experts from the department's Security and Emergency Planning office raced across the country and briefed every single one of the nation's 3,700 federal prosecutors on the ABCs of computer security. In addition, each of the ninety-three offices was provided a hefty package containing a complete collection of nine official orders, twenty-four security awareness memoranda and three special messages that the department had put out on the subject since 1977. Finally, special investigations, ordered in nineteen of the ninety-three offices in a preliminary examination, had uncovered obvious and threatening security shortcomings.[39]

More than fifteen years into the computer age, the United States Justice Department, one of the government's most aggressive collectors of confidential information, had finally realized that its failure to establish effective security controls had left the agency seriously exposed. Bad as it was, if the grave agency-wide shortcomings disclosed by the Lexington snafu had been an exception, perhaps we could close our eyes to the department's systematic laxness. Unfortunately, this is not the case.

LAXITY AT THE FBI, DEA AND INS

From 1982 to 1990, the Federal Bureau of Investigation spent slightly more than $1 billion for what it called ADPT, or automatic data processing and telecommunications equipment and services. But a major audit of the FBI program by the Justice Department's independent inspector general found the massive effort seriously wanting. General controls over the ADPT program, the inspector general concluded, "(a) had not been designed according to management direction and known legal requirements; and (b) were not operating effectively to provide reliability of, and security over, the data being processed."[40]

Among the specific problems, the report said, were: the FBI was unable to account for over 2,000 pieces of ADP equipment, some of which may have contained sensitive information; followup security investigations had not been completed on 40 percent of the FBI employees who at the time were holding critical-sensitive positions in the agency; formal risk analyses to identify data security problems and devise countermeasures had not been conducted, nor had contingency plans been tested; and the bureau's information security policies were incomplete and outdated.

The National Crime Information Center (NCIC) is another FBI computer operation, one of the largest and oldest information sharing systems in the world. Operated jointly by the FBI and the states since 1967, the NCIC provides over 19,000 federal, state and local criminal justice agencies in the United States and Canada with access to over 24 million law enforcement records on a more or less instantaneous basis.

The central purpose of the NCIC is entirely laudatory: to provide police, prosecutors and judges a fast way to determine whether a particular individual is currently subject to an arrest warrant anywhere in the United States.

But the information in the system can be easily misused. A few years ago, for example, a former law enforcement official in Arizona improperly obtained information from the NCIC with the help of three officers and used it to track down and murder his former girlfriend. In another case, a computer terminal operator in Pennsylvania conducted background checks for her boyfriend, who was a drug dealer. He asked her to check the criminal history records of his new clients in an effort to determine whether any of them were undercover police agents.

The security problems of the FBI's NCIC have been a matter of concern since it first began operating. Over and over again, computer experts from industry and the universities, congressional specialists and even paid consultants working for the FBI have warned that the lack of adequate controls meant that more and more serious abuses like those documented in Arizona and Pennsylvania were inevitable.

But according to a 1993 assessment by the General Accounting Office, neither the FBI, the Justice Department nor most of the states have taken the required steps to deal with the long-recognized central problem: misuse of the information by the 500,000 or so "insiders" who can easily access the files for nefarious purposes.

Furthermore, even though just one of the fifty-four state control terminal agencies uncovered one hundred of the hard-to-detect security failures in fiscal year 1992, neither the FBI nor most of the state agencies bother to collect statistics about the misuse of data by law enforcement insiders. In a classic example of the see-no-evil, speak-no-evil theory of government management, the FBI and the state agencies have contended that such data collection was not needed "because there is no policy requirement to report and track incidents of misuse." In addition, the GAO reported, the FBI believes that despite the lack of concrete information about the problem, gathering information about it was not necessary "given the small number of misuse incidents that occur within their jurisdictions."[41]

The circularity of this argument needs no comment. The potential size of the FBI problem, however, is tremendous despite the FBI's refusal to acknowledge it. Indirect evidence of just how bad the situation may be emerged in 1993 when the IRS was forced to admit that it had investigated 1,300 agency employees who were using IRS computers to

browse through the tax returns of neighbors, relatives, friends and enemies. The IRS said that 420 of the cases had resulted in some kind of
discipline, with several hundred more matters under investigation. Because far fewer people have access to the IRS computer system than is
the case with NCIC, and IRS computer security is more stringent, it is
highly likely that many thousands of individuals a year are using the
NCIC for improper and, in some cases, life-threatening purposes.[42]

Like the U.S attorneys and the FBI, a third Justice Department component, the Drug Enforcement Administration, has also exhibited little
concern about protecting its confidential information, even though
some of it could seriously endanger the lives of DEA investigators and
their employees. In early 1992, the attorney general was provided with yet
another secret report by the General Accounting Office. In this report, the
GAO identified a variety of serious security problems in computers
handling confidential information at the DEA's national headquarters in
Washington and two of the agency's larger field divisions. In one case, the
absence of required security measures allowed an agency communications operator to obtain sensitive criminal investigative information
which he sold to suspected drug traffickers.[43]

SAFEGUARDING THE BORDERS?

The Immigration and Naturalization Service, a branch of the Justice
Department, has 13,000 employees and an annual budget of just over $1
billion. The two main units in the INS have different, almost opposite,
goals. One unit is charged with guarding the borders, preventing illegal
aliens from entering the nation. The other unit is responsible for facili-
tating the legal entry of visitors.

The challenges are genuine, the pressures tremendous: nearly 6,000
miles of unfortified frontier and 610 air, land and sea ports of entry.
Each year, the INS inspects and admits, or denies entry to, more than a
quarter of a *billion* individuals. In one recent year it apprehended 1.2
million illegal aliens and intercepted 700,000 pounds of marijuana and
over 38,000 pounds of cocaine. At the same time, the agency processed
the papers of 280,000 persons who became naturalized citizens and the
benefit applications of 2 million aliens.

Despite the impressive-sounding statistics, the INS may well be the
single worst enforcement agency in the federal government. For at least
twenty years, informed critics have again and again identified critical
failures in how the agency is directed and how it functions. While hundreds of INS officials have been indicted on various corruption and bru-

tality charges, numerous reports indicate that such problems persist to this day. And there would be far more charges if incompetence, mismanagement and nepotism were treated as criminal acts. Critics of the INS have included the National Research Council, the Justice Department's inspector general, the Justice Department's Management Division, the General Accounting Office, numerous civil rights groups and defense attorneys and respected reporters such as John Crewdson, now of the *Chicago Tribune.*

The mess of INS has continued to fester despite occasional concern at the highest level of the United States government. Shortly after his inauguration, President Jimmy Carter decided that the United States had to allow the deposed Shah of Iran to undergo emergency medical treatment in a leading New York teaching hospital. The decision triggered thousands of antimonarchist Iranians who had entered the United States for advanced schooling to mount noisy demonstrations in cities throughout the nation. Irritated by the protests, and assuming that many of the demonstrators no longer were valid students, Carter instructed Attorney General Bell to immediately expel the bogus scholars.

But when Bell called Leonel Castillo, the then commissioner of INS, he learned that the Justice Department agency theoretically responsible for immigration matters could be of no help. The INS, it turned out, had no idea how many Iranians were in the country, how many of them were students, who they were or where they were living.

But neither Bell nor the attorneys general who followed him appear to have tried to improve the situation. In a series of unusually critical reports published in 1990 and 1991, the GAO said the INS computers were filled with inaccurate and incomplete information that hindered efforts to deport aliens who had been convicted of serious crimes, undermined the program to punish businesses who hire illegal aliens and made it impossible to measure the agency's effectiveness. Although spending for the processing of persons requesting asylum, naturalization or temporary work visas more than doubled in one recent three-year period, the GAO said, agency-wide processing did not improve and processing times in several key districts exceeded the INS's own criteria.

A parallel kind of problem was found in the INS's Border Patrol. From 1986 to 1991, while its budget increased 82 percent, the proportion of agent time devoted to patrolling the U.S. border decreased.

More recently, the GAO reviewed a sample of alien names and addresses in four INS offices and found that 22 percent of them had significant errors. Because current law requires immigration judges to order the deportation of aliens who fail to show up for scheduled hearings, the error rate in the address list may well result in the improper harassment of tens of thousands of persons.[44]

In 1993, a team from the *Los Angeles Times* examined court files, federal reports and internal records and conducted more than a hundred interviews in the course of investigating the INS's effort to control the U.S.–Mexico border. "The ignoble record of the 1990s," the team reported, "includes agents prosecuted or disciplined for myriad offenses: unjustified shootings, sexual misconduct, beatings, stealing money from prisoners, drug trafficking, embezzlement, perjury and indecent exposure."

A federal judge in El Paso, they said, had ruled in December 1992 that the Border Patrol had committed "wholesale violations" of the rights of citizens and noncitizens. Shortly thereafter, the Justice Department's inspector general, Richard J. Hankinson, told a House subcommittee that the INS "is often indifferent when it comes to screening its employees and training them, much of their work is unsupervised, and administrative discipline is sometimes haphazard."[45]

Griffin Bell, when talking to Jimmy Carter about the INS some two decades before, had said it straight: "They have a sort of system of non-management over there."[46] But as the record clearly shows, Bell should not have limited his comment to the INS. He might have been speaking of the Justice Department as a whole.

4

The
Numbers Game

A few months after his appointment as the new director of the Federal Bureau of Investigation, Louis J. Freeh delivered a speech at the National Press Club in Washington. Freeh, the nation's top cop, was setting out federal crime policy to a gathering of more than two hundred Washington-based reporters, congressional staffers and interested lobbyists who had come to get a direct sense of this major new player on the American scene.

As such matters are judged within the Beltway, Freeh's December 1993 speech was a significant event; important to him, important to the FBI and important to the man who appointed him, Bill Clinton. And because the speech was carried by C-Span, National Public Radio and the Global Internet Computer Network, and would be the basis for articles in newspapers all over the United States, Freeh was also delivering his message to a much larger national and international audience.

The director's talk that day touched on many matters of concern to the federal law enforcement community, among them the continuing menace of drugs, espionage and international terrorism. But the central focus of his speech was violent street crime.

"The people of this country are fed up with crime," Freeh declared. "The media report it, the statistics support it, the polls prove it."

To drive his point home, to authenticate the national menace that the FBI somehow had to confront, Freeh presented what he indicated were the cold hard facts of the case. According to a report by the International Association of Chiefs of Police, he said, "the rate of violent crime has increased 371 percent since 1960—that's nine times faster than our population has grown. In the past 30 years, homicides have nearly tripled; robberies and rapes each are up over 500 percent; aggravated assaults have increased more than 600 percent."[1]

While Freeh's dark vision of America was expressed in an unusually forceful way, his contention that America now faced an unprecedented crime crisis was hardly new. In fact, during the last fifty years, roughly similar statements have been made by literally thousands of politicians, police officers, judges and other civic figures. Led by presidents Clinton, Bush, Reagan, Nixon, Johnson and Roosevelt and chief justices of the Supreme Court like Rehnquist and Berger, official and political America has never stinted when it came to expressing alarm about the nation's crime problem.

It is, in fact, very difficult to overstate the social and political consequences of crime in the United States. The direct costs in terms of untimely deaths, damaged bodies and lost property are considerable. Indirect costs such as the national contagion of fear and hundreds of square miles of devastated neighborhoods are even more massive. Without exaggeration, crime is a scourge that exacts a terrible physical, economic and social toll on the people of the United States.

At the same time, however, crime is a white-hot public issue that has been shamelessly exploited by cynical leaders for their own political and administrative advantage. Here is how these callous manipulators have used the gut-level fears of the American people for their own purposes.

As is suggested by the speeches of Freeh and almost all of the other politicians and officials who have jumped onto this particular bandwagon, for many Americans crime is an indirect experience: glaring headlines, garish television reports and the constant repetition of seemingly irrefutable crime statistics carry the day and, for almost everyone, the armed stickup is an imagined event. Therefore, the rhetoric of crime in the United States is in many ways more important than crime itself.

This chapter is an exploration of some of the oblique ways that a substantial proportion of us gain our perceptions of serious crime. Most particularly, it will focus on crime statistics: how they are compiled, who compiles them and what they tell us about crime.

Partly as a result of the constant repetition of the crime numbers, two distinctly different but related conclusions about crime have been planted in the national psyche as 100 percent true facts: First, violent street crime is today a serious national problem; and second, not only is violent crime a big challenge, but it is an exploding problem that is threatening to destroy our nation. Big problems are bad. But big and exploding problems are much much worse.

While the first proposition cannot be challenged—there is indeed a lot of crime in the United States—there are many important questions about the second. Within the hard-edged rhetoric about crime lurks a startling mystery: America's firm belief that the nation has been and is now engulfed in a rapidly growing wave of street crime, as dramatically summarized by Freeh's National Press Club speech, directly conflicts with America's actual day-to-day experience with crime. In other words, in a very significant way, one of the key national assumptions about crime is contrary to the national actuality of crime.

As we shall see, the knowing manipulation of the crime statistics by the FBI and Director Freeh is only one of a number of reasons for the truly amazing dichotomy between public perception and public experience. Further contributing to this astonishing disconnection has been the media: exploitative broadcasters and publishers who want to boost their ratings or increase their circulation, and ignorant reporters willing to reprint any press release sent to them by a government agency. The final factors contributing to the gap between facts and perceptions are technical in nature. There are, for one example, real methodological challenges to counting street crimes accurately, especially over long periods of time in a large and diversified country like the United States. Yet another obstacle to perceiving the reality of crime in America is the surprising failure of the government to develop a way to measure one of its most important components—white-collar crime.

Despite the serious defects and problems which riddle all crime statistics, the American people, Congress and state and local agencies throughout the country have nevertheless continued to look upon this particular collection of numbers and rates with little skepticism, even equating them with such important social indicators as the monthly reports on unemployment or inflation. It is precisely this misguided faith in crime statistics, and those who produce them, that makes this chapter an essential element in understanding the Justice Department's controlling role in the tumultuous politics of crime.

NATIONAL CRIME VICTIMIZATION SURVEY: THE BASELINE

We begin at the beginning. Hard, consistent and detailed knowledge about one part of the mystery—when, where and how the American people are victimized by crime—has been gathered by the Census Bureau for the Bureau of Justice Statistics, a small Justice Department office, since 1973. Under this program, twice a year, 50,000 Americans are asked dozens of questions about their experience with crime.

The Census Bureau's questions are detailed and probing. During the last six months, "did anyone take something from you directly by using force, such as by a stickup, mugging or threat?" During the last six months, "did anyone beat you up, attack you or hit you with something, such as a rock or a bottle? Were you knifed, shot at or attacked with some other weapon? During the last six months, did anyone break into or somehow get into your home? Was anything stolen? Was anything stolen from you while you were away from home, for instance at work, or in a theater or restaurant or while traveling? Did you call the police during the last six months to report something that happened to you which you thought was a crime? What happened? Did anything happen to you in the last six months that you thought was a crime but did not report to the police? What happened?" If a person responds in the affirmative to being a crime victim, there are then a series of detailed followup questions.[2]

Every year, on the basis of the answers provided by the large sample of survey respondents, the Census Bureau computes crime victimization rates for the entire nation. This technique has long been used by the federal government to determine other important social trends, such as the number of Americans who are unemployed or suffering from various health problems. The procedure is considered highly reliable, and in some circumstances, because of the difficulty of contacting certain segments of the population, even more accurate than a complete census.

Finally, every year, the Bureau of Justice Statistics publishes an authoritative annual report summarizing what the Census Bureau learned about criminal victimization in the previous year. For many Americans, the long-term crime trends uncovered by the survey are startling.

Consider, for example, rape, robbery and felonious assault, the nation's most widespread crimes of violence. These are terrifying events that legitimately generate serious public concern about both personal safety and the overall quality of life in the United States.

In 1992, the most recent comparable year that is available, 15.6 out of every 1,000 persons questioned by the Census Bureau said they had been a victim of a crime. Twenty years before, in 1973, when the Census Bureau talked with a similar sample of Americans, 17.8 out of every 1,000 said they had been the victims of such attacks.[3]

Thus, during two thirds of the period discussed by Freeh in his terrifying speech about the nation's soaring crime rates, the American people were telling the Census Bureau they were actually experiencing a declining number of violent criminal attacks.

Americans, of course, are also worried about property crimes such as those situations where a burglar breaks into a house or an apartment and takes something of value. Although the most fearsome of the property crimes, a burglary is less traumatic than robbery because during a burglary there is no direct contact between the victim and the criminal. Individuals interviewed for the National Crime Survey said the decline in

NATIONAL CRIME VICTIMIZATION SURVEY
Violent Crimes of Robbery, Rape and Felonious Assault 1973–1992

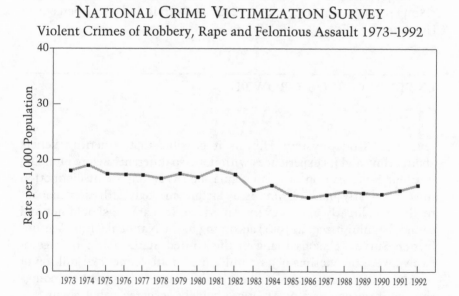

The Justice Department's Bureau of Justice Statistics—with help from the Census Bureau—has conducted a continuous national survey to determine the level of crime victimization in the United States since 1973. Despite the widespread belief to the contrary, the survey shows that many kinds of violent crime are down, and that the chances of being a violent-crime victim in the United States were somewhat higher in 1973 than they were in 1992.
(BUREAU OF JUSTICE STATISTICS)

burglary victimizations during the 1973–92 period was much more substantial than was registered for crimes of violence. In 1973, the survey respondents said there were 92 per 1,000 households. In 1992, survey
respondents said there had been 49 burglaries for every 1,000 households.

Because the United States, more than any other nation in the world,
is addicted to automobiles, car theft is another troublesome property
crime. Here, during the last twenty years, the survey found a very slight
increase: 20 thefts per 1,000 households in 1992, 19 in 1973. But, given
the fact that the average American family today owns more cars than it
did twenty years ago, just how significant was the increase in auto
thefts? Looked at this way, according to a report by the American Automobile Manufacturers Association, the number of motor vehicle thefts,
in relation to the number of registered vehicles, has shown a modest decline. In 1991, there was one auto theft for every 121 registered vehicles. In 1970, there was one such theft for every 116. More recently, the
National Insurance Crime Bureau, another trade association, reported
that auto thefts dropped 3.1 percent from 1991 to 1992. Many big cities
saw larger declines during the same period: 9.61 percent in New York,
5.80 percent in Chicago, 5.58 percent in Detroit and 24.31 percent in
Houston.[4]

EXTENT VERSUS GROWTH

There is our mystery. How is it possible that America's beliefs
about crime and its experiences with it are so different? Before plunging
into our investigation of this enigma, one very important distinction
must be clearly made. Crime is a terrible and ugly affliction that directly or indirectly affects every American. Its damage should not and
cannot be minimized. In 1991, according to the National Crime Victimization Survey, persons living in the United States above the age of
twelve were the victims of 34.7 million separate crimes, 6.4 million of
which were violent—rape, robbery and assault. The survey's findings
thus confirm one part of America's widely accepted belief about this
pathology: There is a great deal of crime in the United States.

On the other hand, the findings of the National Victimization Survey
directly challenge the nation's second strongly held belief: Crime is
skyrocketing. How can this be? Why are so many Americans convinced
that crime is sharply up when their own experience shows the opposite? In his speech to the Press Club, did Director Freeh make up his
scary crime statistics? Given the acknowledged fact that crime is a

"problem," what difference does it make that crime is not an "exploding problem"?

THE ANATOMY OF CRIME

Crime in America today comes in two distinct parts. The first consists of the millions of hurtful or destructive acts that we as a society have decided are criminal. Our first thoughts about crime tend to focus on events like a mugging or burglary or a rape. But crime is highly varied, and includes many kinds of incidents—for example, the acceptance of a bribe by a senator or governor, the beating of a wife by a drunken husband, price-fixing, the deliberate murder of a rival drug dealer, the decision of a group of executives to sell a medical device they have good reason to believe might cause the death of some of the people who buy it.

The second big part of modern crime is crime statistics, the summary method that we as a society have developed to try to record these millions of different events. Despite all their serious shortcomings, it must be remembered that since only a small proportion of Americans are themselves the victims of violent criminal attack in a given period, newspaper and broadcast reports about individual crimes and crime statistics probably play a larger role in determining how the nation as a whole thinks about the problem than does crime itself.

Another key point to keep in mind—and one I'll return to later in this chapter—is that in many important ways the millions of discrete criminal events that occur each year bear little resemblance to the crime statistics that purport to summarize them. To this day, for example, large chunks of America's overall crime experience, such as white-collar crime and family abuse, are either not counted at all or are substantially undercounted.

One final summary observation: Crime statistics don't just happen, they are created; they have to be collected and interpreted and distributed. This is not always a neutral process done by neutral scientific observers. Because the FBI and the Justice Department have been the principal players in the crime statistics game, this chapter will explore the seldom-examined but important question of how these agencies have accomplished their missions. How are the sometimes horrible facts about an individual criminal event extracted from the heart and mind of the victim and transferred to the official statistical reports? Who defines the kinds of criminal events that will be categorized? How does the categorization affect our thinking about crime? What gets emphasized? What does not? Why have the FBI and the Justice Department invested so much effort in collecting and publishing crime statistics?

Accurate crime statistics have long been viewed as a valuable tool for improving the ability of society to control crime. The theory, of course, turns on the truism that information is power. Government officials, armed with detailed information about the patterns and trends suggested by the crime rates, should be able to devise better countermeasures. Ditto for the individual homeowner. On another level, crime statistics should give the public a yardstick for judging the performance of criminal justice officials in dealing with these destructive and antisocial events.

Obtaining reliable measures of crime in a nation as large and diverse as the United States, however, is an extremely challenging task, far more difficult than most Americans understand.

At the present time, there are three major national organizations engaged in various aspects of measuring crime: the FBI's Uniform Crime Reports, the Public Health Service's National Center for Health Statistics and, as we already have seen, the Justice Department's National Crime Victimization Survey. Although all three organizations spend many millions of dollars in the pursuit of what appears to be a similar goal, the events they count and the ways they count them are very different. Through the marketing genius of J. Edgar Hoover, the best known of the three systems is the Uniform Crime Reports (UCR), a publication that the FBI has produced on at least an annual basis since 1930.

WHAT GETS COUNTED AND WHY?

According to the official FBI history of the UCR, the national crime reporting program was initiated at the request of the International Association of Chiefs of Police (IACP), which, despite its rather grand name, has always been an organization dominated by small-city American police executives.

In the late 1920s, the IACP formed a committee to develop a system of uniform police statistics. The committee decided that those offenses that were known to the police would be "an appropriate measure" for its purposes, and set about evaluating which specific crimes should be included "on the basis of their seriousness, frequency of occurrence, pervasiveness in all geographical areas of the country, and the likelihood of being reported to law enforcement."[5]

The committee selected seven offenses to serve as a national index in the overall volume and rate of crime. Four were crimes of violence:

murder and nonnegligent manslaughter, forcible rape, robbery and aggravated assault. Three were property crimes: burglary, larceny-theft and auto theft. In 1930, Congress passed a law authorizing the attorney general to gather crime statistics, and he, in turn, designated the FBI to serve as the national clearinghouse.

It is not entirely clear why the FBI has carried the heavy administrative burdens of the program for all these years. It may be just as stated: a generous federal effort to help local law enforcement develop a reliable set of criminal statistics. Many police officials, however, are skeptical of this explanation. They believe that Hoover saw the UCR as a good source of publicity for himself and the FBI, as an indirect method for developing continuing ties with city, county and state police organizations of the entire nation and, finally, as a powerful engine of propaganda.

While the decisions of the attorney general and the IACP committee about the collection of crime statistics now seem obvious, almost foreordained, this really was not the case. At the very beginning, if the attorney general had given the matter any thought at all, it might have occurred to him to assign the clearinghouse function to a more neutral office in the Justice Department rather than the FBI, an organization with a very big political and bureaucratic stake in convincing the American people that an exploding crime menace exists. Federal health statistics, for example, are not collected and published by doctors, nurses and hospitals—the front-line troops in the area—but by an independent office called the National Center for Health Statistics.

Even more interesting questions were raised by the offenses that the IACP, and then the FBI, decided were worth counting. In fact, the determining factor in the selection process appears to have had little to do with developing a broad index of criminal behavior in America and almost everything to do with choosing a group of crimes that directly concerned the local police chiefs. This meant, and still means, that because few local police agencies ever devote much time to white-collar crimes—commercial fraud, political corruption and serious violations of state and city health and safety laws—the FBI's crime index actually is a very poor measure of crime in America.

It can be argued, in fact, that the very narrow definition of crime implicit in the UCR's eight offenses (arson was added in 1979) has contributed to some of America's confused thinking about crime. While armed robbers frequently are sentenced to ten-year prison terms, for example, the crooked savings and loan executives who steal millions of dollars from their depositors usually end up paying a fine or serving shorter sentences. It seems probable that this disparity in sentencing is partly the product of the public buying into the UCR's implicit judgment that robbery is real crime while bank fraud is not.

In recent years, one aspect of this glaring gap in the FBI's UCR data became a concern of Congress. In 1988, it mandated that all federal enforcement agencies investigating crimes touching on such areas as antitrust violations, the environment, banking and the manufacture and sale of food and drugs begin reporting details of these crimes to the FBI's UCR.

Four years later, in response to an inquiry from Don Edwards of California, chairman of the House Judiciary subcommittee with jurisdiction over the FBI, Freeh said that the project to begin collecting reports of white-collar crimes at the federal level had not moved forward because of budget constraints.[6]

Devising an accurate way to measure white-collar crimes of interest to the federal government is an extremely challenging task. Victim surveys won't necessarily work because many of the victims of white-collar crime may not know they have been victimized.

It should also be remembered that a count of arrests made or cases brought by an enforcement agency almost always reflects the administrative decisions of the agency and not the extent of the crime problem. One Sunday in 1968, for example, the New York Police Department sent the *New York Times* a press release noting a massive increase in drug arrests. The editors, thinking that the increasing arrests indicated a surge in drug use by the public, placed the story about the drug arrests on the paper's front page. The next day, when the department's administrative office was operating, it was discovered that the actual reason the arrests had increased was that the NYPD had doubled the size of the Narcotics Division by transferring officers from other duties.

Despite the very real challenges involved, the failure of the government to establish a system to track the extent of white-collar crime in different parts of the country and how these patterns change over time is extremely important: *It means there is no meaningful yardstick for measuring the effectiveness of the enforcement and regulatory agencies in dealing with such serious problems as bank fraud and stock fraud and life-threatening violations of the nation's environmental, pure food and drug and occupational health laws.*

A few years ago, the glaring absence of a useful yardstick led the Justice Department to mount an intemperate and revealing attack on the General Accounting Office, a congressional investigative agency. The immediate subject of the department's anger was a 1993 GAO report trying to assess how well or poorly federal prosecutors had responded to the nation's savings and loan scandal of the late 1980s and early 1990s. While giving the Justice Department full credit for substantially increasing the number of financial fraud prosecutions, the GAO added that it was difficult to determine the overall usefulness of the effort.

"First, the actual fraud that occurred and the number of individuals involved is not known, thus, the relative significance of Justice's accomplishments cannot be determined. Second, no similar law enforcement effort exists that can be compared to assess the degree of progress or effectiveness. Thus, Justice has not set sufficient goals for measuring accomplishments and evaluating the overall effectiveness of the program. Without such information, it is not clear whether the government's response is as effective as it could or should be and whether changes in the strategy are warranted."[7]

Despite the patent truth of the GAO's assertions, Justice was furious that the auditors had refused to accept its simpleminded definition of success: more prosecutions. In a passionate nineteen-page response, Assistant Attorney General Lee Rawls said the GAO report was "wrong in so many ways that it must be assumed that the inaccuracies are intentional. Release of this draft just five weeks before the presidential election further demonstrates the absence of objectivity. Perhaps it is because of the number of times we have corrected information the GAO has supplied Congress that you have chosen to take this tack, but the report simply fails to meaningfully analyze our program."[8]

FIDDLING WITH THE CRIME REPORTS

From the earliest days, the UCR has been a voluntary system based on the crime complaints that individual citizens chose to make to individual police departments and that these departments then chose to submit to the FBI. In 1931, the year of the UCR's first publication, 400 cities participated. In 1992, over 16,000 city, county and state agencies were involved.

Because of the voluntary nature of the system, the crime reporting procedures of individual police agencies have never been subjected to the rigor of systematic FBI audits. As a partial result of this failing, considerable doubts have long existed about the quality of the crime data that the FBI presents each year in the annual UCR. Experienced police officials from different parts of the country have long acknowledged that until a period beginning in the late 1950s and continuing into the 1960s, many police departments routinely concealed substantial numbers of crimes that came to their attention.

"Police chiefs have always been tempted to fudge their numbers, usually to report fewer crimes than were occurring in the community," said Anthony Bouza, a widely respected New York Police Department executive who went on to be the Minneapolis Police Chief. "I personally wrote Chief Inspector Memo Number 12 in 1967 that ordered the precinct commanders of New York City to stop playing games with the crime numbers. That edict was enforced and there was a real surge—like 200 to 300 percent—in the city's reported robberies and burglaries."[9]

Patrick Murphy is now the director of police policy for the U.S. Conference of Mayors. He is also the most experienced and respected police executive in the United States. Long before Bouza wrote his 1967 memo, Murphy began his career walking a beat in Brooklyn. He eventually went on to head the police departments in Syracuse, New York, Washington, D.C., and Detroit, Michigan. In the early 1970s, Murphy was the top gun of the nation's largest and oldest police agency—the NYPD.

"When I was a rookie cop right after the Second World War, we referred a lot of the crimes in the precinct to the mysterious Detective McCan," he recalled. "The husband would call up to ask about the investigation of the burglary his family had reported the week before. 'Oh yes,' the desk sergeant would reply, 'that case was referred to Detective McCan and he is out of the precinct house right now.' McCan, of course, was a figment, only existing in the sense that he was the large trash basket where we 'canned' a lot of crimes without ever bothering to report them to police headquarters."

The problem of questionable crime statistics remained with Murphy throughout his career. "When the big city chiefs held their annual meetings, there always would be a discussion about what should be done about Philadelphia, which was particularly notorious for its phony numbers," Murphy said. "As I remember it, Philadelphia's rates were about half those of New York's, a fact that of course had nothing to do with the crime patterns in the two cities."[10]

John Dillman, who now runs a private investigative firm in New Orleans, told a similar story about the Big Easy. Dillman began as a New Orleans patrolman in 1967 and retired as a homicide detective in 1986. "When I first came on the job and there was a burglary in a poor area or the projects, you just smoothed over the people. Instead of a crime report, you usually filed what we called a NAT, a necessary action taken." Needless to say, the FBI's UCR has no category for NATs.

By the time he retired, Dillman said, the New Orleans Police Department had come to see complete crime reports as a very important public relations tool. "You got to remember, a whole lot of money is at stake in the crime fighting business. The police budget used to be something like $20 million a year, now it's about $90 million. It has to be justified."[11]

Major cities all over the United States—including New York, Baltimore, Chicago and Philadelphia—have been periodically rocked by scandals in which the police departments were discovered to have been systematically reducing the number of crimes that were being reported by members of the public.

Although these crime reporting scandals continue to occur from time to time, they appear to have been a far more common event in the 1950s, 1960s and early 1970s. Bouza, Murphy, Dillman and other police officials around the country said that widespread administrative efforts within the police world to improve crime reporting were facilitated by technical changes that occurred in the same period, such as the general adoption of centralized 911 emergency service switchboards. With the new systems, the local precincts were bypassed and most incoming calls from the public were channeled to a special communications center where they were routinely recorded on both tape and punch cards.

Assuming, as most police officials do, that there was in fact an across-the-board improvement in police crime reporting procedures between 1960 and 1975, then part of the substantial increases in the crimes reported to the FBI during that period obviously must be attributed to these improvements in the reporting process, and not charged to a cataclysmic collapse in the nation's values.

FBI's UNIFORM CRIME REPORTS
Robbery Complaints to Police 1932–1992

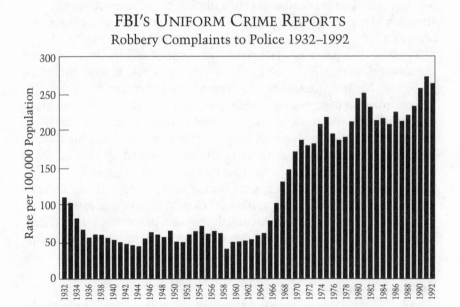

Robbery is defined as the taking of something of value by force or the threat of force. The FBI's annual crime figures are based on those crime events that (1) the public reports to local police agencies and (2) that the agencies then report to the FBI. Because of substantial shifts in public attitudes and major changes in police practices between the mid-1950s and the beginning of the 1970s, many experts believe that the startling increase in robberies suggested here between 1964 and 1974 was largely the product of more complete reporting, and not—as repeatedly claimed by FBI Director Louis Freeh—an actual fourfold jump in these crimes. (UNIFORM CRIME REPORTS)

Some police officials and criminologists assert that changes other than knowing manipulation may have had an even greater impact on the number of crime complaints made to the police by members of the public. These other changes include major shifts in important police policies touching upon how departments are recording complaints and patrolling the streets.

Marvin Wolfgang, a professor of criminology and law at the University of Pennsylvania, has been thinking, studying and writing about crime for forty-five years. "Up until the early 1960s, a constant complaint of all minority communities in the United States was the absence of police," Wolfgang observed. "In many big cities, white police officers were in fact used to surround and cordon off black communities. Police frequently were afraid to enter these areas. The reluctance of the police wasn't limited to black neighborhoods. In New York and San Francisco, for example, there was a tradition that the police would stay out of Chinese areas and enforcement was left to informal groups within them. Partly because of this tradition, the Chinese communities always had a very low rate of reported crime even though there probably was a lot going on that never became a part of the record."[12]

But with the peaceful civil rights demonstrations in the South and the urban riots that followed in the North, the whole nation, including its police, became conscious of a long-ignored segment of society. "A large number of departments became more open and aware of the black community during those years," recalled Patrick Murphy. "The black leadership started to demand better service in their neighborhoods. With more equitable patrol patterns, the police ended up hearing about and recording crimes that in the past had been totally ignored."

Basic police tactics also changed during that period, with an increasing number of departments gradually adopting more aggressive crime fighting techniques. These included the use of "decoy" operations, where police officers would pose as vulnerable victims, and a reemphasis on neighborhood policing where officers were encouraged to abandon their patrol cars and make direct contact with individual residents and small businesses.

In a curious way, the growing efforts of the police to reach the public were mirrored by an increasing willingness of the public to demand police assistance on matters that had long been considered too private for official intervention. The family dispute, for example, has been a major aspect of the patrol officer's daily challenge for many years. With an increasing number of American women asserting their full rights, the long accepted practice of the past, where officers would routinely handle these cases by informal and unrecorded mediation efforts, was gradually abandoned. Because society came to see that spousal rape was a genuine crime, and no longer closed its eyes to battered children, events that had been a horrible and secret part of family life were more and more being recorded in the official statistics.

CONFESSION IS GOOD FOR THE SOUL

Even the FBI, in an indirect way, sometimes admits that police officials like Patrick Murphy, Tony Bouza and John Dillman are right: The UCR is a poor way to measure crime. One such acknowledgment is contained in the remarkably frank cautionary statement that for many years has been printed in the introductory section of its annual crime report.

"Each year when *Crime in America* is published, many entities—news media, tourism agencies and others with an interest in crime in our Nation—compile rankings of cities and counties based on their Crime Index figures," the UCR's small-print consumer warning begins. "These simplistic and/or incomplete analyses often create misleading perceptions which adversely affect cities and counties, along with their residents."

But as the FBI itself goes on to note, it really is very hard to compile anything but "simplistic and/or incomplete analyses" from the UCR's annual reports. "Assessing criminality and law enforcement's response from jurisdiction to jurisdiction must encompass many elements, some of which, while having significant impact, are not readily measurable nor applicable among all locales." Among the thirteen specific elements that can influence local crime rates but are difficult or impossible to quantify, according to the FBI, are: relative stability of the population with respect to the mobility of residents, commuting patterns and number of transients; the investigative and administrative policies of law enforcement agencies within each jurisdiction, including the prosecutors and the courts; variations in the composition of populations, particularly youth concentration; economic conditions including median income, poverty level and job availability; cultural, educational and religious characteristics; climate.

The warning concludes by noting that population size is the only correlate of crime utilized by the UCR, although many of the other listed elements are of equal concern. Here, according to the FBI, is the amazing bottom line: "The reader is, therefore, cautioned against comparing statistical data of individual reporting units from cities, counties, metropolitan areas, states, or colleges and universities solely on the basis of their population coverage or student enrollment."[13]

While the FBI statement warns against using the UCR to compare the crime in one city with that of another, the same problems still exist when it comes to using police reports for comparing crime over a period of time. As noted in the FBI's just quoted statement, the amount of crime in a particular city or county is influenced by the composition of the population living within its boundaries. As discovered by criminologists such as Marvin Wolfgang, for example, young people are more likely to commit criminal acts than older individuals. This means, therefore, other factors being equal, that a city with a small number of teenagers in its total population almost always will have less crime than a city with a large number of energetic, pugnacious youngsters.

The same phenomena appear to occur over time. From 1960 to 1970, for example, Census Bureau data show that the number of fifteen-to-twenty-four-year-olds increased 50 percent, far faster than the population as a whole. It was during this period, of course, that the FBI's rates of reported crime underwent their sharpest increases.

Steven L. Pomerantz is the assistant FBI director who heads the Criminal Justice Information Division, a position that makes him responsible for the overall supervision of the UCR. In an interview, Pomerantz said that while his knowledge of the subject was indirect, it seemed likely that the more aggressive pro-active enforcement strategies adopted by many police departments in the last few decades probably had contributed to some of the apocalyptic increases that his boss had cited in his Press Club speech.[14]

Pomerantz finessed the obvious conflicts between the bureau's official reservations about its own data and Director Freeh's crime claims by neatly changing the subject. The absolute accuracy of the UCR rates, he said, was not the central issue. "What is critical is that compared with many other countries in the world the United States has a terrible crime problem today."

In summary, according to a variety of expert sources, basic changes in public attitudes toward the police and police attitudes toward the public during the 1960s almost certainly contributed to a growing proportion of the nation's crimes becoming a part of the public record. This increase was helped along during the same period by technical developments such as centralized police switchboards. At the same time, partly because of the swelling numbers of young people, the actual number of crimes also moved higher during this turbulent decade.

Albert J. Reiss, Jr., the chairman of Yale University's Department of Sociology, has spent much of his long career thinking and writing about crime and attempts to measure it. "One generality is definitely true," Reiss said. "For a variety of reasons the changes in crime that have occurred in the United States during the last four or five decades are much less dramatic than suggested by the shifts in the FBI's crime rates. It is an established principle that short of major catastrophes such as revolution or war, social fluctuations in a large society simply do not occur at the speed suggested by the FBI statistics. Despite the very slow way that crime patterns change, during this century we have gone through what the public regarded as four major 'crime waves.' I guess the bottom line lesson is that crime can always be fashioned into hot news."[15]

The combined effect of these various factors is that the long-term public impression about crime that emerges from the FBI's annual publications from about 1960 to 1990 is significantly distorted. There is no question that the *reports of crime* increased during these three decades, especially from 1960 to 1985. There are huge questions, however, about what proportion of the increasing number of crime reports were the product of changes in police practices and public attitudes and what proportion related to the *actual criminal events* that were occurring in society as a whole. FBI Director Louis Freeh totally ignored this essential problem in his February 1994 speech to the National Press Club. It was not, as he so vigorously asserted, *violent crime* that had increased 371 percent since 1960, but the *reports* of violent crime.

So why should we care about the reliability, accuracy and completeness of crime statistics? What difference does it make that our understanding of a significant national problem is incorrect? Is it true, as I strongly believe, that a false diagnosis of a disease almost certainly will lead the doctor to prescribe the wrong medicine? Has the manipulation about what we believe about crime led us to turn down the wrong path in our search for possible solutions?

HOMICIDE

Before turning to these questions, we must examine one last important subject: the myths that surround homicide, the most terrifying of all crimes. When Louis Freeh told the National Press Club that homicides have almost tripled since 1960, his audience had to have been disturbed. Freeh's picture of a grim, seemingly inevitable upward surge in what has always been considered among the most heinous crimes is indeed a frightening prospect.

But once again, like a car salesman trying to make his monthly quota, Freeh pushes too hard. First of all, his claim that there are now nearly three times more homicides than in 1960 ignored the important fact that the nation's population grew substantially during that period. When this factor is taken into account, the picture still looks bad, but not quite as bad as Freeh suggested. While the *numbers* of murders did indeed almost triple, the murder *rate* barely doubled: 10.4 per 100,000 in 1992 compared with 4.7 per 100,000 in 1960.

There were other problems with the murder statement in Freeh's speech. More than many other crimes, U.S. homicide rates have undergone major changes over the years; sharply declining during the forties and fifties, increasing during the sixties and seventies, declining some in the middle eighties and once again increasing in the nineties.

So, amazing as it may seem that a leading law enforcement official might try to buttress his cases through the selective use of statistics, when the FBI director selected the years to illuminate his thesis for the National Press Club, he just happened to compare a year when the nation's homicide rate was at one of its all-time lowest points to that of a year when the rate was near its all-time high. Thus, although the rates have gone *down* and gone *up*, Freeh chose to emphasize rate changes from a period that demonstrated the uptick. Such selective use of statistics is dishonest.

An interesting historical reminder about the persistence of homicide is provided by Patrick Murphy, the former head of the New York Police Department. "There of course is a lot of crime in this country, too much," he said. "But you've got to keep a perspective on this. There was one New York street in 1875 or so where 365 murders were committed in a single year, almost all of them by the impoverished immigrant Catholics then streaming into the city."

HOW MANY HOMICIDES?

It might seem that homicide would be the easiest of all crimes to track. Despite the undeniable reality of a dead body, however, even the business of maintaining an accurate and consistent yearly count on homicides turns out to be something of a challenge. While the FBI's UCR has always included homicides as one of the violent crimes it tracks, the bureau modified its definition of this particularly horrible category in the mid-1930s. This means that when it comes to making long-term comparisons, the FBI counts are problematical. On the other hand, the National Crime Victimization Survey, the crime-measuring system based on interviewing victims, is of no help because homicide victims are extremely hard to interview.

Fortunately, a third organization, the National Center for Health Statistics (NCHS), has maintained a meticulous record of U.S. homicides going back more than sixty years. This record is based on reports filed by the nation's medical examiners. While a 1990 statistical analysis found some minor differences in the homicide information reported by the FBI and the NCHS during a recent seven-year period, the annual homicide rates reported by the two systems were highly similar in terms of long-term trends.[16]

Here is the overall picture of homicide in the United States for the last sixty-plus years according to the nation's medical examiners. In the early 1930s, perhaps because of the gangsters of Prohibition or maybe because of the despair of the Great Depression—no one really knows why—there was a lot of killing: 9.8 per 100,000 in 1934 and 9.7 in 1935. During the second half of the thirties, into the war years and through most of the fifties, the annual homicide rates drifted slowly downward, hitting the bottom of the trough, 4.5 per 100,000, in 1957 and 1958. Then the pattern reversed itself, with the rates slowly inching up each year, hitting a peak of 10.2 per 100,000 in 1974. After declining modestly for a couple of years, the rates reached another peak of 10.7 in 1980. During the 1980s, the rates first went down and then up, topping off at 10.9 in 1991 and 10.4 in 1992.

With the involvement of so many overlapping social, cultural, psychological and economic influences, law enforcement officials, crimi-

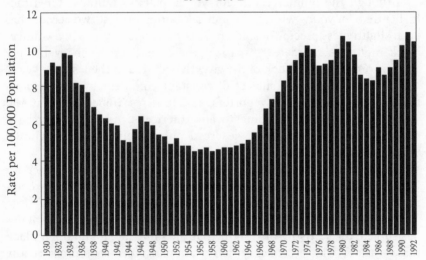

UNITED STATES HOMICIDE RATE
1930–1992

The United States homicide rate has always been high, higher than most other nations of the world. But the high rates of the last few years are about the same as those of the early thirties. Over the years, the nation's most complete and consistent record of homicides has come from information collected by the National Center for Health Statistics from county medical examiners. (NATIONAL CENTER FOR HEALTH STATISTICS)

nologists and others have never been able to develop a consensus theory about the forces that drive the rise and fall of homicide rates. "When it comes to crime rates, there almost always are barely visible forces at work that are extremely hard to quantify," said Albert Reiss, the Yale sociology professor and coeditor of a recent National Academy of Sciences report, "Understanding and Preventing Violence."[17]

"Because of the improved [emergency medical] treatment of traumas in recent years, for example, a larger proportion of all homicide attempts almost certainly are surviving," he said. "This dynamic would seem to lead to a reduction in the homicide rate—deaths in relation to the population—even though homicide attempts may actually have increased. But it is clear that there has been an increasing use of guns that makes such confrontations more deadly. This factor, more guns, would seem to work the other way, to increase homicide rates."

One of the most disturbing recent trends has been the sharp increase of violent mayhem among young American males. The information collected by the National Center for Health Statistics shows that these increases have been found among both whites and blacks. During the last two decades, the death rate for fifteen-to-twenty-four-year-old whites has almost doubled, going from 10 per 100,000 in 1972 to 17 per 100,000 in 1991. A substantial part of this growth came in the last two years.

Although the homicide rate for young blacks is almost ten times higher than for young whites, the increase during the last two decades has been slightly less precipitous. In 1972, 107 out of every 100,000 younger black men was murdered. By 1991, there were 159 such events per 100,000. Once again, much of the growth occurred in the last two years.

These increases—the subject of constant comment by law enforcement officials, politicians, reporters, academic researchers and editorial writers—are deeply disturbing to all Americans. As such, they have clearly contributed to the widespread public belief that the United States is in the middle of a massive and growing crime wave.

Within the homicide data maintained by the National Center for Health Statistics, however, is astonishing information that all the commentators, including Louis Freeh, seem to have largely ignored.

While it is true that the homicide death rate for young black males has surged, the statistics also show that the same rate for all other black males—those who are twenty-five years and older—has dramatically declined. Among black males between twenty-five and thirty-four, for example, homicide rates dropped to 155 per 100,000 in 1991 compared with 180 in 1972. For older black males the declines were even sharper. *For those who were thirty-five to forty-four, the murder rate in 1991 was less than half what it was in 1972, 78 per 100,000 compared with 176. A parallel decline was recorded for those between forty-five and fifty-four, with rates falling to 52 in 1991 from 110 in 1972.*[18]

The explanations for these starkly varied trends—sharp increases for young black males and even sharper declines for their older brothers—are not immediately clear. Was it possible that the major drop in the homicide death rate for a large proportion of black men was the result of the civil rights laws? Had the fair housing laws and the equal employment laws so improved the social conditions of the black community that mindless violence, murder, no longer was an option for many members of the community? Had the "social programs" that so many law enforcement officials and conservative political figures love to loathe actually worked?

This was a possibility that occurred to Chuck Stone, now a journalism professor at the University of North Carolina. At other times in his life, Stone has been the managing editor of a black newspaper in Washington; a senior adviser to the late Adam Clayton Powell, the fiery Harlem congressman; and a syndicated columnist who was directly involved in several hostage situations involving black prison inmates.

"I have written a good deal about the terrible scourge among young black males, but I had never heard about the opposite trends among older blacks," Stone said.[19]

HOMICIDE RATES FOR BLACK MALES, BY AGE
1972–1991

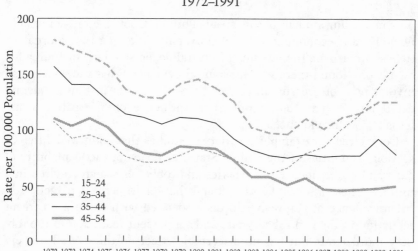

Depending upon age, the homicide rate for black males is currently five to ten times higher than for white males. But among both white and black males, while the homicide rate for the young has sharply increased in recent years, the rate for older men has declined. This is particularly clear among black males between the ages of thirty-five and fifty-four, where homicide rates are about half what they were twenty years ago. (OFFICE OF ANALYSIS AND EPIDEMIOLOGY, NATIONAL CENTER FOR HEALTH STATISTICS)

"You see a lot of despair in the black community, but you also see indications of some advances. The median income of black families, while not keeping up with whites, is indeed up. There obviously are a lot more black professionals. While many of the large number of black families who have moved to the suburbs still live in segregated communities, the people who have escaped the inner cities are in many ways less marginalized. In a very crude way, perhaps this decline in the homicide death rates for all but the youngest blacks indicates some small improvements in race relations."

Much more analysis will be required before all the forces at work can be understood. But what about the opposite side of the coin—the increased homicide rate among all younger males? Without getting into the debate over the effectiveness of gun control measures as a way of reducing violence, there does seem to be overwhelming evidence that the increasing availability of guns is directly related to homicide rates. More guns, more homicides. More lethal guns, more fatalities.

BANG BANG, YOU'RE DEAD

One leading student of this area is Philip J. Cook, a professor of public policy and economics at Duke University. In a long 1991 journal article summarizing the research of several dozen scholars, including his own, Cook found there was substantial evidence "that the widespread involvement of firearms in personal violence is not just an incidental detail but, rather, has an important influence on the patterns and lethality of this violence."[20]

Cook cited, for example, a variety of studies that compared different sections and cities of the United States in terms of the availability of guns and the incidence of robberies and robberies which resulted in a murder. These studies, he said, found that "a 10 percent reduction in the prevalence of gun ownership is associated with about a 5 percent reduction in the gun robbery rate and a 4 percent reduction in the robbery murder rate but has no discernible effect on the overall robbery rate. These results suggest that gun density influences the choice of weapon in a robbery and its lethality, but not the overall volume of robbery."[21]

Cook added that the weapon-specific differences in fatality rates have been clearly established for assaults as well as robberies, that more lethal weapons definitely are associated with higher death rates. In this conclusion, Cook essentially supported the once controversial finding of a 1969 study conducted by George D. Newton, Jr., and Franklin E.

Zimring for the National Commission on the Causes and Prevention of Violence. Assaults involving guns, Newton and Zimring found, were five times as likely to result in death than assaults with knives, despite the apparent similarity of the two kinds of attacks in other respects.

In his analysis, Cook also noted a 1989 international survey of households possessing a firearm. At the top of the nations included in the survey, of course, was the United States, where 48.9 percent of the households had a gun. Among some of the other selected nations, the rate was 31.2 percent in Norway, 24.7 percent in France, 9.2 percent in the Federal Republic of Germany and 4.7 percent in England and Wales.

Although international comparisons are difficult, murder rates in the United States, whether at their peak or their trough, have been higher than almost all other developed nations. According to a 1987 study by the World Health Organization, the homicide rate in the United States during the 1981–86 period was roughly four times higher than those recorded in almost every European country.[22]

The National Victim Survey says the rate of violent encounters—the number of robberies, rapes and felonious assaults in relation to the population—has been slowly declining. At the same time, however, the homicide death rate for the nation is high, in fact just a bit higher than it was in the early thirties and eighties. Considered together, and taking into account the careful research cited by Philip Cook, only one conclusion is possible: The easy availability of guns in the United States has made violent encounters more lethal for a relatively small group of American people.

Although the studies presented in Cook's carefully documented analysis are well known to most criminologists, including some of those working in the Justice Department's Bureau of Statistics, the attorneys general of the Reagan and Bush years seemed to look the other way even while they denounced the problem. Both presidents, after all, were lifetime members of the National Rifle Association, and the politics of the moment required the Justice Department to vigorously oppose federal efforts to control handguns.

BACK TO THE CASE
OF THE MYSTERIOUS DISCONTINUITY

T he conundrum remains. Why does the public currently believe it is in the middle of a soaring crime wave when its experience, in most regards, is the opposite? Although the answer is complicated, one reason has to be the constant repetition of exaggerated claims by people like FBI Director Freeh and other officials and political figures with a personal stake in convincing the public at large that the criminal elements in America pose a continually growing threat.

An essential element in those claims, of course, has been the regular publication of the FBI's Uniform Crime Reports, which year after year focused on *reported crime* without ever acknowledging the revolutionary changes that were occurring within the police departments that were doing the reporting. The success of the FBI strategy in publicizing this spurious evidence was assured by many years of well-engineered press releases and ill-informed reporters who were willing to spout back any "official" statement. When it comes to crime reporting, unfortunately, almost all news organizations transform themselves into low-grade tabloids that systematically play on public fears. Another factor that appears to have helped in establishing the belief in the nation's alleged crime epidemic involves basic shifts in how crime news is presented to the American people. Marvin Wolfgang, for example, theorizes that as a result of the steady development of newspaper chains with outlets in many communities, crime stories that previously appeared in only one city now are being read all over the nation.

"A dramatic violent crime—perhaps involving the brutal slaying of an innocent young person—has always been a big local story in the city where it occurred," Wolfgang explained. "But now, with the steady concentration of newspaper ownership, when there is a grisly murder in Miami, I very well may learn about it the next morning on the front page of my newspaper in Philadelphia. This routine nationalization of crime news is a new thing."

But something else is going on. For reasons that are not entirely clear, in the last few years news organizations, even responsible ones like the *New York Times* and the *Washington Post*, have been giving the crime issue more and more play even though the best available measures of the overall crime rates are holding steady or declining. This is no longer just a question of the tabloids providing the subway straphangers a sleazy scare. Now it is the serious media talking directly to the career politicians who control Congress, the White House and the governors' mansions.

The obsession with crime has been especially noticeable in television, where powerful visual images—the weeping mother, the blood-stained street, the chalked outline of the slain victim—are especially effective in arousing primal emotions and undermining any serious thought. A 1994 analysis by the Center for Media and Public Affairs, focusing on crime reporting by the news outlets of three of the national television networks, tells the story. The center found that the evening news programs of ABC, CBS and NBC broadcast 1,632 stories about crime in 1993. This was twice as many such stories as they broadcast in

1992 and three times as many as in 1989. Murder stories tripled during the 1992–93 period (329 in 1993 versus 104 in 1992).[23]

While the sharp increase in crime coverage by the television networks did not match the national crime picture, it almost certainly had a significant impact on how the public felt about the subject. According to an ABC/*Washington Post* survey, for example, the proportion of Americans naming crime as the nation's most important problem recently underwent a sixfold increase, jumping from 5 percent in May 1993 to 30 percent in February 1994.

WHY?

Has there been a knowing attempt to generate public fears about crime for political and social purposes? Has the news media, partly for commercial reasons, contributed to the confusion? Is the process of trying to measure crime so complicated that the experts who are doing it have become lost in their own information? Does the public for some perverse reason tend to focus on the evil and ignore the good? Or is the general dismay the product of all these factors at the same time?

It is impossible to know what was going through Louis Freeh's mind as he delivered his distorted, exaggerated and fundamentally dishonest crime speech to the National Press Club. We do know, however, that for many decades, law enforcement officials across the nation have advanced their careers and promoted their political agendas by chanting the same mantra of the scary numbers. Police chiefs, prosecutors, judges, FBI directors and the politicians who supported their cause— going back at least to the time of President Herbert Hoover—have long waved the bloody crime flag to rally the public to their various causes.

In his speech to the Press Club, Freeh did not directly assert that the menacing world he described was certain to become even more dangerous if the budget and program needs of the FBI were not satisfied. But a few months later, the new director was less restrained, making explicit what he earlier had only implied. The occasion was a May 1994 speech to the American Law Institute in which Freeh made an impassioned plea on behalf of a controversial change in the nation's wiretap law that he was then trying to persuade Congress to approve. "If you think crime is bad now," he warned the assembled lawyers, "just wait and see what happens if the FBI one day is no longer able to conduct court-approved electronic surveillance."[24]

Although a direct cause and effect relationship cannot be proven, it seems likely that drumfire repetition of such warnings have played a role in persuading local, state and federal legislatures to rapidly expand government spending for criminal justice activities. From 1971 to 1990, for example, government spending for police, prosecutors, public defense, courts and jails grew by 606 percent.[25] During the same period, the number of persons held in state and federal prisons quadrupled, giving America one of the highest incarceration rates in the world.[26] The effects of the overstated crime claims do not appear to be limited to law enforcement. More broadly, millions of Americans altered their basic lifestyles: abandoning evening trips to downtown movie houses; locking all their doors; buying hundreds of millions of dollars' worth of high-priced safety bars, alarm systems and guns, moving to more-and-more distant suburbs.

At an even broader level, the fervent recitation of frightening crime statistics, sometimes spiced by an anecdotal account of a particular grisly crime, has been a favorite rhetorical tactic of those who were worried about all kinds of social change, those who saw a direct causal link between the holdup man and the civil rights laws or America's permissive attitudes toward sex, drugs and rock and roll, not to mention punk, grunge and hiphop.

Some sincerely believe that the surging rates of reported crime are the necessary product of a diseased society. Jerome Daunt, a retired FBI inspector, brings a special perspective to the debate because he was in charge of the UCR during most of the 1960s, the ten-year period when the nation's reported crime rates made their most dramatic leap. In a recent interview, Daunt conceded that the baby boom had indeed contributed to the sharp increases. But the elderly lawman, who for many years was regarded as one of the most intelligent and respected officials within the FBI hierarchy, argued that in his view the gradual breakdown of the nuclear family was the key factor. "Don't forget Woodstock and everything that went with it," said Daunt, referring to the giant rock and roll concert that gave a generation its name.[27]

Many of the statements denouncing the rapid increase in crime have served the interests of the political outs. Such assertions were an important element in Richard Nixon's very close 1968 victory over Hubert Humphrey. Pointing to the apparently authoritative FBI crime reports, Nixon repeatedly attacked his opponent and the Democratic Party for being "soft on crime."

Almost twenty years later, George Bush's brilliant political strategist, Lee Atwater, adopted the Nixon strategy, fully understanding that crime was a perfect "wedge issue" for fragmenting the Democratic Party. Atwater used it for just that purpose in the 1988 presidential campaign when George Bush, fighting for his turn in the White House, overwhelmed Michael Dukakis, partly with the help of the infamous Willie Horton television ad. Four years later, Bill Clinton defeated Bush, helped by the fact that Clinton was the first Democratic presidential candidate in modern history to take what was regarded as a hard-nosed position on the crime issue.

Winning the White House did not lead to a change in the Clinton strategy. The president and Attorney General Reno, for example, read the 1994 polls and openly endorsed a repressive government plan allowing the police to bust into the apartments of the poor without a search warrant.

Senator Joseph Biden of Delaware, the Democratic chairman of the Senate Judiciary Committee, is another supple political figure who was once considered a leading progressive. In 1990, Biden introduced the Violence Against Women Act. Among its provisions was one which, in effect, would make any crime committed against a woman a possible federal offense. Exactly how the comparatively dinky federal enforcement agencies were going to manage this extension of their legal responsibilities to more than half of the nation's population was, and still is, not clear. For Biden, however, his assertions about the alleged surge in crimes against women, despite the strong evidence to the contrary, justified the desperate remedy he proposed.[28] Some Senate staff members who were involved in the redrafting of Biden's unusual rape measure, now a part of federal law, contend the senator's interest was purely political. The trigger, they say, were polls showing that Biden had a low rating among women at a time when he was contemplating running for president.

Keep in mind that during the whole twenty-year period that presidents from Nixon to Clinton were agitating the public about the national crime menace, the best available evidence shows the American people were gradually experiencing less and less crime.

DOES IT ALL ADD UP?

It must always be remembered that crime statistics are highly inflammatory—an explosive fuel that powers the nation's debate over a large number of important social issues—and that Louis Freeh today is the leading official shoveling the fuel into the blazing firebox.

Additional evidence of this observation came five months after Freeh's speech to the National Press Club when the FBI director was confronted with a challenging dilemma. Crimes reported to 10,084 local law enforcement agencies in 1993 had decreased by 3 percent. Furthermore, the 1993 decline had continued the downward trend from the previous year, when crime reports had also decreased by 3 percent.

While the FBI press release announcing the latest crime statistics acknowledged these consecutive declines, Freeh's interpretive statement accompanying the preliminary figures was a truly heroic effort to identify the shining nugget of bad news buried in all the good. "Crime problems are so grave that few Americans will find much comfort in a small reduction in the overall amount of reported crime," he said. "To make matters worse, the number of murders grew larger in 1993—not smaller. The nation must find ways to achieve large crime reductions that are permanent."[29]

Once again Freeh had demonstrated the obvious truth that when it comes to crime statistics the FBI is not an equal opportunity player. During the early days of the UCR, the FBI's manipulative ways may have been inadvertent. More recently, however, this does not appear to be the case. In subtle and clever ways, often through sins of omission and always playing on knee-jerk uninformed reactions of the press, the FBI has consistently sought to terrorize the public about crime. This is because—as it is now and always has been—a widespread public belief that crime rates are increasing in an alarming way directly fosters the political, ideological and budget interests of the FBI.

Given these understandings it is essential for reporters, members of Congress, public interest groups and the American people to become a great deal more skeptical about all generalizations concerning crime. If crime is a "problem," the nation has time to think. If crime is an "exploding problem," a nearly instant response is required. Bad data leads to bad policy. The black and white, oversimplified summary descriptions of crime produced by the FBI tend to demand a black and white, oversimplified response to crime. More crime, more cops. More crime, more laws. More crime, more jails.

In early 1994, House Republican Whip Newt Gingrich and twenty-seven other GOP members of Congress wrote a public letter to President Clinton. Recent public opinion polls and local elections in Virginia, New Jersey and New York City, they said, "demonstrate that the American people are tired of being hostages to violent crime and are looking for action to put a stop to the crime epidemic *now*. They are fed up with discredited theories that 'it is society's fault' or that we have to wait to solve the 'root causes' of crime before we can take action."[30]

Did the congressmen know that for the last twenty years the American people had been repeatedly telling Census Bureau enumerators that fewer and fewer of them were being victimized by crime? Did they know that in more recent years even the UCR summary of crime reports to the police had declined? Did they know that the homicide death rate for all but the youngest black males was sharply less than in previous years?

Or did they fear the truth?

5

Keeping Track of the American People: The Unblinking Eye and Giant Ear

About six times a week, fifty-two weeks a year, a team of highly trained FBI agents secretly breaks into a house, office or warehouse somewhere in the United States. The agents are members of the bureau's Surreptitious Entry Program, and their usual mission is to plant a hidden microphone or camera without tipping off the people who occupy the targeted structure.

FBI officials refuse to discuss, even in the most general way, the operations of these clandestine hit squads. It would seem likely that their reticence, at least in part, is based on the thought that it is dumb to alert the bad guys. Another explanation, however, might be old-fashioned public relations. Gentlemen, after all, do not read other gentlemen's mail.

Whatever the reason for the official silence, the intelligence picked up by the electronic surveillance equipment planted by the special squads must have considerable value to the FBI and the Justice Department for whom the bureau works. Along with the improving technology, how else can one explain the sixfold increase in the number of clandestine break-ins during the last few years: 300 a year in 1993, compared to 47 in 1985? How else can one comprehend the bureau's 1993 decision to invest a substantial sum, about $27 million, in classified research to develop the tools and methods the agents need to defeat the advanced alarms and locks employed by some of those whose property it seeks to invade?

According to a secret FBI budget document, each raid involves a time-consuming four-step process. First, the bureau field office that wants electronic surveillance defines its requirements. Then the Surreptitious Entry agents assigned to carry out the mission prepare themselves by secretly inspecting the target and gathering additional information, such as the building's architectural drawings. Next, the team members assemble the special tools they will need to enter the facility and acquire the custom-made surveillance gear that they will leave behind in the target's home or office. Finally comes "the entry itself, which may include multiple entries over a period of several days/nights."[1]

It appears that in the last few years this unusual law enforcement specialty, now almost always practiced on behalf of a Justice Department prosecutor, has become even more challenging than it was a few decades ago, when such raids were referred to by macho bureau agents as "black bag jobs." The FBI blames its current difficulties on the security industry, asserting that the central problem has been the development of clever new alarm systems that are extremely difficult, if not impossible, to silence. Adding to the bureau's woes, it claims, are computer-controlled locking devices that generate a record each time someone attempts to penetrate a guarded area and instantly transmits a coded warning to a central surveillance post anytime an intrusion is attempted.

The FBI has gone so far as to suggest it is actually losing the security race, that some individuals in the enemy camp are already outfoxing the bureau. "The FBI has traditionally focused on exploiting the mechanical aspects of locks and alarm systems," the bureau explained. "Increasingly, FBI surreptitious entry teams are encountering complex and multiple physical security systems at target locations. Drug traffickers, in particular, are going to extraordinary lengths to protect their premises and property. The FBI has fallen significantly behind in its ability to defeat modern electronics-based locking systems and the latest multi-laser technologies."[2]

This was the central justification offered by the FBI when a couple of years ago it asked the White House for $27 million in public funds to pay the engineering whizzes at the Sandia and Los Alamos National Laboratories and several other government research facilities to develop ways to defeat "any locking system whether it be mechanical or electronic, or computer supplemented" and to identify and overcome the "countersurveillance [equipment] deployed by subjects inside and in close proximity to targets."

The FBI document repeatedly emphasized that the bureau break-ins—undertaken on behalf of itself, the Drug Enforcement Agency and other unnamed government agencies—were carried out only with the permission of a judge under federal laws authorizing the surveillance of individuals suspected of being domestic criminals or spies.

While these official assurances are good to hear, it must be recalled that from the years just before World War II until the mid-1970s there were hundreds, more probably thousands, of instances when the bureau used its very special skills to commit illegal political burglaries of the offices and homes of senators, civil rights activists, former White House staff members, political advocacy groups and other organizations and individuals.

The unlawfulness of these past operations is not in doubt. William C. Sullivan, the FBI official responsible for many of the break-ins during the late 1960s and early 1970s, should have won the frankness award of 1966 when he wrote a famous *"Do Not File"* memo to the bureau's number two boss, Cartha D. DeLoach. "We do not obtain authorization for 'black bag' jobs outside the Bureau," Sullivan explained. "Such a technique involves a trespass and is clearly illegal; therefore, it would be impossible to obtain any legal sanction for it."[3]

In fairness to the FBI, Sullivan overstated his proposition just a bit. While it is true that the black bag jobs of the past were not sanctioned by law, at least some of them were undertaken with the implicit approval and private encouragement of either the president, the attorney general or influential members of Congress.

In recent years, at least, the usual purpose of the secret break-ins appears to have been the installation of various kinds of hidden recording devices. Electronic surveillance, however, has not always been the goal. During the course of the FBI's lengthy investigation of the Socialist Workers Party, for example, bureau agents made 208 illegal raids on the group's offices and the homes of several of its members, during which they removed or photographed 9,864 documents. Most of the raids occurred between 1958 and 1966. Detailed information about the investigation of Socialist Workers was pried out of the FBI in 1985 during New York hearings presided over by federal judge Thomas P. Griesa as a result of the party's suit against the government. In his final opinion on the case, Griesa held that the FBI's investigation, including the bureau's

208 secret raids and its collection of information from 1,300 informants, had been conducted without "statutory or regulatory authority"
and thus was "patently unconstitutional." He ordered the government
to pay the members $264,000 for damages, and noted that although the
group's rhetoric frequently was inflammatory, no party members were
ever charged with a crime.[4]

THE BIRTH OF
A NEW AGE SURVEILLANCE ENTITY

As witnessed by the steady increase in surreptitious break-ins by
the FBI, the vast array of surveillance and tracking technologies is an
important development, a key aspect of the Justice Department's growing power over the American people. Although J. Edgar Hoover's FBI
played a much more profound role in American politics than has been
usually understood, the bureau's actual surveillance activities were
limited by its relatively small staff, the crude technology then available
to the G-men and the genuine resistance of many state and local police
officials to the FBI's expansionist dreams.

But today, rolling along on the back of a number of extremely sophisticated technological changes, the FBI and the other enforcement agencies of the Justice Department—the DEA and the INS—are gradually
deploying across the face of America a truly imposing electronic investigative entity.

It is not easy to quantify the impact of these changes and the speed
with which they have swept over the bureau, the department and the nation. But in 1994, two New York sociologists, Kenneth C. Laudon and
Kenneth L. Marr, came up with a rough proxy. First the researchers obtained from the Office of Management and Budget a detailed year-to-year
inventory of the FBI's stock of mainframe and mini computers. (No centralized tally of desktop computers exists.) Based on their knowledge of
the capacity of these computers, Laudon and Marr calculated the millions
of computer instructions per second (MIPS) that the agency's equipment theoretically was capable of processing on a year-by-year basis.

Their conclusion: In 1980, FBI computers could achieve approximately 5.3 million instructions per second. Ten years later, computers
in the FBI inventory could handle 203 MIPS, nearly forty times more
than in 1980. Given the rapid expansion in the capacities of virtually all
computers during this period, the FBI's growth rate at first glance might
not seem too surprising. As noted by Laudon and Marr, however, the
surge in the FBI's basic computer power was almost twice that racked

up by the Social Security Administration and ten times that of the IRS.[5] The formidable power of the FBI's flourishing computer system has in recent years been enhanced even more by the bureau's intimate collaboration with the intelligence community, particularly the intensely secretive National Security Agency.[6]

The Justice Department's new-age investigative entity, actually a conglomeration of many different technologies, has in a strange way begun to assume some of the basic properties of a living and growing organism. The system boasts a kind of reproductive process, a semi-secret facility specifically established to beget a vast range of sophisticated electronic surveillance devices. It possesses a gigantic maw that uses these devices and other kinds of computerized collection systems to ingest, swiftly and cheaply, hundreds of millions of pieces of information about both the general public and the much smaller number of individuals actually suspected of committing criminal acts.

The entity also is beginning to develop something close to a brain in the form of an expanding stable of advanced computers specifically designed to draw investigative inferences from the organized examination of all the data that the Justice Department and its component agencies are collecting. Finally, it includes a central nervous system in the form of multiple high-speed communications networks. In addition to transmitting intelligence information and commands among the body's multiple parts, the interlocking networks also work to unify the connected agencies, gradually creating a de facto national police force that federal officials in Washington supervise less and less.

FRANKENSTEIN'S MONSTER?

It is often hard to identify the single individual in a large organization who has had the greatest influence on it over a period of time. Usually, the pace of change is too slow and the actors too many. With the ripening of the federal government's current system of investigation and surveillance, however, this does not seem to be the case.

Curiously, the creator and midwife of this largely unheralded Justice Department entity did not begin his professional career as a lawyer, a cop or an FBI agent. Rather, he started out as a physics major whose first job in the federal government was to study the orbits and reentry characteristics of America's earliest space capsules.

William Alfred Bayse—most people who know him call him Al— grew up in Salem, Virginia, a small town on the eastern slope of the Blue Ridge Mountains. His father, with the part-time help of his mother, ran a mom-and-pop trucking business. After graduating from a parochial high school and Roanoke College, young Bayse did graduate work at five other colleges including Virginia Tech and the University of Virginia.

His first real job was at the Langley Research Center of what now is called the National Aeronautics and Space Administration (NASA). "I am a charter member of the space program. I was at Langley when, right after Sputnik, President Eisenhower signed the directive establishing an accelerated space program. I worked on Project Mercury, dealt with the first astronauts and got to know John Glenn when he still was just an unknown Marine Corps major."[7]

Bayse is no longer employed by the government. But for most of his long and remarkable career at the FBI his title was assistant director, Technical Services Division. This meant that the former space scientist was a genuine boss, the FBI official in charge of spending more than half a billion dollars for research, development and computer operations as the bureau and the nation plunged into the computer age.[8] His responsibilities ranged from the real-time production of the James Bond gadgets required by agents who were in the midst of an actual investigation to the broadest kind of conceptual research about the investigative focus of the FBI in the twenty-first century.

Bayse held his position as an assistant director of the FBI from 1978 to 1993. This means that for fifteen years—except for a curious one-year gap when he disappeared on a classified mission, perhaps to improve the surveillance capabilities of several Central American countries—Al Bayse was the highest-ranking outsider inside one of this nation's most clannish and inbred organizations.

Despite his unusual position—a senior manager in an agency in which he had little natural standing and from which he gained almost no public notice—a solid argument can be made that in shaping and directing the FBI's investigative technologies from the late 1970s to the mid-1990s, Al Bayse became the single most important official in both the bureau and the Justice Department that it serves. In fact, because of the FBI's critical role as the lead investigative agency of the federal government, he may well be the nation's single most influential law enforcement official since J. Edgar Hoover.

These, admittedly, are sizable claims. But when the full impact of the many technical innovations nurtured by Bayse is considered in relation to the enforcement community as a whole, they do not appear overstated.

REPRODUCTION

T he three sprawling buildings, linked by a seven-hundred-foot-long glass-enclosed walkway, are located on the edge of the heavily wooded military reservation in Quantico, Virginia. Like many modern structures, the buildings provide the casual viewer no hint as to the activities of the workers encased within their white exterior walls and darkened glass windows. Except for the ten-foot-high chain-link and barbed-wire fence that surrounds the buildings and the reinforced concrete guard post at the gate, the structures might be the home office of a medium-sized insurance company or a university research center or even a suburban hospital.

The buildings, in fact, are the FBI's Rapid Prototyping Facility (RPF), a laboratory and factory dedicated to the design and manufacture of "unique miniaturized devices in direct support of various investigative efforts" of the "FBI and other members of the U.S. law enforcement community."[9]

Operated jointly by the FBI and a high-flying Pentagon operation called the Defense Advanced Research Projects Agency, the FBI facility was created to allow the bureau "to use computer-aided design, engineering and manufacturing tools and equipment (software and firmware, respectively) to design, simulate and fabricate integrated circuits, printed circuit boards, electronic components, packages, systems and concealments in a quick turnaround cost-effective manner."

The establishment of the Rapid Prototyping Facility, Bayse said, was one of the proudest achievements of his fifteen-year career with the FBI. To underline his enthusiasm about this unique government operation, the official displayed a submersible, fist-sized device designed and fabricated by the RPF to collect detailed evidence about the chemical makeup and quantity of toxic wastes that were being dumped in a mountain stream from a nearby factory.

One advantage of Bayse's in-house development and production facility is the improved security that comes when you avoid independent contractors who one day might just leak a sensitive matter to the wrong party. A second advantage is speed, the ability to lessen the manufacturing turnaround time to twenty-four hours "through the use of laser restructuring, high-density interconnect, and reverse milling capability."[10]

Yet another benefit of this fairly new facility, from the point of view of the FBI, is its capability "to produce an integrated microphone ('microphone on a chip') in a single design/fabrication process."[11] Obviously, such a miniature microphone is a great deal easier to conceal from suspicious eyes than the clunky versions that it replaces. And because the new device requires far less battery power to operate, the miniature microphone will go on doing its eavesdropping work for much longer periods of time before it must be replaced.

The FBI technicians often bury their homegrown miniaturized microphones within custom-designed "concealment packages" that the "technically trained agent (TTA)" can leave behind during those raids when there is no time to dally. "The television camera and associated audio/video transmission systems have been successfully concealed in the following: a lamp, clock radio, briefcase, duffel bag, purse, picture frame, utility pole, coin telephone, book and others." The FBI added that other recent technology breakthroughs have "allowed remote control of pan/tilt, zoom and focus to be added in some situations."[12]

The FBI's production facility at Quantico truly is an amazing example of the Dick Tracy school of law enforcement: a high-tech rabbit hutch designed to produce more and more surveillance rabbits for fewer and fewer dollars in less and less time. According to the FBI budget document, for example, the facility achieved a tenfold increase in the output of rabbits between 1987 and 1993.

But in addition to churning out cunning little microphones and cameras for specific investigations, Bayse's dream machine also works on grander projects. In 1993, for example, it received about $5.4 million for research and development. Part of these funds went for a portable tracking system which the FBI can set up in any city in the United States. The purpose of the system is to follow, on a second-by-second basis, the exact movements of electronically tagged automobiles as they are driven from one location in the selected city to another.

In one city, though, the FBI has so much tracking business that the bureau decided a permanent "fully functional real-time physical tracking network" would be cost effective. That city, of course, was New York.[13] It should come as no surprise that the FBI did not announce this handy addition to its investigative bag of tricks: a citywide network of hidden sensing devices that pick up signals from a moving vehicle and immediately project the precise location on a large illuminated map located in the FBI's New York command post.

When Bayse was asked how the new tracking system was working, he looked surprised, and didn't answer the question. "How did you know about that?" he asked.

The FBI denied a request for a tour of its Manhattan command post, where the output from its instantaneous tracking system is displayed for the brass. In 1993, however, the FBI allowed a reporter who was working on what the bureau expected would be a friendly article to visit the inner sanctum. The command center, she later wrote, "looks not unlike the Starship *Enterprise*, of 'Star Trek.' On the rear wall of the room are three giant screens on which neighborhood maps, live field surveillance, and graphs charting the progress of a manhunt can be projected. Law enforcement officials, at stations in three semicircular tiers of desks, can watch—and direct—as criminals are caught in the act."[14]

At about the same time that the engineers at the FBI's Quantico facility were putting the final touches on both the portable and permanently embedded version of the tracking system, they were asked to resolve a second nagging surveillance problem: how to improve the FBI's ability to record those conversations that do not occur in a bugged room or over a tapped telephone.

For many years, the FBI had been placing secret microphones on streetlamps, telephone polls, parking meters and empty automobiles parked near locations where its targets sometimes strolled. Such an array of outdoor surveillance devices planted near the Mulberry Street headquarters of John Gotti, for example, was an important weapon in the FBI's long and eventually successful investigation of one of New York City's most arrogant Mafia bosses.[15]

What the investigators needed, the FBI said, was "a briefcase-size electronically steerable microphone array prototype."[16] Although the FBI budget document did not indicate precisely how this portable piece of equipment would be used, it appears that its purpose would be to give agents a completely portable method of recording the private conversations of people who are sitting on a secluded park bench, walking along a noisy street or standing in any other public place. "The two-year program proposes to exploit the developing technology for solid-state recorders by developing a microphone array based audio collection device concealed on the side(s) of a briefcase. Initially, it would be discreetly steerable by the possessor of the briefcase. The final product would allow beam steering from a remote location."

THE FLY IN THE OINTMENT

T hus has the FBI, with the help of the Surreptitious Entry teams, the technically trained agents (TTAs) and Al Bayse's Rapid Prototype Facility, sought to enhance the government's ability to track the minute-by-minute movements of its suspects and to capture the substance of their conversations, indoors and out. While room always has to be left for bureaucratic hype, it seems obvious that from the bureau's point of view much progress has been made. On the horizon, however, may be a dark cloud in the form of technological changes that the FBI insists could make all kinds of electronic eavesdropping a lot more difficult for the government.

Standing in his sizable office, glancing out across the somewhat barren courtyard of the J. Edgar Hoover Building, Bayse said he was deeply worried that basic transformations in the technical processes by which the nation's telephone calls and computer messages are transmitted already have begun to weaken the ability of all law enforcement to fight crime.

"The nation's telecommunications systems are often used to further serious criminal activities, including illegal drug trafficking, terrorism and organized crime," he said. "One of our most effective tools to combat these crimes is the court-authorized intercept or wiretap. But recent advances in communications technology are now beginning to raise barriers that undercut our ability to investigate crime and protect the public."

A good number of experts, however, believe Bayse's expression of alarm is untrue or highly exaggerated. These experts, in fact, believe the opposite: that the revolutionary communication changes now sweeping through every home and office in the United States in the end will enlarge the FBI's ability to keep track of the American people. The suspicion that Bayse and many other officials are crying wolf is heightened by a secret FBI-DEA analysis of how the next technologies would affect their investigative powers. Although this inquiry has never been made public, its central conclusion was summarized in the FBI section of the four-inchthick Justice Department Congressional Authorization and Budget Submission for Fiscal Year 1992. "In the long term," the FBI said, "digital telephone technology will enhance the FBI's ability to collect, share and analyze information. Many of these enhancements will come without any FBI development effort, driven by consumer demand."[17]

In the view of some experts, the question is not simply whether the technical changes will enlarge or diminish the Justice Department's information collection abilities. The real question, they believe, is much more ominous: whether the remedies now being proposed by the Justice Department and the bureau represent a genuine and long-term threat to individual privacy and freedom in the United States.

To make sense of why and how the FBI and its chief surveillance ally, the National Security Agency, would like to substantially modify the communications systems that will become essential to every aspect of American life in the decades ahead, it is first necessary to understand a bit more about certain aspects of how we communicate today.

Most Americans, for example, believe that under the Constitution they pretty much have an absolute right to hold a private telephone conversation. Similarly, most Americans believe that, in the form of a first-class letter, they have an absolute right to send a private written message. These beliefs are just plain wrong.

Almost three quarters of a century ago, in 1917, Congress passed legislation giving federal agents the lawful right, with the approval of the courts, to read the contents of first-class letters. About fifty years later, after decades of unchecked electronic eavesdropping by federal, state and local enforcement agents, Congress in 1968 approved a second law giving law enforcement the same kind of limited eavesdropping authority in the case of the telephone. A more recent law extended this authority to computers and to such technologies as electronic mail, cellular and cordless telephones, paging devices and video teleconferencing situations.

The nation's postal and electronic surveillance laws have been repeatedly upheld by the Supreme Court. As a result, with the cooperation of postal and telephone officials, federal agents armed with a warrant routinely read the mail and listen to the telephone conversations of targeted suspects. Even though the restrictions in the laws and the high expense of processing the substantive content of individual messages has apparently meant that law enforcement has limited its eavesdropping to a relatively small number of cases, federal officials insist that their ability to conduct a wiretap or place a bug or open a first-class letter is essential to protecting the public from dangerous criminals.

About a decade ago, however, the computer began to alter the basic technology of how we communicate with each other. Right now, the old system of transmission is rapidly disappearing. It is being replaced by digital transmission, a computer-driven technology that makes it far easier and cheaper to transmit voice, data and video images.

The walls of a small windowless conference room down the hall from Bayse's office were plastered with complex charts displaying the FBI's new, worldwide and fully encrypted communication network. As a philosophic matter, did Bayse think there were any spoken or written communications that should enjoy an absolute immunity from interception by government eavesdroppers?

"Sure," he replied, "I believe there is an absolute right to privacy. But that doesn't mean you have the right to break the law in a serious way. Any private conversation that doesn't involve criminality should be private. The central issue is criminality. We get a warrant, we listen, and if the people aren't discussing criminal activities, we turn off the machine, we don't record it. But as law enforcement professionals, we in the FBI are adamant that we need this tool."

In other words, as the debate was framed by Bayse, the right to privacy is at least partly contingent on a determination by an FBI agent or clerk that the conversations they already have intercepted and understood do not involve a crime. And Bayse, the FBI, the Justice Department and the whole American intelligence community are determined that the technical changes now sweeping through communications networks and the improved low-cost encryption and decryption machines now available to individual Americans are never going to prevent them from intercepting those messages that they believe might involve criminal, national security or other important matters.

NTISSC

T he government's effort to guarantee, and in some ways enlarge, its continuing ability to conduct electronic surveillance activities has been led by an interagency group with a mind-numbing name: the National Telecommunications and Information System Security Committee, or NTISSC. This committee, referred to in the conversations of Washington cognoscenti as "entisic," originally was created by a secret directive signed by President Ronald Reagan in 1984. Although the committee has twenty-one member agencies, the two key players are the FBI and the National Security Agency (NSA), a massive Defense Department agency created to eavesdrop on the electronic messages of all other nations. Al Bayse, because of his expertise in the surveillance area, was the FBI's representative.

Not surprisingly, the deliberations of the committee are secret and it rarely issues statements of public policy. But from the public actions taken by the FBI and the NSA in the last few years in connection with the law and technology of surveillance, and a few documents extracted from member agencies under the Freedom of Information Act, the broad thrust of the federal government's campaign in this sensitive area can be discerned.

One of the most far-reaching parts of the overall campaign, first initiated by the Bush administration, was a drive to win congressional approval of a law that the FBI contends has only one modest and reasonable purpose: to ensure that the bureau can go on intercepting phone calls and other electronic messages as it has been doing since Congress passed the 1968 wiretap law.

The bureau's effort, initially code-named "Operation Root Canal," was developed in conjunction with the NSA. As first described by the FBI, the proposed legislation would "ensure the government's ability to lawfully intercept communications unimpeded by the introduction of advanced digital telecommunications technology."[18]

From the beginning, however, some argued that the FBI was being unduly modest, and that what came to be called the "digital telephony proposal" actually was much more ambitious than advertised. One of the principal skeptics was Marc Rotenberg, a lawyer and expert chess

player who was directing the Washington office of Computer Professionals for Social Responsibility when the bureau's telephony proposal
first surfaced in 1992. He believed that the real purpose of Operation
Root Canal was to ease the sharp restrictions on wiretapping established by Congress in 1968.

Secret tapping, he argued, is among the most intrusive of all investigative techniques. Because this basic fact was well understood when
the issue was debated by the House and Senate in the late 1960s, Rotenberg continued, Congress always "intended that wire surveillance be
difficult, that it only be used in the most serious kinds of matters. Now,
the FBI has put forward a proposal to require that all communication
services in the U.S. be designed to facilitate wire surveillance. The FBI
would like to amend the federal wiretap law so that criminal fines will
be levied against private individuals who do not design systems in accordance with FBI surveillance standards."

The nation's existing wiretap law, he added, "was designed to restrict
the government, not to coerce the public. The FBI's proposal would reduce network security, create new vulnerabilities, invite abuse and diminish communications privacy. It is a backward-looking plan that
tries to freeze in place a particular investigative method that is disfa-
vored by the law and disliked by Americans."[19]

Communication industry officials, in both private and public fo-
rums, worried about how the legislation, if it became law, would
change the basic relationship between the government and their sensitive business. In the report accompanying the 1986 revision to the original wiretap law, the Senate Judiciary Committee noted that while
telephone companies had long cooperated with law enforcement, the
relationship had always been at arm's length; telephone company employees did not perform the wiretap itself and telephone company
premises were not used for wiretapping activities. It was important, the
committee said, that the telephone companies not develop into "a
branch of government law enforcement."

Some experts, however, are convinced that this is precisely what the
digital telephone legislation, backed by the Bush and Clinton administrations and approved by Congress in 1994, will accomplish. "The proposal as now drafted is terribly flawed," said Roy Neel, director of the
United States Telephone Association, a trade group representing regional and local telephone companies. "What the FBI is doing is asking
the telephone companies to become the local cop."[20]

There is some irony in the fact that when the Clinton administration
offered Congress its version of the legislation, originally proposed by
President Bush, it was dubbed the "Digital Telephony and Communications Privacy Act of 1994." Orwell would have been amused.

GETTING INTO THE NET

T he evidence supporting a very different scenario than is suggested
by the Clinton administration's original title for the new law is considerable. From the beginning, the Justice Department, the FBI and the
other intelligence agencies had seen that the new communication technologies presented two distinct hurdles to its surveillance activities.
Hurdle number one was presented by the complex communication networks over which individual messages are transmitted. In brief, the
government contended that technical changes in the network itself, inherent in the widespread use of such devices as the cellular phone, were
making it harder and harder for it to intercept messages as they moved
from point A to point B along the information highway. The second
hurdle, and we will explore this aspect a bit later, concerned the ability
of any citizen to use modern technology to express an individual message in a language that no one but the intended receiver can understand.

The FBI's first public move to solve the network problem, which it
argued was weakening law enforcement, came in a March 1992 memo
to Congress. The FBI contended that new communication technologies
based on fiber optics and cellular telephones were making it harder and
harder for law enforcement to install the court-authorized taps. In the
first go-round, however, as a result of opposition from some industry
groups and civil rights organizations, and despite support from the Bush
administration's Justice Department, the FBI was unable to find a single
member of Congress who would introduce its so-called digital telephony legislation.

The FBI had lost a battle, but it certainly was not about to concede
defeat. Several months later, having won the incoming Clinton administration to its cause, the bureau returned to Congress with a new version of the bill. Modified to meet some of the objections to the initial
proposal, the second generation of the government's digital telephony
legislation was considerably less objectionable to the computer and
communications industries.

The leading Clinton administration lobbyist for the new surveillance
legislation was Louis Freeh, the aggressive new director of the FBI. The
government's most important investigative tool, Freeh said, was "wiretapping, court-authorized wiretapping." Unless remedial steps were
taken, he continued, "the country will be unable to protect itself
against terrorism, violent crime, foreign threats, drug trafficking, espionage, kidnapping and other grave crimes."[21]

Freeh's vision, repeating similar claims by his predecessor, William
S. Sessions, indeed presented a frightening scenario. But was it true?

There is evidence that like many law enforcement officials before them, Freeh and Sessions were trying to get their way by resorting to unsubstantiated scare tactics. In fact, at the same time the FBI was telling Congress and the public that the new technologies were already preventing them from conducting essential wiretaps, senior FBI officials from cities across the United States were telling FBI headquarters in Washington the exact opposite.

We know this because in November 1993, reluctantly responding to a federal suit brought under the Freedom of Information Act by Rotenberg and David Sobel, at that time the general counsel for Computer Professionals for Social Responsibility, the FBI provided a short stack of internal documents concerning the digital telephony issue. Among them was a January 6, 1992, message from the head of the FBI's Philadelphia office. "Technically Trained Agents (TTA's) encountered no problems during the month of December, 1991," the official reported. He added that technical experts working for the IRS, the New Jersey State Police, the U.S. Customs Bureau, the Philadelphia district attorney's office and the U.S. Secret Service in the Philadelphia area also had "experienced no difficulties with the new technologies." Remarkably, similar no-problem reports came from FBI offices in Las Vegas and Newark.

Despite the obvious questions raised by the internal memos about the exaggerated FBI claims, Louis Freeh continued his intense lobbying effort on behalf of the legislation. On October 7, 1994, Freeh's efforts paid off when the Senate gave final approval to a law requiring telephone and cable television companies to modify their networks to make it easier for law enforcement to conduct wiretaps and trace other electronic messages.

The technical changes, which are to be developed by industry trade associations under the indirect supervision of the attorney general, are to be gradually adopted between 1995 and 1998 and paid for out of a special $500 million fund authorized for this purpose. In a situation where a communications carrier or manufacturer fails to comply with the new requirements, the attorney general is authorized to seek civil court penalties of up to $10,000 a day.

In addition to successfully pressuring Congress to pass a law forcing the telephone companies and cellular service providers to operate communications systems that the government can easily tap, the FBI was pursuing a secret research program to resolve the "operational, legal, legislative, budgetary, training and technical issues" involved in modern eavesdropping "in a timely and economic manner." In 1993 alone, this research program apparently totaled more than $20 million.[22]

From the viewpoint of Al Bayse and the FBI, however, a thorny problem remained. The government had indeed been successful in forcing the adoption of various technical changes that will greatly improve the FBI's ability to snatch electronic messages from the networks. But what will have been accomplished if the FBI agents are unable to understand the messages they are intercepting?

NO SUCH AGENCY

Here, once again, a little background information is necessary. Until very recent times, the code-making and code-breaking arm of the United States government—the National Security Agency—enjoyed an absolute monopoly on the business of scrambling electronic messages in ways that could not be understood by any of the nation's enemies. The NSA is a large and very secret agency that since the end of World War II has specialized in the worldwide interception of any electronic message it thought significant. With sophisticated satellites circling the globe and massive arrays of listening devices in strategic locations such as Turkey, it was able to pull off such amazing technical feats as picking up the radio telephone conversations of Nikita Khrushchev as his limousine sped through the streets of Moscow. During the Senate's post-Watergate investigation of the intelligence agencies, the NSA was forced to admit that it had also put some of these skills to work to conduct illegal surveillance of American citizens.

In the early 1970s, a handful of independent computer scientists—such as Whitfield Diffie and Martin Hellman of Stanford University, Ralph Merkle of the University of California at Berkeley and Stanford and Ronald Rivest of the Massachusetts Institute of Technology—began to develop effective methods for the coding of written and spoken messages outside the control of the NSA. The new techniques were inexpensive enough to make them attractive to individual corporations and, in some cases, even individual citizens.

The research of the academic entrepreneurs was a terrifying prospect to the NSA. What if every nation in the world were able to guarantee the confidentiality of its important messages? What if this power then became available to individual citizens? At first, in the late 1970s, the NSA tried to suppress the development of low-cost coding methods by bullying the scientists. Partly because the Cold War was coming to an end and partly because the scientists were articulate people who could make a rational argument with reporters from the *New York Times* and a few other papers, the NSA's terror tactics became less and less effective. The genie had escaped the bottle.

Because the official mission of the NSA is to eavesdrop on the communications of the rest of the world—and not on the people of the United States—it was entirely logical that the agency would make an intense effort to prevent the export of the new encryption devices to other countries. But preventing the flow of technology across national borders has always been a nearly impossible task. It is this difficulty that appears to explain why, in the last days of the Cold War, the FBI and the NSA became official allies in a complicated two-step operation. First, the two agencies sought to discourage any use of the new cryptography techniques by private individuals. Second, when it became apparent that this strategy was failing, the FBI and the NSA mounted a joint program to encourage all Americans to adopt a form of cryptology that included a backdoor entrance for the government's use.

If the federal government could force the widespread adoption of a crypto system the NSA knew how to unlock, then the export of the system would be of less concern to the spooks. Because of the FBI's belief that electronic surveillance was essential to law enforcement, the bureau's domestic worries neatly dovetailed with the foreign anxieties of the NSA. Both agencies were in agreement: The widespread adoption of cheap and effective encryption that did not allow easy government access would be a disaster.

The intimate association of the FBI and NSA goes back at least to 1984. That was the year President Reagan signed National Security Decision Directive 145—a then-secret order granting the National Security Agency broad new powers over all computerized communications, both those from classified military systems and those of the civilian agencies of the federal government and even some private-sector companies. Two years later, the head of Reagan's National Security Council, Admiral John Poindexter, issued a directive implementing NSDD 145 and creating the National Telecommunications and Information Systems Security Committee, the secret coordinating body mentioned above in connection with the discussion of digital telephony legislation. Al Bayse of the FBI and Patrick Gallagher of the NSA were named cochairmen of the new committee.

The problem, for them, was clear: If poor third world countries, banks and oil companies could purchase coding devices to protect messages they wished to keep private, so could individual Americans, including those who might be drug dealers or terrorists.

It took a while for the secret research work of the two clandestine agencies to emerge, at least in part, from the highly classified world of signals intelligence. The first public manifestation came from the National Institute of Standards and Technology (NIST), formerly the National Bureau of Standards, a relatively small and little-known federal agency located within the Commerce Department. In August 1991, NIST requested public comment on a proposed cryptographic method by which all civilian agencies could assure themselves that an electronic message they had received actually had come from the agency or person who had signed it. The method was called "digital signatures" and the proposal was labeled the Digital Signature Standard (DSS).

When it formally announced the proposed DSS, NIST did not mention NSA, clearly implying that NIST itself had developed the standard. But heavily censored documents later released under the Freedom of Information Act to Marc Rotenberg, the privacy lawyer, showed that this was not the truth. In fact, most of the work to develop the DSS standard had been conducted by NSA engineers. Other documents released to Rotenberg further showed that the FBI had also been involved in the process and that the bureau viewed the new computer authenticating procedure as "[t]he first step in our plan to deal with the encryption issue."

CHIPPING AWAY WITH THE CLIPPER

T he second important step came in April 1993 when the Clinton administration announced its support for an ambitious program it hoped would minimize the number of Americans who decided to protect their privacy by purchasing the essentially unbreakable encryption devices then being offered on the commercial market.

The government's substitute was called "Clipper Chip," a small, relatively inexpensive device for encrypting messages being sent from any digital phone or computer. Clipper Chip, the White House said, was "a voluntary program to improve the security and privacy of telephone communications while meeting the legitimate needs of law enforcement. This new technology will help companies protect proprietary information, protect the privacy of personal telephone conversations and prevent unauthorized release of data transmitted electronically."

From the point of view of the government, however, the White House–backed initiative had a more important characteristic. Unlike the commercial encryption devices, Clipper Chip had a "trapdoor" that would allow investigative and intelligence agents to decode any message that was processed by the government-developed device. As explained by the White House, each chip would have unique "keys," long strings of numbers that would have to be combined before the messages could be decrypted. Parts of the keys required to make them work would be held in escrow by separate government agencies, only made available to investigators upon presentation of "legal authorization."

The Clinton administration insisted that because government agents would be able to gain access to these keys only when legally authorized to conduct a wiretap, the technology would protect individual privacy and at the same time allow the FBI and other agencies to continue essential surveillance activities. Clipper Chip, it asserted, "provides law enforcement with no new authorities to access the private conversations of Americans."[23]

In February 1994, ten months after the first announcement of the proposal, the Clinton administration announced its formal approval of Clipper Chip, the NSA-developed standard to encrypt the "voice, fax and data communications" of business and government. Although the administration spokesmen acknowledged that almost all business and privacy groups were opposed to the proposal, they insisted this was only because the plan was not understood.

Public concerns about the FBI-NSA program are profound. Whitfield Diffie, a leading cryptographer who now carries the title Distinguished Engineer—Security at Sun Microsystems, Inc., was just one of many critics. "An essential element of freedom is the right to privacy, a right that cannot be expected to stand against an unremitting technological attack," Diffie told a congressional committee. "Where technology has the capacity to support individual rights, we must enlist that support rather than rejecting it on the grounds that it might be abused by criminals. If we put the desires of the police ahead of the rights of citizens often enough, we will shortly find we are living in a police state. We must instead assure that the rights recognized by law are supported, rather than undermined, by technology."[24]

Marc Rotenberg put it more directly. "The government's plan is purposefully intended to weaken privacy protection and facilitate government surveillance," he said. "The government is now seeking to restrict the use of cryptography because it is a technology that may well enhance privacy."

David Sobel, the expert authority on the Freedom of Information Act, has been a leading player in the effort of privacy advocates to use this law to obtain internal documents regarding the government's current drive to enlarge its electronic surveillance abilities. On the basis of his detailed knowledge of what the intelligence agencies have done in the past, Sobel questions government promises that it will not pry without a proper court order. "The National Security Agency, which developed the Clipper technology, shares a long history with the FBI and the CIA of illegal and unauthorized spying on individuals. Its ability to monitor communications is vast, as is its budget, which is probably the largest of any U.S. intelligence agency.[25]

"Why then," Sobel asks, "would the NSA, after having fought against allowing the government to use any cryptography systems that might interrupt its signals intelligence [surveillance] responsibilities, promote a technology that can be broken only with court approval?"

Sobel seeks analogies to explain and further undermine what he views as an organized government effort to dominate and control the public. "Assuming Clipper Chip is widely adopted," he said, "it would be as if we all were required to mail our letters in clear envelopes designed so that government agents could read the message inside. Or, perhaps Clipper can be understood if we compare it to a hypothetical law that required all telephone users to only speak in English because Spanish and Arabic are too hard for the agents to understand."

Al Bayse, whom FBI documents suggest had been involved in the development of Clipper since its inception, was ecstatic about its adoption. Shortly before the White House announced the project to reporters, he telephoned three leading security experts in the academic world—Dorothy Denning of Georgetown University, Lance Hoffman of George Washington University and Peter Neumann of SRI International—and informed them that the FBI's problems had been solved.

Bayse was dead wrong—wrong, that is, if the actual goal of Clipper is to prevent law enforcement from losing its ability to eavesdrop on big-time criminal operations. As noted by security expert Whitfield Diffie in his congressional testimony, because scores of entrepreneurs were then offering competitive cryptographic systems without the trapdoor, it seemed highly unlikely that any serious drug cartel, organized crime family or terrorist gang would code their messages with communications equipment designed by the government to give the FBI easy access to their communications.

William Safire, the conservative *New York Times* columnist, made the same point, only with an additional twist. Smart crooks and terrorists, he wrote, will buy "non-American hardware with unmonitored Japanese or German or Indian encryption chips and laugh all the way to the plutonium factory. The only people tap-able by American agents will be honest Americans—or those crooked Americans dopey enough to buy American equipment with the pre-compromised American code."[26]

This shortcoming of Clipper is so obvious and so gaping, in fact, that it made many wonder whether the stated goal of the program—the targeting of serious criminals—is not simply a ruse developed by the FBI and NSA to hide a much more ambitious objective. The actual purpose of the project, these skeptics are convinced, is to embed Clipper and the related technologies so deeply into the nation's communications systems that law enforcement can conduct electronic surveillance at will.

The suspicion that the government might one day try to outlaw any encryption device which did not provide easy government access was reinforced by comments made by FBI Director Freeh at a 1994 Washington conference on cryptography. "The objective for us is to get those conversations . . . wherever they are, whatever they are," he said in response to a question. Freeh indicated that if five years from now the FBI had solved the access problem but was only hearing encrypted messages, further legislation might be required. The obvious solution: a federal law prohibiting the use of any cryptographic device that did not provide government access.[27]

Freeh's hints that the government might have to outlaw certain kinds of coding devices gradually became more explicit. "The drug cartels are buying sophisticated communications equipment," he told Congress.[28] "Unless the encryption issue is resolved soon, criminal conversations over the telephone and other communications devices will become indecipherable by law enforcement. This, as much as any issue, jeopardizes the public safety and national security of this country."

The FBI director added that he thought he would soon be consulting with Congress to solve the issue. A resolution may be hard to find. In a series of cases in the 1920s the Supreme Court struck down laws restricting the use of non-English languages. "The protection of the Constitution extends to all, to those who speak other languages as well as those born with English on their tongue. Perhaps it would be highly advantageous if all had ready understanding of our ordinary speech, but this cannot be coerced by methods which conflict with the Constitution—a desirable end cannot be promoted by prohibited means," the Supreme Court ruled in one 1923 decision.[29] In a 1995 ruling throwing out a provision of the Arizona Constitution that all government employees must "act" only in English on First Amendment grounds, the United States Court of Appeals for the Ninth Circuit concluded that "Speech in any language is still speech, and the decision to speak in another language is a decision involving speech alone."[30]

TAP, TAP, TAP

A ssuming that the objective of the Clinton administration's dual legislative and research programs are as claimed—exercises only to extend existing surveillance capabilities into the next century—the federal government seems to have invested an awful lot of political energy and a substantial number of dollars for what appears to be a minimum gain. For while Bayse, Louis Freeh, Attorney General Janet Reno and a long line of her predecessors have insisted that electronic surveillance is essential to investigating crime and nabbing spies and terrorists, the public record suggests that the FBI and other investigative agencies actually employ this particular tool, legally at least, on very rare occasions.

During the ten-year period from 1984 to 1993, for example, federal district judges from all over the United States informed Congress that they issued only 3,091 judicial warrants authorizing the FBI, DEA and other such national agencies to operate wiretaps and bugs against individuals suspected of committing domestic crimes such as drug dealing and bank fraud.

In addition, a small, largely secret panel of seven federal judges, operating from a special courtroom actually located in the Justice Department, reported that they had approved an additional 5,490 applications for the electronic surveillance of suspected spies, terrorists and espionage agents during the same decade.[31] The special court never turned down a single request.

Although the tough legal requirements of the law relating to routine criminal wiretaps and bugs partially explain the surprisingly modest levels of electronic eavesdropping by the government, economics almost certainly is the determining factor. This is because of the obvious

TOTAL NUMBER OF COURT-AUTHORIZED ELECTRONIC INTERCEPTS OF CRIMINAL SUSPECTS
1968–1993

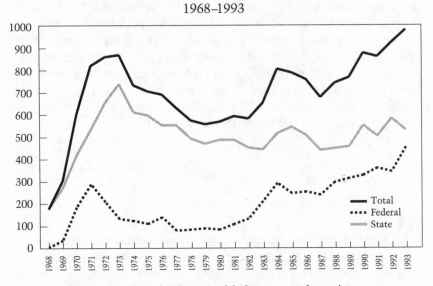

In 1968, Congress approved a law establishing procedures for courts to authorize the surveillance of criminal suspects by electronic means. Most electronic surveillance not authorized by a judge was prohibited. Since that time, the Administrative Office of the United States Courts has published an annual report showing that court-ordered intercepts—by either a wiretap or a bug—are at an all-time high, mostly because of an increase in such actions by federal agents. (EPIC ANALYSIS OF DATA FROM THE ADMINISTRATIVE OFFICE OF THE COURTS)

fact that each tape has to be analyzed. For an average drug case, every hour of raw tape requires three hours of analysis. For example, a court-approved electronic surveillance device that is operated "for ten hours per day over a 30-day period would require 900 work hours to thoroughly analyze the recorded material," says the FBI.[32]

The Justice Department, in the last few years, has taken steps to reduce the high cost of eavesdropping. Under a little-noticed section of a 1986 law, Congress dropped the requirement that only its high-priced special agents could listen to the tapes. The FBI now hires low-cost clerks for what must be extremely tedious work. Because of this minor change in the wiretap law, and another provision authorizing the FBI to intercept nonaural communications such as electronic mail, computer transmissions and video teleconferencing, government eavesdropping is expected to increase in the years ahead.

TOTAL NUMBER OF COURT ORDERS AUTHORIZING ELECTRONIC SURVEILLANCE FOR NATIONAL SECURITY PURPOSES
1979–1993

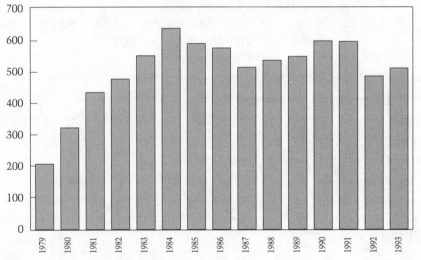

Since 1979, the wiretapping and bugging of suspects in most national security cases—as distinct from criminal matters—has been authorized by a secret federal court that sits in the Justice Department. The public reports by the attorney general—required by law—provide little information other than the number of such operations. The reports, however, do show that in its fifteen-year history, the secret court has never rejected a single one of the federal government's 7,539 requests for authority to conduct a national security surveillance operation. [EPIC ANALYSIS OF DATA FROM THE JUSTICE DEPARTMENT]

While the number of criminal and national security eavesdropping warrants approved by federal judges has remained fairly low, most taps and bugs function for long periods of time and the total number of intercepted conversations is surprisingly high. According to the latest annual report of the federal judges, each law enforcement listening device operating in 1993 picked up an average of 1,801 conversations during its lifetime.

Given the fact that federal judges reported approving 450 eavesdropping warrants aimed at criminal suspects—drug dealers, organized crime figures and corrupt political figures—in 1993, it appears that in that year alone the government agents listened to something like 810,000 conversations. In the quarter of a century since the passage of the original wiretap law, the annual judicial reports about the electronic eavesdropping aimed only at criminals indicate that federal agents have listened to slightly more than 8 million conversations.

It must be remembered, however, that over the years less than half of the government's eavesdropping has been aimed at conventional criminals and that very little information is made public about the national security surveillance efforts. Not reported, for example, are the number

AVERAGE NUMBER OF ALL CONVERSATIONS AND INCRIMINATING CONVERSATIONS INTERCEPTED PER INDIVIDUAL TAP OR BUG
1968–1993

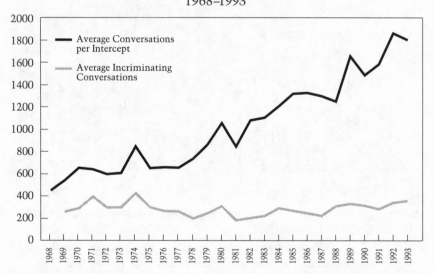

For many years, law enforcement authorities have reported that on average they are recording more and more conversations on each intercept, but that the number of incriminating conversations has remained fairly steady. (EPIC ANALYSIS OF DATA FROM THE ADMINISTRATIVE OFFICE OF THE COURTS)

of conversations picked up on the national security taps and bugs. Thus, even though the government reported planting 484 electronic devices against spies and terrorists in 1992—a total of 6,561 taps and bugs since 1979—there is no way to estimate the number of conversations captured. Projecting from what we know about criminal eavesdropping, it well may be that as many as 20 million conversations have been intercepted for both criminal and national security purposes by federal agencies since electronic surveillance was authorized by Congress.

What about convictions? In 1992, the FBI submitted an eighteen-page analysis of the costs and benefits of electronic surveillance to the White House Office of Management and Budget. The analysis claimed that evidence obtained from 3,428 taps and bugs operated by federal enforcement agencies during the six-year period from 1985 to 1991 led to 7,324 convictions. At first blush this two-to-one ratio of taps to convictions seems quite impressive. It is well to remember, however, that the convictions the FBI attributes to wiretaps represent only a small fraction—less than 3 percent—of the more than 250,000 such judgments obtained by the government during those same years. It is also well to remember that complex criminal cases almost always require a mix of investigative tactics, including the development of inside informants, the subpoenaing of incriminating documents, forensic science and physical surveillance. Thus the FBI judgment that electronic surveillance was the single most important tactic in any given investigation is highly subjective and, without a great deal more supporting information, cannot be taken at face value.

TRANSACTIONAL RECORDS

Surreptitious Entry teams roam the country. The Rapid Prototyping Facility swiftly churns out tiny hidden cameras and bugs. Hundreds of technically trained agents (TTAs), expert in the complex engineering of dozens of different telephone systems, hook up their wiretaps. Low-level clerks spin their tapes and type their transcripts. The NSA, FBI and other federal agencies spend hundreds of millions of research dollars on electronic surveillance. Almost every part of this complex government surveillance effort is aimed at a single and in some ways obvious goal: improving the ability of the government to intercept and understand the actual content of substantive messages.

A substantive message—the voice of a Mafia boss ordering the murder of a rival, the video of a corrupt senator accepting a bribe—almost certainly can be a powerful weapon in the prosecution of a single case.

As already noted, tapes and videos are labor intensive. This simple fact means that, on the average, every wiretap now costs the Justice Department at least $50,000. Such an expenditure obviously is of little concern when it results in the conviction of a murderous organized crime figure or a corrupt U.S. senator. But it is much too much money for casual investigative browsing.

The computer, however, has come to the government's rescue. It has given investigative agencies like the FBI and the DEA an amazing present: a genuinely new ability to organize and analyze gigantic amounts of detailed information about the ordinary transactions of daily life at a minimal cost. What time was a telephone call made? From what number and to what number? How long did the conversation last? At exactly what moment did a specific individual obtain cash from an automated teller machine? When did an individual, using her VISA card, purchase gasoline on the New Jersey Turnpike? Did someone watch a pay-TV movie from a set located in a particular house? What unexpected associations and connections—what conspiratorial webs—are suggested by all these transactions?

There are three basic reasons why this transactional information is so valuable to the enforcement agencies. The universal adoption of computers by large public and private bureaucracies—the telephone companies, state motor vehicle departments, credit companies, voter registrars, insurance companies and county property tax assessors—means that for their own purposes they each have created systems of records containing extremely detailed information about virtually every person in the United States. Because of the technical characteristics of all large computers, the millions and millions of individual records they store can be easily and cheaply transferred from the institution that originally collected them to any interested investigating agency. One blank computer tape, capable of holding information about many millions of transactions, usually costs less than $20. Finally, because the processing of data has become so speedy, once an agency like the FBI has purchased a computer, the incremental expense of examining a tape for revealing patterns and trends can also be negligible.

Thus the computer, as adopted by society in the last twenty years, has profoundly altered federal investigative techniques and, along with that change, dramatically enhanced the power of all federal enforcement agencies. The FBI, as it always has, investigates known suspects by collecting substantive information about their criminal activities. What is new, what the FBI and the Justice Department previously were not able to do on a routine basis, is to make systematic searches of far larger data sets. Sometimes these searches are intended to obtain supporting information about an individual who is already suspected of committing a specific crime. Sometimes, on the other hand, the searches have a very different purpose: determining whether a previously unsuspected crime has been committed.

While it was the computer that powered this substantial change, it was the U.S. Supreme Court that authorized it. The Court's official sanctioning of the new investigative procedure came in several rulings tearing down the constitutional barriers which arguably could have placed some limitations on the government's almost unlimited access to transactional information.

Under the current understanding of the Fourth Amendment—the provision in the Bill of Rights limiting the government's power to conduct searches—government agents usually must obtain a judicial warrant when they want to tap your telephone, open your letters or raid your home. In the days when most of the records of life—a personal letter, a will or a marriage certificate—were maintained in an individual's house, the Fourth Amendment usually meant that the earliest kind of transactional records were protected from casual perusal.

But about twenty years ago, the Supreme Court began to consider the rules it believed were appropriate for the personal information that, more and more, was stored in the computerized files of the bureaucracies. Mitchell Miller, for example, was a Georgia businessman and bootlegger who was convicted in federal court of possessing an unregistered still, conducting his business with intent to defraud the government and possessing 175 gallons of whiskey upon which no taxes had been paid. On appeal, Mitchell's conviction was reversed on the grounds that it was based on the bootlegger's checks and bank records, which the government had obtained from his bank without the judicial warrant required by the Fourth Amendment.

The Supreme Court, however, in a 1976 ruling of major consequence, reinstated Miller's conviction. The Court held that Miller did not have a legitimate "expectation of privacy" because the documents obtained by the government were not his "personal papers" but the "business records" of the bank. Miller's argument that the evidence drawn from his records could not be used against him because the seizure had violated the Fourth Amendment, the Court concluded, "was neither legitimate, warranted nor enforceable."[33]

Three years later, the Supreme Court handed down a second far-reaching decision concerning the government's access to information controlled by another large bureaucracy: the telephone company. In this case, over the strenuous objections of AT&T, the Court held that the Fourth Amendment did not require Baltimore police officers to obtain a warrant before they asked the telephone company to install a device that recorded all the telephone numbers dialed by a burglary suspect named Michael Lee Smith. In a curious bit of mind reading, the Supreme Court concluded that Smith probably had never really had an expectation of privacy regarding "the numbers he dialed, and that, even if he did, his expectation was not 'legitimate.' The installation and use of a pen register [the colloquial name of the device that records these numbers] consequently was not a 'search' [in the Fourth Amendment sense] and no warrant was required."[34]

The Supreme Court had opened the door to the essentially unchecked use of transactional records by law enforcement. But Congress, under heavy pressure from an unusual coalition of privacy advocates and a few powerful corporations, decided the Court had gone too far. The result was the Electronic Communications Privacy Act of 1986. The new law, building on the wiretap provisions of the Omnibus Crime Control and Safe Streets Act of 1968, was extremely complicated. Although the statute expanded the kinds of electronic messages that were covered, it also eased many of the existing restrictions on government eavesdropping. Under the original 1968 wiretap law, for example, only a handful of top Justice Department officials were authorized to apply for a judicial warrant to conduct a wiretap, and these applications could only be sought in the course of investigating a limited number of federal crimes. The new 1986 law expanded the number of officials who could apply for the eavesdropping warrants and enlarged the number and kinds of crimes that could be investigated with this technique.

The new law also leapt into the vacuum created by the Supreme Court's Miller and Smith decisions. Before the Justice Department can install a pen register, for example, the new law now requires the agency to obtain a judicial warrant. These warrants, though, are far easier to obtain than those required for an actual wiretap or bug. One difference is that any attorney in the government can apply for a pen register order. A second difference is that the attorney, instead of being required to establish probable cause, only has to certify that the information sought by the government is "relevant to an ongoing investigation."

The provision of the 1986 law regarding access to individual telephone toll records, while obviously more restrictive than the Supreme Court's totally laissez-faire approach, was minimal. All telephone records were subject to government examination without notice to the customer, providing only that the agency desiring the records present the telephone company with a written request, a warrant or court order.

By its very name, the Electronics Privacy Communications Act of 1986 holds out the promise of greater protection against unnecessary government snooping. The promise apparently was false. Just consider the recent trends in the Justice Department's use of the pen register, the device that keeps track of all calls made *from* a particular telephone, and the "trap and trace" mechanism, the device that records the numbers of all the telephones used *to call* a particular phone. In a recent six-

year period, the yearly installation of pen registers has more than doubled, jumping to 3,423 in 1992 from 1,682 in 1987. All together, for
those years, the FBI, DEA, Immigration and Naturalization Service and
United States Marshals Service planted pen registers on 17,410 telephones that were used to call the telephones owned by 38,450 persons.
During the same period, the use of trap and trace mechanisms saw a
twentyfold increase by the same four agencies, 2,153 in 1993 compared
with 91 in 1987.[35]

One reason agents are much quicker to slap on a pen register or trap
and trace device than they used to be is that the process of monitoring
and recording the transactional information about each call has recently been completely automated. No more scribble, scribble, scribble.
The DEA, for example, has developed an integrated system called
TOLLS that includes a central repository in one of its mainframe computers for all the telephone calls and subscriber information the agents
have acquired. At the retail end of the business, the agency claims to
have developed a "standardized subsystem to electronically upload PC-
based telephone call data from dialed number recorders [pen registers]
into the mainframe TOLLS system."[36]

ELECTRONIC DRIFT NETS

Federal agents typically install pen registers during an investigation
that has led them to suspect a specific individual. The register obviously is an excellent real-time investigative tool for collecting transactional information about specific ongoing cases where agents believe
they know who has committed or is committing a crime. But what
about those situations where the agents don't have a specific suspect or
are investigating a criminal act that occurred in the past?

A few years ago, Alecia Swasy, a reporter in the Pittsburgh bureau of
the *Wall Street Journal*, published several unflattering articles about
Procter & Gamble. The executives were convinced the stories were the
result of leaks from one of the 15,000 employees working in the company's Cincinnati headquarters. But who was the villain? To try to answer that question, Procter & Gamble persuaded the local prosecutor to
open a grand jury investigation into whether the news leaks to the *Wall
Street Journal* had violated a state law prohibiting the disclosure of proprietary business information. Although the decision of county prosecutor Arthur Ney to begin the investigation may have been entirely
based on the merits of the case, *Wall Street Journal* reporter Swasy later
discovered that Procter & Gamble executives had made campaign con-

tributions to Ney. Whatever the motivation, the prosecutors obtained grand jury subpoenas requesting Cincinnati Bell to identify all 513 area code numbers that had dialed the 412 area code telephone numbers of Swasy's home and office.[37]

On the basis of the subpoena, the telephone company used its computer to search through the records of about 35 million toll calls made from 800,000 homes and businesses located in the 2,400 square miles of the 513 area code during the three-and-a-half-month period in question.

As a result, a former Procter & Gamble manager was summoned in for questioning. Had he had any contacts with Swasy after leaving Procter & Gamble? Had he telephoned her? Why had he telephoned her at her home?

After answering questions for several hours—he had called her at home because he couldn't get her at work—the former employee asked one of his own. "Is there a law against talking to reporters?" "No, that's not against the law," the interrogator replied. "Then show me what's got people so concerned." Because no crime had been committed, no charges were ever brought.[38]

Will the wonders of modern science never end? At about the same time that the Wall Street Journal was offending Procter & Gamble, a reporter named Gregory Millman published an article in the September 1991 edition of Corporate Finance that displeased the Internal Revenue Service. Millman's article accused the IRS of failing to collect billions of dollars of back taxes owed the government by companies like General Motors. Once again, the question was: Who is doing the leaking? Almost immediately, without informing Millman, the IRS obtained from the telephone company a list of all the numbers the reporter had dialed from his phone. But then the IRS cast a much wider net, requesting telephone companies all over the country to provide it with the toll records of all of the telephone calls made by those persons whom Millman had called.[39]

In a separate but related action, the Justice Department also went after Millman's telephone records. Because of the many outrages committed by the department during the Watergate years, the agency has unique administrative rules that require it in most instances to inform reporters, and only reporters, when it goes after their telephone records. On January 15, 1992, four months after the government had first begun to pore over his telephone records, the Justice Department finally sent Millman the required notice.

Although the government has never disclosed how many telephone records it obtained and how many people it questioned as a result of its ability to climb this particular electronic tree, the investigative swath was impressive. One person questioned by an IRS investigator was Merton Miller, the 1990 Nobel laureate in economics. It seems that Millman had called Miller during the time he was working on the IRS story.

At about the same time, Millman also called the Alicia Patterson Foundation, an independent nonprofit organization that each year supports the investigative work of a small number of distinguished reporters, editors and photographers. Millman asked the Washington-based foundation to send him an application form. Simply because of this call, the IRS obtained the foundation's telephone toll records for the previous thirteen months. Most of the major telephone companies, like the Justice Department, claim they have policies requiring them to notify customers in such situations. But Margaret Engel, the director of the foundation, told the House Subcommittee on Telecommunications and Finance in May of 1993 that the foundation did not receive a corporate notice of the government's invisible electronic raid until four months after it had happened.

Millman, in his testimony to the same subcommittee, likened the government's effort to the giant, almost invisible, drift nets that Asian fishing boats have begun to stretch across wide reaches of the Pacific Ocean. Sometimes thirty miles long, the drift nets catch every single fish that swims in their path and now are believed to be threatening the ocean's basic ecology.

"This type of investigation opens endless paths to the dogged investigator," Millman testified. "One could assemble a complete chart of a reporter's entire network, map the connections and relationships among all the members of that network—who calls whom, when, how often—in complete secrecy. This sounds extreme, but it is not an exaggeration. In fact, it is exactly what the government attempted to do to me."

Another, more dramatic example of the FBI's addiction to the open-ended tracing of long-distance telephone calls involved Judi Bari, the environmental activist. In May 1990, Bari and a colleague named Darryl Cherney were nearly killed in Oakland, California, when a powerful bomb exploded in the car they were driving. Within hours, despite considerable evidence that Bari and Cherney were the victims of an attack by loggers opposed to an environmental project they were sponsoring, the pair were arrested by the Oakland police for the possession of explosives. Ultimately, because of a lack of evidence, local and federal prosecutors declined to bring any charges.

As a result of what they regarded as a politically motivated investigation, Bari and Cherney filed a federal lawsuit against the FBI and the police for false arrest and the violation of their constitutional rights. During the course of this ongoing legal action, the FBI has been forced to produce documents showing that it believed Bari was a leader of an alleged conspiracy of radical environmentalists. Acting on this suspicion, the FBI obtained the long-distance telephone records of fourteen of Bari's associates and then compiled a list of 634 telephone calls they had made to individuals all over the United States. On November 21, 1991, forty-three FBI division offices were sent these numbers and requested to acquire the names of the relevant telephone subscribers and determine whether any of them had local arrest records.[40] Among those the FBI's New York office discovered had been called was Ramsey Clark, the former attorney general. In the comment next to Clark's name, the New York office noted that "receiving offices are no doubt familiar with Clark."[41]

TRYING TO TRACK THE TRACKERS

Unlike the situation regarding taps, bugs and pen registers, no law requires the Justice Department to submit an annual report summarizing how many long-distance toll records it has examined in the previous year. This means that to learn how frequently the Justice Department employs this particular investigative tactic, it is necessary to ask the people who are providing the toll records, the nation's fragmented telephone companies. On March 19, 1993, Don Edwards of California, then chairman of the House Judiciary Subcommittee on Civil and Constitutional Rights, did just that in an inquiry he directed to the major regional and long-distance companies.

Unfortunately, because of the wide differences in the way the various companies keep their records, the corporate responses to Edwards's questions do not provide a very good national count of how frequently the government is subpoenaing telephone records today, let alone how frequently it was using this tactic in the recent past.

In general, however, the individual corporate reports and supplemental information provided by telephone executives from different sections of the United States did indicate that federal agencies are today acquiring a huge and steadily growing number of toll records for investigative purposes.

NYNEX, for just one example, is the regional Bell operating company in the New York area. NYNEX told Edwards that from 1989 to 1992 the annual number of federal subpoenas requesting individual telephone records had more than quintupled, jumping to 30,692 in 1992 from 5,994 in 1989. As suggested by the Procter & Gamble situation in Ohio, however, a single subpoena can cover a lot more than one telephone line.

This fact was confirmed by the NYNEX report to Edwards, which said that on average each subpoena received by one of its two major divisions—New England Bell—requested the company to provide the government the toll records of 4.5 subscribers. Assuming that the same ratio of subpoenas and records existed for the entire company, it would appear that from 1989 to 1990 government agents examined the telephone records of approximately 300,000 customers.

Bell Atlantic, the regional telephone company operating in the Baltimore–Washington area, said that from 1989 to 1992 it received 25,453 subpoenas or court orders requiring it to provide government investigators access to the toll records of 213,821 customers. Thus the average number of toll records requested by each subpoena received by Bell Atlantic—slightly more than eight—was about twice that reported by New England Bell.

As noted earlier, Roy Neel, the president of the United States Telephone Association, opposes the pending Clinton proposal because he thinks it would be wrong to turn the telephone companies into official government snoops. But he is also concerned about the out-of-pocket costs currently imposed on the companies by the federal government's insatiable demands for long-distance toll information. One of the companies in his association, he said recently, "with only moderate law enforcement obligations, spends $3.7 million a year accommodating over 100,000 enforcement subpoenas, many of which require boxes of documentation."[42]

It is not possible to estimate accurately the extent to which the government is now relying on this investigative technique—and how frequently it did so five or ten years ago. The first problem is that there are nine or ten companies doing the calculating and they do not have a consistent definition of what they are counting. A second problem, mentioned by several telephone executives, is that they do not believe their corporate reporting systems are picking up all the lawful requests for records.

According to conversations with a number of insiders who insisted on anonymity, there is a darker mystery: the extent to which the government obtains toll records on an informal or surreptitious basis. The bootlegging, these experts assert, involves two very distinct approaches. In many cities, for example, federal agents and local detectives maintain close personal relationships with telephone security officials who are delighted to provide their enforcement friends toll records without the fuss and bother of a subpoena, court order or even a notation in a company log.

Moreover, several executives believe that the national security intelligence agencies have somehow worked out clandestine methods for entering the telephone company computers and lifting the records in a completely anonymous fashion. According to several computer security experts, this kind of electronic penetration is relatively easy to accomplish.

Because of these imponderables, any guess about the total number of toll records flowing to the Justice Department and other federal agencies is highly speculative. Certainly, the skimpy evidence that Congressman Edwards was able to extract from the industry would strongly suggest that, at a minimum, many hundreds of thousands of these revealing records are now being scanned each year by federal, state and local law enforcement officials and the intelligence agencies. Given the absence of any serious controls and the ease with which such computerized toll information can be copied and analyzed, the annual total could well be in the millions.

THE ULTIMATE DRIFT NET

Because almost every American household and business has at least one telephone, a national directory of telephone numbers and associated addresses is one of the most useful and obvious investigative tools. Several years ago, for example, a company named Metromail sold the FBI its MetroNet national address lookup service so the bureau wouldn't have to bother calling information when it wanted a number. A national telephone directory, however, has obvious limitations.

This was why, beginning several decades ago, a few creative advertising executives began dreaming about the ultimate directory: a national listing that would contain information about each household so as to enable marketing companies to aim their sales pitches at only those who were most likely to respond.

The process of building these new and improved directories was tedious, but not all that complicated. The beginning point was to transfer the information contained in each telephone book into a computer. Then the marketing experts purchased data tapes from the state motor vehicle departments, the voting registrars, the county tax assessors and the United States Postal Service. In more recent years, the marketing experts began to purchase data tapes from such rich sources of consumer information as credit card companies and banks.

The results are really quite impressive. In a 1991 sales brochure, for example, the marketing division of R.L. Polk claimed its new national listing contained information about 78.2 million named households. Polk said the list had been created by merging over one billion records that it had extracted from twenty-two different data sources. One of the other big guns in the field, Donnelley Marketing Inc., bragged that its national list covered 86 million households and 125 million individual consumers and was based on over 700 million outside records.[43]

The Internal Revenue Service apparently was the first federal agency to use the marketing list for enforcement purposes, in this case the collection of taxes. The IRS's resident genius was Walter E. Bergman, then the agency's deputy assistant commissioner for planning, finance and research, and the year was 1983. Given the speed of computers, his idea was simplicity itself: The IRS would compare its list of the names and addresses of all taxpayers against the names and addresses of all the households identified by the marketing companies.

"If the cross-check suggests a family hasn't paid its taxes," Bergman said more than ten years ago, "we'll make an inquiry to find out why. This is no big deal."[44]

But the situation was not quite as benign as Bergman suggested. In fact, the operation of Bergman's enforcement experiment was just a bit sinister. First, on the basis of scattered information about an individual's lifestyle—where a person lived, what car a person drives, how frequently a person moved—the marketing companies developed inferences about the probable financial status of almost every American, including those who happened to live in several IRS test districts. Then, based on the inferences about these hundreds of thousands of households, the IRS targeted a handful of them for an official audit.

Richard Vincent, then director of marketing for Donnelley, said the IRS experiment was "inappropriate" and "ill conceived" for the simple reason that the lists were not sufficiently accurate. "If a company wants to send a mailer to all American families with incomes over $40,000, we rent it a list for onetime use," Vincent explained. "Depending somewhat on the group that the company wants to target, we guarantee that 75 to 80 percent of those receiving the material will have the correct characteristics."

Although Vincent seemed to be more concerned with protecting his marketing business than stopping Big Brother, the IRS's experiment did not work for the predicted reason that the marketing list contained too many inaccuracies to serve as a cost-effective surveillance device. Put another way, the false suspicions created by those situations when a person's name appeared on the marketing list but not the IRS's taxpayer list for perfectly innocent reasons led the tax agency to initiate a large number of uncalled-for audits, so many that the auditors were unable to handle the cases where there were concrete indications of tax noncompliance.

All of this is relevant today for two reasons. First, marketing experts assert that today's lists—complete with information about one's religious preference, ethnic background, credit card use patterns, political inclination, reading habits and vision problems—are much more accurate than they were when the IRS's Walter Bergman ran his first experiment. Second, both the FBI and the DEA are currently using the commercially developed marketing lists for undisclosed investigative purposes.

To maintain their tactical edge, government investigators always seek to obscure the sources of their information. This was true in the past. It is true now. It was true in the bad old days when some of the government's investigative information gathering was illegal, it is true today when much, if not all, of the government's sweeping surveillance activities have been authorized by Congress or the federal courts, or, as in the present case, when the legal and social implications have never been considered.

The first hint of the FBI's investigative interest in a national directory came in the spring of 1992 when officials from Donnelley Marketing and the Metromail Corporation asserted that the FBI had requested access to their consumer databases. In an article on the front page of the industry's leading trade publication, one source said the FBI agents making their inquiries possessed a "detailed awareness" of the products they were seeking and claimed to have already worked with several other marketers.[45]

As in their brush with the IRS, the major companies strenuously objected to the official use of their marketing lists. The FBI, however, was not to be denied. The formal word came during the congressional testimony of John Cleary, the president of Donnelley. "We have refused requests by the FBI and IRS to install database on their premises because we don't believe marketing lists should be used for investigative purposes," he said. "We told them the only way we would release information to them is if they subpoena us." As the executive explained, however, the refusal had only symbolic significance because the "FBI person who called us said they did have access to other information but they wouldn't identify it."[46]

In response to several inquiries, the FBI refused to discuss the procedures by which bureau agents around the country were able to tap into the national marketing database. They also declined to explain how such a systematically unreliable listing of some 80 million households, along with their ethnic background, religious persuasion and pattern of credit card use, would help agents investigate federal crime.

The proof of the DEA's use of a national marketing list is more extensive. In a budget submission to Congress several years ago, the drug agency reported that one of its most notable recent accomplishments was something it called the National Telephone Directory (NTD). "DEA has installed a commercial-based NTD as part of the central reference system," the drug agency said. "The NTD is derived from public domain information, i.e., mailing lists from direct marketing, publishers, credit card companies, state driver's license files, voting records, other state/local public records, and other public/commercial sources. The NTD is being successfully used in active investigations."[47]

The DEA, like the FBI, would prefer that the public not be informed about its more or less instantaneous access to detailed information regarding every household and corporation in the United States. But in a grudging response to a request under the Freedom of Information Act, the drug agency came up with a handful of internal documents that provide some insights into its astonishing new tracking system.

After what appears to have been a superficial analysis of the proposed project, DEA administrator Robert C. Bonner gave the formal go-ahead in late 1991.[48] A little more than two months later, Donald P. Quinn, an assistant administrator in the operational support division, reported to Bonner's executive assistant that the DEA had already "loaded about 50,000,000 out of a projected 135,000,000 record database."[49]

Quinn said the job would be completed by April 1992, after which "we will be receiving monthly updates for the residential data and quarterly updates for the business data." He added that the work had been "both time-consuming and complex," and had taxed the computer resources of the DEA's parent organization, the Justice Department. "If there are no major system or database modifications needed, the NTD should be available for DEA-wide use by July 1992."

Another document, this one undated but apparently from the same period, indicated that the national subscriber list would be connected to the DEA's Central Reference Files (CREF) and that plans were afoot to expand the directory to include information about those operating cellular and marine phones and the numbers and locations of all pay telephones.

An earlier DEA document estimated the tracking system would cost $1.3 million a year to operate and would be available to special agents and intelligence research specialists on a twenty-four-hours-a-day worldwide basis. The information on each household, it said, "includes sex, age, income, occupation, own/rent home, length of residence and household composition."[50]

A fourth memo, again undated, was a justification for the proposed system from the DEA to the Justice Department. It explained that the automated directory would be used in two ways, the first being to obtain additional information about an individual suspect. The second use, the DEA said, would be "batch requests" for larger numbers of individuals. Although no further explanation was offered, it appears that the DEA is using the directory to collect detailed personal information about groups of people such as all the officers of a single corporation, or all the members of a club or all the residents in a particular neighborhood.[51]

A final curious feature about the purchase was that the DEA arranged for its system to be acquired by the Tennessee Valley Authority. Although the DEA claimed that TVA provided "the avenue to reach the only commercial source known to have current telephone subscriber information," this explanation is doubtful.[52] A more likely reason for the curious arrangement is that the DEA saw TVA as a handy mechanism for avoiding the controversy that had developed at the IRS when it purchased such a system.

THE BRAIN

The Justice Department maw is today swallowing a staggering profusion of data about the American people: the location and lifestyles of approximately 80 million households; transactional information about all toll calls made from hundreds of thousands, perhaps millions, of telephones; substantive information drawn from the secretly recorded conversations of at least 632,000 individuals in just one recent year; the routes followed by targeted automobiles as they zigzag around New York City; "facts" drawn from the hundreds of millions of pages of business and other documents obtained during the course of routine FBI investigations; and all kinds of detailed information about lives and activities of a much smaller number of actual criminal suspects.

Though the Justice Department and the FBI and the DEA routinely decline to discuss the extent of their information gathering, they sometimes can't resist bragging about a particularly dramatic case. The successful investigation and prosecution of the murderer of federal district judge Robert S. Vance was one of those fascinating exceptions. Contributing to the solution, the FBI told Congress a few years ago, was a specially designed computerized system that was able "to analyze, collate, and match 4 million records that were received from 26 different sources" including unnamed telephone companies, prisons and parole boards.[53]

Al Bayse, the ebullient techie who for fifteen years pushed the FBI toward the twenty-first century, stood up and stretched. The long interview was coming to an end. He moved across the windowless room to three oversized computer screens, the business end of a powerful FBI workstation designed to demonstrate the bureau's "expert system" approach to solving its growing information overload problem.

"Artificial intelligence, of course, is not one of my achievements," he explained, as he fired up the workstation and its linked screens. "But it is a technological approach whose time has come, an approach that now is a line item in the FBI's annual budget, an approach that as we talk is sitting on top of a terrorist database that is today helping agents deal with the livest case you've heard of, a case now unfolding a few hundred miles to our north." It was September 16, 1993, just a few months after the bombing of the World Trade Center in New York City, and Bayse's reference seemed obvious.

"This system doesn't just sit around and think about abstract things, it munches away at networked databases and finds all the links and paths," Bayse continued. "I believe that the best link analysis being undertaken anywhere in the United States government is going on right here in this room and I believe I've seen enough of other systems to make this statement."

The colored lights from the high-resolution screens danced on Bayse's face as the demonstration began in the dimly lit room. "The system is called MDES, multidomain expert system," he explained. "This means that it can be used for different areas of criminality, depending upon the data you access. You can focus on terrorism, or counterintelligence or organized crime. We have been able to find a common functionality that allows this system to investigate different kinds of organizations."

In each case, he explained, a small group of agents who had devoted their careers to investigating terrorists, spies or the Mafia were themselves subjected to intense questioning. The goal of these in-house sessions was to get these highly experienced investigators to recall and articulate the often-unwritten rules they had developed in the conduct of their specialized work. Once a comprehensive set of rules had been drawn from investigators, the rules were reduced to computer instructions. These instructions, in turn, guide the specialized computers in making a series of inferential judgments about the possible meaning of discrete events that have been collected by the FBI and recorded in a massive knowledge base. The events would include such matters as a listing of all the toll calls made from a particular person's telephone, precisely when they were made and how long they lasted.

"A rule might be, for example, if a person enters a building and stays in the building and another person enters the building, and both of these persons are criminal suspects, then they probably have a criminal relationship," Bayse explained.

Because the FBI's information about a specific event may lack important details, the expert system includes what are called "fuzzy logic techniques." Fuzzy logic is an attempt to mimic the kind of inexact reasoning upon which a good deal of everyone's life depends. Even when the detailed transactional information in the database does not support an absolute judgment that two individuals were linked in some specific conspiracy, for example, the fuzzy logic process will indicate there is some level of likelihood about the suggested association.

Bayse demonstrated another simple, but still nifty, little service provided by the expert investigative system. Over a period of time, he explained, the patterns of calls made from a particular telephone can sometimes provide investigators with a powerful insight about a case. The problem had always been that spotting these patterns in a long, densely printed list of telephone numbers was almost impossible. But with the assistance of a computer program that displays the information in graphic form on a brightly colored screen, the patterns become instantly obvious. "Here is a bar chart showing you on a day-by-day basis exactly how this phone was used over a two-month period," he said. "The chart shows there were nine calls in the first month, thirteen calls in the second. The gray areas you see on the screen are the weekends. Because this is a business telephone, it may be significant that the chart shows that most of the calls were made on Saturday and Sunday. We can ask for more details about the calls made on any given day. For those four calls made on the last Sunday of the two-month period, for example, we can see what numbers were dialed, when they were dialed, how long each one lasted."

The three expert systems and their associated knowledge bases—one for terrorism, one for counterintelligence and one for organized crime—also contain personal profiles on active suspects. "Where he went to school, where he has worked, where he has lived, any phones he has used, criminal history record, all aliases, any identification numbers, approach restrictions, contact restrictions, criminal specialties, physical characteristics, personality traits and persons and organizations he has been associated with," Bayse said.

"Any area of the screen that is shaded is mouse sensitive. If you put the cursor on organization X and click on it you will be provided detailed information about that organization. Here on the left in the magenta field is our subject. Across the screen are the names of four suspect individuals and five organizations he appears to be associated with. To help the agent working on a particular case avoid information overload, any new data added to the personal profile since that agent last used the expert system is colored a bright red.

"All the transactional information we obtain is entered into the system every day. The data builds up very quickly and everything is linked according to the networks I've shown you. We ran this system twenty-four hours a day during the war in Kuwait—Operation Desert Storm—and it was very helpful," he said.

More than two years after Desert Storm, however, the FBI only had three operational workstations linked with the expert systems—one in Washington, one in New York and one in Houston, Texas.

If the systems were so effective, if they had helped the FBI prevent terrorist acts during Desert Storm and assisted the FBI's investigation of the bombing of the World Trade Center in New York City, why were there only three installations? "It is very expensive to buy and operate, expensive to develop, expensive to build, expensive to do the required training," Bayse said. "I guess it is somewhat a matter of demand and supply. For some years there was a recommendation that the expert systems be kept in research until we were able to give them more functionality. But after our last inspection, we were told to go into implementation. Right now, the question is on the director's desk."

Day after day, month after month, year after year, the federal government continues to sharpen its ability to track the daily activities of the American people. Whatever the decision in this particular case—and the FBI refuses to discuss such matters—it is obvious that in future years Justice Department investigative agents will more and more be guided by various forms of expert systems. The embryonic brains are the only possible way the FBI, DEA and INS can process the vast quantities of transactional data they are now collecting about all Americans.

Perhaps these new techniques will improve the ability of the agents to ferret out individual criminals. The FBI, of course, justifies the steady growth of its tracking abilities in the name of combating crime, and there is no doubt that from time to time these powers aid the bureau's investigations of drug dealers and spy rings. But as the expert systems become more skillful in sensing the subtle patterns and trends within the data and drawing inferences about the possible future actions of the targeted individuals, they may also lead their masters to ever higher levels of official paranoia. Given the supersaturated levels of suspicion that already may be found among FBI agents, it is far from clear whether—in the balance—these developments will make the nation a safer place.

The obsessive law-and-order mind-set should never be discounted, even when expressed in a mildly silly way: The cursor on the FBI's terrorist expert system is shaped like a tiny pistol, with the barrel always pointing toward the particular chunk of data about the individual who then is under the electronic surveillance microscope of the expert systems.

6

The Justice Department's Big, Bad, Dumb War on Drugs

Six times the cops came. Six times they seized the liquor, the gambling equipment and the other contraband. Six times Charlie Matta, the owner of the 37 Club, a dingy after-hours club operating in the middle of a solid working-class neighborhood of Boston, was brought to court.

But somehow, despite the hard work of the police, the active support of the neighborhood and the on-the-record backing of several city councillors, state representatives and the mayor of Boston, Charlie Matta's 37 Club did not close down. At first, exhilarated by the challenge, the neighbors came together at the monthly meetings of the Treadway Road Crime Watch group; sometimes to get the latest report from Tom Crowley, the local police commander, other times to hear a speech from their state representative or to trade the latest horror stories about Charlie Matta's friends.

"The real problem was the night," recalls Mike McGinn, founder of the crime watch organization and an exuberant, hard-working family man who until a few years ago lived half a block from the 37 Club.

"You'd be trying to sleep. But outside, night after night, there'd be prostitutes and drug dealers shouting to each other, and double-parked limousines, their engines running, and gangs of guys pissing into your frontyard," McGinn continued. "It was hard to sleep."[1]

"This guy Matta was so arrogant," said Hendrick "Salty" Solar, a retired truck driver whose house was directly across Savin Hill Avenue from the 37 Club. "He'd stand out there on the sidewalk, all these gold chains around his neck, his hands on his hips, looking at us as if to say, 'What are you going to do about it?' "[2]

"Although a lot of people were fearful, we thought that with all this support and all the work of Tom Crowley and his police officers, that we could put Matta out of business," McGinn said. "But the process turned out to be too slow, way too slow, and the neighborhood began to fall apart."

As the months—and then the years—slipped by, the families living in the Dorchester neighborhood began to lose faith in themselves, the crime watch group and the power of the local authorities to get rid of Charlie Matta and his troublesome customers. A few even began to wonder whether the police raids were a sham, thinking that maybe some of the cops were on the take.

After a time, as the doubts grew stronger, families living near the club began to move away. First one, then another, then a third. Although the neighborhood and its crime watch group were starting to disintegrate, Captain Tom Crowley refused to give up. Officers were dispatched to ticket illegally parked cars and sometimes arrest the club's disorderly customers. Meanwhile, detectives continued to gather the evidence they needed to obtain a judicial warrant for another raid.

"The cops did everything they could," McGinn remembers. "Captain Crowley was always here. It was almost as much of a headache for the police as it was for the people who lived in the area."

On August 21, 1988, in what eventually turned out to be the punch that brought Charlie Matta to his knees, Crowley and his officers once again raided the unlicensed club, this time confiscating four gallons of liquor, four cases of beer, twenty-seven packs of cards, three hundred poker chips and twenty-seven grams of cocaine. The drug seizure made during this raid was pivotal because with it, for the first time, Charlie Matta faced a serious threat of being sent to prison. The club owner was indicted on felony drug charges in March 1989 and was brought to trial almost a year later, on February 21, 1990.

By that time, Matta had decided on an unusual defense: He was not guilty of violating federal drug laws, he told the jury, because he was in fact a paid informant for the FBI. All of his activities at the 37 Club, he claimed, were designed to provide him with a cover while he collected intelligence for the federal government's war on drugs.

Tom Crowley was upset. "This was a truly regrettable situation," Crowley said. "Matta and his customers really messed up the neighborhood. I have no evidence that someone was intervening on his behalf, but he sure did seem to have a special immunity. The FBI, needless to say, never told me what they were up to. You really have to wonder about this operation. What was the goal? Given the world we live in, a few drug arrests don't mean that much. What in the world did the agents think they were accomplishing with their little project?"[3]

Maureen Feeney, now a Boston city councillor, asks the same questions. "What were they doing? What should be important to the federal government? That was a whole solid block that was destroyed, and once you lose a neighborhood like that it is very hard to regain."[4]

Matta's lawyer at the trial was Robert J. Zanello. "From the beginning, I wasn't sure the strategy would work," Zanello said. "The government acknowledged making significant payments to him—for his mortgage, for his living expenses, even for his vacations. And if the FBI and DEA had followed up on this admission by testifying that Mr. Matta had been an important informant and that the drugs he was accused of possessing were directly related to his undercover operations, then maybe this would have been an effective defense. But if my client was involved in drugs on his own hook, then calling in the FBI and DEA probably wasn't going to help."[5]

Zanello's doubts proved on the mark. For while the FBI sent Matta's lawyer a letter acknowledging that the owner of the 37 Club had indeed been paid for providing information that the bureau claimed had helped it seize several million dollars' worth of heroin and arrest a number of drug traffickers, the agency was not willing to say that the twenty-seven grams of cocaine were part of these operations. (For its part, the DEA admitted that Matta had been one of its informants some years in the past.)

At the trial, FBI Special Agent Roderick Kennedy testified that he had been Matta's handler for almost ten years. Kennedy, however, directly disputed Matta's claim that the drugs seized in his club really belonged to the government, or that Matta had never done a drug deal except under the supervision of federal agents.

What, Matta's lawyer asked, had FBI Agent Kennedy requested the club owner to do in return for all the secret payments? "The instructions were to attempt to gather information concerning any large-scale narcotics dealers operating in the Boston area," Kennedy replied.

Neither the jury, which convicted Matta on drug charges, nor the judge, who sentenced him to nine to twelve years in prison, gave credence to his defense. McGinn, who attended the Matta trial when he could get time off from his job at Polaroid, had won the battle. In a broader sense, however, McGinn and his neighbors had lost the war.

"We tried to use the system and do things the right way," said McGinn. "But all along it turns out that the system, our government, was using us.

"My wife was scared," he continued, "scared for herself and our two little girls, and I concluded that for the safety of the family we would have to move out of the city."

After leading the energetic four-year neighborhood campaign to marshal the neighborhood against Matta, McGinn called it quits. "We decided to move out, way out, out to central Massachusetts," McGinn said. "We had shut down the club, but my wife was concerned, afraid of retaliation, afraid to go to the pizza shop around the corner. She had had it."

Born and raised in nearby South Boston, McGinn had originally bought the one-family house at 12 Treadway Road in Dorchester in 1985. "Except for the club, the neighborhood was real solid; decent people, a lot of little kids, and an elementary school almost in our backyard," he said. "What the FBI did was to force a group of hard-working taxpayers out of the city."

In the end, through the intervention of Senator John Kerry, the new FBI special agent in charge of the Boston office met with McGinn and several of the other activists from the Treadway Road Crime Watch group. "This new guy, Tom Hughes, was in a tough spot," McGinn recalled. "What had happened, after all, hadn't been on his watch. While he was nice enough, he was real hard ball. Hughes said he couldn't confirm or deny anything and the FBI certainly never apologized to us."

Bill Walzcak, a leader of the Columbia–Savin Hill Civil Association, is still upset by this tiny skirmish in the federal government's vast war on drugs. "The neighborhood was destroyed by the FBI and it has never really recovered," he said in an interview six years after Tom Crowley's final and successful raid. "The building where the club was located is still empty, the property a wreck."[6]

No one for a moment thinks FBI Agent Roderick Kennedy was trying to drive working-class taxpayers from Dorchester when he funneled thousands of federal dollars to Charlie Matta in exchange for information about the unlawful activities of Charlie's customers. Kennedy's goal, it seems certain, was to get information that would lead to another drug arrest. In fact, it is almost inconceivable that anyone in the FBI's Boston office even considered the broader consequences of the Justice Department's drug enforcement campaign. Their mission, after all, was to develop cases and make arrests, not to ask questions about whether their work was contributing to a safer and more productive city and nation.

DOES IT WORK?

When medical researchers discover a new drug that appears to protect patients from a dangerous disease, there is always great excitement. But before the new product is allowed to go on the market, medical ethics and federal law require the researchers to conduct a complex series of tests designed to establish two important facts. First, is the drug effective: Does it work to reduce or eliminate the targeted medical problem? Second, is the drug safe: Are there situations when the new medicine causes unacceptable side effects?

As demonstrated by the elaborate peer review procedures followed by most scientific disciplines, this healthy skepticism regarding new medical cures has become deeply embedded within the culture of the Western world. The same questioning attitude, of course, also manifests itself in a legal way through the structured medical evaluations undertaken by such agencies as the Food and Drug Administration.

Sensible as these mandatory reviews are for the screening of powerful new medical products, the American people have never been as demanding when it comes to broader social questions, such as how the nation might best deal with the problems surrounding drugs like heroin and cocaine. Perhaps because the drug issue touches on sensitive matters of morality, family, race and class, rational consideration of alternative drug control policies is extremely difficult. It seems that once the president of the United States or the director of the Drug Enforcement Agency or the police commissioner of New York City makes a forceful pronouncement about drugs, whatever its merits, the American people abandon any effort to determine whether the pronouncements make any sense.

There have been, however, a few exceptions to this widespread head-in-the-sand approach. About twenty-five years ago, for example, one of America's brightest and most successful police officials decided to undertake a hard-nosed examination of the response of the NYPD to the use of heroin and other illicit drugs by a substantial number of New Yorkers. Just as with a new medical product, the study would focus on two simple issues. Was the department's strategy effective? Did the department's strategy entail unacceptable side effects?

The official who undertook this unique analysis, Joseph D. McNamara, went on to become the police chief in Kansas City and San Jose, California, and is now, after a long and distinguished career in law enforcement, a research fellow at Stanford University's Hoover Institution. But back in the late 1960s and early 1970s, McNamara was a young lieutenant in the New York Police Department who had obtained a leave of absence to get his doctoral degree in public administration at Harvard University's John F. Kennedy School of Government. McNamara was an uncommon candidate for a doctorate because he was an experienced cop who had begun his career by making drug arrests as he walked his beat in Harlem.

The research for McNamara's groundbreaking thesis was based on two major sources of information. He first undertook a meticulous examination of the records of the police department concerning the enforcement of the drug laws—its formal orders, policy statements, arrest statistics and other communications—going all the way back to the beginning of the twentieth century. What was the 30,000-officer department doing today? What had it done in the past? What had the department's senior officials claimed would be achieved?

His second central source of information was a comprehensive set of surveys, interviews and medical examinations conducted in the Bedford-Stuyvesant and Fort Greene areas of Brooklyn by a team of Harvard, Yale and Columbia University researchers for the Addiction Research and Treatment Corporation's Methadone Maintenance project. These surveys and examinations, when combined with police and health department records, provided McNamara with uniquely detailed and reliable information about the addicts and dealers who lived and operated in the Bedford-Stuyvesant/Fort Greene community. What types and amounts of drugs did the addicts use? How old were they when they became addicted? How were the addicts introduced to their drug of choice? How many times had they been arrested? How many of the arrested addicts and dealers actually went to prison? How frequently were addicts involved in murders, robberies or other violent crimes? How frequently did they engage in property crimes like shoplifting and burglary?

McNamara's final judgment regarding the NYPD's long-held drug strategy was both shocking and characteristically outspoken. For more than half a century, he said, the senior leadership of the police department had viewed arrests as the appropriate response to drugs. In the period immediately preceding his leave of absence, the department's brass had decided to reemphasize this approach, and New York City narcotics arrests jumped from 16,599 in 1967 TO 49,455 in 1970.

New York police commanders had pursued this single-minded enforcement policy, McNamara charged, despite the existence of persuasive evidence proving that the department's past increases in arrests "had not only failed to lower drug use, but had failed to halt increases in the number of users."[7]

His data, McNamara concluded, pointed to a second finding that in many ways was even worse. In addition to failing to curb illicit drug use, the department's policy of emphasizing drug arrests probably had contributed to a steady increase in New York's burglaries and auto thefts. "An arrest takes an officer, perhaps two officers, off the street for purposes of booking, reporting, investigating, handling evidence and appearing in court," he noted. "An arrest represents an expenditure of limited police resources (four man-days in New York City) and the failure to calculate the benefits of arresting a drug misdemeanant in light of overall organizational objectives is a managerial lapse. Its analogy in the business world would be the corporation which expended $12,000 worth of resources merely to get a $6,000 order."[8]

In addition to concluding that the department's policies had failed to reduce drug usage and contributed to increasing levels of property crimes, McNamara said his research had uncovered a third big problem: The senior managers of the largest and most sophisticated police department in the United States did not have the management skills required to develop a rational drug enforcement policy.

New York police officials, he said, "had little knowledge of drug use or how to control it, and almost no capacity for conceiving of and evaluating potential alternative approaches to drug control. In short, the police decision-making was and is limited by unconscious influences of police skills, habits, reflexes and ignorance regarding the phenomena of drug use and the impact of attempts to control it."

New York's drug control policy, he concluded, flowed "from an idealized concept of reality built into the police decision-making model. The premises underpinning the model reflect not what is, but the police preference of what should be."

A NATIONAL WAR ON DRUGS

There is irony in the fact that at about the same time that a street-smart and book-smart New York police lieutenant was beginning to develop the information he needed to challenge the lock-'em-up drug strategy of the nation's largest police department, the politicians in Washington were preparing to adopt the very same policy for the entire federal government.

Although it was not apparent at the time, President Nixon's 1969 decision to launch a national war on drugs probably became inevitable during the two or three years leading up to the November 1968 election. The nation was going through a period of confused unrest and many Americans, especially the older generations, were upset. One force contributing to the turmoil was the increasingly strong resistance to America's military presence in Vietnam. Another key factor was the national debate over race, triggered in part by a long series of peaceful demonstrations led by Dr. Martin Luther King, Jr. With King's assassination in 1968, and the resulting rash of inner-city riots, substantial numbers of voters grew fearful about the future of the United States. A third component of the unrest was the coming-of-age of the baby boomers, that brash generation who saw the world from a very different perspective than their parents—sometimes through a disconcerting haze of marijuana smoke.

With the polls showing that large numbers of Americans were disturbed by these different, but sometimes related, developments, Nixon and his campaign experts decided that the surest way to the White House was a campaign focused on the supposed failure of the controlling Democratic establishment to curb all the protests, demonstrations, riots and increasingly rebellious baby boomers.

Thus was born Richard Nixon's righteous-sounding war on crime. With little thought about what they would do should their strategy succeed, Nixon and John Mitchell, then the campaign manager but soon to be the attorney general, began pounding Vice President Humphrey and Attorney General Ramsey Clark for being "soft on crime." In September 1968, during a campaign appearance in Anaheim, California, Nixon sought to make the focus of his war on crime even sharper. Drugs, the Republican candidate declared, were the "modern curse of American youth." As soon as he was elected, the candidate grandly promised, he would "take the executive steps necessary to make our borders more secure against the pestilence of narcotics."[9]

Within a few weeks of his inauguration, the new president began trying to live up to his campaign rhetoric by issuing a steady stream of press releases on crime and drug control. One of the first described how he had just instructed his new attorney general to take unspecified steps to combat illegal drug traffic in the District of Columbia. That was followed by a special message to Congress on the control of narcotics in which Nixon called for increased federal efforts to reduce the worldwide production of drugs, a stepped-up campaign to prevent the importation of drugs and an intensified enforcement program aimed at major organized crime groups engaged in selling drugs in the United States. Nixon also requested heavier criminal penalties for convicted drug dealers and a new law giving agents the power to smash into a suspect's home without knocking on the door or identifying themselves.[10]

Two years later, on June 17, 1971, Nixon sent yet another special message to Congress on drug abuse, this time declaring that the nation's narcotics problem had now assumed the dimensions of a "national

emergency" that required a massively stepped up federal enforcement program and the creation of a special new presidential office to direct and coordinate all rehabilitation, prevention and education efforts.[11]

With the publication of Nixon's authoritative-sounding statements,
directives and special messages to Congress, it might be assumed that
the White House staff and other responsible government officials had
actually made a systematic effort to collect the information they
needed to build a sensible federal drug program.

As documented in a confidential study on heroin by the Pentagon's
most serious think tank, however, this assumption would not be correct. In fact, according to the 1972 study conducted by the Institute for
Defense Analysis at the request of the president and his White House
staff—a full three years after coming to power—the top levels of the
Nixon government still had very little concrete information about the
dimensions and the dynamics of the drug problem in the United States
and what remedial steps should be taken.

The seriousness with which the policy thinkers at the Institute for
Defense Analysis regarded the absence of useful information can be
judged by the fact that they made this deficiency the very first substantive finding of their three-hundred-page report to the White House.

"Much of the information needed for a comprehensive quantitative
national overview of the heroin abuse problem is not now available,"
the report said. After completing the survey of existing law enforcement data, program treatment data and public health statistics, the policy experts continued, "it was found that this information varies widely
in quality and quantity, suffers from a lack of uniformity in reporting
across the country, and has been subject to very little analysis."[12]

THE EMPEROR IS NAKED

It was not very long before the profound failings of the traditional
law enforcement response to drugs, outlined so powerfully in Joseph
McNamara's 1973 study of the New York Police Department, became
obvious at the federal level to anyone who cared to examine the actual
performance of the responsible agencies.

In October 1979, for example, the General Accounting Office, the
profoundly sober investigative arm of Congress, made public a massive and
upsetting report assessing the achievements of the federal government's
drug enforcement campaign of the previous ten years. Although it is
true that the GAO was then under the thumb of congressional Democrats
who were never reluctant to criticize the Republican-controlled White

House, it also must be noted that the office has always exhibited a profound countervailing faith: a belief in the efficacy of most government programs, even those operating under the control of the opposition party.

The 1979 GAO verdict, after the traditional polite opening, was bleak. "Law enforcement and diplomatic accomplishments have shown some positive results in reducing the availability and adverse impact of some drugs, yet the drug trade flourishes," the report began. "Most evidence indicates that these gains have not permanently reduced overall drug availability, but have instead shifted trafficking and distribution patterns and caused users to switch to other drugs when their preferred drug becomes hard to get. The drug problem [in the United States] persists because of enormous consumer demand, tremendous profits, little risk and the characteristics of the underdeveloped source countries. In addition, the Federal drug supply reduction efforts have yet to achieve a well-integrated, balanced and truly coordinated approach."[13]

As the years have gone by, most law enforcement officials and their political supporters at all levels of government have continued to profess their faith in the theory that arrests and detention someday will solve the drug problem. Most independent critics, however, including the GAO, have become more and more convinced that the current enforcement activities of the DEA, FBI, the Customs Bureau, the IRS and state and local police agencies are doomed to failure.

In 1986, for example, the GAO reported to Congress on its investigation of U.S. efforts to stop the cocaine, marijuana and heroin then flowing across the nation's borders. The report said that while government drug seizures had indeed increased, "the amounts of illegal drugs captured by federal interdiction efforts are believed to be small compared to the amounts of drugs successfully smuggled into the United States. Consequently, smuggled drugs remain widely available in the United States."[14]

Two years later, the GAO investigated another aspect of America's supply reduction effort: the State Department's highly publicized campaign to cut down on the availability of illegal drugs in the United States by reducing their production in third world countries. "Despite increased assistance to the source countries [from the United States] for eradication, crop control and law enforcement," the GAO said, "opium, coca, and marijuana production continue at high levels and narcotics supplies remain plentiful."[15]

Even some of the experts involved in the development of federal drug enforcement policies now admit that important aspects of the government's strategy were flawed. Mark A. R. Kleiman, now at Harvard's Kennedy School of Government, has analyzed national drug enforcement efforts for both Democratic and Republican administrations. The goal of reducing the flow of heroin and cocaine into the United States,

he recently observed in a backhanded criticism of past and present policies, "would be best served if the U.S. government concentrated on demand reduction and on enforcement efforts other than crop eradication
and interdiction."[16]

In addition to criticizing the core of the United States government's
international strategy, Kleiman has also begun to question a central
tenet of federal enforcement policy: keeping the FBI and DEA focused
on the senior ranks of the drug dealers.

As in the case of the federal government, "the belief that high-level enforcement is the real drug war, and that enforcement nearer the street is
merely a series of holding actions, is also common among state police forces
and the elite special narcotics units of some big-city police departments," Kleiman said.[17] "Targeting the higher ups," he continued, "is supported by two notions without much theoretical or empirical support, but
with powerful emotional appeal: that drug dealing is a vast conspiracy, in
which lower-level dealers are mere tools of the shadowy drug lords, and that
the goal of drug enforcement is to interrupt the flow of drugs."

ROOTING OUT DRUGS AT THE SOURCE

Despite the years of criticism, the federal government during 1993
spent about $523 million on international programs intended to reduce
the worldwide supply of illegal drugs. A significant part of this international effort was aimed at the discredited policy of trying to persuade
very poor farmers not to grow two enormously profitable crops, coca
and poppies. During the same year, the government spent $1.5 billion
on the equally questionable effort to interdict the resulting product—
cocaine and heroin—as it was being smuggled into the United States.

In the abstract, both efforts seem sensible enough. But an insight
into the overwhelming challenge of these two exercises can be gained
by considering two relevant points. First, it has been officially estimated that all the illicit heroin consumed by all of America's addicts in
a given year could be manufactured from opium poppies grown on
about twenty square miles of arable land. That is an area a bit smaller
than the island of Manhattan. Second, it also has been reckoned that a
year's supply of cocaine for all of America's users could be concealed in
only thirteen truck trailers.[18]

Given the number of hungry farmers in the world, given the number
of square miles on the earth that could be used for the cultivation of
opium poppies and coca leaves and given the impossibly porous nature
of our thousands of miles of borders, it is not at all surprising that the

government's international and interdiction efforts, which cost U.S. taxpayers about $300 billion between 1981 to 1994, have given little evidence of working.

"The average purity of cocaine at the retail level has remained high for several years, averaging 64 percent in 1992," the 1994 report from the White House's Office of National Drug Policy concluded. "Domestic retail prices, adjusted for purity, declined steadily throughout the 1980s, but increased temporarily in 1990. Since 1990, however, cocaine prices have continued to decline and cocaine has remained readily available."

The office's national assessment regarding heroin was equally dismal. "Regarding street price and purity, the heroin available now is more pure than it was a decade ago. Heroin purity, at the street purchase level, increased from 7 percent in 1982, to 35 percent in 1992, indicating increased availability."

In addition to tracking drug pricing and purity, the government also operates several different kinds of surveys that try to determine the actual drug usage of individual Americans. The patterns uncovered by surveys have been quite erratic, sometimes indicating increased usage, sometimes declines. One survey, for example, suggests that casual drug use among all Americans may be somewhat lower today than it was a few years ago. But another survey found evidence that high school students, college students and recent high school graduates in 1993 appeared to have increased their use of marijuana, hallucinogens and cocaine. Yet another yardstick found that in 1992, after years of decline, heroin-related hospital admissions had increased 34 percent over the previous year.[19]

One other indicator is worth mentioning. A number of years ago, the federal government instituted a program under which the urine of all persons arrested in a small sample of American cities has been routinely tested for the presence of drugs. As noted recently by Alfred Blumstein, the director of the Urban Systems Institute at Carnegie Mellon University, while the percentages of cocaine found in the bloodstreams of the arrestees varied from city to city, "the measurements from 1988 through 1991 "show no consistent downward trend."[20]

WHAT, ME WORRY?

Despite the overwhelming evidence that the government's enforcement programs were a bust, national leaders refused to reconsider their chosen strategies. Instead, annual federal spending by such agencies as the Defense Department, the Coast Guard, Customs, DEA, FBI and the Bureau of Prisons for interdiction, enforcement, prosecution and prisons continued to soar, increasing from somewhat under $1 billion in 1981 to $5.4 billion in 1994. As the yearly drug enforcement expenditures went up, so did the heat of the official rhetoric.

"There are few clear areas in which we as a society must rise up united and express our intolerance," said George Bush in his 1989 inaugural address. "The most obvious is drugs. And when the first cocaine was smuggled in on a ship, it may as well have been a deadly bacteria, so much has it hurt the body, the soul of our country. And there is much to be done and to be said, but take my word for it: This scourge will stop."[21]

Against the hard reality of the drug world, Bush's word cannot be taken at all, and his promise to end the plague was just plain foolishness. Perhaps understanding how such hot language can sometimes trap a politician, Bill Clinton appears to have adopted a somewhat less flamboyant tone in his drug statements. While giving some emphasis in his statements to efforts to reduce drug abuse problems through better education, treatment and rehabilitation programs, Clinton never forgets to include a gung-ho cheer for the enforcement side. "Our aim is to cut off the demand for drugs through prevention," Clinton said in the summer of 1993. "At the same time, we want to strangle supplies by putting more officers on the streets, by enforcing the law in our communities, at our nation's borders, and by helping our friends and allies to do the same thing beyond our borders."[22]

While the tone of Clinton's remarks was a bit more measured than that of his two immediate predecessors, a comparison of their drug spending shows that the Democrats were not prepared to back away from the hawkish and largely discredited priorities of the past. Under Clinton, the federal government's annual average expenditures for international drug programs, drug prosecutions and drug investigations either substantially increased or remained steady in comparison to the Bush years. The only major area of enforcement that saw a modest funding decline involved the costly and largely ineffective deployment of Defense Department resources to interdict drug shipments on their way to the United States.

For the Justice Department alone, spending for drug-control purposes has grown at an astonishing pace, increasing more than eleven times, from $360 million in 1981 to slightly more than $4 billion in 1994.[23]

This incredible growth in spending—by the DEA, FBI, INS, U.S. Marshals Service, the Bureau of Prisons and other agencies—means that during the last five or six years slightly more than fifty cents out of every Justice Department dollar, in one way or another, is aimed at narcotics control.[24]

It also means that offenders sentenced for violating drug laws have now become by far the largest category of criminals convicted in the federal district court. This distinction has been achieved rather quickly, with the number of federal drug cases growing at ten times the speed of all other cases. "Between 1980 and 1990," one Justice Department study has found, "the number of offenders convicted of federal drug law violations more than tripled, while the number of all other offenses combined increased by 32 percent."[25]

ANTICIPATED AND UNANTICIPATED CONSEQUENCES

T he evidence is overwhelming. Experienced police officers like Joe McNamara, the super-insiders like the White House Office of National Drug Control Policy and numerous reports and studies from rigorous outside analysts like the General Accounting Office and Mark Kleiman all agree that the nation's war on drugs—launched a quarter of a century ago by Richard Nixon—has been a fizzle. It just hasn't worked.

What about the second part of the test: the examination for unwanted side effects? Have the government's chosen enforcement policies caused incidental harm? Did the FBI's secret payments to a Boston informant named Charlie Matta, for example, cause the destruction of a working-class neighborhood in Dorchester?

Paolo Alvarez, as I will call him because of his continuing fear of the government, is a handsome thirty-eight-year-old man with dark glowing eyes, a neatly trimmed beard and a polite, almost courtly, manner. Because of his name and soft accent, most Americans would probably guess that Alvarez had been brought up in Central or South America. Actually, he was born on one of the Azores, the Atlantic Ocean islands belonging to Portugal, coming to the United States with his mother and father when he was only sixteen.

"I believe in God," Alvarez said, sitting on the couch of his comfortable ranch house a few blocks south of the salt flats at the southern end of San Francisco Bay.[26] "But the government's seizure of all my savings was really horrible. I felt trapped and I almost flipped out."

Here, briefly, is his story. For many years, Alvarez operated a small company that maintained the lawns and gardens of Bay-area apartment houses and office buildings. A cautious and frugal man, he slowly managed to build up his financial reserves, even while caring for his wife and daughter. Several years ago, however, Alvarez began listening to the speeches of Ross Perot, especially Perot's exaggerated warnings that the nation's savings and loan institutions were about to collapse. As a result of mounting anxiety generated by the Texas businessman, Alvarez decided to move the nest egg from his savings and loan. He placed some of the money in a regular bank and hid the balance in small caches around his house.

When the sky did not fall, when Ross Perot's predictions did not come true, Alvarez began slowly moving the cash in his house back into a bank. Partly because of his fear of a possible robbery, he chose to redeposit his money in relatively small amounts, $5,000 or so at a time.

While Alvarez had come to know that Perot's gloomy predictions were off the mark, he did not know that the federal government, in its hysteria about drugs, had persuaded Congress to greatly expand the government's civil and criminal powers to seize the assets of individuals it felt might be up to some illicit business. The government's concern was so overwhelming that in 1986 Congress was prevailed upon to add a provision to the seizure law forbidding any "structuring" of financial transactions in a way so as to evade an existing requirement that cash transfers of more than $10,000 had to be reported to the government.

On November 11, 1993, apparently tipped off by a friendly bank clerk who thought Alvarez's redeposits looked like "structuring," the Internal Revenue Service seized $88,315.76, the life savings of a hardworking immigrant.

The government, of course, had no evidence that Alvarez was using the money for improper purposes, or was in any way connected with drugs or drug dealing, for the simple reason that he wasn't doing any such thing. In this case, under the astonishing provisions of our nation's asset forfeiture laws, the mere administrative finding that Alvarez had "structured" his transactions was enough to justify the seizure. To the government, the question of whether the money had been legally earned or was the product of a nefarious drug sale was of no concern.

Maybe worse than the nebulous structuring provision is a feature of the same group of laws that places the burden of proof on the victim. In other words, rather than the government having to prove that Alvarez had violated the statute before it seized his money, Alvarez had to prove that he was innocent of any wrongdoing before he could get it back. Further adding to the profound unfairness of the seizure process is an incredible provision that anyone who wants to challenge an action, who wants his day in court, must file a bond with the government of either $5,000 or 10 percent of the value of the seized property. In Alvarez's case, because the government had seized all of his savings, he was forced to borrow the $5,000 from his credit card accounts.

The government's abrupt assault shocked Paolo Alvarez to his core, leaving him with powerful feelings of fearful despair and isolation. While the fear was obviously justified, the feeling of isolation was way off the mark. In fact, as the target of what the government eventually would indirectly acknowledge was a wrongful action, Alvarez turns out to have a lot of company.

A BRIEF HISTORY

While forfeiture laws were unpopular in colonial America—they were one factor in the growing opposition to British rule—the first session of Congress authorized the procedure as a civil sanction against those who failed to pay their customs duties. This federal statute remained essentially unchanged until 1970, when Congress decided criminal forfeiture should be made a sanction under the Racketeer Influence and Corrupt Organizations (RICO) Act. In 1978, responding to widespread public concerns about illegal drugs, Congress authorized the seizure of all profits from drug trafficking and all assets—such as houses, cars and boats—purchased with the proceeds of drug trafficking. In 1984, the law was further broadened. From that point on, federal agencies could use the civil forfeiture process to seize "all real property . . . which is used, or intended to be used, in any manner or part, to commit, or to facilitate the commission of a violation [of the act]."[27]

The widespread public belief that drug abuse is among society's most pressing problems made understandable Congress's decision to authorize the government to seize the profits of drug dealers. The congressional action extending this same sanction to all real property that in any possible manner "facilitated" the violation of the drug laws, however, has been far more problematic.

In 1991, for example, a federal district court judge in Illinois upheld the government's seizure of a company car that was used by an employee for both business and personal transportation. It seems that at 4:08 A.M. on November 11, 1988, while parked in Oak Lawn, Illinois, the car had "facilitated" a violation of the drug laws by being the place where the employee happened to be sitting when caught in the act of ingesting cocaine. In approving the seizure of the company car, the judge ruled that the "innocent owner" exception to the forfeiture law did not apply because, prior to the seizure, JPM Industries, Inc., "had no corporate policy restricting illegal drug use by company officers in company cars, nor were any measures taken to prevent such drug use."[28]

Another example of such a "facilitation" occurred in Hamden, Connecticut. In this case the federal government seized the home of an elderly couple, Paul and Ruth Derbacher, after marijuana and cocaine belonging to their teenaged grandson was found in the house. The couple, who were in their eighties, had raised the boy since he was ten. The government sold the Derbacher house. In this particular case, however, because of the judge's reservations about the whole procedure, the government reluctantly agreed to return to the couple $25,104.46, about half the value of their former house.[29]

The U.S. attorney said the settlement was "about as fair as you could get." The Derbachers' attorney had a very different view. "This was not a question of good law enforcement, this was prosecution for profit," said Robert Castle, a lawyer with an office in nearby Bradford.[30]

"The whole program is a nightmare," he continued. "I have no problem with seizing the Miami Beach mansion of a cocaine wholesaler, but that is not what is happening. This program has very little to do with going after the bad guys and everything to do with going after what is valuable. If it keeps up, the Justice Department is going to be the largest property owner in Connecticut."

At the time of his sentencing on April 17, 1992, Anthony F. Zak was seventy-one, and his ailing wife, Peggy, was seventy-six. Zak was a World War II veteran with no prior criminal history. Some months before, however, federal agents had discovered that he was growing 118 marijuana plants in his garden. Now it was time for District Court Judge Alan A. McDonald—sitting in Yakima, Washington—to pronounce the sentence. McDonald was upset because the mandatory minimum sentences approved by Congress required him to send Zak to federal prison for five years.

Referring to the "very sad issue at hand"—the imposition of a five-year prison term on a seventy-one-year-old man—McDonald turned to Pamely Byerly, the assistant U.S. attorney who was handling the case.

"Now I'm informed by Mr. Zak's attorney that the government has gone farther and they've forfeited all his property, is that correct?" the judge asked the prosecutor. "Who in the world called that shot?"

"Your honor," Byerly replied, "we have a separate forfeiture attorney, and I don't know how that—I was not involved in the case at that time. I do not know how that decision was made."

After observing that it was Good Friday, Judge McDonald said that "the timing is certainly appropriate. We've had crucifixions before, haven't we?" The judge then asked the prosecutor to inform the person in the U.S. attorney's office who was responsible for the Zak forfeiture that he was highly displeased. "Tell him that it's this kind of heavy-handedness, this kind of harshness, that's rapidly alienating the government and its law enforcement policies from the people; would you do that for me?"

Critics of the unbounded character of the seizure laws consider Willie Jones another of the program's classic victims. On February 27, 1991, Jones, a second-generation African-American nurseryman in his family's Nashville florist business, was about to board an American Airlines flight. As he had done many times before, Jones was on his way to Houston to buy flowers and shrubs. Because the wholesalers prefer cash, he was carrying $9,600.

This time, however, apparently because Jones fit a "profile" of what drug dealers are supposed to look like, two police officers stopped him, searched him and seized his $9,600. The businessman was given a receipt and told he was free to go.

Andrew Schneider and Mary Pat Flaherty, the two Pittsburgh *Press* reporters who told Jones's story in their powerful 1991 series on the government's aggressive seizure program, summarized it this way. "No evidence of wrongdoing was ever produced. No charges were ever filed. As far as anyone knows, Willie Jones neither uses drugs nor buys nor sells them. He is a gardening contractor who bought an airplane ticket. Who lost his hard-earned money to the cops."[31] After a long legal battle and a lot of publicity, Jones got his money back.

As those in power always do, Justice Department officials have consistently defended their use of the asset forfeiture process. Asset forfeitures, said Attorney General Janet Reno, have "proven to be an effective tool in stripping criminals of the instrumentalities and proceeds of their illicit activities."[32] Several years earlier, George Terwilliger III, an associate attorney general during the Bush administration, argued that the overall program was good and the problems isolated. While acknowledging that in a few cases "dumb judgment" might have created difficulties for individual citizens, Terwilliger said the safeguards were more than adequate. "That's why we have the courts," he said.[33] The Justice Department also has challenged the accuracy and completeness of some of the horror stories about seizures, insisting, for example, that the Pittsburgh *Press* articles, including the story about Willie Jones, "were highly slanted and misleading."[34]

But it is not only defense attorneys, a few federal district court judges and reporters who have concluded that the asset forfeiture laws have led to destructive abuse. In several recent decisions the United States Supreme Court appears to have begun to reverse its general support of the program and chip away at some of its worst features.

The flat-out opposition of Congressman Henry J. Hyde, a powerful and conservative Illinois Republican, may be of even greater long-term significance. Hyde, who became chairman of the House Judiciary Committee as a result of the Republican takeover of Congress after the 1994 election, has sought to inform the public about the asset forfeiture process by writing a highly critical book on the subject.

"Federal and state officials now have the power to seize your business, home, bank account, records and personal property, all without indictment, hearing or trial," Hyde began. "Everything you have can be taken away at the whim of one or two federal or state officials operating in secret."

The so-called war on drugs, the congressman continued, "has been perverted too often into a series of frontal attacks on basic American constitutional guarantees—including due process, the presumption of innocence and the right to own and enjoy private property."[35]

Despite the criticism by Hyde, other members of Congress, the Supreme Court, defense attorneys and published reports from all over the country, the seizure of the profits and assets from illicit drugs by federal, state and local law enforcement agencies remains one of the fastest-growing businesses in America. One central repository of the federal government's seizures, for example, is the Justice Department Asset Forfeiture Fund. In 1993 alone the department took in $556 million, twenty times more than it did when the program began in 1985. Between 1985 and 1993, as the result of more than 200,000 forfeitures, this fund took in over $3.2 billion.[36]

THE BOUNTY HUNTERS RETURN

T he swift growth in drug seizures, civil and criminal, is partly an outgrowth of changes in the drug laws mandated by Congress. Also contributing has been the policy of recent presidents, both Democratic and Republican, to respond to public concerns about drugs by emphasizing enforcement. But there is a third, obviously corrupting, factor at work. Under a 1984 provision of the law, a substantial part of the dollars seized by federal, state and local enforcement agencies each year is returned to these organizations for the purchase of new vehicles, radios and surveillance equipment and, in some instances, to pay for the overtime racked up by individual agents.

Once again, Henry Hyde put it straight. Some enforcement authorities, he said, were guided by greed because the property and cash expropriated from private citizens goes directly to their agencies. "The more they seize, the more they get for their own 'official use,' " he said.[37]

In a 1992 brief filed with the Supreme Court, the National Association of Criminal Defense Lawyers made the same argument, contending that "this dubious system" operated in such a way that it gave federal, state and local agents "an undue incentive to seek forfeiture penalties which are not in the interest of justice solely for the purpose of raising revenues for law enforcement agencies."[38]

The association charged that both police and prosecutors "are in thrall to a reward system that resembles [a] bounty system." It added that the incentives for abuse were not merely pecuniary, citing one situation in the Justice Department as an example. Because the Justice Department considers district forfeiture activities when deciding how many federal prosecutors will be allocated to each U.S. attorney, the association said, areas with little criminal activity may pursue wrongful forfeitures as a way of justifying higher staffing levels.

The belief that the Justice Department's obsession with forfeitures is partly driven by interests other than the enforcement of the drug laws is also supported by direct evidence. In June 1989, Acting Deputy Attorney Edward S. G. Dennis dispatched an administrative bulletin ordering the nation's U.S. attorneys to take all possible actions to make their forfeiture cases "current," even if that effort required federal prosecutors to drop matters they were already pursuing. If inadequate resources are available to meet the forfeiture goal, Dennis said, "you will be expected to divert personnel from other activities or to seek assistance from other U.S. Attorneys' offices."[39]

One year later, the attorney general himself warned U.S. attorneys that the Justice Department had fallen far behind its budget projection in the collection of assets. "We must significantly increase production to reach our budget target. . . . Failure to achieve the $470 million projection would expose the Department's forfeiture program to criticism and undermine confidence in our budget projections. Every effort must be made to increase forfeiture income during the remaining three months of [fiscal year] 1990."[40]

While the Justice Department now seems to be more discreet in the wording of its policy directives, the popularity of this particular cash cow with law enforcement officials means that the fund-raising potential of the forfeiture program is always mentioned. "Although the primary mission of the [Justice Department's] program is to maximize the effectiveness of forfeiture as a law enforcement tool in the fight against crime, revenue is an ancillary benefit," a recent annual report delicately declared. Since fiscal year 1986, it added, more than $1 billion in cash and tangible property "have been reinvested into law enforcement efforts at the state and local levels."[41]

ALVAREZ LUCKS OUT

In relation to hundreds of millions of dollars seized by the federal government in 1993, the move on the $88,315.76 of Paolo Alvarez was small potatoes. "From the government's point of view it was almost nothing, to me it was my life savings," he said.

Unlike many other such victims, Alvarez was extremely lucky, partly because, in a stroke of great good fortune, he was referred to a lawyer in Oakland, California, named Montie S. Day. A former college football star who had a brief professional career with the Chicago Bears, Day became a lawyer after a career as a criminal investigator with the IRS. Perhaps because of his experience as a serious football player or maybe because of his years with the IRS, Day is a tough infighter with a great deal of detailed knowledge on how the Justice Department functions.

From the moment the matter was referred to Assistant U.S. Attorney Jonathan R. Howden for initiation of the forfeiture proceedings, Day began flooding the government with Alvarez's financial records, arguing that his client was innocent of any wrongdoing and establishing that the money was merely the life savings of a hard-working individual. As a result of this effort, seven months after the government had seized the savings, Howden advised Day in July 1994 that the Justice Department would not go forward with the forfeiture.

Despite his refusal to take the case before a judge, however, Howden made an astonishing attempt to keep half of the $88,000 the government had seized from Alvarez's bank account. In a July 28, 1994, conversation, Day said, Howden had offered him two options.

"Under the first option," explained the defense attorney, Howden said "we could resolve the matter with the Justice Department and the U.S. attorney's office by agreeing to the forfeiture of 50 percent of the seized funds and I thus would not have to negotiate with the IRS, the agency that made the original seizure. Under the second option, the U.S. attorney would refuse prosecution and send the money back to the IRS. Hinting that option two just might result in the loss of all of the seized money, Howden told me it was possible the IRS would pursue other ways of keeping Alvarez's savings."

After some legal research, Day decided that Howden was bluffing in a crass attempt to hold on to part of the money that he had tacitly acknowledged did not belong to the government. With the consent of his client, the lawyer rejected option one and demanded the return of everything. On November 7, 1994, one year after the seizure, the IRS returned the $88,315.76. The government, of course, did not offer any explanation for this unusual action. Was it tired of hassling with Montie Day? Or had it decided Alvarez was a needy case?

While the victory was sweet, it was not complete. As noted in Day's November 18, 1994, claim against the government, Alvarez was out one full year's interest on his savings and about $5,000 in legal fees. The lawyer also requested a modest $50,000 in damages, contending that the seizure had constituted a "wrongful conversion of funds without due process." Day is not hopeful the government will ever honor this claim. And because any appeal would be extremely costly, the possibility that Alvarez will recover his out-of-pocket costs, let alone his claimed damages, seems slim.

A QUESTION OF RACE

In the United States, racial and ethnic minorities have frequently been blamed for the nation's drug problems. During the last few decades of the nineteenth century and the early years of the twentieth, for example, Chinese immigrants were the focus of concern for opium abuse, although numerous physicians of the day were plying their middle- and upper-class patients with narcotic preparations. Another popular image of the period involved the cocaine-crazed black. The negative link between cocaine and blacks existed despite the fact that cocaine was the primary ingredient in many widely used elixirs, restoratives and tonics, most particularly, in its early days, Coca-Cola. A few decades later, Mexican immigrants were singled out for allegedly promoting marijuana use.

For tens of millions of Americans, the derogatory connection between minority groups and illicit drugs continues to this day. Although poor urban areas are obviously troubled by high levels of alcohol and drug abuse, it is also true that a substantial portion of those living in these areas are white, not black or Hispanic. Furthermore, although the subject of alcohol and drug problems in the suburban and rural areas is largely ignored by the media, research indicates that substance abuse problems are by no means limited to urban ghettoes.

Despite the reality that drug abuse plagues almost all races and ethnic groups, law enforcement's war on drugs has come down much harder on black Americans than whites. Local and state police, for example, currently arrest four times more blacks, in relation to population, than whites. Even more revealing is the fact that since 1985, while drug arrest rates for white juveniles have substantially declined, the rate for black juveniles has quadrupled.[42]

Racial disparities have also been discovered at the federal level, where black offenders are sent to prison more frequently and for longer periods of time than whites.[43]

The fact that all levels of drug enforcement come down unusually hard on blacks does not, by itself, prove the system is racially biased. One explanation for the disparity, for example, is that a disproportionate number of African Americans are engaged in the drug business. Unfortunately, however, because of the illegal nature of such activities, hard evidence indicating the race of drug dealers does not exist.

Some, possibly relevant, information is available which suggests this supposition about blacks is wrong or at least highly exaggerated. According to the government's National Household Survey on Drug Abuse, the percentage of whites, blacks and Hispanics who have recently *used* any kind of illicit drug is quite similar. Considering just one drug, and looking at the use statistics from a slightly different perspective, the survey found that of all those reporting they had smoked crack at least once in their lifetime, 65 percent were white, 10 percent black and 10 percent Hispanic. Although government surveys that seek information about unlawful activities have obvious limitations, there is a consensus that approximately three quarters of those who have used an illicit drug in the recent past were white.[44]

But can the survey information about the race of illicit drug *users* be used to infer the race of *traffickers*? This question was discussed in a 1994 memorandum written by Jan Chaiken, the director of the Justice Department's Bureau of Justice Statistics. In arguing for the proposition that more blacks were involved in drug trafficking than would be suggested by the user surveys, Chaiken cited unpublished 1990 FBI data that 56 percent of all adults arrested in the United States for "trafficking in opium or cocaine and their derivatives [crack] were black."[45]

Chaiken's memo, however, did not discuss a basic limitation of all arrest statistics. This problem is that the race and other characteristics of those who are arrested for crimes like drug dealing sometimes tells us a good deal more about an enforcement agency's policies—for example, the neighborhoods where officers have been ordered to patrol—than they do about the characteristics of all dealers.

While there is no doubt that when it comes to drugs the entire criminal justice system of the United States is much harder on blacks than it is on whites, sorting out the reasons why this is so is not easy.

Is simple racism—among police officers, prosecutors, juries and judges at all levels of government—the determining factor? Or does the disproportionate number of blacks arrested for drug dealing simply mirror the reality of the drug business? Are drug enforcement tactics unconsciously biased? Or have court administrators, in drafting official guidelines, somehow written regulations that resulted in blacks being treated in a tougher way than whites?

All federal judges, upon assuming office, take an oath to "administer justice without respect to persons" and to "do equal right to the poor and the rich." Biases about the economic circumstances, race and other such factors should play no role in the functioning of the federal courts. It then was hardly surprising that a few years ago—as a result of the concerns of federal judges, members of Congress, defense attorneys and civil rights organizations—a small team of researchers, headed by Douglas C. McDonald and Kenneth E. Carlson, were asked to undertake a sophisticated statistical analysis of the racial disparities that had been discovered in federal sentencing.

Using data drawn from the Federal Probation Sentencing and Supervision Information System, the researchers charted the outcome of all the cases where offenders were convicted of federal drug violations from 1986 through June 1993. When the outcomes were compared by the race of the defendant, the data showed that from 1986 till the end of 1988, "white, black and Hispanic offenders received similar sentences, on average, in Federal district courts."[46]

Looking at the sentencing information of a more recent period, however, McDonald and Carlson found a very different situation. According to their analysis of drug offenders sentenced in federal court between January 20, 1989, and June 30, 1990, 85 percent of the African Americans and 78 percent of the Hispanics were sentenced to prison, while only 72 percent of the whites received this penalty.[47]

The two researchers also discovered that during the second test period the average sentence for black drug offenders was 41 percent (almost two years) longer than for whites.

In their initial analysis, McDonald and Carlson had examined the sentencing outcomes for all federal drug cases and the separate outcomes for those convicted for their involvement with four different drugs—cocaine, marijuana, heroin and other controlled substances. As a result of recent changes in the consumption of drugs and the enforcement of the drug laws of the United States, however, the researchers decided a more exacting analysis might be revealing.

The particular change that intrigued them was the rapid development of crack cocaine as one of America's favorite drugs. Powder cocaine had long been a favorite of a relatively small number of urban artists, musicians and other sophisticates. Gradually, however, its popularity grew among young, middle-class professionals all over the country. Then, in the mid-1980s, a new form of cocaine—crack—was placed on the national drug market.

Because crack is relatively cheap to manufacture and can be easily ingested without injection, it quickly caught on among low-income users. It also caught on with the media. The first published mention of crack was in the *Los Angeles Times* on November 25, 1984. "In the months leading up to the 1986 elections, over 1,000 stories appeared on crack in the national press, including five cover stories in *Time* and *Newsweek*. NBC ran 400 separate reports on crack (15 hours of airtime)," one federal study observed.[48]

The centerpiece of this media feeding frenzy was the June 1986 death of Len Bias, the University of Maryland basketball star who had just been drafted by the Boston Celtics. Although Bias's death was widely reported to have resulted from the smoking of crack, it was later determined that this was not the case: Bias died the old-fashioned way, snorting powder cocaine.

As Congress rushed toward adjournment and the looming November 1986 elections, the crack that allegedly had caused Bias's death became its central obsession. Senator Paula Hawkins, a Republican from Florida, described the problem in sweeping, almost apocalyptic, terms as she called for the approval of the then-pending drug legislation, the most important provision of which concerned crack. "Drugs pose a clear and present danger to America's national security," she declared. "This is a bill which has a far-reaching impact on the future as we know it as Americans and as we mature into the next century."[49]

Senator Jesse Helms, the right-wing North Carolina Republican, also weighed in on the debate. Cocaine in general and crack cocaine in particular, he told the Senate, "causes the crime rate to go up at a tremendously increased rate." Other senators suggested that ingesting crack made its users uniquely violent. Although this certainly was the conventional wisdom of that fall, there was little evidence in 1986 and there is scant evidence today that cocaine powder or crack cocaine contains any unique crime-causing substances.

In the media-generated hysteria of the final frantic hours of Congress, without benefit of hearings, the Anti-Drug Abuse Act of 1986 was approved. The legislation set mandatory minimum penalties for trafficking, depending upon the amount and type of drug involved. For the first time, a distinction was made between crack cocaine and powder cocaine. Under the law, federal judges were required to impose a minimum sentence of at least five years upon anyone convicted of dealing in five or more grams of crack. When it came to powder cocaine, however, the law required the minimum five-year sentence only for those who were convicted of trafficking in five hundred grams or more. In essence, the 1986 legislation established that when it came to traffickers, the courts had to consider crack a hundred times more dangerous than powder cocaine.

Under the same law, the 100-to-1 ratio was also applied to convictions leading to a mandatory ten-year minimum sentence—in this case, 50 grams of crack versus 5,000 grams of powder cocaine.

Two years later, still preoccupied by crack, Congress approved the Anti-Drug Abuse Act of 1988, this time requiring judges to impose a *minimum* five-year sentence for anyone convicted of the simple possession of five grams or more of crack. To appreciate the degree to which crack had captured the imagination of national lawmakers, it must be understood that the *maximum* sentence allowed by the same law for the possession of other drugs such as heroin and powder cocaine was one year.

It was this recent history that prompted McDonald and Carlson to undertake the extra work of sorting out the cocaine defendants into one of two categories, those dealing primarily in crack and those dealing in powder cocaine. After achieving this separation, the researchers determined that when the sentencing patterns were looked at this way, the race of the defendants no longer was so significant. All crack dealers—white, black and

Hispanic—were treated by the courts in fairly similar ways. Likewise for all dealers in powder cocaine. The judges apparently were following the law in a relatively color-blind way. The hitch, of course, was that for a variety of class and economic reasons, most crack dealers are black and a substantial majority of powder cocaine dealers are white.

"The single most important reason for the longer average sentences given to blacks was their predominance in the crack trade (or, more precisely, among those brought into federal court for trafficking in crack)," the researchers concluded. "Because they were disproportionately convicted of a crime that Congress had chosen to penalize especially harshly, the average sentences of all black traffickers were longer than those imposed for whites."

Here is the situation in a nutshell. Largely because of laws adopted by Congress in 1986 and 1988 during a period of public hysteria about the nation's drug problems, tens of thousands of small-time crack dealers, mostly black, are receiving substantially longer prison sentences than the mostly white wholesale dealers who specialize in marketing much larger amounts of powder cocaine.

The United States Sentencing Commission, an independent agency within the federal court system, was created by Congress in 1984 to establish sentencing policies for the federal criminal justice system. In a draft report to Congress in late 1994, the Sentencing Commission observed that because powder cocaine is the drug of choice of white, middle-class communities, while crack is more popular in minority and lower-class communities, critics have contended that the harsher penalties for crack under the statutory 100-to-1 ratio "are racially discriminatory."[50]

While the 1994 draft report was cautiously written, the Sentencing Commission appeared to agree with the critics of the drug law. Because the penalty difference for powder cocaine and crack cocaine was not supported by the research, the draft said, the disparity raised serious questions of fairness. The commission recommended that Congress eliminate the law mandating the dissimilar penalties for the two forms of the same drug.

Behind the scenes, according to several of the players, the Justice Department was displeased and brought heavy pressure on the commission to abandon its heretical position. By the time its final report was issued in February of 1995, the commission had given in to these pressures to the extent that it now recommended that the disparity between the sentences for the two drugs should be lessened. The original call for the outright elimination of the differential was abandoned.[51]

Curiously, even though Reno has given scores of speeches proclaiming her deep concern for social justice, the attorney general was not satisfied with the commission's modified position. "I strongly oppose measures that fail to reflect the harsh and terrible impact of crack on communities across America," she said. The attorney general voiced her opposition shortly after a group of U.S. attorneys meeting in San Antonio voted to oppose the commission on the matter.[52]

Neither the McDonald-Douglas study nor the draft report of the commission discussed one other example of how the federal government is treating black Americans much more harshly than whites. One special provision of the 1988 drug law authorized U.S. attorneys to seek the death penalty for murders committed by anyone involved in a "continuing criminal enterprise" that sells drugs. From the time the law was approved, until March 1994, former Attorneys General Thornburgh and Barr and present Attorney General Reno have approved the prosecution of thirty-seven defendants under the so-called kingpin law. Of these, according to a staff report by the House Civil and Constitutional Rights Subcommittee, 78 percent have been black, 11 percent Hispanic and 11 percent white.[53]

The report went on to say that the Justice Department had been challenged at a congressional hearing to provide an explanation for the racial disparities, and the chairman asked for additional relevant data, but the "Department has offered no response."

AT THE LOCAL LEVEL

As laid out in the United States Constitution, enforcement of the criminal law is supposed to rest mainly with state and local authorities. More and more, however, the federal government has come to be a dominant force, especially in such areas as drugs. In the joint task forces, where local and state police officers are teamed with agents from the DEA, the FBI and other federal agencies, U.S. attorneys are becoming de facto police chiefs. Through agreements to accept local drug cases in federal courts, U.S. attorneys are becoming de facto local district attorneys. Through the distribution of dollars flowing through the Justice Department's asset forfeiture program, U.S. attorneys are increasingly able to influence, even direct, the drug enforcement strategies of state and local enforcement agencies.

Given this powerful federal role, it is fair to ask whether the Justice Department should be held partially responsible for the drug enforcement programs of local authorities. At question here is the previously mentioned analysis of Alfred Blumstein, the Carnegie-Mellon professor, showing that the drug arrest rate for nonwhites is currently four times higher than for whites.

"The difference in the rate of arrests for whites and nonwhites for drug offenses is far greater than the nonwhites' relative representation among drug users," Blumstein said.[54] "To the extent that self-reported drug users are a racially representative sample of drug sellers (and many drug sellers are also users), there could well be a serious distortion in the distribution of drug arrests."

After observing that it was likely that a somewhat larger number of nonwhite dealers were in the marketplace than suggested by the user surveys, Blumstein examined a number of factors that probably contributed to the much higher rate of arrest for nonwhites. Drug markets operated by blacks, for example, "tend much more often to be outdoors and vulnerable to police action, whereas whites tend much more often to be inside and thereby less visible and more protected from police surveillance and arrest." Blumstein also related how the police presence is often far more dense in nonwhite areas because of the higher levels of reported crime.

But Blumstein said the higher arrest rates for nonwhites might also be the product of racially biased police profiles and the policy decisions

ARREST RATES FOR DRUG OFFENSES, JUVENILES, BY RACE
1965–1991

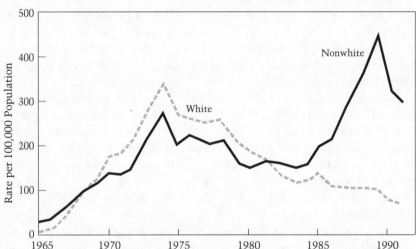

Since the mid-1980s, the drug offense arrest rate of nonwhite juveniles has been far higher than that of white juveniles. Because there is no clear proof that the arrest rates reflect differing levels of drug usage, it appears that a large part of the discrepancy is the result of enforcement policies such as those that dictate which neighborhoods officers are assigned to patrol. This variation in state and local arrest rates is just one aspect of a number of racial disparities in the nation's war on drugs. (ALFRED BLUMSTEIN, PROFESSOR OF URBAN SYSTEMS, CARNEGIE MELLON UNIVERSITY)

of many local police authorities to focus a large share of their enforcement resources on crack cocaine rather than powder cocaine.

Whatever the possible explanations, Blumstein concluded, the national pattern of drug arrests does in fact constitute "a major assault on the black community. One can be reasonably confident that if a similar assault was affecting the white community, there would be a strong and effective effort to change either the laws or the enforcement policy."[55]

CORRUPTION

Many Americans, when they think about corruption at all, focus their attention on the person who has taken the bribe. How can it be, we wonder, that this flawed individual could succumb to what often seems like a very small reward? While contemplating the ethical collapse of a single corrupted person can be a useful pastime, it is also sometimes an obstacle to understanding, because we are distracted from examining the broad institutional impact of corruption. An excessive interest in the "occasional rotten apple in the barrel"—whether the apple is an individual police officer, a DEA agent or a senator—can eclipse the larger question: Is there something wrong with the barrel? In addition to signaling the moral failure of an individual, corruption almost always indicates administrative failures within the institution where the individual functioned.

Tank and Slim were addicts in Harlem. To support their chemical needs, Tank and Slim had gone into the business of helping the police by setting up low-level street dealers for arrest. In return for their contribution to a more just society, the police officers would pay the two informants. But because the NYPD did not fully trust its officers, "buy money" was scarce, and the police officers often paid Tank and Slim in an unusual currency: heroin that the police officers had stolen from other addicts.

This was not a pretty picture. In the name of the war on drugs, New York police officers had somehow begun to provide illegally confiscated drugs to drug addicts. Here is how it looked to a special commission created to investigate police corruption in New York. "The commission found that police officers were involved in possession and sale of drugs in a variety of ways, including financing transactions, recruiting informants and addicts as pushers, and share-selling, where the pusher is given drugs on consignment and retains part of the proceeds as payment."[56]

But when the commission, headed by a Wall Street lawyer named Whitman Knapp, hired Tank and Slim to assist them in its investigation, and the two addicts were rigged with hidden microphones during their sidewalk chats with friendly police officers, the investigators uncovered ironclad proof of something that was much much worse.

"The commission found it common for police officers to use narcotics as a medium of exchange for goods and services," the report said. "Among the completed drugs-for-merchandise transactions [captured on audiotape] were several involving whiskey and other alcoholic beverages. In one of these transactions a plainclothesman gave the two Commission informants a written list specifying thirty-one quart bottles by name. He told them to make sure to 'come through because I need them for my daughter's wedding shower.' The patrolman paid for the liquor with a quantity of white powder containing heroin, starch, quinine, and manitol."[57]

Clearly this police officer was a moral leper. But for the city as a whole much more was at stake. In an incredibly perverse and counterintuitive way, this member of New York's finest was contributing to the city's crime problem by confiscating illegal drugs from the addicts he was arresting and then using the contraband to *pay* the addict-informants who were in his employ to go out and *steal* for him.

In all, during a few weeks in the summer of 1971, under the supervision of a retired FBI agent named Ralph Cipriani, the commission recorded ten transactions where different police officers gave Tank and Slim illicit narcotics in return for various goods that the police officers believed had been stolen from some merchant or householder. All transactions were recorded on the body mikes worn by Tank and Slim. Many were filmed by commission surveillance cameras. In the same period, meetings involving twenty similar arrangements were scheduled but then not consummated because of various conflicts. "One scheduled sale was, according to the informants, postponed by the plainclothesman involved because he had to attend a Department anticorruption meeting."

Growing out of the Knapp Commission's far-reaching investigations, the New York Police Department mounted a sustained campaign to reduce corruption. Led by Police Commissioner Patrick V. Murphy, training methods were substantially changed, anticorruption forces were enlarged and police strategies for sensitive enforcement subjects such as drugs and gambling were revised. And the number of sergeants and lieutenants supervising patrol officers was substantially increased.

While these efforts resulted in a far more honest and effective police operation for two decades, a second commission found evidence in the early 1990s that at least some of New York's corruption problems had returned. A series of investigations in other cities, including New Orleans, Chicago, Miami, Washington, D.C., Los Angeles and many smaller places, has proven that significant corruption is yet another of

the almost inevitable undesired consequences of aggressive drug enforcement programs.

It would be nice to believe that the patterns of corruption found
within the drug units of police departments and sheriff's offices all over
the country were not a serious problem at the federal level. But this is
not the case. A few years ago, for example, a highly regarded former
DEA agent named Darnell Garcia was convicted of trafficking in drugs
and laundering at least $3 million of his profits through secret Swiss
bank accounts. The evidence at the trial showed that Garcia and two
other renegade agents had, for a long period in the 1980s, stolen cocaine, heroin and cash directly from dealers, traded in seized contraband and pilfered additional drugs from the DEA's evidence vault.[58]

Six months before, a DEA agent who had been a supervisor in the
agency's Los Angeles office was indicted for stealing a relatively small
amount of cash from a suspected cocaine trafficker. Eddie Hill, the DEA
supervisor, had been in charge of a special fifteen-agent unit that specialized in investigating Colombian and Mexican cocaine dealers.[59]

Michael Levine, for many years one of the DEA's most inventive and
successful undercover agents, quit the agency in disgust in 1989.
Levine, through direct experience, had become convinced that officials
in the Central Intelligence Agency, the State Department, the Justice
Department and the White House were betraying DEA investigators because efforts to jail some of the world's most powerful dealers appeared
to conflict with certain foreign policy goals of the United States.

Writing about his DEA career in 1991, Levine said he personally had
known many of his "colleagues who had gone bad and every one of
them was the last guy in the world you would have suspected. The past
decade has brought with it the worst epidemic of corruption in the history
of law enforcement—and almost all of it related to our war on drugs."[60]

Within the ranks of the DEA alone, Levine continued, "cases of 'misconduct' have increased during the past several years by a whopping
176 percent, 40 percent of which involve bribery, fraud, obstruction of
justice and the selling of drugs."

For many years, FBI Director J. Edgar Hoover and the men who followed him resisted efforts to engage the FBI in the war on drugs because
of their concern about the corruption potential. But in 1982, the Reagan
administration persuaded the FBI to change its policy, and the bureau
was given concurrent jurisdiction over federal drug laws with the DEA.

The FBI works very hard to keep the public from learning about its
corruption problems. But every once in a while an FBI official will let
down the bureau's guard. A few years ago, for example, one of the most
senior FBI officials attended a formal dinner where he ended up sitting
next to Patrick V. Murphy, the highly regarded former commissioner of
the New York Police Department. Because Murphy was known as the

police executive responsible for the largely successful anticorruption drive that followed the shocking disclosures of New York's Knapp Commission, the problem of maintaining the integrity of large enforcement institutions came up.

Murphy said the FBI official was genuinely disturbed. " 'I've been in the FBI a long time and I never thought it would come to this,' " Murphy recalled the senior official saying to him. " 'As we're sitting here tonight we have 12 to 14 active cases of corruption under investigation in the bureau.' "

DOES ANYONE REALLY CARE?

T he first two questions remain: Does the program work, does it achieve its stated goals? And does the program cause unacceptable side effects? But when a government program costs many billions of dollars a year, it is proper to ask a third question. On its own terms, has the program been reasonably well managed?

As noted elsewhere in this book, the nation's U.S. attorneys are the key players in the functioning of the federal criminal justice system. While the FBI or the DEA propose, it is the semi-autonomous U.S. attorneys who dispose. While the attorney general gives the national speeches and establishes the national guidelines, it is the U.S. attorneys who make most of the day-to-day decisions.

The spirited exercise of this discretion means that even in an enforcement area described as top priority by the last five attorneys general, there are vast regional differences in how the drug laws are executed. Some of these differences, which become visible through the analysis of case-by-case information originally collected by the Justice Department, appear to be entirely sensible. It is hardly surprising, for example, that federal prosecutors in Miami pay a great deal more attention to drug matters than do their counterparts in Boise, Idaho. Or that federal prosecutors in San Diego, a federal district on the U.S.–Mexico border, devote a substantial portion of their working hours to drug enforcement. This is a very large and varied country and it would be foolish to expect districts along the southern border of the United States to devote the same effort to drug enforcement as districts in other parts of the nation.

Nevertheless, some of the variations that have emerged from an analysis of Justice Department information are exceedingly curious. Perhaps as interesting as the specific details of the district-to-district variations are the broader questions these differences raise about the basic operations of the Justice Department. Given the goal of treating similarly situated citizens in similar ways, for example, should individual U.S. attorneys be granted what appears to be almost unchecked discretion in the prosecution of federal crimes? On the other hand, given

FEDERAL DRUG PROSECUTIONS 1984–1993
Most Active Districts

	RANK	% CRIMINAL DRUG CASES	DRUG CASES PER MILLION POP.	DRUG CASES PER FED. PROSECUTOR
West Virginia North (Wheeling)	1	56	104	9
West Virginia South (Charleston)	2	48	120	6
New York East (Brooklyn)	3	44	46	3
Maine (Portland)	4	43	44	4
Florida South (Miami)	5	43	102	3
Iowa North (Cedar Rapids)	6	42	34	4
Delaware (Wilmington)	7	38	51	4
Texas South (Houston)	8	37	104	8
Washington, D.C.	9	37	244	1
Florida North (Pensacola)	10	35	63	4
New Mexico (Albuquerque)	11	34	91	6

During the Reagan and Bush administrations the public became unusually alarmed about drugs and the attorneys general of the period claimed that drug enforcement was their top priority. The response of the frontline troops, however, was highly varied. Some districts with relatively small drug problems—including West Virginia North (Wheeling), West Virginia South (Charleston), Iowa North (Cedar Rapids) and Delaware (Wilming-

the obvious dangers of arbitrary and overly centralized enforcement, should the attorney general in Washington micromanage the activities of each U.S. attorney?

FEDERAL DRUG PROSECUTIONS 1984–1993
Least Active Districts

	RANK	% CRIMINAL DRUG CASES	DRUG CASES PER MILLION POP.	DRUG CASES PER FED. PROSECUTOR
California Central (Los Angeles)	80	14	10	1
California East (Sacramento)	81	14	15	2
Washington East (Spokane)	82	14	15	2
New Jersey (Newark)	83	14	6	1
California North (San Francisco)	84	12	12	1
Oklahoma East (Muskogee)	85	12	14	1
South Dakota (Sioux Falls)	86	11	33	2
Nevada (Las Vegas)	87	10	27	1
Tennessee Middle (Nashville)	88	10	15	2
Louisiana West (Shreveport)	89	8	9	1
Idaho (Boise)	90	7	8	1

---

ton)—*devoted a large proportion of their enforcement efforts to drugs. On the other hand, several districts which might be expected to have major drug problems—California Central (Los Angeles), New Jersey (Newark), Nevada (Las Vegas) and the middle district of Tennessee (Nashville)—appeared to pay relatively little attention to the problem.*
(TRAC analysis of Justice Department and Census Bureau data)

Here are a few of the particulars. Of all the cities in the United States, according to both the DEA and FBI, Miami and Los Angeles are among the four or five most active centers of big-time drug smuggling. Yet Justice Department data suggest that the federal prosecutors in these two cities have a different view of their responsibilities.

From 1984 to 1993, in the Southern District of Florida, 43 percent of all criminal cases involved drugs. There were 102 drug cases per million population or 4 cases for every assistant U.S. attorney. But in the Central District of California, Los Angeles, only 14 percent of the criminal cases brought from 1984 to 1993 involved drugs. That meant that in this California district there were 9.8 cases per million persons and 1.1 drug cases per federal prosecutor.

When questioned about such extensive variations, the less active prosecutors almost always claim that while the assistants in his or her office may indeed be bringing fewer cases, the cases that are brought are much more complex and important. Because the significance of individual cases is not easy to quantify, this usually silences the skeptics.

In this case, however, there is at least one indication that the kinds of cases brought by federal prosecutors in Miami and Los Angeles are not so different. In 1992, the United States Sentencing Commission calculated the proportion of drug cases in each district that involved a substantial amount of cocaine, heroin or marijuana. For both the Southern District of Florida and the Central District of California, the proportion of cases involving large amounts of drugs—55 percent—was almost exactly the same.

Let's look at another part of the country. Five different U.S. attorneys share the federal enforcement responsibilities along the northeastern border between the United States and Canada. In many ways, these districts are quite similar. None of them has a major U.S. city. None of them has a substantial minority population. All are quite rural.

Federal drug enforcement activities within these districts, however, are distinctly different. From 1984 to 1993, along the border from east to west, here is the number of cases brought in each of the districts per million people: Maine, 44; New Hampshire, 9; Vermont, 36; the Northern District of New York, 10; and the Western District of New York, 19.

Another curiosity. By almost all measures, Idaho ranked as the Justice Department's least active drug enforcement district. Given the nature of the state, this does not seem surprising. But right down there in the cellar with Idaho were three districts which common sense suggest should be very different: the Middle District of Tennessee (Nashville), the northern district of California (San Francisco) and Nevada.

Joseph Russoniello, the U.S. attorney in San Francisco during most of the 1980s, insisted that his drug enforcement effort was a serious one; it appeared small only because he left the street-level cases to the local prosecutors. While acknowledging that he had refused a DEA request to form a special controlled substance unit in his office, he denied that considerations of San Francisco's laid-back lifestyle and its dependence on tourists had in any way influenced his enforcement policies.[61] It is worth noting that the central cities in the Middle District of Tennessee and Nevada—Nashville and Las Vegas—are like San Francisco in their reliance on happy-go-lucky tourists as an important source of income.

Questions about the possibly dubious exercise of prosecutorial questions have been raised in other quarters. The U.S. attorney's office in Los Angeles, for example, has stated in court documents that it generally does not prosecute cases involving fifty grams or less of crack. In 1993, there were only five such convictions in this district. During the same period, federal prosecutors in the Southern District of West Virginia, a far less populous area, convicted eighty-nine individuals for trafficking in fifty grams or less of the drug.

Considered together, what generalizations do these variations allow? First, during a period when presidents and attorneys general were claiming a unified war on drugs, U.S. attorneys across the country were very definitely marching to their own drummers. Some were on the team; others were not. Second, while some of these variations appear to properly reflect differences in the enforcement environment, other variations suggest that certain offices may have been overzealous while still others may have been overly lax. Third, given the strenuous law and order rhetoric of the period and the wide variations in district enforcement priorities, it appears that the Justice Department in Washington had little control over its U.S. attorneys.

Behind these specific observations lies a larger point. The patterns and trends of federal drug enforcement during the last decade are based on information that the Justice Department has long collected. Although this information appears to raise obvious and important questions about the effectiveness and fairness of the war on drugs, the Justice Department, at least through 1994, never sought to develop the information in a statistically useful way. Did the attorneys general of the period not care how the government's massive and sometimes brutal war on drugs was functioning? Or did the attorneys general understand that simply knowing what the U.S. attorneys were doing might generate conflict with the senators who dominate the appointment of federal prosecutors?

THE GODFATHER

T here is no question that the father of America's modern war on crime was Richard Nixon. The honor of being the godfather of this quasi-religious crusade, however, must be given to Charles Henry Brent, a well-connected Episcopal bishop who, from 1901 to 1918, provided missionary services in the Philippines. Upon his arrival on the islands, Bishop Brent became concerned about opium. With the appointment to a commission on the opium problem and the publication of a highly moralistic report, Brent very quickly became a leader of a small but influential group of missionaries who became convinced that the answer to opium abuse was the criminal law. Their first success was a statute prohibiting the importation of opium to the islands.

Through his contacts with President Theodore Roosevelt, Brent then began lobbying for a world conference on opium. In 1906 the bishop was one of the three commissioners who represented the United States at an international convention on the subject in Shanghai.

"The original idea was that the opium traffic and habit as it existed in the Far East was to be investigated," said Dr. Hamilton Wright, in a study published in the *American Journal of International Law* in 1909. "But during the passage of the diplomatic correspondence it developed that the opium habit was no longer confined to Far Eastern countries, and that the United States especially had become contaminated through the presence of a large Chinese population."

A few weeks before the 1909 meeting in Shanghai, Congress rushed through the approval of the Opium Exclusion Act. Then, in 1914, three more antiopium bills were approved, the most important of which was the Harrison Act. It was this law that served as the original springboard for America's long-lived war on drugs, a campaign that from its earliest years has involved a unique reliance on criminal sanctions—arrest and incarceration—to suppress the use of culturally undesirable drugs.

Although the United States decided in 1933 to back away from a quite similar, religiously inspired, criminal enforcement campaign against alcohol, the drug problem to this day generates a blinding moral passion among substantial numbers of Americans and their representatives in Congress.

While growing numbers of experienced people challenge the wisdom of the American government's heavy reliance on criminal enforcement, the White House and Congress continue to call for more investigations, more arrests, more prosecutions and, in the end, longer prison sentences. In early 1995, for example, the Clinton administration's National Drug Control Strategy recommended that 64 percent of federal drug dollars be spent on supply reduction through the failed policies of interdiction and international and domestic enforcement, and 36 percent on demand reduction.[62]

What, then, do we know? We know there are some very ugly and dangerous people who deal in illicit drugs. We know it would be much better for the United States if these people, some of them pathological murderers, could be sent to prison. We know that, led by the Justice Department, the United States has spent many billions of dollars arresting substantial numbers of these people and seizing vast quantities of their drugs.

We also know that, because millions of Americans are willing to pay huge amounts of money for illegal drugs, new dealers immediately replace the old ones and new drug supplies almost instantly supplant the seized contraband. In a very important sense, the enforcement policies we have pursued have not worked. We further know that as a result of sloppy management, overzealousness and corruption, the war on drugs has resulted in a serious erosion of the basic rights originally promised in the Constitution.

Finally, we know that it is much easier to be critical than correct and that choosing the correct course, especially in a representative democracy, will be extremely difficult. Many smart people—Kurt Schmoke, the mayor of Baltimore and a former prosecutor and Rhodes Scholar; Patrick Murphy, the former New York City police commissioner; George Shultz, the former secretary of state; Daniel Patrick Moynihan, the Democratic senator from New York who once worked on drug problems for President Nixon; George Will, the newspaper columnist; Whitman Knapp, the former chairman of the New York City commission on police corruption who is now a federal judge; William F. Buckley, the publisher and television commentator; Joseph McNamara, the Hoover Institution fellow and former police executive; Milton Friedman, the Nobel laureate in economics; Max Frankel, the former executive editor of the *New York Times*; and Joseph A. Califano, the former secretary of health, education and welfare who now heads Columbia University's Center on Addiction and Substance Abuse—agree that the programs of the last quarter of a century have failed.

There is a good deal less consensus when it comes to deciding what should be done. Some critics support the legalization, the outright decriminalization of all drugs. A majority of the skeptics recommend less drastic reforms that would stop short of eliminating criminal sanctions against drug dealing but would still involve a massive change in emphasis.

"We now spend about two thirds of the nation's drug budget on the interdiction and enforcement side, on trying to use the criminal law to reduce the supply of drugs coming into the United States," said Murphy. "Most of the balance goes for various programs to reduce the demand for drugs. I think there is good evidence this proportion should now be turned around."

Like Murphy, Senator Moynihan opposes the legalization of drugs but believes that much could be accomplished with treatment and education programs aimed at reducing demand. Looking to history, he notes that in the first decades of the United States distilled whiskey became so widely used that it posed a serious risk to the society. "Laborers digging the Erie Canal were allotted a quart of Monongahela whiskey a day," he wrote.[63]

With a growing public awareness of the threat came the development of the temperance movement, which by the end of the nineteenth century had managed to reduce the per capita alcohol consumption by two thirds. But then, Moynihan observed, came America's experiment with Prohibition, "a convulsive event that, among other things, led to the creation of a criminal underworld of exceptional influence and durability."

Baltimore mayor Kurt Schmoke has become one of the most outspoken critics of the nation's current drug policies. From the beginning, he argued, the war on drugs was "doomed to failure—doomed not for lack of effort, money or good intentions (the latter still paving the road to hell), but because of the internal and inescapable contradictions posed by the war."[64]

Schmoke urges the United States to decriminalize drugs, not legalize them. Under his proposal, drugs "would not simply be made available to anyone who wants them, as is now the case with nicotine. Decriminalization is in effect 'medicalization,' a broad public health strategy—led by the surgeon general, not the attorney general—designed to reduce the harm caused by drugs by pulling addicts into the public health system."

Whether our current crop of political leaders can learn from history is not clear. The puritanical insistence that all sins must be punished, even when the punishment does not work, has always been one of the most powerful currents in American life. The political breadth of the challenge was described a few years ago by Dr. Herbert D. Kleber, a director of the Office of National Drug Control Policy during the Bush administration, in a private communication to Senator Moynihan.

"Funding for the treatment of substance abuse has been a bipartisan failure," the Kleber statement said.[65] "Our Republican President has requested substantially less money than is needed; and the Democratic Congress gave him only one third of what he asked for," Kleber declared, adding that essential federal drug research projects had also been seriously shortchanged. "Both government leaders and the general public," he concluded, "need to be made aware of the potential promise that can occur by adequately funding treatment and research, and of the many harms to society that will occur if it does not happen."

7

Corporate
Enforcement?

I n recent years, the war on white-collar crime has become an essential element in the rhetoric of attorneys general, both Republican and Democrat. Despite aggressive sniping by the corporate world, the politicos who run the department have felt compelled to talk up the government's avowed campaigns against medical fraud, bank fraud, official corruption and other such evils. Yes yes to the war on drugs. Yes yes to the war on violent crime. But yes yes also to going after corporate criminals.[1]

Surprisingly, this emphasis is quite new. The very concept of a class of people who were categorized as white-collar criminals—middle- and upper-class price-fixers, corporate swindlers, insider traders, big-time tax cheats, crooked real estate speculators—simply did not exist until just before the beginning of World War II, when the concept was conceived and the phrase coined by a famous sociologist named Edwin Sutherland.[2]

Until then, the word "criminal" was pretty much restricted to riffraff—the poor, the immigrants, the thugs, the gangsters and the pickpockets. Sutherland argued that although the police, the prosecutors and other enforcement agencies had never paid any systematic attention to white-collar crime, the unlawful actions of legitimate business posed a greater danger to America than all of its murderers, muggers, burglars and rapists.

Sutherland based his conclusion on an analysis of the criminal activities of seventy of the nation's largest corporations that he had pieced together from a careful study of the published decisions of federal and state judges and the findings of such regulatory bodies as the Securities and Exchange Commission. The financial cost of white-collar crime, he said, "is probably several times as great as the financial cost of all the crimes which are customarily regarded as the 'crime problem.' "[3]

Forty years later, a University of Wisconsin sociologist named Marshall B. Clinard and a small team of researchers completed a three-year, $248,000 study for the Justice Department on illegal corporate behavior and its cost to the American people. Clinard's analysis was the first systematic effort to follow up on Sutherland's groundbreaking work. Largely based on an examination of the criminal, civil and administrative charges brought against all of the 582 largest publicly owned corporations by twenty-four federal agencies during 1975 and 1976, Clinard concluded that Sutherland had it right. The economic losses suffered by consumers and government as a result of corporate crime, he said, dwarfed the losses taken from street crime victims by the nation's car thieves, burglars and robbers. As for physical hazards, the sociologist found that "far more persons are killed through corporate criminal activities than by individual criminal homicides. . . ."[4]

Exact comparisons, however, remain difficult. From detailed information provided by local medical examiners, it is known that just under 15,000 persons were murdered in the United States in 1992. No such precise victim counts exist for other kinds of traditional street crime. But from the responses of a sample of 50,000 Americans to a national survey of crime victims, government experts estimate that during the same time period, 1992, about 257,000 men, women and children were injured while they were being robbed. Using the same survey technique, the experts calculated that 173,000 women were victims of rape.[5]

Sample surveys and medical examiners, however, aren't very helpful when it comes to counting the victims of white-collar crimes. One problem is that the cause of death in most white-collar-crime situations is nowhere as clear as a bullet hole or knife wound. A second problem is that the victims of white-collar crime are often unaware of their special status and how they achieved it. Individual lung cancer patients, for example, are almost never able to determine whether their disease was caused by the polluted air in the factory where they worked, their addiction to tobacco, their genetic makeup or a combination of these factors. Furthermore, because cancers typically take decades to develop, the victims may have no recollection of which conditions triggered their tumors.

What can be determined, however—thanks in part to the pioneering studies of Sutherland and Clinard—is that, over the years, thousands of corporations have knowingly sold defective, life-threatening products including automobiles, heart valves, home appliances and foods and drugs to millions of consumers. What can be determined is that, over the years, corporations have knowingly exposed their workers to job hazards that have caused millions of serious injuries and deaths. What can be determined is that, over the years, corporations have knowingly operated their factories, their chemical processing plants and their reactors in ways that shortened the life spans of the millions of Americans who breathed the air or drank the water polluted by these facilities. These corporations, of course, were managed by executives who, assuming their individual knowledge, were all white-collar criminals.

THE LAW AND WHITE-COLLAR CRIME

In 1215, under pressure from the great barons of England, King John signed the Magna Carta. Although primarily celebrated for establishing the concept of due process, the Magna Carta also included language regarded as one of the earliest consumer protection laws: a provision establishing a uniform measure for the sale of ale, wine and corn. In 1630, according to the records of the Massachusetts Bay Colony, a certain Nicholas Knopf was sentenced to pay a fine or be whipped for selling "a water of no worth nor value" as a cure for scurvy. A century and a half later, in 1785, Massachusetts passed the first general law in the United States making it a crime to sell "corrupted, contagious or unwholesome provisions." In 1906, Congress approved and President Theodore Roosevelt signed the original Food and Drug Act prohibiting the interstate shipment of misbranded and adulterated foods, drinks and drugs.[6]

Thus, as a matter of law, Sutherland's powerful concept of the white-collar criminal has an extremely long history. But it was the rapid expansion of federal regulatory powers beginning with Franklin Delano Roosevelt's New Deal that demonstrated the broad political appeal behind the vision that the federal government had an affirmative responsibility to deal with the corporate criminal in America. With the passage of dozens of additional economic, health, safety and environmental laws during the 1960s and 1970s, the theoretical reach of the federal government became truly formidable.

Absolutely in the middle of this massive tangle of law and rhetoric is the Justice Department. For while Congress during the last hundred years or so was busily creating a series of specialized regulatory agencies such as the Food and Drug Administration, the Environmental Protection Agency and the Occupational Safety and Health Administration, it determined that one central enforcement power would be retained by the attorney general and the individual U.S. attorneys. And that power is: the authority to bring, or not to bring, criminal and civil actions against the white-collar violators who were selling fraudulent medical devices in Indiana or polluting the Chesapeake Bay or looting a savings and loan bank in Texas.

Regulatory agencies like the Nuclear Regulatory Commission and the National Highway Traffic Safety Administration can be important to the health and safety of the American people because they have the authority to set national standards and impose administrative penalties upon those who violate them. But with only a few exceptions, when a utility or one of the big three auto manufacturers is thought to have violated the law in a major way, the Justice Department is the controlling agency. No criminal charges can be brought against a business executive, no civil suits filed against a corporation, without the approval of the attorney general or a U.S. attorney. For good or evil, the department serves as the clearinghouse—more frequently stumbling block—for almost all federal litigation.

Given the physical and economic havoc that white-collar criminals each day impose on the American people, given the truly vast numbers of federal laws that are now on the books to control various kinds of white-collar crime and given the Justice Department's rhetoric about its war on white-collar crime, the federal government has woefully failed to meet the authentic demands of this challenge. As a result of unacknowledged class biases, outright political deals, poorly drafted laws and incompetent investigators, the Justice Department itself could be convicted of fraud when it comes to white-collar crime.

BLOOD MONEY

Every year, dishonest doctors, crooked health-care providers and a variety of other big-time con artists are believed to siphon off $3 to $10 out of every $100 you spend for medical care. Because the nation's annual overall medical bill is so large—about $1 trillion—the part being extracted for fraudulent purposes in a single year is breathtaking: at least $30 billion, perhaps as much as $100 billion.[7]

With the right enforcement activities and bookkeeping procedures, of course, a significant part of the billions of dollars now flowing into the bank accounts of the crooks could be poured into more worthy purposes, such as the funding of vitally needed inner-city clinics, national vaccination projects or additional AIDS research.

In many ways, however, the billions of dollars lost each year to fraud is not the important story—after all, it's only money. The true outrage of medical fraud lies in the disabling pain and death that come to thousands, perhaps tens of thousands of Americans every year at the hands of the white-collar medical criminals.

The horror stories are compelling. In Indianapolis, for example, an aggressive entrepreneur named Michael Walton was in the business of selling faulty pacemakers, some of which had been "explanted" from patients, to doctors and hospitals who then would "implant" the defective devices in new patients. All in all, between 1984 and 1990, Walton presented fraudulent bills totaling $1.2 million for the faulty equipment and about 150 of the items were actually implanted in patients. Although no deaths are known to have resulted, problems with Walton's equipment forced numerous patients to undergo additional surgery.[8]

In Baltimore, a physician named Mark Davis operated the Popular Manor Nursing Home. To maximize his profits, Davis did not provide his patients with the most basic kinds of medical care. As a result, Davis was able to steal about $100,000 in Medicaid and Medicare funds. Because of Davis's actions, some of the elderly residents in his nursing home developed serious bedsores, dehydration, severe malnutrition, kidney failure and, in a few situations, loss of limbs.[9]

Medical fraud—the billions of dollars of illicit gains, the pain and suffering and death of tens of thousands of Americans—has been a national concern for at least twenty years. Since the early 1970s, experts in Congress's General Accounting Office, executives of some major insurance companies and the attorneys general in several of the larger states have recognized that the United States was confronted by a large and growing crisis. Because Medicaid and Medicare dollars made up such a significant portion of the nation's medical expenditures, it was clear to many that medical fraud should have long been a central concern of the federal government.

It was not until 1992, however, that the Justice Department began to see the light. As is often the case in Washington, the first signal was a self-serving press release in which Attorney General Barr announced what he called "a major initiative against health care fraud." But the new national effort, it turned out, was downright anemic. In Washington, with all the huffing and puffing, a grand total of six attorneys were assigned to a new health-care fraud unit within the Justice Department's criminal division. At the FBI, fifty agents specializing in foreign counterintelligence and domestic terrorism were "reprogrammed" to the health-care initiative. Across the United States, in twelve federal districts where the problem seemed unusually serious, one hundred assistant U.S. attorneys were assigned to "criminal and civil health care matters."[10]

To grasp the thoroughly puny nature of Barr's "major initiative" against medical fraud, it is necessary to comprehend the size and complexity of the health-care system that gives the crooks so much room to maneuver. According to the General Accounting Office, the basic numbers look like this: Approximately 210 million Americans are now covered by some kind of health insurance. During a recent year, they received a huge range of services from about one million "medical providers"—534,200 physicians, 157,800 pharmacists, 142,000 dentists, 16,000 nursing homes, 6,400 hospitals and a never-counted number of entrepreneurs who sell or rent wheelchairs, walkers, oxygen and other kinds of equipment.

To pay for all these services, the providers generated about 4 billion claims that they sent to "processors"—the state agencies, employers, commercial insurers and other third-party administrators responsible for sorting out all the claims and passing them on to the "insurers." (Some claims processors also are insurers.) The insurers include "private payers" like the 33 Blue Cross and Blue Shield plans and the 1,250 commercial insurance companies as well as the "public payers" like Medicare, Medicaid and the Veterans Administration. Finally, the insurers send off their checks, a substantial number of which are paying for fraudulent claims.[11]

In its February 1992 flurry of press releases and special reports on the problem, the Justice Department poured on rhetorical steam. "Health care fraud hits hard at the poor, the injured and the innocent and the federal enforcement agencies are going to hit back even harder at these unscrupulous predators, whether businessmen who steal insurance premiums or professionals in white coats who do not deliver the quality of care they promised and got paid for. Through vigorous enforcement, we hope to punish wrong doers and deter health care fraud."

The windy claims of Attorney General Barr and the Justice Department promised much. But when the resources he committed—six more lawyers in Washington, fifty more FBI agents and one hundred more assistant U.S. attorneys—are compared with the hulking target, the attorney general's promise to confront medical fraud seems only a feeble wheeze.

The negative judgment on Barr's promise to mount a serious effort against medical fraud is reinforced by an examination of data summarizing the Justice Department's enforcement activities during the last ten years. This analysis shows that cases the department itself classified as involving white-collar crime did, in fact, undergo a modest increase: 9,016 in 1984 compared with 12,837 in 1993. During the same period, however, the data indicate that the Justice Department more than doubled its drug enforcement activities. In 1984, federal prosecutors brought 10,433 narcotics cases, in 1993 there were 23,984. Talk, of course, is cheap; the investigation and prosecution of real cases is not. In comparative terms, the records show that Barr's Justice Department was far more concerned about drug violators than about white-collar criminals.

This judgment becomes even stronger when drug and white-collar-crime cases for the period are examined in relation to the number of assistant U.S. attorneys employed by the Justice Department. For drugs, the cases handled per prosecutor were sharply up: 4.7 in 1984 compared with 6.1 in 1993. For white-collar crime, the trend was exactly the opposite: 4.1 in 1984 and 3.3 in 1993.[12]

No one believes that prosecuting white-collar criminals is easy. But given the plethora of federal laws in the area, the relative sophistication of federal investigators and other considerations, the declining proportion of Justice Department resources committed to corporate lawbreakers seems to be a highly questionable, probably partisan, decision.

THE BIGGER PICTURE

Medical fraud, of course, is just one category of white-collar crime where the Justice Department's commitment seems to have been a hoax. During the late 1970s and early 1980s, for example, the owners and senior managers of a few hundred banks and savings and loan institutions—such as Penn Square, United American Bank and Empire Savings and Loan—engaged in tens of thousands of fraudulent acts that allowed them to loot their institutions of billions of dollars. Although the Justice Department eventually managed to obtain evidence leading

to the indictment of a number of these bankers, questions remain about
why it took U.S. attorneys around the country so long to get going and
whether, in the end, too many of the bad guys were allowed to escape
criminal sanctions.[13]

After a single financial brokerage house, E. F. Hutton, pleaded guilty
to more than 2,000 counts of mail and wire fraud that cost its customers, its banks and the Federal Reserve Bank as much as $256 mil-
lion, the company was required to pay a $2 million fine. The Justice
Department, however, somehow failed to bring criminal charges
against a single one of the company's executives who had devised and
implemented the illegal scheme.[14] How was this possible?

Going back as far as 1983, the Justice Department and other federal
agencies began receiving tips that the Bank of Credit and Commerce International, better known as BCCI, was a gigantic scam. But it wasn't
until 1988 that the first BCCI indictment was handed down in Tampa
and 1991 that the Justice Department managed to organize a coordinated national investigation of the massive bank fraud. Why did it take
the Justice Department so long to pick up on the information it was receiving from its own agents?[15]

Clinard's 1979 study indicates that the federal government's casual
attitude toward big-time corporate crime in the 1980s and 1990s was
not a new development. Although over 40 percent of the corporations
he studied were found to be repeat offenders, "few members of corporate management ever go to prison even if convicted; generally they are
placed on probation. If they do go to prison, it is almost always for a
very short period of time [2.8 days]. For crimes committed by the large
corporations, the sole punishment often consists of warnings, consent
decrees [under which the accused agrees not to do thereafter what the
executive doesn't admit doing in the past], or comparatively small
fines."[16]

Brave-sounding promises about the government's all-out war against
white-collar criminals have been made by a lengthy string of attorneys
general: Carter's Griffin Bell and Benjamin Civiletti made them; so did
Reagan's William French Smith and Edwin Meese and Bush's Dick
Thornburgh and William Barr. Yet despite the repeated assurances that
the war is a genuine one, the pledges ring hollow. Even a cursory examination of the Justice Department's recent record uncovers weak-kneed,
politics-ridden enforcement activities that almost always concentrate
on the small fish while allowing the big ones to get away.

THE POWER OF CLASS, CORRUPTION AND POLITICS

T he hard question is why? How does it come to pass that an agency with the power and investigative resources of the Justice Department so regularly strikes out? We all know that the police officer on the beat can only act on a small percentage of crimes that occur in his neighborhood. We all know the same is true for the Justice Department. But why is it that the department and the FBI, despite the presence of many well-intentioned lawyers and investigators, do not even come close to achieving their stated goals?

Long before white-collar crime became a must subject for inclusion in Justice Department statements and press releases, long before Sutherland invented the term, long before Congress and the courts vastly expanded the reach of federal enforcement efforts, corporate criminals had developed a series of strategies designed to prevent federal prosecutors from doing anything so unpleasant as charging them with a criminal offense. Many of these strategies were and are completely legal, even enjoying the blessing of the Constitution. Others were not. The record suggests, however, that the white-collar criminal's best approach has always been the straightforward one of persuading the Justice Department that white is black, that hot is cold, that despite all the evidence to the contrary, no crime has been committed. Perhaps the single best reason this technique has proven so effective is that the men and women appointed to the thousands of influential patronage jobs in the Justice Department, usually through the intervention of their senator, almost always come from the same social circles as the white-collar criminal. The resulting class solidarity has always been helpful for two obvious reasons. First, the similar experiences and values of the business executives and the Justice Department lawyers means that the two groups quite frequently agree as to how society should function, especially on the critical issue of crime and punishment. Second, because the individuals involved often share the same language, have gone to the same colleges, belonged to the same clubs, worked in the same law firms or have mutual friends, businesspeople engaged in white-collar crime are perfectly positioned to persistently, informally and secretly influence the thinking of those who will decide whether they should be prosecuted. The actual victims, of course, almost never know about these informal preindictment contacts and seldom get a chance to respond.

From time to time, however, the quiet little talks are not successful and less agreeable methods are required, such as the payment of bribes. Sometimes the illicit payments have gone directly into the pocket of the Justice Department official who delivered the favor. More frequently the payments for halting an investigation or bending the law in some other way have gone to the political party then in control of the Justice Department through the White House.

While the long, echoing halls of Justice have thus certainly provided the backdrop for the old-fashioned out-and-out bribe, both direct and indirect, such blatant transactions do not seem to be an everyday event, mainly because they violate the upright image that many lawyers have of themselves and their profession. That is why, as we shall see, more subtle arrangements, some just as crooked as the straightforward bribe, are worked out by the offending parties.

Every year, a large number of young Justice Department lawyers join private law firms after having honed their legal skills as government prosecutors. Because the negotiations that precede their departure are private, the underlying ethical questions of these understandings are among the most difficult to explore and document. I am willing to grant that a substantial number of the arrangements are aboveboard. The possibility of less edifying agreements, however, is very real. The individual prosecutor in charge of a specific business case, for example, is informed by the target company's law firm that a high-paying job is a real possibility when he or she leaves the Justice Department. On many occasions, no doubt, the Justice Department lawyer brushes aside the flattering offer. On many occasions, no doubt, the job offer is not explicitly linked to a specific favor, and the quid pro quo remains an unstated and totally deniable understanding. But on too many occasions, a deal, either implicit or explicit, is cut and the law firm's goal of maximum leniency for the client has been discreetly achieved.

Outright or indirect understandings, however, explain only some of the Justice Department's persistently flawed efforts to control corporate crime. The United States is a giant country with a giant economy that presents gigantic opportunities for corporate fraud. In comparison to the substantial dimensions of the white-collar-crime problem, the federal enforcement personnel available to fight it are few. This is not necessarily to argue that it would be desirable for Congress to quadruple the size of the Justice Department, but only to note that the hundreds of overreaching laws favored by Congress have created a vast disparity between the enforcers and the enforcees, and that this disparity requires federal prosecutors, willy-nilly, to ignore thousands of true violations of law. So, to the extent that white-collar crime is allowed to flourish in the United States with relatively little fear of punishment, one important explanation is that nowhere near enough investigators and prosecutors are available to probe all the hidden nooks and crannies where the white-collar criminals wait to pounce on their innocent victims.

Another confounding force that should be kept in mind is that the Justice Department, like many large bureaucracies, is so poorly managed that it has great trouble locating sufficient evidence to make corporate cases, especially when the law is complex and the suspect has almost unlimited resources to hire aggressive defense attorneys. In other words, corrupt conspiracies are frequently not the determining force. Often the culprit is incompetence.

An unlikely but convincing proponent of this view is Peter Stockton, a brilliant and energetic investigator who, for the last two decades, has specialized in uncovering evidence of Justice Department failures large and small for a number of congressional committees. "I know we have detected a good number of cases involving genuinely corrupt failures in the Justice Department," he said. "But after too many years in this business, I have come to understand that in many cases, especially the very big and important ones, the Justice Department is in fact undermanned and underminded."[17]

This point was reinforced by an experienced Justice Department lawyer who over the years has brought a substantial number of cases against corporate executives. "There are some wonderful exceptions, but you would be amazed by the number of FBI agents who are either unwilling or unable to read a business document during the course of an investigation. This problem is truly maddening."

FRIENDS IN HIGH PLACES

As noted above, there are incidences of out-and-out bribery in the Justice Department. One of the most flagrant ever to become known involved a lawyer named T. Lamar Caudle. On June 15, 1956, Caudle was found guilty of accepting oil royalties worth many thousands of dollars from the lawyer of a St. Louis shoe manufacturer named Irving Sachs. The lawyer wanted Caudle to help his client avoid being charged with criminal tax fraud. At the time the bribe was paid, Caudle was among the highest officials in the Justice Department, the assistant attorney general in charge of the Tax Division. Four years before Caudle's conviction, President Truman fired him for engaging in unspecified outside activities that the White House said were "incompatible with the duties of his office." A few months after his conviction, still protesting his innocence, the former assistant attorney general was sentenced to two years in prison and fined $2,500.[18]

A payoff, however, does not have to go directly into the pockets of the corrupt official to be considered a bribe. In early 1971, Harold S. Geneen, then the president of ITT, agreed to provide the Nixon team with a large campaign contribution to help support the 1972 Republican convention, which the president hoped to stage in San Diego. The promised contribution was offered at the same time that ITT and the Justice Department were engaged in complex negotiations over whether the giant corporation had violated the antitrust laws. According to a later memo about the contribution, written by ITT lobbyist Dita A. Beard, the Washington office of the corporation was convinced "our noble commitment has gone a long way toward our negotiations on the mergers coming out as Hal [Geneen] wants them." Certainly, she concluded, "the President [Nixon] has told [Attorney General John] Mitchell to see things come out fairly."

Although there was some dispute later about the precise dollar amount of ITT's noble commitment—whether the original offer was for $400,000 or $200,000—there is no question that Nixon intervened on behalf of the corporation. During a conversation with John Ehrlichman, captured by the White House taping system on April 19, 1971, Nixon displayed his delicate way with words and his usual deep concern for the underlying issues. "I don't know whether ITT is bad, good or indifferent," he said. "But there is not going to be any more antitrust actions as long as I am in this chair . . . goddamn it, we're going to stop it."

Shortly after Nixon's elegant pronouncement, the president telephoned Deputy Attorney General Richard Kleindienst, the senior Justice Department official then supervising the negotiations. The man handling the day-to-day talks was Richard McClaren, the assistant attorney general for antitrust matters. "I want something understood, and if it is not understood McClaren's ass is out within an hour," Nixon told Kleindienst. "The ITT thing—stay the hell out of it. Is that clear? That's an order."

Kleindienst apparently was so startled by Nixon's call that he started to ask the president exactly what he meant. Nixon interrupted him. "The order is to leave the goddamn thing alone . . . I do not want McClaren to run around prosecuting people, raising hell about conglomerates, stirring things up at this point. Now you keep him the hell out of there. Is that clear?"

Nixon's improper intervention in the Justice Department's handling of the ITT case, and the subsequent false testimony about the matter by both Kleindienst and Mitchell, eventually became one of the specific cases cited by the House Judiciary Committee in support of its 1974 resolution to impeach the president.[19]

By any measure, the House committee's impeachment vote must be considered a uniquely powerful lesson, so powerful in fact that it would deter future presidents from helping corporate political supporters when they got in trouble with the Justice Department. Is it possible that the import of such a lesson would be missed? Perhaps.

Almost twenty years after President Nixon intervened on behalf of a major corporate political supporter, the Justice Department granted a reprieve to another giant corporation, raising suspicions that the ghost of ITT had returned—this time to haunt the Bush administration. The new case began in February 1988 when Gary Gilman, an accountant for Georgia Power, approached the Internal Revenue Service and claimed that the giant utility and its parent, Southern Services, were apparently involved in a massive fraud that had allowed them to avoid paying at least $50 million in taxes. Gilman agreed to become an undercover agent for the IRS, secretly taping hours of incriminating conversations with several company officials. According to an affidavit subsequently filed by IRS Special Agent Arthur McGovern, the companies had improperly written off some $61 million in spare parts, creating a special "off the books" accounting system to hide this fact from the IRS. "I mean, if the IRS comes in . . . you're dead," one middle-level official told Gilman in a secretly recorded conversation.

On the basis of the conversations and other evidence, the IRS and the office of the U.S. attorney in Atlanta began the painstaking job of bringing a criminal tax case. More than five hundred subpoenas were issued and approximately two hundred witnesses were called to testify before a grand jury. Although the process was not easy—corporate lawyers fought them every step of the way—Special Agent McGovern persevered. Sometime in late 1989, after winning the final approval of his IRS supervisors and most of the intermediary bosses in the Justice Department, the case reached the office of a high level political appointee, Shirley Peterson, the assistant attorney general in charge of the Tax Division. The time had come for the final "go" or "no-go" decision.

Peterson's ruling shocked most of those who had been working on the case. On May 25, 1990, she decided the Justice Department would not bring criminal tax charges against the utility and its holding company. The last-minute escape from criminal prosecution was unusual for several reasons. First, department officials admit that only a handful of criminal tax cases ever get rejected at the political level after they have successfully negotiated the torturous preliminary reviews required by the regulations of both the Justice Department and the IRS. In an interview with Jeffrey Denny of *Common Cause Magazine*, for example, Stanley Krysa, a thirty-five-year department veteran who heads the Tax Division's criminal enforcement section, acknowledged that over the years only 6 to 10 percent of such cases ever were declined.[20]

Even more curious was the fact that a senior executive of the utility, just as in the ITT affair, had made an extremely large campaign contribution to the administration whose Justice Department would provide him comfort. In 1988, a few months after Gilman had approached the IRS with his accusations, Edward L. Addison, the CEO of the Southern Company, joined a select number of other big-dollar donors and became a member of "Team 100." Addison achieved this status by contributing $105,000 in "soft dollars" to the Republican National Committee. George Bush was then running for president and the millions of dollars contributed by Team 100 members were passed on to state party politicos with instructions to use the funds to help the presidential campaign in their areas.

Ultimately, 248 other wealthy individuals joined Addison in coughing up at least $100,000 each to the special Bush campaign fund.

There is no question the Team 100 donors obtained easy access to the White House, Vice President Dan Quayle, White House counsel C. Boyden Gray and the various federal regulatory agencies in return for their generous campaign contributions. There is no question Addison was among those who enjoyed some of these perks.

But there is no specific evidence proving that Addison's $105,000 campaign contribution in 1988 in any way contributed to Peterson's 1990 decision to reject the advice of all her Justice Department colleagues on the merits of the criminal case against the Southern Co. It should be remembered, however, that the curious circumstances of the Bush administration's handling of this particular case never underwent the kind of intense investigation by congressional Democrats that ultimately led to the forced resignation of Richard Nixon.

All sides deny that the massive political donation had any influence on the failure to bring the tax case. In an April 23, 1992, letter to *Common Cause*'s Jeffrey Denny, Peterson said that privacy laws prevented her from commenting on any individual case. "I will state categorically that neither the White House nor any party's political affiliation affected any decision made by me during my time in the Department. I assure you that, during my tenure as Assistant Attorney General in charge of the Tax Division, all cases with which I was involved were handled in accordance to regular Tax Division procedures." Blanket denials also have come from the company.

A final interesting aspect of the 1990 case, however, concerns Peterson, the political appointee who made the unilateral decision to drop the criminal charges against the politically well-connected company. In January 1992, President George Bush selected Peterson for an important new job, the career-enhancing position of Commissioner of the Internal Revenue Service.

AT&T HITS THE BELL

The variety of goodies available to those who can gain entry to the Justice Department's candy store seems almost endless. On January 14, 1949, after a four-year investigation, the Justice Department filed a complaint charging that AT&T and its manufacturing subsidiary, Western Electric, had for many years engaged in a gigantic, billion-dollar-a-year price-fixing conspiracy in the manufacture, leasing and sale of telephones and telephone equipment. Attorney General Thomas C. Clark, a Truman Democrat, citing various provisions of the antitrust law, demanded that AT&T sell Western Electric and that its operating companies start buying telephone equipment only under competitive bidding.

Because of the vast size of Ma Bell—it was then the world's largest and most powerful corporation—this was a truly momentous case.

Although the government's arguments were convincing, AT&T mounted a no-holds-barred campaign against the Justice Department complaint. One prong of the attack involved persuading a gaggle of high Defense Department officials to oppose the divestiture of Western Electric on national security grounds. On March 20, 1952, for example, Defense Secretary Robert A. Lovett wrote the attorney general requesting postponement of the antitrust suit until the Korean emergency was over. Lovett's letter, and many others like it, were either drafted or cleared by AT&T, one of the nation's largest defense contractors.[21] While the officials were perfectly willing to carry AT&T's water, House investigators later found that not one of them had made an independent investigation to determine whether the suit would do any of the damages claimed by the telephone company.

On January 24, 1956, Attorney General Herbert Brownell, Jr., the leading Republican Party political strategist before his appointment by President Eisenhower, announced the case had been settled. The attorney general claimed the agreement was a major victory for the government. Brownell's claim was false. In fact, a line-by-line examination of the actual document shows that very little of the relief requested by the government in the 1949 complaint was obtained. The settlement's biggest single shortcoming was that it did not require AT&T to sell Western Electric.[22]

What had happened? How had the Justice Department's initial effort to end AT&T's stranglehold on the communication lines of America been short-circuited? Three years after Brownell's settlement, the Antitrust Subcommittee of the House Judiciary Committee began to investigate. The Justice Department, in its usual way, made a major effort to block the probe, finally refusing to provide the subcommittee any of the underlying documents in the case. But AT&T, apparently more fearful of the House investigators than of the Justice Department, did not have the heart for this kind of hard-ball approach and eventually provided the subcommittee thousands of documents.

The records showed that throughout the lengthy negotiations between the telephone company and the government, the staff-level lawyers in the Justice Department had largely rejected the arguments put forward by AT&T and its allies in the Defense Department, contending that if the company would not agree to sell Western Electric, then the case should be brought to trial where a judge and jury would consider the legal issues.

In the middle of the negotiations, however, on June 27, 1953, sitting on the porch of a cottage on the grounds of the luxurious Greenbrier Hotel in White Sulphur Springs, West Virginia, Brownell had a twenty-five-minute chat with T. Brooke Price, the telephone company's vice president and general counsel. Brownell wanted to cut a deal.

According to Price's subsequent memorandum about his secret meeting with the chief law enforcement official in the United States, the attorney general said he "wanted to get rid of this case." Outside the presence of all his legal experts, Price reported, Brownell added that he was sure the way to achieve this goal was for AT&T to sign a consent decree with the government in which certain practices would be enjoined which would cause "no real injury to AT&T's business."[23]

At a subsequent House hearing about the meeting, Price said he got the impression from his conversation with Brownell that the attorney general did not know very much about the details of the complex dispute. All Brownell did, the company lawyer testified, was give AT&T "a little friendly tip as to how we might approach them [the Justice Department] to get something started in the way of a negotiation."

Even with the "little friendly tip" from the department's top man, working out the details of the final consent decree still required two and a half years to negotiate, partly because the permanent Justice Department staff did not agree with Brownell and his political assistants about how the case should be handled.

This fundamental split was highlighted when Edward A. Foote, a young political appointee whom Brownell had brought in to supervise the complex negotiations with the telephone company, followed the attorney general's lead and arranged his own little secret meeting with T. Brooke Price. Again according to the company documents and later testimony, the second private meeting took place in the course of an informal dinner at the Foote family's Washington home on a cold winter night in early 1955. Price once again made some notes. Foote told Price that the Justice Department complaint against AT&T "was a monstrosity, it was badly drawn, it was full of perfect absurdities, and you could not go to trial on that kind of complaint."[24]

Foote's indiscreet comments to Price, which probably violated the American Bar Association's code of ethics, worked to undermine the Justice Department. The remarks also contradicted the views of the three staff attorneys then working on the case who, between them, had more than thirty years of experience in the business of enforcing the nation's antitrust laws. In his subsequent appearance before the House subcommittee, Foote acknowledged as much when he testified that no member of the Justice Department staff "assigned to work on the case or getting the case ready for trial . . . was in favor of settlement without divorcement of Western."[25]

Perhaps the best indication that the final settlement was a gigantic Justice Department giveaway to AT&T comes from the mouth of F. R. Kappel, who was then the president of Western Electric. Talking to a group of Western Electric executives on the day the agreement was reached, Kappel gave them secret instructions as to the spin he wanted to put on the agreement.

According to the shorthand notes of one of the sales managers who attended this meeting, Kappel said: "Use discretion in passing along. Don't brag about having won victory or getting everything we wanted."[26]

Despite the tenacious ability of business to persuade the Justice Department to give corporate criminals a break—as illuminated by ITT, Georgia Power, AT&T and many examples yet to come—it obviously would be unfair and untrue to say that the Justice Department always collapses when it hears from a complaining business executive.

TEDDY TRIES TO TAKE A DIVE

One fascinating story that illuminates such a failed corporate attempt began on August 8, 1908. That was the day that A. J. Fowler, an assistant attorney general, dispatched a confidential letter to the Alphaduct Company of Jersey City, New Jersey, asking the company to provide him with information about the patents and commercial agreements it had obtained or entered into concerning the manufacture of a product described as a "non-metallic flexible conduit." Although Fowler's letter did not say so, the inquiry was part of a much broader

Justice Department investigation of price-fixing by a large number of companies then in the electrical supply business.[27]

Within a very short time span, perhaps in less than a day, a copy of Fowler's inquiry somehow reached the influential hands of W. L. Ward, the Republican national committeeman of New York. Ward instantly fired off a complaining note about the Justice Department inquiry to President Theodore Roosevelt, the man ultimately in charge of both the Justice Department and the Republican Party. Ward, observing that the national political campaign was not running "very smoothly," was extremely unhappy about the Justice Department investigation. The inquiry, he said bitterly, "appears to me to be nothing more nor less than a dragnet plan put out for the purpose of getting hold of some agreement that will make a basis for prosecution. It does seem to me that it is most important that there should be nothing of this kind done for the present."

Theodore Roosevelt, who the newspapers of the day occasionally referred to as a "trust buster," did not take Ward's complaint lightly, perhaps because the Republican committeeman had characterized the investigation as a "dragnet," perhaps because of his own political calculations. In fact, within a matter of only a few hours, the president responded to Ward's letter by dispatching his own message to Charles Bonaparte, his attorney general. Roosevelt's letter shows that the president was only interested in the politics of the case. The possible price-fixing that had triggered the investigation of the electrical equipment business was of very little concern. "I do not know anything about the matter," Roosevelt said, "but of course I feel very strongly that the less activity there is during the Presidential election, unless it is necessary, the better it will be."

The entire transaction, from the mailing of Fowler's initial query on August 8 to the dispatch of Roosevelt's slightly hedged request for the immediate suspension of a Justice Department antitrust investigation, had taken only four days. It is hard to say whether the speed of this particular round-robin should be regarded as a tribute to the influence of this particular industry or to a harder working postal service.

Bonaparte, who then was vacationing in a resort hotel in western Massachusetts, responded to Roosevelt's request on August 14. The attorney general, an elegant Baltimorean and the grand nephew of the second emperor bearing his name, was not at all cowed by his president. He began by asserting the propriety of the investigation, stating that it was being made in a very thorough and quiet way "under instructions to obtain no indictments until the facts are fully understood and such action has been duly authorized by me." Then Bonaparte defended his investigation with a tactically elegant appeal to Roosevelt's own political interests, namely the president's image as an independent fighter against the special interests.

"I may be unduly nervous on this subject," Bonaparte warned, "but it seems to me that the danger to be guarded against in this campaign is any appearance of solidarity with the trusts." The problem, he said, was that intervention by people "like Mr. Ward, who are connected with the management of the Republican campaign, in matters of this description may be called to the attention of the hostile press."

Although the secret intervention on behalf of the electrical companies by Ward and several other political figures continued, and indeed may have slowed the processing of the case, the investigation was not scuttled. In fact, on March 3, 1911, with Taft now in the White House, the Justice Department filed a suit against General Electric, Westinghouse and thirty-two other companies for working in combination to control the market for electric lightbulbs.[28]

In this particular situation, it appears, a smart, tough and honorable attorney general successfully resisted the efforts of the politicians of his own party, working through the authority of his own president, and moved to enforce the nation's price-fixing laws against a large number of powerful companies who were indeed fixing prices.

Sadly, however, the brave resistance of Charles Bonaparte to uninformed political pressure has not always served as the behavioral model for those who subsequently held the hundreds of influential political positions in the Justice Department.

SAFE FOOD AND DRUGS?

T ax and antitrust disputes, even massive ones involving powerful institutions like AT&T, sometimes seem a bit abstract. At first blush it appears that the only thing at stake is money. Yes, billions of dollars are involved. But because the economic costs inherent in such cases usually get spread out over millions of individual consumers and over many years, each separate bite is so small that it is politically invisible.

But when a Justice Department enforcement decision concerns the life and well-being of both you and your children, and millions of other people all over the globe, the stakes are far higher.

The G.D. Searle Company is one of the nation's largest and most successful drug companies. Searle, with headquarters in Skokie, Illinois, manufactures a variety of over-the-counter and prescription drugs relied upon by tens of millions of people. More important for this story, Searle also was the developer of aspartame, the generic name for an extremely popular artificial sweetener called NutraSweet. NutraSweet is now one of the most widely ingested artificial food additives in the world.

Like all drug companies, Searle operates under the general supervision of the Food and Drug Administration, one of the oldest federal regulatory bodies in the United States. In a very general way, the FDA exercises its authority by requiring the drug companies to provide the results of scientific studies that have been undertaken to prove that the new products are safe. The government's efforts to prevent the distribution of dangerous foods and drugs is thus heavily dependent upon the careful and accurate testing by the companies.

In 1974 and 1975, the FDA discovered discrepancies in some of the animal studies that Searle had submitted to the government in support of its plans to market certain drugs and food additives. As a result, the FDA formed the Searle Investigative Task Force.

On March 24, 1976, after more than a year of study, the task force released its final report to the public. It was not reassuring. "At the heart of FDA's regulatory process is its ability to rely upon the integrity of the basic safety data submitted by sponsors of regulated products," the report began. "Our investigation clearly demonstrates that, in the G.D. Searle Company, we have no basis for such reliance now."[29]

The company, the report continued, "has not submitted all the facts of experiments to FDA, retaining unto itself the unpermitted option of filtering, interpreting, and not submitting information which we would consider material to the safety evaluation of the product. Some of our findings suggest an attitude of disregard for the FDA's mission of protection of the public health by selectively reporting the results of studies in a manner which allays the concerns or questions of an FDA reviewer. Finally, we have found instances of irrelevant or unproductive animal research where experiments have been poorly conceived, carelessly executed, or inaccurately analyzed or reported."

The task force concluded the summary of its findings by stating that "while a single discrepancy, error or inconsistency in any given study may not be significant in and of itself, the cumulative findings of problems within and across the studies we investigated reveal a pattern of conduct which compromises the scientific integrity of the studies."

For the public that had long depended upon the oversight of the FDA and the basic honesty and competence of this giant drug company, the task force's conclusions were grim. For Searle, however, the task force's recommendations for action were grimmer.

The FDA, the task force said, should impose all the civil sanctions authorized by law. "In addition, we recommend that FDA recommend to the Department of Justice that grand jury proceedings be instituted in the Northern District of Illinois utilizing compulsory process in order to identify more particularly the nature of violations and to identify all those responsible for such violations."[30]

This was heavy business. While large corporations have learned to shrug off the civil penalties and fines sometimes imposed by federal regulatory agencies, the possibility of criminal charges, especially criminal charges directed at specific corporate executives, is an entirely different matter. Unlike the sanctions available under civil law, which are limited to the payment of tax deductible fines, people convicted of criminal violations can actually be sent to prison. More important, at least to the corporation, a criminal conviction is a very serious public relations setback. At least some newspaper readers and television viewers might be expected to stop buying drugs from a company whose executives had been convicted of crimes connected with the muddying of its safety research data.

Very shortly after the completion of the task force report, on April 7, 1976, the chief counsel of the FDA informed the U.S. attorney in Chicago that the agency agreed with the task force recommendation that a grand jury investigation was required.[31] Upon receipt of this letter, the U.S. attorney appointed two assistant U.S. attorneys, Fred Brandon and William F. Conlon, to take over supervision of the case. Nine months later, the FDA formally requested the grand jury investigation and on February 2, 1977, the U.S. attorney and his two assistants had their first meeting with Searle's lawyers.[32]

The two principal players at the February meeting were serious people. Speaking for Searle was Newton Minow, a senior lawyer in Sidley & Austin, one of Chicago's most prestigious law firms. During the Kennedy administration, he had been chairman of the Federal Communications Commission. Speaking for the United States was Samuel K. Skinner III, who had begun his working life as one of IBM's most successful salesmen. Despite his impressive record, Skinner had grown bored at IBM, gone to night law school and, after an apprenticeship as assistant U.S. attorney, had been appointed U.S. attorney by Jerry Ford. A decade later George Bush would make him a member of his cabinet— the secretary of transportation—and then, for a brief unhappy period, bring him to the White House as his chief of staff.[33]

During his early years as a federal prosecutor, Skinner had been given the nickname "Sam the Hammer" because of his aggressive, no-holds-barred enforcement style. But whatever occurred during the February 1977 meeting called by Skinner and Minow to discuss the Searle case, it apparently did not become a hostile gathering. We can infer this because just a few weeks after the first session, Minow privately offered Skinner a job at Sidley & Austin.

The exact date of the job offer from the Searle law firm to the Searle prosecutor is not known. But on March 8, 1977, Skinner wrote a confidential note informing the two assistant U.S. attorneys handling the Searle case that he was talking with Sidley & Austin about going to work for the firm. Although Skinner then recused himself from further involvement in the Searle matter, the recusal did not prevent him from reminding his two assistants that they had previously agreed that further processing of one of their most important cases then being handled by his possible new employer would be put off until the appointment of a new U.S. attorney.[34]

The official record suggests that Skinner's conditioned recusal did not go down very well with his staff. On April 13, Charles P. Kocoras, the first assistant U.S. attorney, informed Skinner that he now had decided "it would not be appropriate to refrain from conducting necessary investigation by the grand jury" until the new U.S. attorney had been appointed.[35] It appears that Kocoras was in a position to cancel the suggested timetable of his nominal boss because Skinner had in fact recused himself from the Searle investigation.

Despite Kocoras's rejection of Skinner's condition, the Searle matter was in fact not presented to a federal grand jury until a few months after July 1977, the time when Skinner left his federal job to join Sidley & Austin and his successor, Thomas P. Sullivan, had been confirmed as the new U.S. attorney. According to some legal experts, this four-month delay was critical because, for complex legal reasons involving the federal statute of limitations, it meant that powerful evidence supporting the FDA's charges against the drug company could no longer be presented to the grand jury.[36] Whatever the explanation, on January 29, 1979, U.S. Attorney Sullivan informed the FDA that the Searle lawyers had won the day. Sullivan said the evidence against both the company and some of its current and former employees had been investigated by his staff and the grand jury and that he, in consultation with his staff, had decided "to decline criminal prosecution." The prosecutor said the principal reason for his decision was that the FDA regulations spelling out Searle's responsibilities to report negative findings were not sufficiently clear.[37]

Except for the initial sweeping charges by the FDA investigative task force, none of the details of this curious story became public at the time they occurred. But in February 1986, almost ten years after Skinner had first begun talking with Sidley & Austin about joining the firm, the staff of Senator Howard Metzenbaum of Ohio investigated the case. At that time, Skinner denied any impropriety. During his confirmation hearings as secretary of transportation in January 1989, Skinner again denied any wrongdoing, insisting that from the day in 1977 when he had recused himself he had nothing to do with the matter, either as public prosecutor or private attorney.[38]

At the end of this torturous road, the FDA's recommendation that criminal charges be brought against one of America's largest drug companies for systematically violating critically important safety procedures did not go forward. Searle had successfully avoided criminal charges, one of the worst nightmares of corporate America. Despite Skinner's assertions of propriety, the timing of the job offer from the company's law firm—and his acceptance of employment—raises suspicions that cannot be totally erased. A second event contributes to this lingering uneasiness. In October 1978, shortly before the prosecutors decided against going ahead with the charges against Searle, William Conlon, the assistant U.S. attorney who shared responsibility for the investigation during its initial stages, was offered a job with Sidley & Austin, actually joining the firm in January 1979.[39]

Whatever the reason, the lawyers for the G.D. Searle Company had chalked up an important victory. Despite the most serious kinds of allegations of criminal fraud by the investigators, general counsel and commissioner of a respected federal agency, neither the company nor its executives were indicted by a federal grand jury and thus the merits of the allegations were never considered in open court.

INTO THE MOUTHS OF BABES

T he record is clear. Political campaign contributions, personal bribes and other direct and indirect favors have frequently influenced important Justice Department decisions about the enforcement of law. Sometimes, however, the explanation for an otherwise inexplicable decision is a far less specific consideration, a general belief that criminal sanctions are for street criminals, not corporate ones.

On March 23, 1978, the chief scientist and nutritionist of the California-based Syntex Corporation ordered the deletion of all the salt from an infant formula the company manufactured and sold to adoring parents all over the world. For reasons that are still not clear, the senior scientist apparently did not realize that salt is an essential component of infant formula, and that by deleting it he had transformed the formula from a life-supporting to a life-threatening mixture.

Following up on his baffling mistake, the Syntex scientist ordered that the product's label be changed to reflect the absence of salt. But the printing of the new label, which would have informed physicians about the situation, was somehow delayed. The problem was further compounded in December 1978, months after the salt had been deleted, when Syntex ran an advertisement in *Pediatrics Magazine,* a publication directed at physicians, which continued to list the vital substance as one of the formula's ingredients.

As a result of this series of misjudgments and mistakes—none of which were detected by the company's quality control system—20,000 babies were exposed to the defective formula and many infants experienced a condition called metabolic alkalosis, which would leave some of them physically and mentally impaired for the rest of their lives. Government investigators later uncovered evidence that at least 247 infants who had been given the formula who had developed related health problems ranging from minor illnesses to death.

There is almost no argument that Syntex had violated Section 331 of

PERCENTAGE OF FEDERAL PROSECUTIONS INVOLVING DRUG AND REGULATORY VIOLATIONS

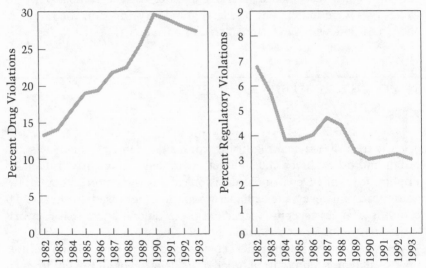

In law enforcement, as in life, there are always trade-offs. The decision to emphasize one enforcement area almost always means that other areas will suffer. From 1982 to 1993, the percentage of all criminal cases involving drugs completed by the Justice Department more than doubled, while those involving regulatory matters dropped by half. Regulatory cases, according to the Justice Department, include health and safety violations, occupational health violations and the illegal discharge of toxic, hazardous and carcinogenic waste. (TRAC ANALYSIS OF JUSTICE DEPARTMENT DATA)

the Food, Drug and Cosmetic Act, which prohibits the introduction into interstate commerce of adulterated or misbranded food. So after an intensive investigation, the Food and Drug Administration (FDA) in 1980 sent a strong recommendation to the Justice Department that it bring criminal charges against Syntex.

Five years later, Richard K. Willard, a Texas lawyer, a true-blue Reagan-era conservative, who was at this particular time a high Justice Department official, flatly rejected the FDA's request that the company be brought to trial.

There really is no logical explanation for Willard's long delayed and unappealable decision in the Syntex case. But at a subsequent Senate hearing to consider his nomination to be the assistant attorney in charge of the department's Civil Division, Willard tried to explain his decision. The accuser was Senator Howard Metzenbaum.

The Reagan administration official claimed that one reason he decided the Justice Department would not prosecute Syntex was that the company never received any prior warnings of its failings. According to Metzenbaum, however, this simply was not true. In 1977, he noted, the FDA had written to George Rosencrantz, the chairman of the board of Syntex Laboratories, saying it was disturbed by evidence that the managers of a Syntex plant in Illinois had failed to cooperate with an agency inspector who was trying to determine the number of cans of infant formula that did not bear the correct code numbers. While not directly related to the deletion of salt, the FDA complaint did raise questions about the company's quality control program.

There was also evidence that a quality control specialist within the company and an independent Oregon pediatrics professor had both expressed early concern about the salt deficiency.

Another reason cited by Willard for his decision not to prosecute Syntex was that the company had inherited an inadequate quality control system when it purchased the infant formula plant. The FDA argued that Syntex had purchased the product line seven years before the incident, certainly long enough before the incident to hold the company accountable for it.

A third reason offered by Willard for not prosecuting Syntex involved the argument that financial losses suffered by the company as a result of disclosure of its serious failure would be an adequate deterrent to prevent similar negligence in other companies. But shortly after the Syntex case exploded in the press and shortly before Willard decided not to prosecute, another major infant formula manufacturer was discovered to have dropped Vitamin B_6 from its product.

Willard would not be moved. At his 1986 confirmation hearing, the Justice Department official denied that the Syntex Corporation had es-

236

caped facing criminal charges because of any secret political connections. But he failed to offer any convincing explanation for his inaction. Senator Metzenbaum pressed him to explain. "And even as I sit here now, Mr. Willard, I say to myself why did this man not go forward? What really motivated him? What slowed him down?"

An examination of cases where the FDA has asked the Justice Department to bring criminal charges against corporate figures shows that the escapes of G.D. Searle and Syntex are hardly unique. While many factors may be at stake, such as murky regulations and inadequate investigations by the FDA, there is considerable evidence that the Justice Department has frequently been extremely solicitous of corporate interests. This mindful watchfulness is especially striking in situations where a U.S. attorney is considering the fate of a business whose corporate headquarters is located in his or her district.

THE PRESS SELDOM STRIKES OUT

As already suggested, virtually every administration has demanded that the Justice Department bend the law in an improper way on behalf of one corporate criminal or another. The lesson is that if a given company or industry is in a position to assist the party that controls the White House, the politicians who manage that administration's Justice Department are willing to give that company or industry a helping hand. The newspaper industry, for example, obviously has many benefits it can bestow on a presidential candidate or his party, so it should come as no surprise that publishers feed very well at the Justice Department's table. Sometimes the mutual understandings are explicit, sometimes not. The positive response of two different administrations to requests from the press for special legal favors illustrates the continuing power of this industry.

One of the best-documented examples concerns a 180-degree Justice Department flip-flop arranged by those two master schemers, Richard Nixon and Attorney General John Mitchell. The switch involved the position the Nixon administration would take on legislation then pending in Congress to give the press an important exemption from the antitrust laws.

Throughout all of 1968 and the first half of 1969, John Mitchell and his antitrust chief, with the full backing of the White House, had opposed the bill in the strongest terms. The proposed newspaper legislation, the Justice Department had repeatedly argued, would entrench

"absolute monopoly," would "flout the basic principles of the free enterprise system" and would weaken the key press responsibility of "acting as a watchdog on government." The denunciations were clear, the
chances for compromise apparently nil.

But looks, as we have all been told, can be deceiving. The White
House records of this matter, now stored at a special warehouse maintained by the National Archives in Alexandria, Virginia, are somewhat
skimpy. It also is unfortunately true that the White House meeting during which Nixon struck his bargain occurred before the president had
ordered the installation of the secret tape-recording system, which
might have caught all the juicy details.

But the available documents are sufficient to gain an excellent understanding of the transaction. On August 7, 1969, Nixon replied to a
July 15, 1969, letter from Richard E. Berlin, the president and chief executive of the Hearst Corporation. Nixon thanked Berlin for presenting
his views on "the pending newspaper legislation." After noting that the
subject was complex, Nixon made the tantalizing and entirely cryptic
observation that, as a result of Berlin's message to him, he had "asked
Attorney General Mitchell to look into the questions you have brought
up as well as those implied by the arrangements described in your letter." What were the questions that Berlin had brought up or implied?
What were the arrangements he described? Nixon does not say.

Shortly thereafter, according to the records, the president and the
press baron held a private meeting at the White House. No documents
apparently exist that describe the substance of this meeting. But on September 23, Nixon sent a brief revealing note to two of his senior assistants that nicely discloses the raw politics driving this particular
enforcement issue.

Nixon's memo, directed to Bob Haldeman and Peter Flanigan, said he
had talked to the attorney general and that Mitchell now understood
that the administration was changing its position and no longer would
actively oppose the pending legislation supported by the industry, a bill
grandly named the "Newspaper Preservation Act."

Now that Mitchell has received his marching orders, Nixon writes,
Flanigan should get back to Berlin, the president of Hearst, and complete the loop. Flanigan, the president said, should suggest to Berlin
"that he get this word around among those publishers who would be affected, on a private basis, so that we get some credit where it counts."[40]

One shoe had dropped in private. The second shoe would drop in a
public forum two days later when Richard W. McClaren, the Justice Department antitrust chief who had led the administration's attack on the
Newspaper Preservation Act, testified he no longer spoke for the president. McClaren said the lead agency was now the Commerce Depart-

ment, which now actively supported the bill. Emanuel Celler, a New
York Democrat and chairman of the House antitrust subcommittee,
told McClaren that in his forty-seven years as a congressman he did not
recall "any such situation." He added that the abrupt switch must be
very embarrassing for him.

"I regret it, sir," the assistant attorney general replied.[41]

Although the subsequent press coverage of Nixon's Watergate scandal suggests that winning some degree of credit from the publishers ultimately did not count for all that much, the industry did very well by
the deal and by the understanding it reached with President Nixon.
With the sudden disappearance of active opposition by the Nixon administration, the politicians in the Democratic-controlled Congress,
who were as interested as the president in currying the favor of the
newspaper industry, decided that the game was up, and the antitrust exemption desired by the press soon became law.

Frequently, the understanding between a particular administration
and an influential business interest like a publisher can be far less obvious than the arrangement ultimately worked out by Nixon and Berlin.
Yet even the most indirect of agreements can be revealing, as was disclosed during a 1963 hearing by the House Judiciary Subcommittee on
Antitrust.[42] In late 1961, according to the testimony of several participants, James McInerney, a former assistant attorney general, requested
an appointment with Attorney General Robert Kennedy. As an attorney
then working for the Hearst Corporation, McInerney was seeking Justice Department approval of a private business agreement worked out
between the Hearst Corporation and the Times Mirror Corporation.
The purpose of the agreement was to slice up the circulation and advertising dollars of the vast and rapidly growing Los Angeles metropolitan
area into two big fat pieces of pie.

As a courtesy due a former high official of the department, Kennedy
briefly met with McInerney and immediately referred him to Lee
Loevinger, the assistant attorney general then in charge of the department's Antitrust Division. On December 1, 1961, Loevinger met the
Hearst lawyer. According to Loevinger's later testimony, the assistant
attorney general told McInerney that the Justice Department could not
approve the plan under which the two publishers would purchase each
other's money-losing second papers, thus leaving the *Los Angeles
Times* with an exclusive hold on the morning market and Hearst's *Herald Express* with control of all the afternoon readers.

Loevinger said the corporate lawyer had been told the proposed deal
would be illegal. "I said it seemed to me that it was perfectly clear the
only purpose of the cross-sale was to effect a division of fields which
would be illegal per se under the antitrust laws," he recalled.[43]

The assistant attorney general, however, apparently confused about his role as a senior federal law enforcement official, then offered the former assistant attorney what turned out to be some very valuable legal advice. While a cross-sale *agreement* between the two giant publishers would clearly be illegal, Loevinger said, the Times Mirror and Hearst could achieve the same goal if they just both shut down their money-losing operations. "The antitrust laws have nothing to do with this," he remembered telling McInerney. "This would be an obvious rational business decision given the circumstances."

McInerney passed on his understanding of Loevinger's remarks to the Hearst organization and within days the executives of the two publishers met with their Washington lawyer in New York. "McInerney said he had met with various officials of the Justice Department to discuss the closing of the morning *Examiner* and the evening *Mirror* due to their heavy continuing losses," Otis Chandler, the Times Mirror publisher testified.[44] The lawyer, Chandler continued, assured them he had "received oral assurance from responsible Justice Department officials that the two companies could cease publication, simultaneously, of the *Examiner* and the *Mirror*."

An ugly little war had been avoided. By giving the deal its extremely discreet blessing, the Kennedy administration avoided offending two institutions which had never been all that friendly in the past but who always might be helpful in the future. The actual cost to the public, in terms of whether the agreement made it easier for the two companies to increase their general advertising charges, was never calculated, at least in a public way. All was well in la-la land, at least for the publishers.

LET'S NOT PROSECUTE THE BANKERS

On June 13, 1987, the witness before the House Subcommittee on Commerce, Consumer and Monetary Affairs was William Crawford, a state official in charge of regulating savings and loan banks in California. "The best way to rob a bank," Crawford observed with some conciseness, "is to own one."[45]

Two other things became clear that day. First, the sloppy and illegal banking practices of the previous decade were going to cost the taxpayers billions of dollars. Second, the federal government had expended precious little effort to head off these unacceptable practices by punishing the wrongdoers.

Just a month or so before, for example, the Federal Savings and Loan

Insurance Corporation had estimated that it would take in excess of $8 billion to meet the obligations of fifty-one failed institutions whose officers or directors at that time had been sued for misconduct in just one state—California.

Despite the widespread knowledge of the truly gigantic damages wreaked by the collapsing savings and loan institutions and banks, however, U.S. attorneys in key cities, some FBI offices and the Justice Department's politicos in Washington were still preoccupied with other, sometimes surprising, matters.

As documented by the investigators of the House subcommittee, Justice Department outposts in California, Texas and Florida—three of the hardest-hit states—gave the investigation and prosecution of large-scale financial fraud, particularly by the financial institutions, an extremely low priority. During 1986 and 1987, for example, while California was stumbling through its darkest banking crisis, the U.S. attorney in San Francisco prosecuted only a single major bank fraud case involving a failed savings and loan institution. The subcommittee found, however, that during the same two-year period, the San Francisco office had over sixty similar cases stockpiled in its files, all of which were ready for presentation to a grand jury or for actual prosecution.[46]

Another area unusually hard hit by serious bank fraud was Texas, especially Houston. Here, a 1990 investigation by the same House subcommittee determined that Henry Oncken, the U.S. attorney for the Southern District of Texas, had "brought only a few major prosecutions against insiders of failed institutions" and "that FBI agents and prosecutors in his own office were frustrated by this reluctance."[47]

The subcommittee report cited a statistical analysis completed by Dee Gill, a reporter for the *Houston Chronicle*, which had determined that nearly 90 percent of all 129 federal indictments brought in the Southern District of Texas for bank fraud and related statutes since 1986 were against individual bank customers and low-level bank employees who had committed such wicked acts as providing false information on an application for a loan.[48]

"This dearth of major prosecutions is not due to a lack of referrals," the subcommittee observed. "The Federal Home Loan Bank Board, hired fee counsel, and investigative organizations have made numerous referrals involving serious allegations of misconduct by insiders and prosecutions. There have been no prosecutions of insiders arising out of two of the biggest bank failures, Mainland Savings and Continental Savings, where serious misconduct has been publicly and privately reported."[49]

The conclusion of Dee Gill and the subcommittee, that the U.S. attorney in Houston was not overwhelmingly interested in white-collar crime despite the financial institution failures then ripping at the economic fabric of the city, is supported by an analysis of Justice Department enforcement data. Recognizing that each U.S. attorney has only a relatively few prosecutors, and that if one category of crime is made a high-priority item another category of crime has to suffer, consider the following facts: During the worst years of the banking crisis, federal prosecutors in the city concentrated on drug enforcement and gave relatively little attention to white-collar crime. More specifically, when all U.S. attorneys are ranked in terms of the number of drug cases they brought in relation to population living in their districts, Houston constantly is among the most active. When the same comparison is made in regards to white-collar crime, federal prosecutors in the district are consistently in the cellar.

The Middle District of Florida, with its principal office in Tampa, was also identified as having an outstandingly poor record in the prosecution of major bank fraud cases. In this instance, however, the subcommittee said the blame should not fall on the U.S. attorney in charge of the office or the FBI but on the Justice Department. "It appears that the DOJ seriously shortchanged the district by allocating it only one new FBI agent and one new prosecutor during the December 1990 allocation, although in mid-1988 that office had the fourth largest caseload in the United States," the subcommittee said.[50]

Why? Why did the Justice Department, most of the ninety-three U.S. attorneys and the FBI miss the boat on what in some ways was the single most important crime wave in the history of the United States? Certainly the Justice Department has never been particularly concerned about corporate crime. Certainly this view did not change when the conservative, even right-wing, lawyers who were a part of the Reagan and Bush administrations came to power.

One factor was the personal enforcement obsessions that led officials like Attorney General Edwin Meese to bend the Justice Department to his own personal purposes. During April 1988, for example, the Fraud Section of the department's Criminal Division had to start declining to provide expert assistance to a number of districts because of a severe lack of travel funds. Among other matters, the absence of expert prosecutors from Washington significantly delayed the timely investigation of cases arising out of a number of S&L failures in the Dallas area.

Subsequent investigation by House investigators found that one reason for the shortage of travel funds for combating bank fraud was that the Justice Department had diverted $1.1 million from that particular account to help finance the operations of its highly questionable Obscenity Unit, a project strongly supported by right-wing ideologues, including the man who was at that time in charge of the department, Attorney General Meese. What was more important? Prosecuting the corporate criminals whose swindles eventually would cost the American taxpayers billions of dollars? Or bringing charges against a handful of admittedly sleazy pornographers, many of which ultimately would be thrown out by the courts on constitutional grounds?[51]

PURE POISON

The Puregro Company, Inc., with dozens of branches operating in eleven states, is one of the largest agricultural chemical application and distribution businesses in the nation. Since 1986, and perhaps for many years before, the managers of the Puregro facility near Richland, Washington, had directed their workers to dump a variety of liquid wastes into a 1,500-gallon open-air evaporation tank.[52]

But sometime in the spring of 1987 a problem developed: The wastes were no longer evaporating into the atmosphere because the liquids in the tank had thickened and developed an oily surface film. What should be done? Puregro hired an outside consultant who suggested two options. The company could undertake a preliminary chemical analysis. Should this test find evidence indicating the mixture contained hazardous wastes, more complex and expensive analysis would then be required and the entire mixture might have to be carefully transported to a special facility licensed to handle the poisonous liquid. But if Puregro decided the mixture only consisted of one of the company's products, such as an insecticide, it could be cheaply disposed of by applying it to a local crop.

For the managers whose annual salaries were partially determined by the branch's profit margins, the choice may have seemed obvious. On Wednesday, May 12, 1987, company workmen, with the knowledge of at least three managers, dumped 3,500 gallons of the waste in the corner of a field near the small farming town of Pasco, Washington. The company had leased the unplowed and semi-arid field, allegedly to grow sweet corn for its annual picnic.[53]

Shortly after the dump, the wind carried a noxious cloud of gas over a nearby farm then owned by Jack and Veda Downs. The cloud caught the elderly couple as they were wrestling with 120-pound bales of hay for their cattle. Veda Downs remembers seeing a wispy fog rising from the field across the road and then smelling a foul odor like rotten eggs. She says she and her husband immediately had trouble breathing and that the cattle refused to eat the hay. The couple spent that night in their house, coughing and feeling ill.

The next day, Thursday, Mrs. Downs reports that she passed out and her husband remained in bed. Their tongues, eyes and ears were burning, they had muscle cramps and headaches and they both experienced great difficulty in breathing. On Friday, the couple finally went to see their doctor, who immediately referred them to an emergency room where oxygen was administered to ease their breathing problems. The doctors were unable to determine the precise cause of the illness.

Shortly after the dump, Veda Downs had called Puregro and asked what had been sprayed on the field. She says the manager said it was Dyfonate, an insecticide manufactured by Stauffer Chemicals. Company officials stuck with this story during a second conversation with Downs. Subsequent testing of the liquid by Stauffer, Oregon State University and the Environmental Protection Agency eventually determined the presence of seven different herbicides and pesticides, sixteen additional compounds and small amounts of Telone, a powerful fumigant related to mustard gas which can only be used legally when injected underground in narrowly circumscribed situations.

Over twenty neighbors reported having similar symptoms to those suffered by the Downses. In the days and weeks after the dumping, a number of the Downses' farm animals died, baby birds were found dead on the ground and trees on their property withered and died. Jack Downs, who before the incident had been physically active despite a mild heart condition, never worked again. On June 8, 1988, after eight months of treatment in the medical center at Walla Walla, he died of congestive heart failure. Veda Downs suffered months of muscle spasms and large open sores. At a hearing before a House subcommittee five years after the illegal dump, she said her health was still impaired.

Because the local county prosecutor took months to decide he did not have the resources to prosecute Puregro, the case did not reach the EPA until 1989. Very quickly, however, criminal investigators employed by the EPA, the Environmental Crimes Section of the Justice Department and an assistant attorney general with the state of Washington began collecting evidence. Apparently understanding the strength of this evidence, attorneys for Puregro offered to have the *company* plead guilty to a felony charge that would have resulted in the assessment of a large fine. But the prosecuting team rejected the offer. They felt felony charges should be brought against the *individual* executives responsible for the dumping as well the company. On September 7, 1990, four officials and Puregro were charged with felony violations.[54]

Then the government's aggressive pursuit of Puregro came to a screeching halt. Rebecca Dewees, the staff attorney handling the case for the Justice Department's Environmental Crimes Section, was involved in a serious bicycle accident that required her to take a leave.

She was replaced by Criselda Ortiz, a lawyer whose primary experience was in civil rights. At about the same time, a new attorney, Neil Cartusciello, was named to head the Environmental Crimes Section. Like Ortiz, he had no previous experience in enforcing federal environmental laws.

Ortiz began a whole new investigation of the Puregro case. After months of internal strife—and over the strong objections of both the EPA and the attorney general of the state of Washington—the Justice Department decided to drop the case completely. This initial decision caused so much dissent that Ortiz and Cartusciello finally agreed to allow Puregro to plead guilty to a single misdemeanor charge and pay a $15,000 fine.[55] This was the company, remember, which several years before had volunteered to plead guilty to felony charges. All charges voted by the grand jury against the Puregro managers were dropped.

In an unusual public challenge to the Justice Department, Ken Eikenberry, the attorney general of the state of Washington, questioned the actions of the two responsible federal lawyers. In a letter to Attorney General William Barr, Eikenberry said he and others in his office were convinced there was "a solid case" against both Puregro and its managers and that "they should not have been allowed to escape with only minor sanctions against the corporation."[56] The criticism had a special bite because Eikenberry, like Barr, was a Republican officeholder.

But the abandonment of a single case, no matter how powerful the evidence appears and how outrageous the decision seems, is rarely sufficient to challenge the judgment of the prosecutor who handled the matter, let alone raise the question of whether the office in which the prosecutor works has a secret political agenda. There are simply too many variables.

Concerning the Environmental Crimes Section of the Justice Department, however, especially during the Bush and Reagan years, a convincing case can be made that the improper handling of Puregro was an example of a much larger problem. In fact, a piercing congressional investigation into the handling of a small sample of environmental cases, a special study undertaken by a team of law students working under their professor at George Washington University and a computer analysis of all environmental cases brought by the federal government in California during the 1980s together suggest that the Justice Department and selected U.S. attorneys failed to enforce the nation's environmental laws in an appropriate manner.

In September 1992, after months of investigation, the House Energy and Commerce Subcommittee on Oversight held hearings about the evidence it had found indicating that the Environmental Crimes Section of the Justice Department "had interfered with the effective criminal prosecution of companies, corporate officials and individuals for serious and willful violations of the environmental laws."[57]

The subcommittee's preliminary staff report, which was supported by both Democratic and Republican members, said its investigation of about a dozen recent cases showed that the department was plagued with serious management and performance problems. Among the shortcomings, the subcommittee said, was a persistent tendency not to prosecute important matters, a serious lack of environmental law expertise, an ineffective use of EPA investigative resources and a general lack of aggressiveness which led many of the government's lawyers to regard any factual or legal challenges from the accused corporation as "reasons to drop it."

Although the Justice Department refused to testify at the hearings, various department officials have contended in press interviews that the bipartisan criticism of the Bush administration's prosecutorial performance was politically motivated and that the cases that had been selected for review, including the Puregro situation in Washington, "all boil down to legitimate disagreements between government officials acting in good faith about what the weight of the evidence shows."[58]

A year and a half after the publication of the interim report, however, the Justice Department released a nine-month, 325-page review by four career lawyers, confirming that the Environmental Crimes Section had indeed been plagued by serious management problems. While highly critical of the House subcommittee's findings, the internal review acknowledged that some of the admitted problems had been caused by Republican appointees in Washington who were "philosophically more reluctant" to prosecute than some of their subordinates.[59]

"As general characterizations go," the reviewers said in their March 1994 report, "we think it is fair to say that from 1989 to 1992, Assistant Attorney General [Richard] Stewart and Acting Assistant Attorney General [Barry] Hartman took a more cautious approach to prosecuting particular cases than others—including some career attorneys—would have followed."

Some of the specifics discussed by the Justice Department's reviewers were actually downright funky. The department noted, for example, that Hartman had attempted to prevent the attorney general of New York State from signing a plea agreement and attending a postsentence press conference concerning a particular environmental case. Hartman pursued this course even though the state had been actively involved in the investigation and prosecution of the matter. Hartman's effort, the Justice Department acknowledged, apparently had nothing to do with the merits of the case and everything to do with the fact that the New

York attorney general "was a Democratic candidate for the Senate at the time."[60]

After nearly three years of investigations, two hearings, staff interviews with dozens of witnesses and the examination of hundreds of documents, many of which could only be obtained by subpoena, the House oversight subcommittee issued a final staff report on the unfortunate impact of the Justice Department on the environmental enforcement efforts of the federal government over a three- or four-year period.

"The PureGro case was replete with evidence of managerial failure and dysfunction," the report said.[61] But when considered along with the handling of a sample of other cases, the report concluded that the department's "environmental crimes program during the early to mid-1990's was in a damaging state of disarray. Morale was poor. Relationships were strained. Management policies both with respect to personnel and case management were inadequate and, at times, even destructive."[62]

To appreciate the significance of the Justice Department's seriously flawed environmental enforcement program, some understanding of how frequently American corporations are violating the nation's environmental laws and regulations would obviously be helpful. By its very nature, such information is hard to obtain. In 1993, however, the *National Law Journal* and Arthur Andersen Environmental Service, a consulting firm, conducted a fascinating confidential survey of the senior attorneys of more than two hundred corporations. Two out of three of the corporate counsels, 66.8 percent of the respondents, said that their businesses have operated, at least some time in the last year, in violation of federal or state environmental laws.[63]

8

Uncivil
Wrongs and
Civil Rights

On November 12, 1992, during the waning days of the Bush administration, the federal prosecutor in the Northern District of Alabama sent a brief, churlish letter to Jonathan Rose, a lawyer working for Birmingham mayor Richard Arrington. The federal investigation of Arrington, U.S. Attorney Jack Selden announced, was over. "Based on a thorough evaluation of the evidence," he wrote, "the Public Integrity Section and the Tax Division of the Department of Justice determined, with my concurrence, that prosecution should be declined."

Considering the full circumstances, the response of Birmingham's first black mayor to Selden's letter was extraordinarily restrained. "As I have stated repeatedly throughout this protracted investigation, I have never engaged in any crime or wrongdoing," Arrington said in a brief announcement.

Thus ended an amazing on-again off-again string of federal investigations of Arrington that had begun two decades before with the racist paranoia of FBI Director J. Edgar Hoover and then resurrected by the Republican political operatives who seized control of the federal government in Alabama with the 1980 election of Ronald Reagan.

The full story of the Justice Department's unwarranted pursuit of Mayor Arrington, a former biology professor and mainstream political figure, is by itself a repellent tale of unjustified official harassment. But when considered along with the government's flawed attacks on a half-dozen civil rights activists in Birmingham and other parts of Alabama, the combined events suggest something even uglier: a systematic and partly successful effort by conservative white Alabamians to harness the enforcement muscle of the Justice Department for the purpose of subduing the black Democratic politicians who challenged their domination of the state.

So far, no single memorandum describing this long-lived effort has been located. Quite likely, none was written. Of course, the federal officials who were responsible for the Arrington investigations and the other, even more noisome, acts insist that partisan, racial and class calculations had nothing to do with their ugly guerrilla war. And many thoughtful Americans, imbued with a sense of idealism about how their Justice Department sometimes has worked to protect the basic rights of individual Americans, shrink from considering the disturbing ease with which the Justice Department over the years has pursued other goals.

"During a good part of my working life, many of my friends and I have regarded the Civil Rights Division as the crown jewel of the Justice Department," said Mark Lynch, a highly respected Washington lawyer who for many years was on the staff of the American Civil Liberties Union (ACLU).[1]

At one level, Lynch's point is well taken. Few Americans doubt that the Justice Department's enforcement effort under the Voting Rights Act of 1965, leading to the enfranchisement of black voters across the South, was a major, essential and even glorious event in American history. Similarly, a strong majority of the American people agree on the critical importance, both in real and symbolic terms, of the department's complex campaign against segregated public services and facilities.

As Lynch acknowledges, however, when the Justice Department's short-term and long-term civil rights record is carefully scrutinized, an optimistic reading of the Civil Rights Division must, at a minimum, be carefully qualified. One essential distinction to keep in mind is that the Civil Rights Division is only one part of the Justice Department, and the two institutions have very different records. The department's performance in Alabama—encompassing the activities of senior officials in Washington, the state's three federal prosecutors and the FBI—is just one recent and particularly powerful reason why considerable skepticism is required when it comes to judging the department's overall civil rights record.

Because the discrete parts of what might be called the Alabama conspiracy were many, and were mostly cloaked in secrecy, the overall pattern of the scheme was not immediately obvious. The true picture began to emerge a few years ago when the government, in response to a request from Mayor Arrington under the Freedom of Information Act, provided Arrington with 292 pages of his 518-page FBI file.[2]

Among the most interesting parts were a set of sixteen heavily censored pages concerning a secret FBI investigation of Arrington that had been started more than twenty years ago, on January 26, 1972. The FBI said an additional forty pages of this particular section of his file were being withheld. The bureau justified both the censorship and the withholding on a number of legal grounds, including the need to protect the identity of confidential sources.[3]

Arrington was the brilliant son of sharecroppers who had gone on to earn his doctorate in biology and become a college professor. At the time the FBI's original investigation began, he was the director of the Alabama Center for Higher Education, a consortium of Alabama's black colleges, and had just been elected to the Birmingham City Council. In those days, of course, Birmingham was special: probably the South's most segregated city, the place where Public Safety Director Eugene "Bull" Connor would shock the world by unleashing snarling police dogs and violent streams of water on peaceful, young and mostly black demonstrators.

Although most of the notations on the sixteen pages have been blacked out, it appears that with Arrington's election, the FBI concluded that the new councilman in this relatively small southern city had been magically transformed into a national leader of a dangerous "black-extremist organization." The reward for the FBI's mystifying decision to elevate him to this exclusive brotherhood was that Arrington became the target of the FBI's formal and highly secret program to "track, expose, disrupt, misdirect, discredit, or otherwise neutralize the activities of black nationalist, hate-type organizations and their groupings, their leadership, spokesmen, membership and supporters, and to counter their propensity for violence and civil disorder."[4]

As noted in a later chapter on the Justice Department and its handling of national security problems, every federal court that considered the merits of the FBI's various COINTELPRO (Counter-Intelligence Program) projects has concluded that they were unlawful. The statutory responsibility of the FBI, after all, is to investigate specific criminal acts, not to disrupt, misdirect, discredit and neutralize individuals who are criticizing various aspects of life in the United States.

According to the decisions of several appellate courts, the COINTELPRO projects aimed at black activists had another repugnant feature. "The blatant racial overtone of the FBI program, coupled with the plaintiffs' various organizational efforts, make clear the entanglement of race and politics that characterized the implementation of the COINTELPRO conspiracy," said one such critical decision.[5]

This general condemnation is reinforced by the specifics of the Arrington case. At precisely the same time that the FBI made Arrington a COINTELPRO target, the newly elected councilman had become a vocal critic of the brutal way the Birmingham Police Department was then treating many African-American citizens. He also was directly involved in a strenuous and intensely resented effort to persuade the city to improve its employment and promotion policies for black Americans.

The highly censored documents the FBI provided Arrington do not disclose whether the bureau initiated the kinds of actions against him that it routinely employed against other COINTELPRO targets. The documents do not show, for example, whether the FBI sent out slanderous unsigned letters designed to disrupt Arrington's budding political career or break up his marriage or destroy his credit rating. Nor do they show if FBI agents provided unscrupulous reporters with incorrect or misleading information designed to undermine his reputation. At the very minimum, all persons rated as "key black activists" were subjected to intense surveillance which resulted in the writing of FBI reports that were then shared with the Secret Service, military intelligence units and the appropriate federal prosecutor.

On August 8, 1972, for example, the FBI dispatched such a report about Arrington to the U.S. attorney in Birmingham. In the copy of the report provided to Arrington, all the substantive details have been obscured. The censors, however, kindly left untouched a mystifying official claim that any disclosure of the information contained in the original report on City Councilman Arrington "could be prejudicial to the defense interests of the United States."

Even before Arrington had become an official COINTELPRO target, however, the whole project had begun to unravel. One key event in its eventual demise was the March 1971 burglary of an FBI office in Media, Pennsylvania, during which a number of embarrassing COINTELPRO documents were stolen by a group of political activists and subsequently leaked to reporters. Then, in May 1972, came the death of J. Edgar Hoover, the program's principal architect. Though manipulative FBI actions to foil political activism did not completely disappear from the FBI's bag of tricks after Hoover's death, the post-Watergate leaders of the Justice Department established new and far more restrictive guidelines to control them. One development outside the control of the Justice Department which surely contributed to the end of COINTEL-PRO was the growing strength of African-American voters. With their increasing voice in the elective politics of America, the demonstrations and sit-ins that had so upset the authoritarian mind-set of Hoover and the governors, mayors and police chiefs of the South began to decline.

THE REAGAN ADMINISTRATION

Arrington's days as an FBI target were far from over. The former college professor was thrust back under the FBI–Justice Department microscope by three separate political events that had no apparent connection with any criminal or national security concerns of the government. First, in November 1979, Arrington was elected mayor of Birmingham. Second, exactly one year later, a right-wing Vietnam War hero named Jeremiah Denton was elected to the United States Senate. Third, in the same election, Denton's fellow Republican, Ronald Reagan, captured the White House.

Within months of their election, Senator Denton selected and President Reagan approved three new U.S. attorneys for Alabama. Frank Donaldson became the federal prosecutor in the Northern District of Alabama (Birmingham), John C. Bell the prosecutor in the Middle District (Montgomery) and Jefferson Beauregard Sessions III in the Southern District (Mobile).

For a while, it appears, there was a lull in the Justice Department's interest in Arrington. But then, with increasing ferocity, the U.S. attorney for the Northern District and the FBI agents in the Birmingham area once again focused their official gaze on the city's mayor. The official records obtained by Arrington show the FBI initiated the first of its new wave of investigations in 1984. The FBI undertook a second and third investigation in 1985 and 1986, three in 1987, one in 1988, three more in 1989 and a final probe in 1990.

Given the amazing number of FBI investigations of Mayor Arrington between 1984 and 1990, the campaign obviously was not a casual, unplanned series of unrelated events. And given the government's complete failure to charge him with a single crime, and the final 1992 clearance letter, it's also impossible to believe that the campaign was anything but a political vendetta.

Some of the FBI investigations of Arrington were routine, others extremely elaborate. In one of the more complex probes, U.S. Attorney Donaldson and a team of six FBI and IRS agents offered a deal to an Alabama real estate developer named Robert Moussallem who had known Arrington for nine years and worked for him during his 1983 reelection campaign. If Moussallem, while wearing a hidden recorder, could persuade the mayor to take a bribe, the U.S. attorney promised the real estate dealer that he "would get full immunity from prosecution" for a criminal tax case that was pending against him.

After several months of unsuccessful efforts to entrap the mayor, Moussallem confessed to Arrington that he was a secret undercover agent working for the federal government. The informer also provided the mayor with revealing tapes of some of his conversations with his FBI handlers. When his federal handlers learned that Moussallem had warned Arrington of his duplicitous assignment, the real estate developer was immediately indicted, tried and convicted on the tax charges. On September 16, 1989, while awaiting sentencing, Moussallem was murdered by the blast from a shotgun that blew away most of his face. Found at the scene of the murder was a copy of the July 3, 1989, *Newsweek* article that had described Moussallem's undercover role in the Arrington investigation and speculated on whether the federal government was systematically targeting black political figures.[6]

Other evidence of the almost nonstop federal investigation of Arrington included dozens of censored FBI documents describing "Bowtye," the code name for a Washington-approved undercover corruption investigation. The Bowtye documents included inventory control records of audio- and videotapes used secretly to record several conversations and meetings, apparently in connection with the investigation of the mayor.

Arrington's aggressive use of the Freedom of Information Act to investigate the investigators was not his only response to the continuing probes of his personal and professional life. In July 1989, for example, Arrington's special counsel, a Birmingham lawyer named Donald V. Watkins, submitted a formal complaint to the Senate Judiciary Committee accusing the FBI, the IRS and the Justice Department of systematically harassing the mayor. Six months later, Watkins followed up his complaint with a lengthy report analyzing the government's many investigations of the mayor.[7] Watkins filed other harassment complaints with the Justice Department's Office of Professional Responsibility (OPR) in Washington; the chief U.S. District Court Judge in Birmingham, Sam C. Pointer; and even the federal prosecutor leading the charge, U.S. Attorney Frank Donaldson. Finally, charging selective prosecution, the lawyer asked the federal courts to quash a December 1991 grand jury subpoena for Arrington's records detailing all of his appointments and meetings for the previous five years.

Arrington's barrage of complaints yielded few tangible results. The department's Office of Professional Responsibility, for example, informed Watkins in November 1992 that allegations that U.S. Attorney Donaldson had abused his investigative powers "have not been substantiated." Given OPR's see-no-evil track record, the finding was not surprising. It should be noted, however, that a heavily censored copy of OPR's report, which was eventually obtained by Arrington under the Freedom of Information Act, showed that OPR failed to investigate some of the allegations made by the mayor and the city.

But in the end, as announced in the November 1992 letter to Jonathan Rose, a wobbly bottom line was finally drawn. The failure of the Justice Department's essentially nonstop wave of investigations to uncover evidence of wrongdoing by the mayor had become an overwhelming reality that could no longer be ignored. Even in a day when grand juries almost always serve as the passive playthings of the prosecutor, and even when the record indicates that the Republican U.S. attorney who had directed most of the effort was gripped by an obsession to break the Democratic mayor's political hold on Birmingham, there was no way that even superficially believable charges could be brought against Arrington.

Of course, the letter announcing the government's remarkable retreat contained no apologies. Such letters never do. In fact, the letter made one last lame attempt to defend the indefensible. "It is regrettable that unfounded allegations have been made about the conduct of this investigation and certain prosecutors," U.S. Attorney Selden said. "It is equally unfortunate that there have been public misperceptions concerning this investigation. As I have previously stated, justice is served only by investigations driven by facts and evidence, objectively gathered and reviewed, and not by sentiment. This is the manner in which this investigation was conducted from the beginning."

IF YOU CAN'T STOP A BLACK POLITICIAN, HOW ABOUT BLACK VOTERS?

Selden's statement about the department's sorry guerrilla war against Arrington was ridiculous on its face. But when that particular struggle is considered alongside what appears to have been a carefully coordinated Republican campaign aimed at a handful of African Americans working to get out the vote, the corruption of the Justice Department's enforcement actions in Alabama during the Reagan-Bush years becomes even more obvious.

On June 2, 1987, during the period that Arrington was under attack, a three-judge panel of the conservative Court of Appeals, Eleventh Circuit, vacated the conviction of Spiver Whitney Gordon, a black voting activist in the Tuscaloosa, Alabama, area. The panel said Gordon's trial, in which he was convicted of fraud for allegedly mailing an invalid primary ballot, had to be thrown out for two reasons. First, the district court judge handling the trial had denied Gordon a hearing on his claim that the prosecution brought by U.S. Attorney Donaldson had been tainted with improper political calculations. Second, the district court judge did not hold a hearing on Gordon's assertion that the prosecutor had used his peremptory challenges to remove every African American from the jury that went on to convict him, thus violating his constitutional right to be judged by his peers.[8]

The evidence cited by the Appeals Court panel to support its decision to vacate the conviction included the statement by a Justice Department spokesperson in Washington that investigations of the voting activists in Alabama were part of a "new policy . . . brought on by the 'arrogance on the part of the blacks' in these counties." Equally demanding of exploration, the court wrote, were the affidavits and other evidence presented by Gordon's lawyers that the Justice Department had chosen "to prosecute him and other black political leaders in Alabama's 'Black Belt' counties for voting fraud, while not prosecuting county residents who were members of a rival white-dominated political party and [who were] committing similar election offenses."

The court also cited evidence that the government had focused its investigation only in those counties "where blacks were a majority, specifically targeting those counties where blacks since 1980 had come to control some part of the county government."

In regard to the jury selection process, the Court of Appeals panel found that in addition to improperly preventing any black citizens from serving on Gordon's jury, the government had followed the same pattern "of exclusions of black venirepersons in the government's other voting fraud cases against black leaders."

It was a stinging rebuke to both the prosecutor who had originally brought the case and to the district court judge who had denied Gordon a full evidentiary hearing on his allegations of selective prosecution and the improper selection of his jury. For whatever reason, Donaldson did not seek a second trial of Gordon.

ANOTHER PRECINCT IS HEARD FROM

T he Republican U.S. attorney in Birmingham, however, was not the only Reagan-appointed prosecutor in Alabama who demonstrated an intense interest in the Democratic black voting activists of the state. A couple of hundred miles to the south, in the small, crumbling, Gulf Coast city of Mobile, Jefferson Beauregard Sessions III led a parallel charge. As noted earlier in this chapter, Sessions had achieved his influential position as the chief federal law enforcement official of the area thanks to his political connections with the right-wing senator Jeremiah Denton.

Sessions's apparently fervent concern about election fraud reached its official peak on January 25, 1985, when the prosecutor announced that a federal grand jury in Mobile had indicted three longtime black civil rights activists—Albert Turner, Albert's wife, Evelyn, and Spencer Hogue, Jr.—for voting fraud.[9] The charges were based on allegations that the two Turners and Hogue had sought to help elderly, often illiterate and bedridden, black voters cast absentee ballots in improper ways.

While Sessions described the prosecution as a straightforward application of federal law, the circumstances of these indictments suggest he had mobilized the power of the federal government for personal reasons and to satisfy the political interests of those with whom he wished to curry favor.

From the very beginning of the case, the defense lawyers for the three plaintiffs made repeated public statements charging that the indictments were nothing but a political hatchet job and that their clients had not committed any federal crimes. This argument gained considerable strength on July 5, 1985, when a jury of seven blacks and five whites acquitted the three defendants after less than three hours of deliberation.[10] The jury appears to have decided that while the Turners and Hogue had indeed helped elderly, disabled people vote—activities they had openly engaged in since the civil rights demonstrations of the early 1960s—their actions had not violated federal criminal law.

Despite the inconvenient acquittals, Sessions continues to justify the prosecution. "This was a horrible crime, someone taking absentee ballots and changing them," he earnestly recalled a few years later, as he sat in a red leather armchair in his dark gray office. "I considered this case a clear example of major fraud, not at all a gray area."[11]

A careful examination of the social, political and bureaucratic circumstances in which this case was brought, however, raises profound questions about Sessions's version of the prosecution.

The record indicates, for example, that Jefferson Beauregard Sessions III was very much a product of his world. Born, raised and educated in Alabama, Sessions's first real job was as a lawyer in Russellville, a small town in the northwest corner of Alabama. After two years of handling the civil cases normal to a small-town law firm, he was appointed an assistant U.S. attorney in Mobile. Sessions's political career had begun. His stint as an assistant U.S. attorney lasted two and a half years. Then came four years with one of Mobile's more prestigious law firms. With the election of Ronald Reagan in 1980, and the sponsorship of Senator Denton, Sessions was ready to take the next step up the political ladder, appointment as the U.S. attorney for the Southern District of Alabama. The Mobile office, with only eight assistant U.S. attorneys, was one of the Justice Department's smallest outposts. But Sessions had now become a player, positioned to leap into elective politics should the right seat open up or, with a lot of luck, available for appointment as a federal judge, a respected and respectable post with lifetime tenure.

The conclusion that Sessions was extremely sloppy in how he expressed his views on racially charged subjects is based on a series of statements he made after his appointment as U.S. attorney, many of which he later acknowledged. Given his responsibilities as the chief federal law enforcement officer in a district with a substantial number of African-American citizens, his proven penchant for making disparaging racial remarks was revealing, surprising and outrageous.

We have a rather complete understanding of Sessions's unfortunate way with words because in March 1986, nine months after the collapse of his dubious election fraud prosecution, the Senate Judiciary Committee quizzed him about a number of his comments at a public hearing. The occasion was a remarkable session called by the committee to consider Sessions's controversial nomination to be a federal district judge. Once again, the prosecutor's chief patron was Senator Denton.

Under questioning by the senators, for example, Sessions acknowledged that he had once told one of his assistants that he thought several Klan members accused of lynching a young black man "were OK until I learned they smoked pot."[12] Looking back, Sessions testified at the Senate hearing, he now realized that he had made "a silly comment."

Sessions also admitted that he had once said he thought the National Association for the Advancement of Colored People (NAACP) was "un-American." In his attempt to defend this characterization of one of America's most middle-of-the-road civil rights organizations, Sessions seemed only to dig himself into even deeper trouble. What he had intended to say, the prosecutor explained, was that to the extent an institution like the NAACP "gets involved in political activities and international relations that people consider to be un-American, they lose their moral authority and ability to function, or to speak with authority to the public because people see them as political."

The chairman of the committee, Senator Joseph Biden of Delaware, then asked the prosecutor whether on yet another occasion he had told one of his fellow federal prosecutors that the NAACP hated white people, that it was out to get white people and that it was "a commie group and a pinko group as well."

On this question, Sessions went from a firm denial to a quivering waffle in less than fifty words. "I do not recall saying anything like that," he began. "I will admit that I am pretty—in my office, in talking to people I associate with, I am loose with my tongue on occasion, and I may have said something similar to that or could be interpreted to that."

The record laid bare in the Senate hearing was sufficiently disgraceful that Sessions won the distinction of being Reagan's first nominee to the post of federal district judge who was rejected by the Senate Judiciary Committee. To understand the degree of displeasure felt by the committee toward Sessions, it is worth noting that before his defeat the committee had approved 269 other Reagan nominees to the federal bench. This particular distinction, however, did not prevent him from returning to Mobile and continuing his responsibilities as a U.S. attorney.

THE VIEW FROM WASHINGTON

The evidence suggesting that the investigation of Mayor Arrington and the prosecutions of the Democratic voting activists were spiteful and politically motivated actions is quite strong. Yet there are indications that the situation was actually something worse: that the Alabama Republican prosecutors were the local hit men of a larger plan.

On September 27, 1984, at approximately the same time the U.S. attorneys in Birmingham and Mobile began to crank up their investigations of Spiver Gordon, the two Turners and Hogue and some other blacks, a secretary from the Justice Department's Public Affairs Office in Washington slid a few dozen copies of a press release into the slanting wooden rack reserved for the department's latest handouts.

This particular release, a three-page statement by the Reagan administration's first attorney general, William French Smith, described what the department said was a stern new federal enforcement strategy to combat election fraud. Because the proclamation of policies, even new and stern ones, is a fairly routine part of the busy Washington news day, most of the reporters who saw the release put it aside without bothering to write an article. The item definitely did not make any of that night's network news shows.

On its face, the collective news judgment of the reporters and editors about Smith's windy high-toned statement was correct. "The right to vote as one pleases and the knowledge that the vote will count—and be counted—form the cornerstone of our democratic system of government," the attorney general intoned. "Any activity that disrupts this electoral process rips the fabric of American society as we know it."[13]

Smith, an upscale Los Angeles lawyer who had been named to head the Justice Department on the basis of years of service as Ronald Reagan's personal attorney, noted that the department had long prosecuted various easy-to-recognize election crimes such as bribing voters, intimidating voters and fraudulently altering vote tallies.

But the time had now come, the attorney general said, for federal prosecutors to attack more subtle forms of election fraud. "For example, federal law prohibits political participants from intentionally seeking out the elderly, the socially disadvantaged, or the illiterate, for purposes of subjugating their political will. Federal law also gives every voter the right to mark his or her ballot in private, free from the watchful eye of political leaders or officials."

After his lengthy preamble, Smith got to the news, although many months would pass before its actual significance would become apparent. "The Department of Justice considers election fraud in any of its forms a crime of the first magnitude. As Attorney General, it is my responsibility to see that those who commit such offenses are dealt with swiftly and sternly."

To try to assure that his newly announced concern about voter fraud was not ignored by his own department, Smith ordered the immediate adoption of a nine-point action program. He instructed each of the ninety-three U.S. attorneys, for example, to appoint a District Election Officer who would be responsible for ensuring that FBI agents and assistant U.S. attorneys were available in every district "to respond to complaints of election irregularities." Smith also directed each district to publicize a local Justice Department telephone number where complaints of voter fraud would be received.

To further emphasize his concerns, Smith directed that voter fraud be the subject of special presentations at the Justice Department's next annual get-together with its district prosecutors. In addition to a special lecture on the subject, attending U.S. attorneys were presented with a new department enforcement manual spelling out the department's policy on the prosecution of election fraud cases.[14]

CHANGING THE RULES

The new manual called for a fundamental shift in Justice Department enforcement policy. First, up until then, in a world with too much crime and too few assistant U.S attorneys, federal prosecutors had been advised to let local district attorneys handle local election problems and to focus their attention on federal matters. Second, up until then, the department had recommended that its prosecutors concentrate their fire on cases where the evidence suggested that the fraud had changed the actual outcome of the election. Third, up until then, the targets of virtually all federal election fraud prosecutions had been insiders—political officials who had conspired to pervert the election machinery they controlled. In sum, cases that primarily involved state and local election fraud, particularly in situations where the attempted fraud had not been successful, should be left to state and local prosecutors.

But, as the September 27 press release and the new Justice Department manual made clear, Smith now wanted to change all that. Federal prosecutors should concern themselves with all elections, not just those that were primarily federal. Federal prosecutors should investigate any allegations of fraud, not just those that changed the outcome of an election. Federal prosecutors should probe outside attempts to influence elections, not just the improper rigging attempts of elected and appointed insiders. Given the Reagan administration's continual rhetorical attack on unnecessary federal regulation, Smith's call for a focused new election fraud enforcement program policy seemed a little out of place.

Despite this contradiction, the Reagan administration's top law-and-order man gave every appearance of being deadly serious about the problem of election fraud. In fact, Attorney General Smith's ranking of election fraud as a crime of the "first magnitude" suggested that he and the Justice Department viewed the outside political fixer who made an unsuccessful attempt to rig a local election almost as much of a threat to the American people as the South American drug dealer, the Middle Eastern terrorist and the made-in-the-U.S.A. serial killer.

THE FAILURE TO HUNT HUNT

Thus it was that the specific Justice Department prosecutions of black Democrats working to increase the turnout of black Democratic voters seems to have been very much in line with departmental policy. Curiously, however, the aggressive approach to election fraud does not appear to have been pursued when it came to white Republicans.

On March 1, 1985, Richard F. Allen, the Agriculture Department's inspector general for the southeast region, dispatched a six-page summary report to Washington recommending the immediate removal from office of Harold Guy Hunt, a born-again Christian who then held the fairly senior federal position of executive director of the department's Agricultural and Conservation Service in Alabama.[15]

The inspector general said his recommendation was based on "significant evidence of substantive and continuing participation in prohibited political activities." The allegation that Hunt had violated the Hatch Act, the federal law prohibiting federal employees from direct involvement in politics, was serious enough. But there was something worse. According to the inspector general, Hunt had also made "repeated and continuing efforts to interfere with the ongoing investigation through direct and indirect contacts with subordinate ACSA employees and other witnesses seeking non-cooperation and withholding of information by these persons." In other words, Hunt appeared to have taken actions which would make him vulnerable to federal charges of obstruction of justice.

On March 4, less than a week after the inspector general had sent his preliminary report to Washington by express mail, Hunt abruptly resigned and announced that he was now running for governor as a Republican candidate. His three-year career as an executive in the Agriculture Department, a patronage position won with the support of Senator Jeremiah Denton, was finished.

But Hunt's resignation failed to satisfy the inspector general. On April 25, 1985, following up on his summary account, Allen filed a comprehensive, inch-thick investigative report, spelling out all the gory details of Hunt's alleged improper and illegal activities from March 1982 to January 1985. The allegations, Allen wrote, were based on the sworn statements and supporting evidence provided him by eight different witnesses, six subordinates of Hunt and two members of the current ACS Committee.[16]

Allen said Hunt had caused subordinates "to prepare on government premises, during official duty hours, voluminous political mailing lists, political correspondence, a political campaign budget, and listings of persons involved in Hunt's campaign for governor in 1978 and in a possible second such campaign in 1986." The high Agriculture Department official also ordered that political fund-raising letters be mailed to his subordinates in the agency, interviewed candidates for his campaign committee in his Agriculture Department office and instructed one subordinate "to prepare typed correspondence containing instructions to his campaign workers."

The Hatch Act specifically prohibits an executive branch employee like Hunt from using "his official authority or influence for the purpose of interfering with or affecting the result of an election" or taking "an active part in political management or political campaigns."

By prompting Hunt's resignation, the Allen reports had served the limited purpose of ridding the Agriculture Department of an official accused of violating important government rules. But the reports, along with a thick appendix of sworn statements, incriminating telephone records and other documents, also provided strong ready-made evidence suggesting that Hunt had violated a number of federal criminal statutes. For this reason, Allen sent his investigative material to John Bell, then the U.S. attorney in Montgomery, the Middle District of Alabama. Like Hunt, the federal prosecutor was a patronage appointment of Senator Denton.

Can anyone be surprised that Hunt, who went on to win the 1986 Alabama gubernatorial election for the Republican Party, was never indicted by the Republican U.S. attorney? Bell is now a trust officer with the First Alabama Bank in Montgomery. In 1990, an investigative reporter named Glynn Wilson contacted the former prosecutor and asked him about the Allen Report and why Hunt was never brought to trial. Bell refused to make any comment to Wilson, other than to claim that he "prosecuted every case that warranted prosecution and never gave special treatment to anybody."[17]

There thus is a wide range of evidence, some direct, some circumstantial, showing that the vast enforcement powers of the Justice Department were specifically harnessed to combat the lawful political gains of black Americans in Alabama during the Reagan and Bush administrations. There were several levels in this campaign. National enforcement policies were altered in such a way that the perceived enemies of the white Republicans in Alabama were subject to investigation. Federal prosecutors persuaded grand juries to bring numerous cases, most of them flawed, as a result of the changed policy. The leading black Democratic figure in the state, Richard Arrington, became the subject of numerous fruitless investigations. The proven serious misdeeds of the leading white Republican figure in the state, Harold Guy Hunt, were ignored. A minimum of four highly influential Justice Department officials, Attorney General William French Smith and Alabama's three U.S. attorneys, were active players in the drama. Finally, there is an extensive public record proving that one of the four, U.S. Attorney Sessions, frequently made racist comments to his colleagues, including a black assistant U.S. attorney.

THE BIG PICTURE

Understanding the true reasons why an individual performs a particular act is tough business. Understanding the reasons why large organizations like the Justice Department or the FBI make the choices they do is even more arduous. This is true partly because individuals and organizations often have overlapping motives.

Attorney General William French Smith, for just one example, may have ordered the full-bore federal prosecution of every voting fraud allegation that came to the Justice Department's attention solely because of his concern for the integrity of the ballot box and as a matter of high conservative principle. In addition, Smith's decision may have involved certain partisan calculations: a determination, for example, that the prosecution of Democratic political operatives in Alabama for activities the department had previously chosen to ignore would benefit the state's Republican office seekers. Finally, it is also possible that Smith, or some of his lieutenants, was an out-and-out racist who believed that black Americans were inherently inferior beings who must be prevented from voting and holding important elective positions.[18]

Ultimately, because of the difficulty of plumbing the inner recesses of any individual's mind, the judgment about motive must remain a matter of speculation. What can be calculated, however, are the consequences of a specific policy or action—how an administrator's decision to take one course rather than another affects the relative well-being, economic status and political influence of the target populations. In this sense, through many administrations, the Justice Department has been amazingly consistent in coming down on the side of the established and against the poor, the black and the disenfranchised.

ACTION VERSUS INACTION

As suggested here and other places in this book, the decision not to investigate and not to prosecute your friends is frequently more important than going after your enemies. Sometimes this discretion is exercised on behalf of a specific person like Harold Guy Hunt, sometimes on behalf of a more general cause.

For at least the last thirty years, for example, most new attorneys general have promised the nation vigorous enforcement of the nation's civil rights laws. President Clinton's Janet Reno, President Carter's attorneys general Griffin Bell and Benjamin Civiletti and President Johnson's Ramsey Clark, of course, were among those who made this politically correct promise. Interestingly enough, President Bush's last attorney general, William Barr, took the same pledge.

At his confirmation hearing before the Senate Judiciary Committee in 1991, Barr told Congress, and thus the American people, that drugs, violent crime and civil rights were his top law enforcement priorities.[19] A few months later, in early 1992, Barr sounded the same note before the House Appropriations Committee. "Another high priority is civil rights enforcement," Barr testified. By limiting his discussion to the growth in requested funds, rather than to the department's actual record, the attorney general managed to suggest an aggressive and growing effort. "We are seeking a 13.8 percent increase in the Civil Rights Division, which is, I believe, the highest increase of any of the litigating divisions."[20]

Once again, computer analysis of the records of the Justice Department and the FBI provides a unique insight into the vast gulf that sometimes develops between the department's rhetoric and its actions. For if Barr ever intended to make civil rights one of his "high priority" enforcement efforts, he surely defined this phrase in a curious way.

Here is the overview: In 1992, the Federal Bureau of Investigation, an agency under the nominal control of Attorney General Barr, received 8,599 civil rights complaints from the public. The FBI made unilateral administrative decisions that well over half of these complaints—5,387 of them—had so little merit that they were not worth any investigation at all. Of the remaining 3,212 complaints, the bureau determined that about two thirds—2,400—were sufficiently serious to be forwarded to the Justice Department with a formal recommendation that they be prosecuted. Finally, of the 2,400 matters the FBI sent to the department, federal prosecutors throughout the country brought a grand total of forty cases.[21]

The federal enforcement of the civil rights laws was a high priority matter for Barr? If that were so, acknowledging that many citizen complaints do not involve federal crimes and others may lack sufficient supporting detail, why was it that Justice Department prosecutors brought criminal charges in less than half of one percent of all civil rights complaints that came to the attention of the department's investigating arm, the FBI? If that was so, why did federal prosecutors bring charges in only about 4 percent of the complaints that the FBI said should be prosecuted? Given the FBI's historic reluctance to investigate police brutality and other civil rights matters, why did Attorney General Barr and John Dunne, the assistant attorney general for civil rights, fail to undertake a formal audit of the 5,387 complaints that the bureau in 1992 decided did not even require preliminary investigation?[22]

Finally, if civil rights enforcement was a top priority matter for Attorney General Barr and the Bush administration, why was federal enforcement in most other areas of law so much more vigorous?

Because acquiring corroborating evidence in civil rights cases is unusually difficult and the whole area is highly controversial, it would not be fair to compare the prosecution of persons accused of violating the civil rights laws with far more common matters such as drugs or bank fraud. But might not the Justice Department's processing of official corruption be roughly analogous to its processing of civil rights matters? Would not the political sensitivities be approximately parallel? Would not the challenge of collecting evidence of corruption among state and local government officials be similar to the difficulty of developing proof against brutal cops?

Despite these affinities, Justice Department records show that federal prosecutors handled the two categories of criminal matters in distinctly different ways. In 1992, in fact, the Justice Department was nine times more likely to prosecute when an official corruption matter was referred to it than when the referred matter involved civil rights. Here are the 1992 percentages: While federal prosecutors filed formal charges on 39.7 percent of the official corruption matters with which they were presented, the same action occurred in only 4.1 percent of the civil rights matters.

Both Attorney General Barr and Assistant Attorney General Dunne contended separately that the explanation for the extremely low rate for department civil rights prosecutions reflected their belief that it was essential to encourage local and state governments to deal with the civil rights violations of their communities. "The federal government should only step in when local authorities have failed their lawful responsibilities," said Dunne.

But if the policy of encouraging local activism is appropriate for civil rights, would it not be equally valid for official corruption? Barr declined to answer this question, insisting several times that he did not understand the point. Dunne adopted a different response, defending his personal record and the department's leave-it-to-the-locals policy for civil rights cases. He added, however, that as the assistant attorney general for civil rights he was not responsible for the Justice Department's far more vigorous official corruption effort.

A much more devious explanation for the Bush administration's double-decked enforcement policy suggests itself. One relatively important group of supporters for President Bush were the nation's police officers and prison guards—a large, growing and mostly conservative collection of voters who are relatively easy to reach through such labor groups as the National Association of Police Organizations and the Fraternal Order of Police. On the other hand, African-American and Mexican-American voters, the victims in a substantial number of civil rights abuses, were never among the Bush administration's biggest fans. Finally, because state and local governments throughout the 1980s were more likely to be controlled by Democratic than Republican politicians, the federal prosecution of official corruption was, in the balance, an advantageous strategy for the Republicans.

Given the mix of these various forces, can anyone be surprised that Justice Department tapes show that the Bush administration's Justice Department viewed official corruption as a much more important problem than police brutality?

DONALD DUCK STRIKES OUT IN NEW ORLEANS

T he highly questionable attacks on specific black Democratic political figures in Alabama and the low priority given to the prosecution of civil rights matters suggests that the Justice Department under two Republican presidents engaged in a systematic effort to undermine black Americans. The evidence supporting this ugly proposition becomes even stronger with the examination of a third department program, this one involving a systematic effort that sought to disenfranchise millions of African-American voters.

One of the most egregious examples of this more expansive dirty business took place in Louisiana following the 1980 census. The chief actors were William Bradford Reynolds, then the assistant attorney general for civil rights, and Governor David C. Treen, the former chairman of the central committee of the racist Louisiana States Rights Party. The main platform of the party was the preservation of segregation.[23]

Immediately after publication of the 1980 census figures, the Louisiana legislature recognized that the growth in population mandated changes in the boundaries of the state's eight congressional districts. On November 6, 1981, following statewide hearings, the legislature approved a reapportionment plan. A major feature of the plan would have been the creation of a New Orleans congressional district in which 54 percent of the population was black.

That very evening, Governor Treen announced the proposal was unacceptable to him and that he would veto it. For complex historical and procedural reasons, the Louisiana legislature has never overridden a veto. As a result of Treen's threat, the legislature immediately began work on a second redistricting plan. This plan, the details of which were hammered out during a private all-white meeting in the computer room in a subbasement of the state capitol, did not provide the New Orleans congressional district with a majority of blacks. Instead, black voters were split into two districts, which guaranteed they would remain a distinct minority in each. Because of the weirdly contorted boundaries of one of these substitute districts, the proposal became known as the "Donald Duck Plan."

Under Section 5 of the Voting Rights Act, the final plan had to be cleared by the Civil Rights Division before it could go into effect. During the federal review, the staff prepared a letter for Assistant Attorney General Reynolds in which the Justice Department asked Governor Treen for additional information about his role in the redistricting negotiations, specifically about his statements that he was opposed to a black-majority district. Reynolds refused to send this letter, substituting one that avoided asking the governor any potentially embarrassing questions about why he had blocked the first plan.[24] (A senior county tax official who supported the creation of a black-majority district had told Justice Department investigators that one of Treen's key allies in the Louisiana legislature would not support the original plan for the stated reason that "we already have a nigger mayor [in New Orleans] and we don't need another nigger bigshot."[25]

Upon the completion of the Justice Department's investigation, even without answers to the questions Reynolds refused to ask, the staff of the Civil Rights Division recommended that the Justice Department reject the second plan because it was intentionally discriminatory. "It is clear in our view that the Governor was acutely aware of the racial consequences of his actions, and those racial consideration[s] formed the basis for his actions," the staff concluded.[26]

A subsequent examination of Reynolds's calendar, telephone logs and other Justice Department material—uncovered by Lani Guinier, then with the NAACP's Legal Defense Fund, and William I. Quigley, a New Orleans lawyer—discovered that during the time the staff of the assistant attorney general was investigating the adoption of the second plan, Reynolds had two face-to-face meetings and at least nine telephone conversations with Governor Treen. Guinier says the same records showed that Reynolds had no meetings or telephone conversations with any Louisiana black legislators or community leaders who opposed the plan.

Reynolds's repeated contacts with Treen may have been crucial to the Republican desire to create new districts that would assure the election of additional conservative white Republicans to the House of Representatives while preventing the creation of a "nigger bigshot." Although the handwritten notes of the meetings between the assistant attorney general and the governor are sketchy, they clearly indicate that the former official in the States Rights Party argued against what he called "racial bloc voting." The notes also make it clear that Treen defined bloc voting only in terms of what blacks do when they vote for black candidates. Whites voting for whites, of course, was not the governor's concern.

Whatever the explanation for Reynolds's final action, the assistant attorney general rejected the recommendation of his staff and approved the suspect plan. There was no evidence of racial intent on the part of the governor or the legislature, Reynolds concluded in his June 20, 1982, decision.

Fifteen months later, however, a three-judge panel ruled that the plan approved by Reynolds was unlawful and had to be replaced by a new one. "We are convinced that in the present case, the division of the black population [into two districts] was not designed to enhance the effectiveness of the black electorate, nor is it likely to occasion such," the judges held. "Based on the totality of relevant circumstances, the court concludes that the contours of the First and Second Congressional districts, as established by Act 20, operate to deny or abridge the rights of minority voters, who are accorded less opportunity than other members of the electorate to participate in the political process and to elect representatives of their choice."[27]

That, of course, was the precise goal of the redistricting plan pushed through the legislature by Governor Treen and approved, against the recommendations of his staff, by Assistant Attorney General Reynolds.

NORTH CAROLINA

If Reynolds's decision in Louisiana had been an isolated event, it might be possible to argue that the case did not reflect the general attitude of the Justice Department and the Reagan administration that controlled it. The Donald Duck determination, however, was not an isolated case. In 1985, for example, the Justice Department again astonished most of the legal community by filing a friend-of-the-court brief supporting an appeal by the North Carolina attorney general from a federal court decision holding that the state's 1982 redistricting plan violated the Voting Rights Act.

As is customary, the administration's submission had been written by the Office of the Solicitor General, the departmental unit which specializes in representing the views of the federal government before the Supreme Court. In this case the brief was signed by Assistant Attorney General Reynolds and Charles Freid, the acting solicitor general.

The Justice Department, siding with the attorney general of North Carolina, called on the Supreme Court to throw out the decision of a lower federal court that the multimember legislative districts created by the North Carolina legislature diluted black voting strength in ways that violated the Voting Rights Act of 1965.

One indication of the wrongheaded nature of the Justice Department's brief was the astonishing fact that the department's arguments were opposed by North Carolina's governor, the Republican National Committee and a bipartisan group of House and Senate members including Republican senators Robert Dole of Kansas and Charles Grassley of Iowa and the senior Republican on the House Judiciary Committee.

A second, even stronger, indication of the questionable and highly political quality of the Justice Department's decision was that the Supreme Court unanimously rejected the department's interpretation of the law.

THE POLITICAL NEXUS

As already suggested, it is nearly impossible to imagine that the Justice Department's complex overlapping enforcement efforts aimed at black Democratic political leaders, black Democratic political activists and black voters during the Republican years from 1980 to 1992 were motivated by straightforward considerations of right and wrong, or were the random actions of isolated government officials just going about their job of enforcing the law. The various activities within the Justice Department were too widespread, too cohesive and too advantageous to the party then in control of the government.

It therefore should not come as a complete surprise to learn that the Republican National Committee (RNC) was a part of the same campaign. The RNC, of course, is a private organization with no legally mandated control over any federal agency. Yet when Republicans control the White House, the committee reflects the social and political attitudes of many if not most of the thousands of political appointees selected to head the federal agencies of the executive branch. As noted elsewhere, the Justice Department, in relation to its size, has more political appointees than any other major agency of the government.

The first question about Republican activities came on December 14, 1981, when the Democratic National Committee (DNC) brought a civil suit charging that the Republican National Committee, the New Jersey Republican State Committee and various Republican Party officials had engaged in "a concerted effort to threaten and harass black and Hispanic voters" in New Jersey in direct violation of the Constitution and several federal election laws.[28]

The gist of the suit was that the Republicans, working through an organization called the National Ballot Security Task Force, had improperly challenged the right to vote of some 45,000 New Jersey voters in predominantly black and Hispanic areas. The task force's method for selecting the individual voters to be challenged was simple. Using computerized mailing lists, postcards were sent to all registered Democrats living in the state's heavily Democratic neighborhoods. The names of those whose postcards were returned to the task force as undelivered were then placed on a voter challenge list. Less than two weeks before the November 1981 election, Republican representatives formally requested the New Jersey Commissioner of Elections to remove those persons on the challenge list from the voter registration rolls on the grounds that they no longer lived in the district in which they were registered.

While the Republican research obviously identified some bogus voters, it also resulted in thousands of questionable challenges which tended to reduce black voter turnout. There are many reasons, after all, why a postcard may be returned as undelivered, especially in low-income areas. After extensive exploration of the Republican program before federal judge Dickinson R. Debevoise, the two parties signed a consent decree on November 1, 1982. A key provision of which stated that the Republicans would refrain from undertaking any ballot security activities where the purpose or significant effect was "to deter qualified voters from voting" in areas with substantial numbers of black and Hispanic residents.

Just a few years later, however, political reporters and the staff members of the Democratic National Committee discovered that the RNC had hired an organization called the Ballot Integrity Group, Inc. The year was 1986 and this time the object was to expand the RNC's New Jersey project to minority voters all over the United States. In Louisiana, for example, lawyers for the Democrats found that the Ballot Integrity Group had mailed preliminary postcards to 350,000 registered voters in the state, three quarters of whom were black. The lawyers also discovered a memo written by a Republican National Committee executive on August 13, 1986, stating that the official assumed the postcard program "could keep the black vote down considerably" in Louisiana.

As a result of the discovery, the Democrats renewed their complaint with Judge Debevoise. On July 27, 1987, a second consent agreement was signed. This time the judge ordered the Republican National Committee not to engage in any so-called ballot security activities unless they were specifically authorized by the first decree or he had been given an opportunity to review and approve them.[29]

Four years later, in November 1990, Judge Debevoise issued yet another ruling, this one suggesting that the Republican National Committee was not terribly concerned about his judicial restrictions relating to its postcard operation. The judge said the committee had failed to live up to his orders when it did not show him the instructional materials it had sent state Republican parties relating to ballot security programs.

The 1990 order was issued in response to a Democratic complaint that Jesse Helms, the right-wing Republican senator from North Carolina, was using the prohibited ballot security technique in what turned out to be his come-from-behind effort to win reelection. Judge Debevoise said he had not issued an order against Helms's use of the questionable political technique because the DNC had failed to prove that the RNC "had participated in, or assisted ballot security activities in North Carolina."[30]

THE PAST IS INDEED PROLOGUE

T he twelve-year record of the Justice Department under Presidents Reagan and Bush in dealing with sensitive racial issues demonstrates the extent to which cynical political motives can corrupt federal prosecutors. But the impression should not be left that the men and women who controlled the department during the Reagan and Bush years were unique. Partisan calculations, frequently based on naked racial concerns, have almost always played an important role in both the policy and enforcement decisions of the Justice Department, even in administrations generally considered to be friendly to the cause of racial equality.

Franklin Delano Roosevelt, for example, is widely remembered as a president who courted the support and votes of black Americans by making the federal government more responsive to their interests. This memory, based partly on the generous concerns of his wife, Eleanor, has become an article of faith among both the liberals who revered FDR and the conservatives who hated him and his caring wife. As always, the truth is much more complicated.

Roosevelt himself, like many men of that age and class, sometimes talked like a racist. Thurgood Marshall, the brilliant legal theoretician and first African American to be appointed to the Supreme Court, certainly believed that Roosevelt was a racist. And he apparently had cause. On one occasion, Marshall recalled, he went to talk with Francis Biddle, Roosevelt's second attorney general, about a case where a black Virginia man had been accused of shooting a sheriff. While they were meeting, Biddle called Roosevelt, and asked Marshall to pick up an extension so he could hear the conversation. "I warned you not to call me again about any of Eleanor's niggers," Marshall recalls FDR saying, apparently unaware that the lawyer was listening. "Call me one more time and *you* are fired."[31]

The powerful racism of the period, along with the flinty political calculations of the Roosevelt team, meant black American citizens could not expect much help from the federal government. Consider, for example, the response of Roosevelt and his Justice Department to the sudden surge of vicious lynchings that swept the South shortly after he was elected president in 1932. According to an authoritative analysis published by the Commission on Interracial Cooperation, 3,745 people were lynched in the United States between 1889 and the year of Mr. Roosevelt's election. The commission said that more than four out of five of the victims were black, practically all the lynchers were white and that the lynchers were subsequently convicted in only eight tenths of one percent of the barbarous murders.

Historical analysis has found considerable variation in the annual count of lynchings committed in the United States since the Civil War. A special congressional commission on the Ku Klux Klan reported in 1872, for example, that between 1869 and 1870 there were at least 124 lynchings in Mississippi alone. The commission also found that during an eighteen-month period beginning in 1866, 197 persons were lynched in North and South Carolina. Meanwhile, in the year ending July 1, 1868, mobs in Tennessee staged 168 lynchings.

Although there were several periods of social unrest when the annual number of lynchings surged to levels that could be compared with the Reconstruction period, the national trend was generally downward, reaching the unusually low figure of only eight in 1932. As the Great Depression began to sweep the nation, however, the number of lynchings suddenly surged, increasing to twenty-eight in 1933. One case that attracted special attention that year concerned the lynching of two white men in San Jose, California.

The incident was sensationalized, of course, because of the race of the victims. But what made the case unusual was the reaction of California's governor. In the days after the lynching, he promised he would pardon the members of the lynch mob for the good job they had done. As noted by J. Eugene Marans in his 1962 honors thesis for Harvard College's Department of History, the "San Jose lynchings and the governor's statement became a cause célèbre overnight. The issue of mob violence was clearly shown as a nationwide, interracial problem."[32]

At that time, Roosevelt's White House staff had declined several requests from the NAACP to discuss the wave of violent killings and the fact that the president had not made a public statement on the issue. But eight days after the California murders, on December 6, 1933, Roosevelt did speak out. In an eloquent speech to a Federal Council of Churches convention in Washington, the president strongly denounced that "vile form of collective murder" which "has broken out in our midst anew. We know that it is murder and a deliberate and definite disobedience of the commandment, 'Thou shalt not kill.' We do not excuse those in high places or low who condone lynch law."

Roosevelt's statement thrilled Walter Francis White, the gifted executive secretary of the NAACP. White, along with Edward Costigan, a progressive Democratic senator from Colorado, and a handful of other liberal lawmakers, had launched a national campaign to make lynching, and the failure of local law enforcement officials to prevent a lynching, a federal crime.

But FDR's speech to the churchmen turned out to be rhetoric: comforting to hear but free of substantive remedies. Despite the shocking ferocity of the lynchings and the absence of lynch laws in most of the states, especially in the South, the president, his White House advisers and his attorney general very definitely had other fish to fry. In fact, Attorney General Homer Cummings, a former chairman of the Democratic National Committee, was absolutely opposed to any Justice Department involvement in lynching cases.[33]

The Roosevelt administration and Cummings expressed negative views in two ways: flat opposition to Walter White's proposed antilynching law, and an explicit Justice Department decision not to use the Lindbergh kidnapping law against lynch mobs that dragged their victims across state borders.

Shortly after Roosevelt's stirring speech, Cummings issued his own statement denouncing lynching as "reprehensible, inexcusable, unjust and un-American." But, he added, lynching was a problem that had to be handled by local authorities, and the Department of Justice was "not interested in lynching legislation."[34]

Although a federal lynching law would have presented several possible constitutional hurdles, the administration's decision was pure politics. The Justice Department, at Roosevelt's request, was developing proposals to control interstate crime, and no one in the administration

wanted to support a federal law on lynching for fear of creating southern opposition in Congress to the crime package. Louis Howe, a top assistant to the president, expressed this concern in a note attached to his
copy of an early version of the Costigan lynching bill. "Not favored at
this time—may create hostility to other crime bills."[35]

The Justice Department's enforcement decision was equally political. In 1934, Congress modified the existing Lindbergh law, making kidnapping a federal crime when the subject was transported across state
borders and "held for ransom or reward or for otherwise." During Senate hearings, Cummings endorsed the addition of the words "or for otherwise" and indicated that he understood the importance of the
seemingly insignificant phrase. Under the original law, kidnapping was
a federal crime only when a ransom was demanded. Now, dragging a
person across a state line was a federal crime, whatever the reason.
Clearly, the new version of the Lindbergh law applied to interstate
lynchings.

A short time later, a man named A. B. Young was captured by a mob
in Tennessee and brought back to Mississippi, where he was lynched.
Walter White asked Roosevelt to prosecute the killer under the Lindbergh law. Cummings, however, in his opinion to Roosevelt on the
case, rejected the broad interpretation he had provided Congress only a
few months before, now inexplicably arguing that prosecution was not
possible because there had been no ransom request. A federal indictment, he said, also might be viewed as an attempt to circumvent Congress and might cause it to "react unfavorably in connection with
future legislation of an interstate character which the necessities of our
people might require."[36]

In any case, Cummings's concerns about his people, apparently the
officials in the Justice Department, easily won the day over the
NAACP's worries about its people, dozens of individual victims of mob
violence.

THE KENNEDY MYSTIQUE

J ohn F. Kennedy is another president who is remembered as a vigorous champion of civil rights. This memory is partly based on such ges-
tures as his telephone call expressing sympathy to Coretta Scott King
about the plight of her jailed husband during the 1960 presidential campaign. It is reinforced by the substantive and sometimes heroic efforts
of Justice Department officials like Burke Marshall, John Doar and John

Seigenthaler in Birmingham and Jackson and other infamous crisis points of the South.

But as with Roosevelt, partisan calculations were always present. On March 4, 1963, New York governor Nelson A. Rockefeller, an undeclared candidate for the Republican presidential nomination, attacked the civil rights record of President John F. Kennedy and his brother Attorney General Robert Kennedy. His forum was a rally sponsored by the New York State Conference of the NAACP. One of the specific charges by the governor was that the Kennedy brothers had recently appointed four federal judges in the South "who were well known at the time of their appointment for their segregationist views."[37]

Although the governor's criticism was not completely fair—senators by long tradition have played a key role in the selection of federal judges within their states—his condemnation still hit a raw nerve. The next day, President Kennedy responded by asserting that his judicial appointments generally had "done a remarkable job in fulfilling their oath of office. There may be cases where this is not true, and that is unfortunate, but I would say that on the whole it has been an extraordinary and very creditable record."[38]

Subsequent research by a large number of serious scholars indicate that Rockefeller's criticism of Kennedy's judges had merit. According to the analysis of Victor Navasky, a liberal lawyer, editor and the author of the definitive book on the operation of the Justice Department during the Kennedy years, at least five of the twenty white lawyers that the Kennedy brothers appointed to lifetime federal judgeships in Florida, Texas, Georgia, Alabama, Louisiana and Mississippi were singled out by students of judicial decision-making as "anti–civil rights, racists, segregationists and/or obstructionists."[39]

The results, in both legal and social terms, were disastrous. Judge W. Harold Cox, for example, refused to find a pattern of discrimination in Clarke County, Mississippi, even though only one African American, the high school principal, had been able to register to vote in thirty years. On another occasion, Cox asked who was telling black residents "they can get in line to register and push people around, acting like a bunch of chimpanzees." He also referred to litigants as "niggers." A second infamous Kennedy appointee, Judge Robert Elliott of Georgia, ruled against black litigants in 90 percent of the civil rights cases that came before him during the years Robert Kennedy was attorney general. Ten years after the famous Brown decision, he was still refusing to enjoin the operation of segregated public schools.

The damage was severe. As argued by Navasky, the opinions of the racist judges, while usually overturned on appeal, seriously postponed justice. The opinions also weakened the civil rights movement by fragmenting and radicalizing both its leaders and the rank and file. Finally, the decisions undermined the administrative processes of the Justice Department. "No aspect of Robert Kennedy's Attorney Generalship is more vulnerable to criticism than these appointments," Navasky concluded.[40]

As already noted, the appointment of judges has always involved a subtle power struggle between the man in the White House and the Senate. But in the end, a choice is made by the president and his staff, and on too many occasions, they made awful choices. According to an article in *The Nation* by Robert Sherrill, the appointment of Harold Cox was achieved after his chief supporter and college roommate, Senator James Eastland of Mississippi, had a brief conversation with Attorney General Kennedy in the hallways of the Capitol. "Tell your brother that if he will give me Harold Cox I will give him the nigger," Sherrill reported.[41] In this particularly inelegant transaction, the black pawn referred to by Eastland apparently was Thurgood Marshall, the brilliant NAACP lawyer whom the Kennedys then wanted to appoint to the Federal Court of Appeals.

A second theory about Cox's appointment turns on Robert Kennedy's obsession with organized crime. To wage a successful war against the Mafia, Kennedy believed, it was essential that Congress quickly approve a legislative package making it a federal crime to travel in interstate commerce to aid racketeering or gambling. William Geoghegan, the number one assistant to Byron White, then the deputy attorney general, recalled that the bargain for immediate approval of the crime proposals went this way: "It was one of those little deals with Senator Eastland. He got five anti-crime bills moved through the Judiciary Committee so quickly that nobody had a chance to read them. Eastland mumbled some words on the floor and the bills were passed by unanimous consent. Maybe this was the price for appointing Cox in Mississippi."[42]

Geoghegan is not the only observer to believe that Cox was the price Kennedy had to pay for his crime legislation. Assuming this theory is correct, the parallels are striking between the Kennedy-Eastland deal and the political arrangement apparently worked out thirty years before by Roosevelt's attorney general. In both cases, liberal administrations were willing to duck their moral and legal responsibility of protecting a defenseless segment of the American people in order to increase their basic enforcement powers.

THE SECRET ROLE
OF PROFESSOR J. EDGAR HOOVER

Contributing mightily to the Justice Department's questionable civil rights record was J. Edgar Hoover, a narrow-minded and fearful racist who for many decades injected his spiteful views into the highest reaches of government. The strong and consistent evidence regarding Hoover's racism includes his long refusal to hire any black FBI agents except as personal servants, and the FBI's systematic failure, for many decades, to investigate outrageous attacks against blacks by individual citizens, organizations like the Ku Klux Klan and many state and local enforcement officers. Although Hoover's racism clearly paralleled that of many Americans, the FBI director had a special obligation: He headed a powerful federal agency that at least in theory was under the control of a series of presidents and attorneys general who gave speeches touting their solemn belief in the principle of equal opportunity for all citizens.

It is hard to exaggerate the truly sinister role played by Hoover and his FBI, and thus the Justice Department, in the way the United States government responded to the organized efforts of black Americans to achieve equal treatment under law. The sheer scope of Hoover's efforts to shape the racial beliefs of generations of government officials, to protect local and state law enforcement officials who were personally involved in attacking black citizens and to undermine the federal response to these social upheavals can only be described as malevolent.

Internal administrative records of the FBI provide incontrovertible evidence concerning hundreds of specific situations supporting these generalities. One small but ugly example involved the Freedom Riders, a small group of civil rights activists who had decided to challenge the segregationist laws of the South. The Ku Klux Klan's attack on this group in May 1961 was a brutal exercise in mob violence that paradoxically alerted many Americans—at least for a while—to the dimensions of that era's racial conflicts.

Appalling FBI documents later made public by a federal district judge proved that Thomas Jenkins, senior agent in charge of the bureau's Birmingham office, failed to make any effort to protect the Freedom Riders from the mob even though he had long known that the violent KKK attack would occur, and that Birmingham police chief Eugene "Bull" Connor was engaged in a conspiracy to protect the KKK thugs. But the FBI's involvement in the conspiracy to terrorize the Freedom Riders was not merely a passive failure to act. Even worse, the documents show that Jenkins actually told the KKK when the FBI expected the Freedom Riders to arrive in Birmingham.[43]

Because so many similar events are stored in the FBI's closet of racial horribles, it is easy to become hardened to them, to begin discounting their significance in American history. On the other hand, when considering the individual atrocities of the FBI, it becomes easy to lose track of a bigger truth. Hoover did not limit the expression of his racial animosity to concrete situations in which the FBI encouraged individual police departments to do the wrong thing or undertook to harass successful black political figures like Richard Arrington. Hoover also mounted an organized campaign to disseminate his racist views throughout the administrations of the Democratic and Republican presidents he in theory served.

On September 24, 1943, for example, Hoover delivered a secret report to President Roosevelt. The report's title was ambitious: "Survey of Racial Conditions in the United States." In a covering letter to Major General Edwin M. Watson, secretary to the president, Hoover said the 429-page document included "information received by this Bureau as late as August 5, 1943, and represents data concerning un-American forces, as well as social, economic and political factors that affect racial conditions."[44]

Hoover pretentiously called the massive document a "monograph," perhaps in the hopes of persuading its readers in the White House that this was a serious work of sociology. But the FBI offering was infected with the same simplistic outside-agitator theory of racial tension that had dominated Hoover's personal thinking throughout his life. "As evidenced from the foregoing details and as apparent in the appendix of this survey, there are and have been subversive forces at work among the American Negroes causing unrest and dissatisfaction," the report declared. "The most outstanding force, as evidenced from the information received by this Bureau, is the Communist Party."[45]

The ponderous FBI tome was extremely condescending, at one point referring to the "pseudo leaders" of "the Negro people." "In the matter of Negro leadership throughout the country, a number of opinions have been expressed, both by Negro and white sources of information, that it [the Negro leadership] is weak and not capable of acting in the best interest of its race. The practice of exploiting and enlarging beyond each alleged incident [of racial discrimination] which acts to the detriment of Negroes by some Negro leaders is cited as an influential factor in stirring up unrest and discontent rather than promoting the best interest of their race."[46]

It was the middle of World War II and President Roosevelt had more important things to worry about than Hoover's distorted, though hardly unusual, racial views. But a decade later, beginning in the early 1950s, the war was over and race returned to its position as one of the most important and difficult issues facing the American people. One of the first outward signs of the coming storm was a little-noticed 1953 bus boycott in Baton Rouge, Louisiana. At about the same time, a series of suits challenging the legality of segregated schools was brought in federal courts across the country that in May 1954 would culminate in the Supreme Court's momentous decision in *Brown* v. *Board of Education.* It was also in this period that a young unknown minister named Dr. Martin Luther King, Jr., first became involved in a bus boycott in Montgomery, Alabama.

On the morning of March 9, 1956—apparently at the invitation of Attorney General Herbert Brownell—J. Edgar Hoover once again brought his racist soapbox to the White House. This time the occasion was a briefing Hoover gave President Eisenhower and his cabinet on the bureau's views regarding "Racial Tension and Civil Rights." Although a transcript of the talk has never surfaced, Hoover spoke from a fifteen-page FBI position paper that showed his racial views had undergone little change since he dispatched his monograph to Roosevelt some thirteen years earlier.[47]

"Racial tension has been mounting almost daily since the Supreme Court banned segregation in public schools on May 17, 1954, and later, on May 31, 1955, required that integration be established at the earliest possible date 'consistent with good faith compliance,' " Hoover began.[48]

The FBI's presentation, however, did not maintain this measured tone for long. One reason for the mounting tension, he told the cabinet, was the "clash of culture" inherent "when the protection of racial purity is a rule of life ingrained deeply as the basic truth."

Hoover said the South, moved in part by the paternalistic spirit that was a holdover from the days of slavery, "recognizes the need to provide greater opportunity for Negroes . . . but does not yet consider that mixed education is the means whereby the races can best be served. And behind this stalks the specter of racial intermarriages."

Among the chief causes for southern resentment toward the Supreme Court's rulings, the FBI chief continued, was health. "The claim is made that colored parents are not as careful in looking after the health and cleanliness of their children [as white parents]. The claim of a higher incidence of venereal disease among Negroes is also cited as a reason for segregation in the use of lavatory facilities and gymnasiums."

Hoover also recalled for Eisenhower and his most senior advisers that "race relations still are affected by the deep and bitter feelings which have been handed down from generation to generation in the deep South. Memories of the Civil War are being revived. There is still talk among some cultured and educated Southerners of the rule by 'blacks,' 'carpetbaggers' and 'scalawags.' "

While Hoover acknowledged that the persons leading "the crusade for integration" based "their position on legal, moral and ethical grounds," he immediately undercut this admission by noting that the leading proponents of integration were the National Association for the Advancement of Colored People, what he called the Muslim Cult of Islam and the Communist Party USA, an organization that sought to weaken the United States by "pitting class against class."

The Communist Party, he continued, "which had long been clamoring for a March on Washington to bring pressure on both the Executive and Legislative Branches of Government," had adopted a program demanding that Congress enact "antilynching, antipoll tax and fair employment practices legislation."

Hoover incorrectly minimized the importance of those he called the "prosegregationists" in stirring up racial tensions. Whether this failure was from poor FBI intelligence or some unknown tactical consideration of Hoover is not known. "In no instance have we been advised that any of the so-called White Citizens Councils advocate violence," he told the assembled cabinet members. Hoover also said the Ku Klux Klan "was pretty much defunct" after a series of prosecutions in the early 1950s, although an effort had recently begun to reactivate it.

With the death of Hoover, and the repugnant disclosures of the post-Watergate years, a new and more professionalized FBI is said to be in the making. Because of the profound secrecy that surrounds many FBI activities, however, it is not clear that this optimism is well founded.

During the 1980s, for example, a group of black FBI agents charged that white agents had frequently subjected them to racist harassment. In 1993, after several independent investigations had concluded that the internal harassment of black agents was a substantial problem, the FBI agreed to a settlement, one provision of which allows a federal judge to supervise the bureau's employment practices to ensure the fair treatment of black agents.[49] A few years earlier, a federal district court judge in Texas ruled in favor of a group of Hispanic agents who charged the FBI had systematically discriminated against them in job assignments, promotions, transfer and discipline.[50] And as mentioned previously in this chapter, the FBI in 1992 made a unilateral decision not to investigate more than 5,000 civil rights complaints. Of the 3,000 complaints it did investigate, the FBI determined that an additional 1,000 were not worthy of referral to the Justice Department.

While it seems certain that many of these FBI rejects were for good cause, the bureau's handling of some individual complaints was highly questionable. One notorious failure involved a situation in which the FBI office in Jackson, Mississippi, refused, for a period of nine months, to investigate serious allegations that the guards in a city prison were repeatedly raping juvenile female prisoners. When Justice Department

officials finally ordered the reluctant FBI field office to investigate the
matter, a reporter later determined that bureau agents had never interviewed the jailhouse rape victims.[51]

IN THE LONG HAUL

P artly because of the very different expectations we have about various administrations, liberal and conservative, it is not easy to keep the
Justice Department's civil rights enforcement activities in proper perspective. The canvas is large, the players many and the secrets profound. It is clear, however, that department policies and enforcement
activities have always been influenced by complex partisan calculations, sometimes tinged with outright racism, as well as by a concern
for the law. Although the final outcome of the calculations might differ
slightly, the basic process has remained remarkably similar regardless
of who was in the White House.

One man with an intensely informed view of the Justice Department
during the last thirty years of racial turmoil is J. L. Chestnut, Jr., a
short, chunky, opinionated and very direct African-American lawyer
who was born in Selma, Alabama, on December 16, 1930. With a fringe
of white hair around his bald head, bushy eyebrows and a deep throaty
laugh, J.L., as he is widely known, has been practicing law in Selma
since he returned after graduating from Dillard College in New Orleans,
serving a two-year stint in the army and completing his studies at
Howard University Law School in 1958.

In 1985, for example, shortly after Albert and Evelyn Turner were indicted by Jefferson Beauregard Sessions for voter fraud, Chestnut and
several other lawyers working for the voting activists requested a conference with Attorney General Edwin Meese. A meeting was set up
under the auspices of the National Education Association. Chestnut
said that during the pretrial discovery process they had uncovered evidence of whites providing their supporters exactly the same kind of
voter assistance that had prompted the government to bring charges
against Turner and his wife.

"We actually met with Ed Meese, Brad Reynolds and eight other
high-echelon Justice Department lawyers around a huge table in the attorney general's conference room," Chestnut remembered during a long
interview in his dark, cluttered office that, curiously enough, is located
on Jeff Davis Avenue in Selma. "Meese himself furiously took notes
even though he asked that no one else take notes. I guess he thought as
attorney general he was entitled.

"At first Meese said he could only spare us fifteen minutes, but then he stayed for an hour and a half," Chestnut continued. "We laid out the evidence we had obtained, and asked Meese how the government could justify prosecuting us when it was not prosecuting white people who were doing exactly the same thing. Meese said he did not know that was going on, that no one had told him. He promised to look into it and get back to us."

Chestnut was not surprised when Meese failed to call back. But talking about the long meeting with high Reagan administration officials jogged the Alabama lawyer's memory about other trips to Washington and other disappointments.

Many years before, for example, Chestnut and another delegation of civil rights activists came to beg Robert Kennedy to bring federal charges against the corrupt and ruthless police officers who were brutalizing civil rights demonstrators in Alabama. While the lawyer had nothing but praise for John Doar and some of the other Justice Department officials who were trying to keep the peace in Alabama at that time, Chestnut and the others felt that somehow the federal government could do more to check the official brutality of the local police.

"Robert Kennedy listened to us," Chestnut recalled. "He said he wanted to help us. But then he said his hands were tied, that he was doing all he could do right then, that we would have to wait until after the election before the Justice Department could do any more."

President Kennedy was not to be elected to a second term and Robert Kennedy thus would not be able to deliver on the promises he had made to J. L. Chestnut shortly before the assassination. Robert Kennedy's pledge, however, remains a poignant reminder to us all of both the fragile nature of life and the continuing influence of politics on all Justice Department enforcement policies.

9

In the Name of
National
Security

On a warm spring afternoon in 1989, several months into the Bush administration, fourteen armed agents of the United States Customs Bureau smashed through the front door of the Miami apartment of Ramon and Nercys Cernuda. The agents who charged into the elegant suite overlooking Biscayne Bay were not seeking the usual contraband—plastic bags of cocaine, lethal collections of assault weapons or banded stacks of illegally laundered money. Instead, they were searching for works of art—specifically the hundreds of paintings and other objects that Ramon Cernuda had collected during the thirty years since he and his family had fled Castro's Cuba.

By the time their search was completed, a full twenty-five hours after the front door of the Cernuda apartment had first been knocked from its hinges, the agents were in possession of 259 art objects. They also had laboriously photographed the spines of all of the couple's books.[1]

Cernuda and his wife were traumatized. "The raid was a shocking, brutal and terrorizing event," the forty-five-year-old art collector and publisher later recalled. "This was the government of the United States coming down on us in a very tough way and it was scary as hell. My wife and I, under extremely close surveillance, were required to stay in our home during the entire period. We could not move about. If we wanted to go to the bathroom, an agent would follow us right to the door. The search was amazingly detailed. In addition to seizing our art and making a photographic record of all of our books, the agents looked into the nail polish bottles of my daughter, apparently to see if she was a drug user."[2]

As the lengthy onslaught was drawing to an end, acting U.S. attorney Dexter Lehtinen, the man who had given the final go-ahead for the novel raid, held a press conference which would win him extensive coverage on that night's television news shows and splashy headlines in the next day's papers. The top federal law enforcement official in southern Florida, a protégé of one of President Bush's biggest financial supporters in the state, Lehtinen told the assembled reporters that the raid was part of a broad government investigation of individuals who had violated the Trading with the Enemy Act. This law, originally passed by Congress just before the United States entered World War I, gave the president legal authority to impose comprehensive trade embargoes in times of both peace and war.

The art bust, made in the name of the old national security statute, was an unusual event. So was Lehtinen's decision to hold a press conference to announce it. While U.S. attorneys routinely meet with reporters to inform them about the formal charging of newsworthy figures, it is considered unprofessional, even unethical, for federal prosecutors to trumpet the execution of a search warrant that usually marks the beginning of an investigation, not its formal conclusion.[3]

"We have an across-the-board investigation that is not limited to paintings," Lehtinen said. Only those who had deliberately violated the Trading with the Enemy Act would be prosecuted, so that "innocent purchasers have no need to fear arrest," he added.[4] By citing the embargo law, the prosecutor managed to suggest that the seizures were part of a national security investigation of some consequence.

But Cernuda, whose boyish unlined face contrasts with his prematurely white hair, sees the 1989 raid in a starkly different light. "It was, quite simply, a political prosecution," he said. The opinions of three

federal judges in this and two related cases, and a powerful mix of circumstantial evidence, strongly support Cernuda's opinion.

It is an accepted fact that since the beginning of the modern nation-
state, spies and espionage agents have played a small but significant
role in the conduct of international relations. Let it also be conceded
that as a result of these dangerous activities, almost all national governments have created special investigative units that have a legitimate
duty to detect, investigate and sometimes prosecute such troublesome
people. Let it finally be acknowledged that over the years the United
States government has uncovered hundreds, perhaps even thousands, of
individuals and groups who committed, or were about to commit, acts
that seriously threatened the security of the American people.

The record, however, also discloses numerous occasions when federal enforcement officials have waved the national security flag to justify the prosecution of individuals where the government's actual
motivation was flagrantly and improperly political. In addition to providing excellent cover for indecent political hits, the record further
shows that the national security flag has often served as an effective device for hiding wasteful, ineffective and even ludicrous gumshoeing by
the Justice Department, the FBI and other members of the national security family.

On that spring day in 1989, when Customs agents smashed into the
Cernuda apartment, most Americans understood that the long Cold
War against communism was a relic of the past. Even Ronald Reagan,
who a few years before had described Iron Curtain nations as the "Evil
Empire," had come to regard Soviet leader Mikhail Gorbachev and his
allies as generally enlightened men who were working with the United
States to reduce the chances of an all-out nuclear war. National security, that long-lived force in both the proper and improper calculations
of the White House, Congress and the Justice Department, had lost a
great deal of steam.

But the new wave of international forbearance had not yet washed
over many of the Cuban Americans who immigrated to Miami with
Fidel Castro's rise to power in 1959. And it was this politically influential segment of the Cuban community that had become enraged by the
art collection of Ramon Cernuda. It was this community that mobilized the federal government in an effort to crush him.

The event that initially triggered their anger was the 1988 vote by a
majority of the board of directors of Miami's Cuban Museum of Arts
and Culture to auction off some of its art to raise operating funds. The
problem was that a few of the artists represented in the auction were allegedly "compromised" because at one time or another they had supported Castro.

The prime target of the passionate conservatives was Ramon Cernuda, the publisher, art collector and museum board member. Cernuda had offended them by being the leading proponent of what they regarded as the museum's heinous financial plan. (The politics of the Cuban community are Byzantine. "Some people in Miami think of me as a liberal," Cernuda observed. "There of course are many others who see me as a 'Communist sympathizer.' In Havana, however, I am labeled a counterrevolutionary.")

Immediately after the plan to hold the auction was approved, Cernuda and other board members who had supported it began receiving anonymous death threats. On the day of the auction, a large crowd of boisterous picketers—shouting "Art yes, Communist propaganda no," and "Repatriate the Board Members"—angrily milled around the museum's entrance. During the auction, the protestors purchased one painting and then, in a spooky reminder of Nazi Germany, set it on fire. A few days later an unknown person set off a bomb that damaged the front door and wall of the museum. That was the unofficial reaction.

By approving the Customs Bureau raid one year later, and then holding his extraordinary press conference, acting U.S. attorney Dexter Lehtinen publicly demonstrated that now he and the federal government had chosen sides in the long-festering art controversy. This is true even if, as Lehtinen has contended in later interviews, the investigation and resulting seizure of Cernuda's art was a routine matter, the natural outcome of an unsolicited recommendation from the Customs Bureau.

Maybe that is the way it happened. But even Jorge Mas Canosa, a Lehtinen supporter and a powerful figure among the passionate Cuban-American conservatives of Miami, has acknowledged that the prosecutor's interpretation of the great art raid is not the whole truth.

Mas Canosa is a millionaire, a successful businessman and the chairman of the Cuban American National Foundation. He was also an important contributor and fund-raiser to the 1988 presidential campaign of George Bush. Three days after the agents seized Cernuda's art collection, Mas Canosa bragged in an interview on a Spanish-language talk show about his role in triggering the raid. Because he had exposed those who were trading with Cuba and continually urged the government to investigate them, Mas Canosa said, "my answer to Cernuda's accusation [of arranging the raid] is 'yes.' "[5]

How could a businessman, even a wealthy and influential one like Mas Canosa, persuade the federal government to serve his personal political interests? What was the process that allowed Mas Canosa to influence the official actions of Dexter Lehtinen and the powerful agencies under his command?

As already noted, Mas Canosa and his right-wing Cuban-American friends in Miami were a significant source of campaign contributions to Bush's campaign. In addition, partly as a result of the lavish contributions, Mas Canosa had developed an intimate relationship with John Sununu, the White House chief of staff.

According to two former staff members of the Senate Judiciary Committee in Washington and several former assistant U.S. attorneys in Miami, the appointments staff in the Bush White House allowed Mas Canosa to have a powerful voice in the selection of the new federal prosecutor in Miami. Mas Canosa's choice was Lehtinen, a gung-ho Vietnam veteran, a professional politician, an eight-year Republican member of the Florida State Senate and a lawyer with almost no experience trying criminal cases.[6]

"This was very much a White House appointment," said one Washington lawyer with direct knowledge of the Senate Judiciary Committee's consideration of Lehtinen's nomination. "Neither of the Florida senators were actively behind him, even though his backing by the Cuban-American community meant the senators would never raise any public objections. The Justice Department professionals were positively hostile to him."

Lehtinen was obligated to Mas Canosa in another very important way. Canosa had thrown his considerable influence behind the budding political career of Lehtinen's wife, Ileana Ros-Lehtinen. Then a member of the Florida State Senate, Ileana Ros-Lehtinen had decided to seek the Republican nomination for the seat in the House of Representatives held by Claude Pepper, an elderly Democrat. With the crucial backing of Mas Canosa and his Cuban American National Foundation, Ros-Lehtinen was elected.

There was one other political link between the Lehtinens and the White House patronage dispensers that is worth noting. The manager of Ros-Lehtinen's congressional campaign was one of President Bush's sons, John Ellis "Jeb" Bush, a Miami businessman not entirely without influence at the White House. (Three days after arriving in Washington to take the oath of office, Ros-Lehtinen was granted a private fifteen-minute meeting with President Bush, an unusual high-publicity event for a just-elected member of the House of Representatives. At a reception arranged for her that evening by Mas Canosa's Cuban American National Foundation, according to an article in the *Miami Herald*'s Spanish-language paper, Ros-Lehtinen showed she understood the political realities of her success. "The goals of the foundation are mine," she declared.[7]

It is these overlapping connections between Mas Canosa and Miami's then hottest political couple, and Mas Canosa and the White House, and Mas Canosa and Jeb Bush, that fully convinced the Miami legal community that Mas Canosa was directly responsible for both the Bush administration's decision to keep Dexter Lehtinen as the U.S. attorney and Lehtinen's subsequent decision to execute the 1989 art raid. Lehtinen himself did not respond in any way to several requests for interviews.

The seizure of Cernuda's paintings thus was an improper political hit, a raw exercise of federal power on behalf of a wealthy businessman who had arranged the appointment of the controlling federal official.

But the seizure was more, much more. It was a wrongful and unconstitutional act that appears to have been the first step in a long, carefully organized campaign of official harassment aimed directly at Ramon Cernuda.

Although Ramon and Nercys Cernuda were profoundly disturbed by the government's violent seizure of their artworks, they were determined to fight back. Almost immediately, they filed an emergency motion in federal court demanding the return of their property. Their argument was based partly on the fact that the Trading with the Enemy Act did not apply because the Cernudas had purchased the disputed objects in the United States. More to the point, however, was their contention that the raid was a blatant violation of the free speech provision of the First Amendment and the end-product of the "political maelstrom in which prominent ultra-conservative Cuban-Americans have vowed to squelch Cernuda as a perceived opponent."

Three months later, District Court Judge Kenneth L. Ryskamp, in a ruling that directly challenged Lehtinen's legal judgment in authorizing the raid, ordered the Customs Bureau to return the art.

The ruling by the conservative Miami judge was devastating. Under the law and the Constitution of the United States, the judge held, the government had absolutely no right to dictate what paintings the Cernudas and the Cuban Museum of Art and Culture hung on their walls or offered in an auction. "Such activity is not illegal," the judge said. "On the contrary," he continued, such activities are "protected by the First Amendment and exempted from regulation under the 1988 amendment to the Trading with the Enemy Act.[8] In the previous year, Congress had modified the old law by removing the government's authority to regulate "informational materials" whether commercial or not.

With the help of an effective and well-paid lawyer, Cernuda had persuaded the court to rebuke Lehtinen for the arbitrary and unlawful application of an obscure national security law against one of the enemies of his friends. Ryskamp's order and opinion represented a clear victory for Cernuda. But unknown to the art collector, his war with the federal government had just begun.

Several months after the favorable decision, Cernuda traveled to Canada to attend a conference on Cuba. As he was returning to the United States, immigration officials stopped him, claiming his travel documents were forged. A bit later, Lehtinen's office brought criminal charges against a friend of Cernuda who had openly supported him when he was attacked by conservatives in the Cuban-American community. A federal judge ruled there was insufficient evidence and threw the case out of court.

The next suspicious action came shortly thereafter, when federal inspectors entered Cernuda's publishing company and conducted a disruptive search for illegal workers who might be working for him. Finally, the Internal Revenue Service initiated extensive audits of Cernuda, Cernuda's father and brothers and Cernuda's company.

It is barely possible, of course, that all these federal investigations of Cernuda and his friends and family were random events. But it is highly unlikely. The suspicion of something else—of a well-orchestrated campaign of official harassment—begins with an understanding of the absolutist mentality of some of the conservative Cuban Americans and their connections to Lehtinen. The suspicion is heightened by the timing of the investigations, all of which were initiated shortly after Judge Ryskamp's embarrassing ruling. The suspicion of official misuse of power is increased even further by the fact that not one of the investigations of Cernuda, his family or his friends turned up any evidence of wrongdoing.

Federal agents do not normally like to waste their time investigating matters of little consequence that are not likely to result in formal charges. This is true in part because investigating insignificant cases is less fun than important ones. A second consideration, assuming everything is on the up-and-up, is that cases that go nowhere do not create the performance statistics that advance professional careers. Thus, in the normal course of events, agents do not undertake investigations unless they see indications that the case has some potential or they have been ordered to do so by someone in power. When it comes to the federal enforcement agencies, the U.S. attorney who controls almost all of the prosecutions that go forward in each district is certainly in a position to encourage the investigation—right or wrong—of any individual who has caught his or her attention.

In the Cernuda situation, the government's failures were clear and unambiguous. The allegations about Cernuda's travel documents simply evaporated. A federal judge, not the one who issued the ruling in the art case, dismissed all charges against Cernuda's friend and supporter on the first day of the trial on the grounds that there was insufficient evidence to bring the case. The decision was a rare one because judges normally bend over backward in allowing prosecutors to present evidence to a jury. The Labor Department found that all of Cernuda's employees were legally entitled to work in the United States. After months of probing, the IRS informed Cernuda that neither he, his relatives nor his company owed the government any additional taxes or penalties.

Fighting back against a broad campaign of improper official harassment, however, involves heavy financial, as well as psychological, costs. Cernuda estimated that his legal and accounting fees during the period came to well over $200,000.

It is unlikely that the individual conspirators who organized the harassment campaign ever wrote orders, memos or other documents that would prove that Dexter Lehtinen was behind the Cernuda investigations and that Mas Canosa was behind Lehtinen. Moreover, even if such evidence exists, it is even more unlikely it will ever see the light of day. But the full circumstances of Lehtinen's appointment and the subsequent investigations strongly support this scenario.

In January 1992, three and a half years after his appointment as Miami's interim chief federal prosecutor, Lehtinen announced his resignation. Although he denied suggestions that he had been forced to quit, his departure came shortly after the completion of an investigation of his performance by the Office of Professional Responsibility. Because of Lehtinen's controversial handling of the Cernuda matter and several other cases, the Senate twice returned his nomination to the White House, actions that were tantamount to rejections without a formal vote. "From the very beginning he had a lot of problems and the committee did nothing about his nomination," said a Senate insider.[9]

The harassment of Ramon Cernuda, initially begun under the Trading with the Enemy Act, is an extreme example of the way a federal prosecutor can bend national security law for personal political advantage. But it certainly is not an isolated event in American history. In fact, false or exaggerated national security claims have repeatedly provided the government a handy smokescreen for questionable prosecutions and other official actions ever since the United States was created.

IN THE BEGINNING: SEDITION

Almost two hundred years ago, in the summer of 1798, Congressman Mathew Lyon of Vermont was indicted by a federal grand jury sitting in Rutland on charges of criticizing President John Adams. Lyon had committed this alleged offense in an article he published in the *Vermont Journal*. During the Adams administration, Lyon wrote, every consideration of the public welfare had been "swallowed up in a continual grasp for power, in an unbounded thirst for ridiculous pomp, foolish adulation and selfish avarice."

Compared to the negative television spots favored by today's politicians, the congressman's words were pretty quiet stuff. But after a brief autumn trial before a hostile federal judge, Lyon was convicted and sentenced to four months in prison, a $1,000 fine and $60.96 in court costs. Instead of being imprisoned in the federal jail in Rutland where he was tried, Lyon was taken to a jail forty-four miles distant and held in a cell with one small window, a smelly indoor toilet and neither a fireplace nor a stove.

At about the same time, federal marshals in New York City arrested John Daly Burke and James Smith, the owners of the *Time Piece*, a politically outspoken newspaper, on charges of printing "seditious and libelous" utterances about President Adams.

On June 26, 1798, Benjamin Bache, the editor of the *Aurora*, a paper published in Philadelphia, was indicted for his articles attacking Adams and the other leading members of the Federalist Party. Bache, a grandson of Benjamin Franklin, was extremely outspoken, respecting almost no one. He once accused George Washington of taking more salary than he was allowed while president and advancing his own financial well-being during the Revolutionary War at the expense of his half-starved soldiers.

The federal charges brought against Lyon, Burke, Smith, Bache and approximately two dozen other editors and individuals who dared to criticize the Federalist establishment represented a deliberate effort by the Federalists to muzzle their political enemies—Thomas Jefferson and other members of the Republican Party.

The attacks were authorized under the Sedition Act that President Adams signed into law on July 14, 1798. (The Federalists were so anxious to nail Bache that common law charges had been brought against him three weeks before the Sedition Act was rushed into place.) It should be recalled that Congress approved the Sedition Act exactly seven years after the required number of states had ratified the Bill of Rights, including the constitutional amendment which forbade Congress from making any law that abridged "the freedom of speech, or of the press; or the right of the people peaceably to assemble, and to petition the Government for a redress of grievances."

The Sedition Act made it a crime for persons to combine or conspire to "oppose any measure or measures of the government of the United States, which are or shall be directed by proper authority, or to impede the operation of any law, or to intimidate or prevent any person holding a place or office in or under the government of the United States, from undertaking, performing or executing his trust or duty." For these acts, the maximum punishment was five years in prison.

The other substantive section of this short but extraordinarily sweeping law allowed the government to bring criminal charges against persons who "shall write, print, utter or publish, or shall cause or procure to be written, uttered or published, or shall knowingly and willingly assist or aid in writing, printing, uttering or publishing any false, scandalous and malicious writing or writings against the government of the United States, or either house of the Congress of the United States, or the President of the United States" with the purpose of stirring up the hatred of the people or opposing or resisting the laws of the United States. Ominously, Congress did not bother to define what it meant by the words "false," "scandalous" and "malicious."

The Federalist Party and its leaders—George Washington, Alexander Hamilton and Adams—had controlled the United States government since it had come into existence only ten years before. As political leaders frequently do, the Federalists convinced themselves that it was essential to the well-being of the nation that they remain in office. But there was a cloud on their horizon. At that time, the presidential candidate who received the second highest number of votes became the vice president. Thus it was that Vice President Thomas Jefferson, head of the opposition Republican Party, was a vocal critic of President Adams.

Worried about the possibility of losing the forthcoming presidential election, the Federalists began searching for a way to silence their domestic political enemies. It was at this precise moment in American history that the forces of revolution began to erupt in France and war between the United States and France became a remote but still serious possibility. Shrewdly, the Federalists began to play on the public fear of this war, picturing Jefferson and James Madison and the other Republicans as taking their orders from the French directory. "At one stroke, the entire party was placed under suspicion of treason, and Jeffersonian ideals were stamped with the dread trademark, MADE IN FRANCE. The purpose of the opposition party was made to appear to be not the advancement of American interest, but of those of France; it became axiomatic [to the Federalist believers] that no Republican could be a true American."[10]

Fanned by the propaganda of the Federalists, including a harangue from the president's brilliant wife, Abigail Adams, Congress's reaction to highly exaggerated public concerns about the French Revolution and the alleged infiltration of the United States by foreign spies was all too predictable. During the late spring and summer of 1798, over the objections of the Republican minority, Congress approved four laws that became known as the Alien and Sedition Acts. The unstated goal of the Alien Acts was to curb the growth of Jefferson's Republican Party by slowing the entry of immigrants, especially Irish immigrants, to the United States. The objective of the Sedition Act was to silence public criticism of Adams and his colleagues so the Federalist Party could maintain its control of the government in the upcoming election.

President Adams himself, apparently understanding that the Sedition Act violated the spirit of the new government and its singular constitution, tried to distance himself from its enforcement. Curiously, the lead role in persuading the U.S. attorneys to enforce the new law fell to Secretary of State Timothy Pickering. It should be remembered that at this point the Justice Department had not yet been created and the attorney general was a second-ranking figure in the president's cabinet.

Pickering, an austere and humorless law-and-order man from Massachusetts, had a strong, even fanatic, faith in the usefulness of the Sedition Act. "Of all the United States District Attorneys, Pickering demanded close scrutiny of the Republican newspapers published in their districts and prompt prosecutions of offenses, even of seditious material copied from other newspapers."[11]

The Republicans feared the Alien and Sedition Acts, feared the additional restrictions that the Federalist Party could be expected to impose should they win control of the government for another term, and feared the expansive way that Federalist judges had been interpreting the laws already on the books. Despite these justifiable fears, however, the U.S. attorneys in the end only indicted about twenty-five persons for sedition. Approximately half of these were ever brought to trial.

In spite of the Federalist efforts to suppress critics—and, paradoxically, partly because of them—Jefferson was narrowly elected president in 1800. In one of his first official acts, the new president granted full pardon to those still in prison under the Sedition Act. In his inaugural address, without directly mentioning the law, Jefferson explained why he felt it unnecessary. "If there be any among us who wish to dissolve this union, or to change its republican form," Jefferson said, "let them stand undisturbed, as monuments of the safety with which error of opinion may be tolerated where reason is left free to combat it."[12]

By any statistical measure, the passage of the Alien and Sedition Acts and the subsequent indictment of a handful of editors were not major events. Considered from the idealistic perspective of the free-speech promises of the Bill of Rights, however, the cynical manipulation of the government by the political bosses of that day looms somewhat larger.

Doubts about the activities of the Federalists against Jefferson's supporters are further heightened by the historical situation in which they occurred. The Alien and Sedition Acts were not passed and the editors were not charged in the midst of a shooting war. Much can be forgiven when the nation is fighting for its life. Although the laws of 1798 were approved at a time of great international tension, when the United States was fearful it might be drawn into a major war, direct conflict with France was avoided. Furthermore, 3,000 miles of stormy sea meant the threat was always quite remote. It is the want of a genuine war, combined with the blatant targeting of the government's political enemies, that made these laws and their enforcement an infamous moment in American history.

AMERICA'S ULTIMATE HOT WAR AND AFTERWARD

The Civil War, the single most devastating period in American history, was very different. Approximately 600,000 people lost their lives during the struggle. To put these losses into perspective, the Civil War casualties were ten times those of the Vietnam War. When the size of the American population during the two periods is taken into account, of course, the relative impact was far greater. Major battles of the Civil War took place so close to the Capitol that booming cannons could be heard in Washington, D.C. The borders of the two combatants were contiguous. Significant parts of some northern states were actual war zones, and thousands of spies and lesser collaborators infiltrated the governments of both the North and the South.

The Civil War was indeed the most profound threat to national security in the history of the United States, before or since. Given the horrific circumstances, the response of Lincoln and his generals can be understood, even though their systematic, widespread and ruthless suppression of dissent represented a terrible assault on the Constitution and the Bill of Rights. Antiadministration newspapers were closed down and hostile editors were jailed. Complete censorship was imposed on all telegraphic communications. A former member of the House of Representatives, a critic of Lincoln, was arrested for treason and exiled to the Confederacy. Lincoln unilaterally suspended habeas corpus, the right of all Americans to a court hearing on the legality of their arrest.

The extent of the suppression was unlike anything before or since. "During the course of the Civil War, the United States arrested and jailed somewhere between 10,000 and 30,000 people, denying them the benefits of habeas corpus hearings. Kept in military custody, without charges, for as long as the government felt necessary, many were never brought to trial."[13]

A good deal of burden fell on the willing shoulders of the military. Homer Cummings, Franklin Roosevelt's first attorney general, caught the horror of this abusive period in his sweeping 1937 history of the federal justice system. The suspension of the writ of habeas corpus, he said, served as an effective instrument for curbing the influence of prominent sympathizers with the southern cause whose activities were "of such character that prosecution for specific violations of the law were not expedient. The mayor and police commissioners of Baltimore were taken into custody and lodged in Fort McHenry without being charged with any offense. Influential members of the legislature in Maryland and elsewhere received the same treatment."[14]

At the same time, Cummings said, the attorney general and the U.S. district attorneys throughout the country busied themselves with other tasks. Treason charges, which called for the death penalty, became extremely popular in some districts. In a special July 1861 term of the federal district court in St. Louis, Missouri, twenty-five treason indictments were returned. Cummings reported that the federal prosecutor in what is now called West Virginia was even more enthusiastic about treason and that, at one point during the war, seven hundred to eight hundred of such capital punishment cases were pending in his district.

The end of the long bloody war, however, did not mean the end of the abuses of federal enforcement powers that the savage fraternal struggle had almost made defensible. Perhaps the most intriguing failure of federal prosecutors to adjust their actions to the conclusion of the war was the decision of James Speed, Lincoln's second attorney general, to have the conspirators involved in Lincoln's assassination tried before a military tribunal rather than in federal district court. Given the rights available to any defendant whose case is tried in federal court, it is likely that a great deal more information about the president's assassination would have surfaced had the case been handled in an open court operating under normal rules of evidence, rather than by the military.

Three leading Republican newspapers in New York City—the *Times*, the *Tribune* and the *Post*—immediately criticized Speed's decision regarding the conspirators. Also horrified was Edward Bates, who had immediately preceded Speed as attorney general. Writing contemporaneously in a journal that would not be published until the following century, Bates said Speed must have known that handing the case to the military was a bad idea, even though he was a weak man who was not qualified to be attorney general. Bates's entry on August 21, 1865, was only one of several discussing the issue. "Such a trial is not only unlawful, but it is a gross blunder in policy: It denies the great fundamental principle that ours is a government of *Law,* and that the law is strong enough, to rule the people wisely and well; and if the offenders be done to death by that tribunal, however truly guilty, they will pass for martyrs with half the world."[15]

Several months earlier, immediately after the trial decision first became known, Bates wrote in his diary that he had been told Speed acted in response to intense political pressure from Secretary of War Edwin Stanton and Secretary of State William Seward. "It seems, that when he came into office a new man, with not much reputation as a lawyer, and perhaps, no strong confidence in his own opinions, he was caressed and courted by Stanton and Seward, and sank, under the weight of their blandishments, into a mere tool—to give such opinions as were wanted. Tho' my indignation rises at seeing the corruption and degradation of the *Law Department* of the Government, I cannot help pitying my poor imbecile successor!"[16]

The outspoken Bates believed that Stanton, who he viewed as both a bully and coward, was the key manipulator in the matter. The former attorney general's judgment about Stanton is of interest because of the lingering suspicions about him. Some scholars have argued that the secretary of war did not want a federal court trial because it would prove he had provided Lincoln inadequate security. Others have gone so far as to speculate whether Stanton actually may have been the chief conspirator in Lincoln's assassination. This dark suspicion has lingered partly because Stanton was a fanatic opponent of Lincoln's plan to welcome the South back into the Union. While Vice President Andrew Johnson ultimately would follow Lincoln's approach for dealing with the South, it is believed that John Wilkes Booth originally hoped to kill both Lincoln and Johnson. If Booth had managed that, Stanton might well have become the dominant figure in the Union government. The quick execution of the four conspirators after the brief military trial approved by Speed, and the possibly suspicious death of Booth while he was being captured by federal troops under the control of Stanton, worked to assure that the full circumstances of Lincoln's assassination were never explored.

At that time, the Supreme Court had not yet ruled on the general question of the legal reach of military tribunals. Nor would it ever consider the specific facts in the trial and execution of the Lincoln conspirators. But shortly after the end of the Civil War, the Supreme Court did decide a landmark case holding that many of the military trials resorted to by the federal government both during and immediately after the Civil War were illegal.

The decision involved Lamdin P. Milligan. Milligan had been sentenced to death by hanging after his conviction by a military tribunal in Indiana for giving aid and comfort to the rebels, inciting rebellion and several other charges. In asking the Supreme Court to uphold Milligan's conviction and death sentence, Attorney General Speed found comfort in unspecified "laws of war" and the fact that the president was commander in chief, just as he had in his after-the-fact 1865 order justifying the military trial of Lincoln's assassins.[17]

The Supreme Court did not agree with Speed's argument. "The laws and usages of war can never be applied to citizens in states which have upheld the authority of the government, and where the courts are open and their process unobstructed."[18] The federal courts in the District of Columbia, of course, were fully functioning when Speed ordered the conspirators in Lincoln's assassination to go before a military tribunal.

There is no indication that any of the Supreme Court justices who fashioned the five-to-four Milligan decision ever considered the history of the government's handling of the Lincoln trial. And, as in almost all such decisions, the court's focus was on the facts concerning a single case in Indiana. But in the sweeping analysis, a majority of the Supreme Court vividly documented how easy it was for national security claims, some of them completely specious, to justify the arrest, prosecution and internment of tens of thousands of citizens who had committed no crime.

THE BOLSHEVIKS ARE COMING

The armistice ending the shooting part of World War I went into effect on November 11, 1918. But with the defeat of the Germans and the end of the mass killing in the muddy trenches of Europe, the United States became obsessively fearful of another kind of enemy. These new adversaries were the radicals, the immigrants, the Socialists and the Bolsheviks, and the ordinary labor leaders whom many powerful Americans saw as a threat to their comfortable way of life. The war against the Huns had just been won, but the battle against the Bolsheviks was only beginning.

Actually, under the cover of patriotic fervor, the first skirmishes of the ideological war had gotten under way while the shooting war against the Germans was still proceeding. On June 15, 1917, Congress enacted the Espionage Act, which authorized the government to bring criminal charges against both those who transmitted military secrets and those who published antiwar commentaries. A year later, Congress amended the Espionage Act, once again making almost any criticism of the government a crime. The amended law became known as the Sedition Act.

Many of the prosecutions brought by the Justice Department under the Sedition Act were ridiculous. Rose Pastor Stokes, for example, was convicted of espionage for the act of stating that "I am for the people and the government is for the profiteers." She was sentenced to ten years in federal prison.[19] Historians report that about 2,000 individuals were prosecuted under the Espionage and Sedition Acts, mostly for speaking out against the war, and that not a single person was convicted of spying.[20]

Especially hard hit was the leftist press that did not support the war. With President Woodrow Wilson's uneasy consent, for example, the Justice Department and the Post Office destroyed *The Masses*, a Socialist magazine with a monthly circulation of about 20,000 readers. The journal was published by Max Eastman, an old friend of the president.

As in the struggle between the North and South more than fifty years before, the government's unlawful use of federal enforcement powers to silence dissent during the actual course of war is understandable, even if not legally defensible. But the Wilson administration's extensive and highly political misuse of federal criminal powers in the period following the end of the shooting war are much harder to justify. What made the postwar campaign especially notorious is that it was orchestrated by A. Mitchell Palmer, an ambitious politician who was at the time attorney general of the United States.

On December 27, 1919, a bit more than a year after the beginning of the armistice, Frank Burke, chief of the Justice Department's investigative arm, then known as the Bureau of Investigation, dispatched a long letter to George E. Kelleher, the head of the bureau's office in Boston. The letter, marked "Strictly Confidential," provided Kelleher with precise details of a Justice Department plan for the arrest and deportation of all the aliens living in the Boston area who belonged to either the Communist Party of America or the Communist Labor Party.[21]

"Particular efforts should be made to apprehend all of the officers of these two parties if they are aliens; the residence of such officers should be searched in every instance for literature, membership cards, records and correspondence," Burke wrote.

"If found in groups in meeting rooms, they should be lined up against the wall and there searched; particular effort being given to finding the membership book, in which connection the search of pockets will not be sufficient," he continued.

After describing a variety of other possible contingencies and how he wanted them handled, Burke ended his long letter with some housekeeping details. These included one of the first known references to a very young and, most assuredly, up-and-coming federal bureaucrat.

"On the evening of the arrests this office will be open the entire night, and I desire that you communicate by long distance to Mr. Hoover any matters of vital importance or interest that may arise during the course of the arrests. I desire that the morning following the arrests you should forward to this office by special delivery, marked for the 'Attention of Mr. Hoover,' a complete list of the names of persons arrested, with an indication of residence, or organization to which they belong, and whether or not they were included in the original list of warrants."

Mr. Hoover, Mr. J. Edgar Hoover, was not, however, just a glorified telephone operator or clerk, as Burke's confidential instructions seemed to suggest. In fact, a short time before, Attorney General Palmer had selected the twenty-four-year-old lawyer to direct the General Intelligence Division (GID), a brand-new, high-priority unit within the Bureau of Investigation. The GID was the first unit ever established within the Justice Department that had the specific mission of gathering information about the political activities of those who questioned government policies. Within a hundred days, according to Hoover historian Athan G. Theoharis, it had amassed files on 60,000 persons.[22]

The swift rise of Hoover and the GID was part of the nation's broad postwar worries about the radical threat. These had been triggered by Lenin's seizure of the Russian government in 1917 and the wave of strikes and other labor troubles that swept the United States during the difficult economic period following World War I. But the general concerns were abruptly sharpened on May 1, 1919, when postal inspectors in New York uncovered a plot to assassinate a number of leading Americans, including Attorney General Palmer. Then, on June 2, the bomb of an angry radical exploded on the front porch of Palmer's Washington home. It was a shocking bloody business—the bomber killed himself in the blast—and Palmer, not surprisingly, immediately ordered a massive Justice Department dragnet. It was two months after the attack on his house that the attorney general selected Hoover to create and direct the GID. Hoover immediately became the controlling force behind the Wilson administration's two-pronged campaign against all radicals—both the reasonable part that was aimed at the bombers and the questionable one that focused on the talkers and the writers.

Prosecutors, of course, are rarely required to explain the motives behind their actions. When the question is considered at all, commentators seem to work on the assumption that the prosecutors' only concern is sorting out the bad from the good; indicting the criminals, letting the innocent go free. But Palmer's direct involvement in national politics of the day suggest that his motives for mobilizing the prosecuting power of the federal government had very little to do with the problem of guilt and innocence.

Doubts about Palmer are largely based on the fact that at the time he was directing the department's official enforcement campaign against the nation's radicals and other malefactors, he also was actively engaged in a campaign to win the Democratic nomination for president. As a former member of the House of Representatives from Pennsylvania, every action he took as attorney general during 1919 and the first half of 1920 directly influenced his standing among the delegates who would soon assemble at the Democratic convention in San Francisco.

The Boston roundup described in Burke's December 27 instruction to Kelleher, one of the major Palmer raids, took place January 2, 1920. At about 6:00 P.M. that evening, 300 to 500 Justice Department agents and a handful of local policemen spread out through twenty Boston-area cities and began arresting suspects, including 39 people meeting in Lynn to discuss a cooperative bakery. The Bureau of Investigation subsequently reported that a total of 600 people were arrested that night in the Boston region, but it appears the government deliberately understated the haul, that between 800 and 1,200 people were actually detained. There were federal raids in dozens of other cities and historians believe that the total arrests came to at least 3,000. An additional 3,000 suspects were taken into custody for periods of up to several months without ever being formally charged.[23]

The mass roundup was at first hailed by the mainstream press. But very soon questions were asked about the purpose of the raids and the arbitrary way they had been carried out. On June 23, 1920, following a fifteen-day hearing, George Anderson, a federal district court judge in Boston, issued a ruling on the habeas corpus petition of twenty aliens arrested in the raid who had been confined in a federal detention center at Deer Island pending deportation.[24] Anderson held that the arrests were not valid because the basic theory behind them was incorrect. "There is no evidence that the Communist Party is an organization advocating the overthrow of the government of the United States by force or violence," he wrote. "Hence all the petitioners ordered deported are entitled to be discharged from the custody of the immigration officials."

Judge Anderson's observation about the manner in which the Justice Department carried out the raid was even more blunt than his comments about its motivation. "I refrain from any extended comment on the lawlessness of these proceedings by our supposedly law-enforcing officials. The documents and acts speak for themselves. It may, however, fitly be observed that a mob is a mob, whether made up of government officials acting under instructions from the Justice Department, or of criminals, loafers, and the vicious classes."

Not surprisingly, the Justice Department had a very different view of the administration's war on radicalism. In the department's December

1920 annual report, Palmer lavishly praised Hoover's General Intelligence Division and its sophisticated system for collecting and analyzing detailed information about the activities of "agitators connected with the ultra radical movement." As had been the case before and would be the case later, Attorney General Palmer expended little effort to make the crucial distinction between those who actually had committed crimes and those who talked or wrote about their strong opposition to the government. The GID, he wrote, would give the government a single focus for combating "the unlawful activities of certain persons and organizations in the United States whose sole purposes were to commit acts of terrorism and to advocate, by word of mouth and by circulation of literature, the overthrow of the government of the United States by force and violence."[25]

Palmer's drive for the Democratic nomination for president was not successful. Although a variety of forces were at work, it appears that one important factor was the cooling passion of American voters against the alleged menace of the Bolsheviks and their allies. Perhaps the most dramatic moment in Palmer's fall from political grace was a hearing by the Senate Judiciary Committee in the first months of 1921. The nation's changing mood was illuminated by the title of the hearings: "Charges of Illegal Practices of the Department of Justice."

Just two years after the Justice Department's massive roundup, the collective verdict of almost all the committee's witnesses was that the Palmer raids had been a legal and social disaster. But the attorney general who gave his name to one of the darker moments in American history was not repentant.

"I apologize for nothing that the Department of Justice has done in this matter," Palmer said. "I glory in it. I point with pride and enthusiasm to the results of that work; and if, as I said before, some of my agents out in the field . . . were a little rough and unkind, or short or curt, with these alien agitators whom they observed seeking to destroy their homes, their religion and their country, I think it might well be overlooked in the general good to the country that has come from it."[26]

Palmer did not get it. Ambition seems to have blinded him to the reality that if the nation he sought to protect was to survive, then the law enforcement agencies of the nation would have to act in a lawful manner.

The attorney general's personal blindness was distressing, but Palmer's reasons for ordering up the dragnet raids are far more troubling because they illuminate the very fragile quality of representative government, American style.

"I remember, Mr. Chairman, the morning after my house was blown up, I stood in the middle of the wreckage of my library with Congressmen and Senators, and without a dissenting voice they called upon me in strong terms to exercise all the power that was possible in the Department of Justice to run to earth the criminals who were behind this outrage," Palmer testified. "I say that I was shouted at from every editorial sanctum in America from sea to sea; I was preached upon from every pulpit; I was urged—I could feel it dinned into my ears—throughout the country to do something and do it now, and do it quick, and do it in a way that would stop this sort of thing in the United States."[27]

Palmer, armed with the unwavering convictions of an established political figure and law enforcement official, was unable to understand how his driving ambition to be president had blinded him to the vast distance between undertaking a sharply focused criminal investigation of criminal terrorists and launching the unlawful roundup of thousands of immigrants.

THE BOLSHEVIKS ARE COMING AGAIN

In 1945, with the end of World War II, the United States was the supreme power of the world, overwhelming all other nations in food production, industrial resources, technological know-how and sheer wealth. In a way that has rarely occurred before in recorded history, the United States was the absolute king of the hill. Almost immediately, however, serious doubts began to gnaw at the American psyche.

The principal cause, of course, was the Soviet Union and Joseph Stalin, its ruthless dictator. While the propaganda experts in Moscow aggressively hawked the Soviet Union and the dream of humane communism as the inevitable wave of the future, the Red Army brutally occupied Latvia, Lithuania, Estonia, East Germany, Poland, Czechoslovakia, Hungary, Bulgaria, Romania and other territories. Moreover, Stalin, in both open and clandestine ways, made grabs for all of Berlin, for Northern Iran and for Greece and Turkey, and operated one of the most aggressive and best-financed intelligence-gathering systems in the history of the world. In a famous speech in May 1946, Winston Churchill described the Iron Curtain that now separated East from West and called for a great world struggle, which later came to be known as the Cold War, to resist the expansion of Soviet communism.

In ways that made President Adams's worry about the revolutionary French look downright silly, and Palmer's concern about the first generation of Bolsheviks seem ridiculous, official American anxiety about the menace described by Churchill was based on numerous documented actions of the Soviet Union and its allies. Fifty years later, with the total disappearance of the Soviet Union from the maps of the world, it is almost impossible to remember just how grave the challenge had seemed to the political leaders of the United States in the years after the end of World War II. But a top-secret report on world communism submitted to President Harry Truman in September 1946 provides contemporaneous evidence about the profound fear that then gripped the leaders of the world's wealthiest and most powerful nation. The report, summarizing the official views of the secretary of state, the secretaries of war and navy, the director of Central Intelligence, the chairman of the Joint Chiefs of Staff and the attorney general, was prepared by Clark M. Clifford, then a special counsel to Truman. The content and tone of this document were extraordinarily bleak.[28]

"Soviet leaders believe that a conflict is inevitable between the U.S.S.R. and capitalist states, and their duty is to prepare the Soviet Union for this day," Clifford told Truman. "The aim of current Soviet policy is to prepare for the ultimate conflict by increasing Soviet power as rapidly as possible and by weakening all nations who may be considered hostile." The ability of the United States to resolve the conflicts between the foreign policies of the two nations, Clifford wrote, "may determine whether there is to be a permanent peace or a third World War."

In the section analyzing Soviet activities that directly affected American security, Clifford included a lengthy discussion of the Soviet government's active efforts to direct "espionage and subversive movements in the United States." After describing the two major espionage units operating in the United States and how they functioned, the presidential aide turned to their ideological allies.

"The Soviet government, by utilizing the membership of the Communist Party in the United States [CPUSA], has thousands of invaluable sources of information in various industrial establishments as well as the departments of the Government. In this regard it must be remembered that every American Communist is potentially an espionage agent of the Soviet government, requiring only the direct instruction of a Soviet superior to make the potential a reality."

Clifford's terrifying vision of the threat of internal subversion would have a far-reaching impact on almost every aspect of American life for the next few decades. It turned out, however, that the smooth young presidential adviser from Missouri had greatly overstated the perils of infiltration. This was partly because many of the party members in the United States were naive political activists with neither the position nor the skill to serve as useful espionage agents. But there was a second reason which Clifford either ignored or was not told: The FBI had so thoroughly infiltrated the CPUSA that it was useless to the Kremlin.

Clifford, very much the captive of the unreasoned paranoia that was sweeping through the defense and intelligence establishment, was not engaged in an exercise of informed and reasoned analysis. The threat was everywhere, he concluded. The directing force behind "the recent soldier demonstrations relating to demobilization and the recent anti-caste agitation," for example, were operatives of the Communist Party. Even more alarming than the CPUSA's opportunistic support of full civil rights for black soldiers, he alleged, was the party's effort to subvert the United States Army. "A definite campaign, in the making at present, is being sponsored by the Communist Party to indoctrinate soldiers to refuse to act in the event the United States Army is called upon to suppress domestic disturbances, to take over essential industries or to operate public utilities."

The notion that the U.S. Army, one of the world's most stable and conservative institutions, was actually threatened by subversion, illuminates the level of fear then sweeping the nation.

Clark Clifford, who later would present himself as a detached and level-headed adviser who resisted the excesses of the Cold War, had begun his extremely influential report to Harry Truman with an objective summary of the expansionist foreign policies of the Soviet Union. He ended it with a passionate, overheated and highly political statement which managed to suggest that the racial and economic problems of the United States somehow were the creation of the CPUSA. The profound analytic failure at the heart of Clifford's 1946 report would bedevil the Truman and Eisenhower administrations for the next fourteen years.

Two months after Clifford handed Truman his top-secret report, the Republican Party won a major victory in the mid-term elections, seizing control of the House of Representatives partly on the basis of GOP charges that the Democrats were not capable of confronting the Communist menace. Truman got the message. As a first step to avoid being personally buried by the national avalanche of doubt and concern, the president, on November 25, 1946, issued Executive Order 9806 creating the President's Temporary Commission on Employee Loyalty.

Its chairman was A. Devitt Vanech, special assistant to Attorney General Tom Clark. Vanech told the commission that in his view the "serious threat which *even one* disloyal person constitutes to the security of the United States" was insupportable.[29] The commission would be the architect of a draconian government loyalty program which perversely came to threaten the very freedoms—the right to free speech, the right to peaceably assemble, the right to due process—which in theory it was trying to protect.

As noted by the historian David Caute, a substantial number of the witnesses summoned to testify before Truman's loyalty commission represented the intelligence agencies, individuals obsessed by both the need for comprehensive security measures and a hatred for many of the New Deal's social programs. The testimony of one commission witness reflected the twisted political logic of many: "A liberal is only a hop, skip and a jump from a Communist. A Communist starts as a liberal."[30]

Thus the government's effort to combat espionage, a legitimate response to a genuine hazard, quickly grew from a narrowly focused campaign to identify enemy agents into a massive official struggle to guarantee the "loyalty" of millions of Americans. But because "loyalty" is a quality that defies precise definition, especially when it is applied to almost every person who works for or is licensed by government—federal, state or local—the endeavor quickly turned sour: a massive, clumsy, ineffective and menacing operation that sought to impose a rigid brand of political correctness upon the whole nation.

Without doubt, some of those who supported or directed the federal government response to the Cold War kept their eye on the prize: confronting the real espionage challenges of the Soviet Union and its allies. But for many others, the program offered a splendid way to advance their personal careers and promote their political agendas. Like the Federalists of 1799, like Secretary of War Stanton and his allies in 1866 and like Attorney General Palmer in 1919, a number of the most outspoken Cold War warriors latched onto the federal government's investigative and prosecutive powers as a tool for knocking down their opponents, personal and ideological, and building their empires. Granted, some did believe the perils of the day required bitter medicine. But the inevitable product of their collective obsession was a steady growth in the national security state and the power of the Department of Justice and its component agencies.

The serious departmental excesses of the period are too many to list here. The story of one—the disgraceful tale of how Hoover, the FBI and Truman's Justice Department together developed a secret unlawful program to detain thousands of Americans without trial in the event of a national emergency—was described in the first chapter of this book.

Since Hoover's death in 1972, many books and articles about the director have argued that he was personally responsible for most of the FBI abuses during his long reign. According to this reading of history, Hoover was, at least in his later years, a rotten apple, the cunning bureaucrat who more or less single-handedly led the FBI and the Justice Department astray.

There are good reasons to believe that this view is incorrect or at least far too simple. The director was indeed a man possessed; a racist; a personal despot with the narrowest possible worldview. In addition, however, he was a brilliant political infighter who almost always obtained the formal or informal approval of his supervisors before taking his troops into action. Though it was not emphasized at the time, the post-Watergate investigations discovered that Nixon was far from the only president who knowingly played Hoover's game. The FBI, for example, was found to have sent President Roosevelt, President Truman, President Kennedy, President Johnson and President Nixon the transcripts of wiretapped conversations of their political enemies. The acceptance of this material by a long line of presidents provided Hoover useful cover. All the presidents either knew, or should have known, that the transcripts were based on questionable FBI activities. Like Adam and Eve, once each president partook from this particular apple of tainted knowledge, he lost his innocence and could hardly attack Hoover for picking the fruit from the tree.

One of the classic true stories of this genre began on March 8, 1956, when President Eisenhower called a secret meeting to discuss the potential power of American Communists to damage the United States through either espionage or subversion. Attendees included FBI Director Hoover, Attorney General Herbert Brownell, Vice President Nixon, Secretary of State John Foster Dulles and Secretary of Defense Charles Wilson. During this session, Hoover for the first time disclosed that he had initiated a new kind of FBI program to systematically penetrate the Communist Party, using such activities as secretly intercepting and reading the first-class mail of party members and breaking into their homes and offices to plant hidden listening devices.[31]

At least as important as the specific details of Hoover's disclosure, however, was the director's formal announcement that the FBI had fundamentally altered its strategy for trying to control Communist activities in the United States. No longer, Hoover explained, was the bureau going to limit itself to the traditional police role of collecting evidence to help prosecutors bring criminal charges against party members in federal court. In the interest of protecting national security, he said, the FBI was now seeking to "infiltrate, penetrate, disorganize and disrupt" the party.

The tactical change was not a casual decision for the FBI. It was undertaken because the bureau had come to believe that several Supreme Court rulings had reduced its ability to combat the Communist Party through the techniques required by the Constitution: the formal prosecution of party members for specific criminal acts. In the general war against the CPUSA, the FBI would no longer bother with the legal niceties of indictment by grand jury and proving beyond a reasonable doubt the guilt of the accused during a public trial.[32]

According to the later recollection of Attorney General Brownell, none of the participants at Eisenhower's March 1956 meeting raised any objections to Hoover's decision to revolutionize the FBI's basic modus operandi. Hoover apparently viewed the silence as approval, because five months later, without obtaining the blessing of either the attorney general or the president, he formally launched the already-functioning project, calling it COINTELPRO (counterintelligence program)—Communist Party. The mission of COINTELPRO was to "harass, disrupt and discredit" the party by initiating thousands of dirty tricks against party leaders and members and other political activists whom the FBI judged to have parallel interests.

During the twenty-five-year period following the Palmer raid debacle of the early 1920s, a chastened FBI had mostly stuck to the business of gathering facts about specific criminal acts. Beginning in the early 1950s, however, Hoover, with at least the implicit approval of his president and attorney general, ordered bureau agents to devote more and more of their time to combating the Red menace by secretly manipulating and censoring the political activities of the American people. The writing of anonymous letters designed to wreck the personal and professional lives of the selected targets, the leaking of derogatory information to friendly reporters and editors, the triggering of selective IRS tax audits and the creation of false records incorrectly suggesting that dedicated party members were government informants were only some of the new techniques that COINTELPRO added to the FBI's basic operating repertoire. It was, according to the man directly in charge, "a rough, tough, dirty business."[33]

For a time, COINTELPRO spewed most of its lies and deceit on party members. But as the effectiveness of the new program became clear, Hoover decided to expand the FBI's aggressive political control efforts to other areas of American life. According to most accounts, the director ultimately authorized seven distinct COINTELPROs. One particularly effective program was primarily aimed at the Ku Klux Klan. (It should be remembered that the FBI's effort to *disrupt* the KKK was separate and in addition to its effort to *uncover evidence* which could be used in court against Klansmen who had planted bombs and murdered civil rights activists.) Other groups selected for secret disruption and discrediting included those criticizing the House Un-American Activities Committee, those supporting greater rights for black citizens and those who opposed America's war in Vietnam.

The FBI's paranoia was extraordinary. In the spring of 1970, for example, one of the bureau's internal security agents in Baltimore dispatched a six-page memo to Washington about the city's women's liberation movement. The heading indicates the report was also shared with military intelligence. "It [the movement] started out as a group therapy session with young women who were either lonely or confined to the home with small children, getting together to talk out their problems," he explained.[34] "Along with this, they wanted a purpose and that was to free women from the hum-drum existence of being only a wife and mother. They wanted equal opportunities that men have in work and society."

In the defensive period immediately after Watergate, the supporters of the intelligence community often contended that most if not all of the FBI's Cold War excesses were lawful because they had been authorized by the president and undertaken in the name of national defense. In a number of cases, this argument was accepted by the Supreme Court. But a Justice Department committee that studied the COINTELPROs in 1974 decided that at least some of the FBI activities under them "may" have violated various federal laws and regulations, including the civil rights statute, the mail and wire fraud statutes and the prohibition against divulging information from wiretaps. In addition, internal FBI documents show that bureau officials believed that some of the threats aimed at COINTELPRO targets might have violated federal extortion statutes.[35]

While it is obvious that Hoover's lawless COINTELPROs can in no way be compared with the political horrors of Nazi Germany, Fascist Italy or the Soviet Union, they did cut a wide swath across the face of the United States, disrupting the lives of thousands of Americans whose only crime was to hold beliefs the director did not like. Their impact, however, was not always limited to a general stifling of free speech, the undermining of academic freedom and the creation of a poisonous atmosphere of paranoia that infected the entire nation. On at least a few occasions, the projects personally approved by Hoover in the name of national security and under the COINTELPROs led to both vicious and deadly outcomes.

At 4:00 A.M. on December 4, 1969, for example, a special fourteen-man squad of Chicago police officers raided a house used by the Black Panther Party. During the shoot-first-ask-questions-later raid, police fired at least ninety-eight rounds into the apartment. Illinois chairman Fred Hampton and Peoria chairman Mark Clark were killed. Three other Panthers were wounded. Hampton's bodyguard, William O'Neal, was an FBI informant who had provided the bureau specific information about where Hampton probably would be sleeping and a detailed floor plan of the house which the special squad used during its raid. There are some indications that O'Neal also sought to guarantee that Hampton would not fight back by giving him a glass of Kool-Aid laced with a substantial dose of secobarbital.

Exactly one week after the raid, on December 11, the Chicago office of the FBI informed Hoover that O'Neal's help had been essential to the success of the attack and requested the informant receive a $300 bonus for services rendered. Thirteen years later, in November 1982, District Court Judge John F. Grady determined there was sufficient evidence of an FBI-led conspiracy to deprive the Panthers of their civil rights, and awarded the plaintiffs $1.85 million in damages.[36]

As described above, President Eisenhower and his attorney general, through their silence, went along with the FBI plan to launch the unlawful twenty-year-long campaign of dirty tricks against the Communist Party. Hoover subsequently sent reports about that and other COINTELPROs to most of the attorneys general, including those with liberal credentials like Robert F. Kennedy, Nicholas Katzenbach and Ramsey Clark. Even while Lyndon Johnson fought for far-reaching civil rights legislation and spoke out against racism and government eavesdropping, the Johnson White House—as noted in the second chapter—created a special squad of FBI agents to place wiretaps and bugs on most of the African Americans who came to Atlantic City during the 1964 Democratic convention.

Yes, J. Edgar Hoover aggressively sought to expand his empire. Yes, Hoover personally instigated many of the FBI's illegal or improper forays into the political process of the United States. Yes, Hoover was ruthless. But one also must acknowledge that the presidents and attorneys general who theoretically were responsible for directing Hoover's actions almost always were aware of these efforts, frequently took advantage of the political leverage they offered and often had formally approved them. The point here is that most of the time, Hoover enjoyed at least the tacit blessing of those above him who had taken solemn oaths to uphold the Constitution and laws of the United States.

AFTER WATERGATE

With the forced resignation of Richard Nixon, the death of J. Edgar Hoover and the conviction of John Mitchell, the disgraced attorney general, the American people heaved a sigh of relief. The nightmare was over. The nation could now return to normalcy. But as the history of the Justice Department proves, large institutions—encrusted by law, tradition and a particular social view—are persistent hard-to-control beasts more responsive to the momentum of the past than the realities of the present. This is true when the White House is advised by idealogues like CIA Director William Casey, Assistant Secretary of State Eliot Abrams, National Security Council Directors Robert MacFarlane and John Poindexter and Marine colonel Oliver North. It also was true during the periods when the federal investigative and prosecuting units were controlled by men like President John Adams, Attorney General James Speed, Attorney General A. Mitchell Palmer, and many of the fifteen individuals who commanded the Justice Department during the Cold War.

One measure of the FBI's continuing national security concerns was the 1990 finding by congressional investigators that from January 1982 through June 1988 the bureau opened and closed about 19,500 investigations of possible terrorist activities in the United States. Just under four out of ten of these investigations were focused on American citizens or permanent resident aliens.[37]

In an attempt to better understand the purpose of these investigations, the General Accounting Office selected a small sample of the cases for detailed analysis. This study showed that the FBI claimed it opened only 12 percent of the investigations because it had received information that the subject or target group had committed, planned or was otherwise involved in a terrorist act. Involvement was defined as taking part in a specific act like a bombing, providing materials to carry it out or raising funds for that purpose.

The FBI said that most of the other cases, 74 percent of them, were opened on much more tenuous grounds: because it had some indication to believe that the targeted individual was a leader or member of a group that the bureau defined as sponsoring terrorism, or had some other less direct association with such a group. In the balance of the sample, the FBI was not able to explain to the GAO why the cases had been opened.

The GAO study was ordered by Congress because of questions that had been raised about the propriety of the FBI's intensive investigation of the Committee in Solidarity with the People of El Salvador (CISPES). The questions became concrete when, in January 1988, a lawyer for the Center for Constitutional Rights won the release of about 3,500 pages concerning the FBI's long investigation of CISPES, some of which indicated the probe had violated Justice Department guidelines.

Then, in September of the same year, William S. Sessions, the new FBI director, reported to committees in both the House and the Senate about the CISPES investigation, admitting error. He insisted, however, that the situation was "an aberration . . . an unfortunate aligning of mistakes in judgment at several levels [of the FBI] of which the FBI is not proud." In July 1989, after an extensive study of its own, the Select Senate Committee on Intelligence concluded that the FBI investigation

of CISPES had been based on unfounded allegations that the people opposed to the Reagan administration's aggressive policies in Central
America were linked to international terrorist groups.

The basic conclusion of both the FBI and the Senate Intelligence
Committee was that gung-ho lower-level FBI executives, carried away
with their national security mandate, had mistakenly led the bureau
into an improper political investigation. But a case can be made that
something much more sinister was at work. In his carefully documented analysis of the CISPES matter, *Break-ins, Death Threats and
the FBI: The Covert War Against the Central American Movement*,
Boston writer Ross Gelbspan argues that a much more extensive conspiracy may have been at work. Far from being a low-level operation,
Gelbspan reports, hundreds of the documents in the CISPES file had
been initialed by Oliver "Buck" Revell, then the number two official in
the FBI.[38]

Gelbspan believes that the CISPES waters may run even deeper. Noting such matters as the direct involvement in the case of the National
Guard of El Salvador and the scores of unexplained break-ins at the offices of antiwar groups all over the United States, he speculates that the
mastermind behind the whole affair may have been William Casey,
Ronald Reagan's Machiavellian CIA director.

Gelbspan discussed the question with Robert White, the Carter administration's ambassador to El Salvador. "You're only looking at the
FBI," White said. "That's just one piece of it. What Ronald Reagan has
done is to mobilize the entire government around his policies in Central America."[39]

The CISPES investigation received a good deal of congressional attention in the late 1980s. But the persistent way the FBI continued its
old bread-and-butter investigative techniques also is worth noting. It
was March 30, 1989, just before April Fool's day, and at first Virginia
Bernard thought the caller was one of her friends pulling a practical
joke. Why in the world would an FBI agent want to talk to her, a grand-
mother, a retired nurse and a substitute schoolteacher in the parochial
schools of Phoenix, Arizona? Virginia Bernard handed the telephone to
her husband, George, who had been an IRS official until his retirement
a few years before. George knew how to handle these things. After a
brief discussion, the man on the phone convinced George he was a genuine FBI agent and that he must talk to Virginia immediately. Less than
an hour later Special Agent Stephen C. Emmett knocked on their door.[40]

"Agent Emmett was wearing a tie and a shirt but no coat," Mrs.
Bernard recalled. "He was a nice-looking young man, I guess about
thirty, and he showed me his credentials and gave me his card. Then he
asked me whether my name was Virginia Bernard and whether my

birthday was March 1, 1916. I don't know how, but he even knew my Social Security number."

The seventy-three-year-old, part-time teacher then asked the agent why he had come calling. "Well, you subscribe to *Soviet Life*, don't you?" Emmett replied, consulting a notebook. "When you subscribed to *Soviet Life*, that was mark one against you. Then you wrote to the Russian embassy. That was mark two. I need to clear this up. It's in the interest of national security."

With the invocation of the sacred words "national security," one of the most powerful mantras of the long-lived Cold War, Mrs. Bernard's seventy-nine-year-old husband burst out laughing. At any time, it would have been hard to imagine the connection between his wife and the fearsome world of espionage, the arms race and Check Point Charlie. But it was now 1989, when the spirit of glasnost was sweeping through the Soviet Union, East Germany and central Europe. The agent's linkage of his wife to "national security" seemed absurd. The agent, however, did not share George's amused astonishment. "Don't mock me," the couple remembers Emmett warning them.

Virginia Bernard was not impressed. "When I realized what the FBI man was driving at, I looked him right in the eye and said, 'I'm pissed. I'm very angry that my tax dollars are going for this kind of crap.' I then asked him whether he really truly thought Russian spies took out subscriptions to *Soviet Life* and put their return addresses on the envelopes they mailed to the embassy? He replied that he was just doing his job." It was the classic dishonest cop-out of all bureaucrats, great and small, who have been granted great discretionary power.

Soviet Life, which ceased publication shortly after the formal abolition of the Soviet Union on the last day of 1991, was a glossy, English-language magazine distributed in the United States under a 1956 cultural-exchange agreement between the U.S.S.R. and the United States. A friend had given Mrs. Bernard a copy of the magazine and she then took out a subscription because the photography was impressive. Although she knew the articles were misleading, they presented an interesting picture of life in Russia and the other so-called republics. The magazine thus was quite similar to the Russian-language publication that the United States distributed in the Soviet Union.

Mrs. Bernard said her second alleged national security infraction, writing to the Soviet embassy in Washington, was easy to explain. A few months before the agent's visit she had sent a note congratulating the Soviets for dispatching an icebreaker to free the two whales that had become stranded in the thick ice near Barrow, Alaska. The congratulatory message, she said, had been suggested by the host of a television talk show she happened to see.

The FBI, of course, would not acknowledge that it just might have been a waste of time to question all the individuals like Mrs. Bernard who put their return name and address on the envelopes of the letters they sent to the Soviet embassy. Responding to an inquiry from one of her senators, John E. Collingwood, the inspector in charge of the bureau's Congressional Affairs Office, limited himself to noting that Agent Emmett's visit was part of the FBI's broad counterintelligence responsibility "to resolve unexplained contacts between persons in this country and officials of the Soviet Union and certain other foreign countries."[41]

The patently silly counterintelligence program that led the FBI to knock on Mrs. Bernard's door and the doors of thousands of other subscribers to *Soviet Life* was hardly the only indication of the bureau's intrusive interest in the reading and writing habits of the American people in the waning years of the Cold War. In fact, approximately two years before, agents drawn from the FBI's 2,500-person counterintelligence division launched an investigation of this specific subject at libraries all over the country, including those connected with the University of California at Los Angeles, the University of Utah, the University of Wisconsin, the University of Houston, the Broward County Public Library in Florida and a number of academic and public libraries in and about New York City. Subsequent investigations by Congressman Don Edwards, a liberal California Democrat and chairman of the House Judiciary Subcommittee on Civil and Constitutional Rights, and several library organizations discovered that most of the requests made by the FBI agents during their visits to the targeted libraries were vague and highly varied, suggesting that the bureau wasn't quite sure what it was doing. Occasionally the agents asked about the reading habits of a specific individual. More frequently they requested all the names of those using the library facilities to obtain certain kinds of nonclassified technical information. At some of the libraries, the agents instructed the staff to call them in the future about any suspicious activities such as the theft of microfiche and other library resources.

As noted in the later congressional testimony of Duane Webster, the executive director of the Association of Research Libraries, an after-the-fact report by a slightly defensive FBI showed that the bureau still did not understand why its unfocused Library Awareness Program raised so many hackles in the library and academic communities. The report, Webster said, failed to acknowledge that some of the bureau's library requests were in direct conflict with the laws of many states, with the formal policies of almost all libraries and with the ethical values of the library profession that for many years has viewed the privacy of readers as an essential freedom guaranteed by the United States Constitution.[42]

One aspect of the silliness of the FBI's investigation of Mrs. Bernard was noted two years later by Congressman Edwards. At about the same time that the FBI agent was knocking on Mrs. Bernard's door in Arizona, the bureau had 21,000 allegations of savings and loan fraud it was unable to investigate, and at least 2,400 inactive financial crime investigations awaiting consideration. In the San Diego area, for example, lack of available agents meant the FBI would not even consider investigating bank fraud cases unless they involved losses of at least $1 million.[43]

On April 19, 1995, a massive car bomb exploded outside of the federal office building in Oklahoma City. In addition to taking the lives of 168 men, women and children, the bombing—at least for a time— seemed to alter the perceptions of a substantial number of American people. Obviously, the national security threat of the Soviet Union was gone. But now, according to President Clinton, Attorney General Reno and FBI Director Freeh, a new menace has raised its head that called for the enhancement of important government powers.

Two weeks after the horrific Oklahoma event, Clinton sent to Congress the "Antiterrorism Amendments Act of 1995," an eighteen-page grab bag of recommendations which the president said were intended "to combat domestic and international terrorism."[44] But many of the amendments had very little to do with terrorism and a great deal to do with expanding the general investigative tools of the FBI. Wiretapping, which under the existing law can be used to probe a quite lengthy list of specific felonies, in some circumstances would now be authorized for all felonies. A second amendment would weaken a section of the wiretap law that penalizes the government if it fails to follow certain restrictions involving how its wiretaps are conducted.[45]

In addition to the proposed changes in law, Deputy Attorney General Jamie Gorelick and FBI Director Freeh announced that they had decided to reinterpret twenty-year-old Justice Department guidelines originally put in place to restrain the FBI from violating the constitutional rights of political dissidents.[46]

"If those guidelines are interpreted broadly and proactively, as opposed to defensively, as has been the case for many many years, I feel confident . . . we have sufficient authority," Freeh told a Senate Committee.

William Safire, the conservative *New York Times* columnist with libertarian leanings, was appalled, asking if there wasn't anyone in the government who remembered how the FBI played the game in the bad old days?

"To the applause of voters fearful of terrorism," Safire wrote, "the proactivists declare their intent to prevent crime. This would be followed by surveillance of suspect groups by new technology; the infiltration of political movements deemed radical or violence prone; and the stretching of the guidelines put in place 20 years ago to restrain yesterday's zealots."[47]

Ramon Cernuda in Miami, the CISPES supporters in Texas, Virginia Bernard in Phoenix and the librarians at a half dozen major institutions in cities around the United States all can bear witness to how easily national security concerns can be perverted, even at a moment in the nation's history when the United States was relatively secure from enemy attack. This recent testimony must, of course, be considered alongside the lengthy history of similar abuses by the Justice Department and, before its creation in 1870, by the attorney general and the separate U.S. attorneys of more distant administrations.

The list is long. It begins with Adams and the almost nonexistent threat posed by revolutionary France. It includes the paranoid fear of Eisenhower, Kennedy, Johnson and Nixon that the just grievances of black Americans were being fanned by the Communist International to weaken America's response to the Cold War. In between there was Stanton and the passionate fervor of the Radical Republicans, Palmer and the isolationist hatred of the middle European immigrants, Roosevelt and his authoritarian demand for secret intelligence about domestic politics and Truman and his acceptance of unconstitutional loyalty programs. For aggressive presidents who wished to expand their political authority over the American people through the machinations of the Justice Department and the FBI, the dubious national security claims have repeatedly provided excellent camouflage for more agents, more laws, more surveillance, more investigations, more centralizing of power within the federal government. Let the buyer of justice beware of shoddy goods; let the citizen be wary about false claims that the security of the nation is threatened.

10

Taking on the Ethically Challenged

Sometime during the late summer of 1992, a man came to the office of Jim Oberwetter, the Dallas campaign chairman for President Bush and Vice President Quayle. The man was a salesman of sorts. Would Oberwetter be interested, the visitor asked, in purchasing some audiotapes and documents that he had secretly obtained from Ross Perot? It was the Perot presidential campaign, of course, that then threatened to derail Bush's hopes of capturing Texas in the November election. The price for the purloined material was a mere $2,500.

Oberwetter said no to the mysterious salesman, refusing to buy the tapes, which presumably would have provided him useful political intelligence about the operations of the businessman-turned-candidate who was giving the Republican campaign so much trouble.

Several months later, a furious Oberwetter informed reporters about the offer. The Bush campaign manager, it turned out, was not so angry about the proposition itself. After all, politics is politics. What truly enraged him was that he had just learned that the man offering the stolen tapes and documents was not just another disgruntled campaign worker but an FBI undercover agent who had been sent to test his honesty. Employing such tactics to secretly trap Communists, drug dealers and other lowlifes was one thing, Oberwetter seemed to suggest. But when aimed at respectable people, that was going way too far.

The FBI, which confirmed its investigative probe of Oberwetter's integrity, said it had initiated the secret "sting" operation as a routine response to a complaint of criminal conduct, in this instance unsupported allegations by Perot that the Bush-Quayle team had engaged in dirty tricks by conspiring to tap his telephones. "That allegation was investigated and no evidence of criminality was found," the FBI said.

The FBI's investigation of the political ally of a sitting president shocked the sensibilities of Oberwetter and some others. The *New York Times*, for example, wrote an editorial denouncing the "Federal Bureau of Temptation" and its clandestine probe. But William S. Sessions, the FBI director at the time, disagreed with the criticisms. The FBI's use of undercover agents was "carefully circumscribed in law, guidelines and policy," he said. In this particular case, he added, if the FBI had failed to act, "we would not have carried out our Federal law enforcement responsibilities. In the end, our investigation clearly saved innocent people from unfair and inaccurate public depictions."[1]

In a curiously revealing way, both the editors of the *Times* and FBI Director Sessions were right: The FBI has indeed developed an investigative tactic which is extraordinarily intrusive, and this tactic has, in fact, been approved by Justice Department officials of several recent administrations.

For many years after its formation during Theodore Roosevelt's administration, the FBI mostly limited itself to investigating specific criminal acts that had been committed already. The bureau's one exception to this rather narrow vision of its responsibilities involved out-of-bounds organizations such as the Communist Party or the KKK. In these situations, always in the name of disrupting the operations of the targeted groups, the FBI planted large numbers of undercover operatives who provided intelligence and took steps to embarrass or confuse their putative colleagues.

Then, in the wake of Watergate, and with the formal blessing of President Carter's Justice Department, the FBI was authorized to employ the undercover sting techniques it had perfected for an entirely new purpose: gathering evidence for criminal trials—most particularly, bringing criminal charges against corrupt public officials.

Abscam, the bombshell 1978 investigation which ultimately resulted in the convictions of seven members of Congress, was the beginning point of this new campaign. But soon, in the name of combating public corruption wherever it occurred, the FBI had set up hundreds of complex stings aimed at all kinds of public officials—federal judges, governors, state legislators, mayors, city council members—the business executives that sought to bribe them, and even suspect campaign officials like Jim Oberwetter. By the early 1990s, the FBI had initiated thousands of such operations.

For the Justice Department and the FBI there was one very important advantage to using undercover agents to gather evidence. Unlike its other favorite surveillance technique, electronic eavesdropping, the law did not require the FBI to obtain the written permission of a federal judge when it initiated an investigation involving a human operative. Sting operations were almost totally free of outside review.

The Carter administration's decision to allow the FBI to undertake this very new kind of criminal investigation was a matter of major consequence. Previously, as already briefly noted, the FBI had viewed the goal of its investigations as collecting evidence against individuals it had reason to believe had committed specific crimes. Now, the FBI had been authorized to insert itself into the middle of criminal transactions, and even to commit criminal acts, in the name of preventing the individuals who walked into its subtle web from committing a criminal act sometime in the future.

The Justice Department, the prosecuting attorneys and the FBI were all highly enthusiastic about this mutually advantageous enlargement of their basic powers. During one recent twelve-month period, for example, according to a bureau report submitted to the House Judiciary Committee on September 30, 1991, FBI headquarters in Washington approved 171 separate long-term criminal sting investigations in which its "salesmen" were offering selected targets an opportunity to do things in front of hidden television cameras and undisclosed recording devices that might later cause them to be charged with a federal crime.

The bureau's official report, however, substantially *underestimates* the number of stings it undertook that year. This is because the report does not include information about such operations that were completed in less than three days or were aimed at spies. With the addition of these two additional categories, it is likely that the FBI is running several thousand stings a year.

By itself, the decision of Jimmy Carter's Justice Department to au-

318 ABOVE THE LAW

thorize the FBI to begin using undercover sting investigations on a routine basis was a big deal, a major expansion in the Justice Department's reach into every level of American life. But because the new FBI investigative technique was approved at roughly the same time as two other, apparently unrelated, changes in the department's basic approach to crime, a significant revolution was accomplished with hardly anyone noticing it. The two other changes, described in greater detail below, were, first, a vast expansion in the laws under which corruption cases are brought; and second, the creation of special new units within the Justice Department centralizing the control of corruption investigations.

IN THE BEGINNING

But first, a little history is required to appreciate the dimensions of this revolution. Government corruption—the sale of political favors for bribes and other things of value—has always been an important part of the American scene. Bribery has speeded up the destructive plundering of the nation's natural resources, fixed elections, allowed dangerous criminals to avoid prison, permitted wealthy businessmen to evade paying billions of dollars in taxes, facilitated the illicit collection of useful political intelligence, contributed to the construction of shoddy highways and other public facilities and eased the distribution of illegal drugs. Even more important, perhaps, bribery has weakened the collective integrity of the local, state and federal bureaucracies upon which we depend for all manner of vital services.

Until very recent times, federal prosecutors have chosen to ignore official corruption, usually deciding it was unworthy of national attention. The problem, it was thought, was best left to indignant clergymen, special commissions of earnest do-gooders, local district attorneys and scandal-seeking newspaper reporters.

The extended period of federal indifference does not appear to be in any way related to the extent to which corrupt officials held positions of power. Everyone remembers the massively crooked political organizations of Boss Tweed's New York or Mayor Curley's Boston or Al Capone's Chicago in the late nineteenth and early twentieth centuries. But, as recounted in the fascinating and exhaustive history of bribery by Court of Appeals Judge John T. Noonan, Jr., and despite the idealized accounts of early American political life by many historians, federal officials stooped to striking corrupt deals a long time before the rough-and-tumble days when the poor immigrants from Ireland, Italy and Eastern Europe began pouring into America's big cities.

When James Monroe was secretary of state, for example, the distinguished Virginian borrowed $5,000 from John Jacob Astor, the aggressive and successful fur trader then on his way to becoming one of this nation's first millionaires. Astor had an intense commercial interest in obtaining a variety of favors from the federal government, which Monroe was in a unique position to provide, both as secretary of state and later as the fifth president of the United States.

The amount of the credit Astor extended to Monroe was considerable, the equivalent of Monroe's annual salary as the nation's most senior cabinet member when he first took the loan. The loan was also unusual because it was made without security and allowed to run for three years without interest.

Letters between the enormously successful entrepreneur and the federal official show that during the many years the loan remained in place, Astor never hesitated to ask his well-placed debtor for the assistance of the government. Whether this assistance was in the national interest and whether Monroe would have been so helpful to Astor in the absence of the loan is not clear.

But the timing of the wealthy businessman's decision to terminate the arrangement is suggestive. Astor's generous loan, first granted to Monroe when he was secretary of state during the War of 1812, remained in force until 1825. At that time, shortly after Monroe had left the White House and could no longer provide the businessman any favors, Astor demanded repayment.[2]

This was not Monroe's only dubious relationship with a high-powered business executive. During part of the same period, the politician also accepted a $10,596 loan from the Bank of the United States, a private institution whose success was totally dependent upon federal deposits and a friendly Congress. As noted in the account of Nicholas Biddle, the forceful president of the bank, a number of other federal officials were also willing to accept the suspicious loans. Henry Clay, for example, was down for $7,500 and Senator Daniel Webster for $17,782.86.

Favorable loans, however, were not the only under-the-table way eighteenth-century tycoons sought to assure themselves of the support of their government. The Bank of the United States, for example, also liked to hire influential officials as consulting lawyers, apparently to provide it with the very best legal advice money could buy. Among the many well-placed lawyers who accepted a retainer from banker Biddle was William Wirt, the nation's ninth attorney general.[3]

Other dubious arrangements were worked out by the young nation's political leaders, less obvious than those put together by the likes of

Monroe and Webster. Consider, for example, the election of 1824, when citizens failed to give a majority of electoral college votes to any one of the three presidential candidates and, as provided in the Constitution, the matter headed to the House of Representatives for final resolution. In the months between election day and the final House vote, even according to his friendly biographers, John Quincy Adams managed to defeat the only other serious candidate, Andrew Jackson, by purchasing the electoral college votes he needed to become president.

In this case the currency of payment was patronage, a series of secret commitments for generous federal favors once Adams was installed in the White House. The loser, who himself would gain the presidency in the next election, was outraged by the corrupt understandings that assured the victory of his opponent. One of Jackson's suspicions of fraud was confirmed when Adams named Henry Clay, a key player in the election fix, to be his secretary of state.

The acceptance and offering of questionable payments and loans by Monroe, Clay, John Quincy Adams, Webster and Attorney General Wirt—even those suspected or known about by their contemporaries—never resulted in criminal charges. That was partly because there were no federal bribery laws back then. Although the leaders of the young country were fully aware of the problem of government corruption—bribery and treason, after all, are the only two specific crimes mentioned as grounds for impeachment under Article III of the Constitution—Congress did not get around to enacting a federal bribery statute until shortly before the Civil War. This law, approved in 1853, authorized a three-year jail term and disqualification from office for any congressman or other federal official who was convicted of accepting a bribe, present or other reward to influence his vote, decision or opinion.

THE FIRST TO FALL

As most of us find it hard to remember, lawbooks are full of statutes that for one reason or another are seldom enforced. In this particular case, it would be more than three quarters of a century after the passage of the first bribery law before a high federal official, Albert Bacon Fall, would be convicted of taking a bribe—a $100,000 payment from two oilmen. The official took the money in return for helping the businessmen gain access to the naval oil reserve at Teapot Dome, Wyoming. Fall, who was convicted on October 25, 1929, had been serving as President Warren Harding's interior secretary at the critical moment. The spectacular payoff might well have become yet another in a long line of similar illegal transactions that routinely escaped the public ugliness of prosecution except for two accidents of history. First, the case was investigated by an unusually intelligent and aggressive Democratic senator from Montana named Thomas J. Walsh. Second, the figure who probably would have been able to provide Fall the necessary protection, President Harding, unexpectedly died.[4]

In addition to marking the end of the long period when crooked officials of the federal government were exempt from criminal sanctions, the Teapot Dome scandal is of historical interest for other reasons. Partly as a result of public resentment generated by the failure of the Harding administration to confront the scandal, the hard-drinking Harry Daugherty, one of the worst attorneys general in the entire history of the Justice Department, was forced to resign.

The second noteworthy precedent of the scandal was the appointment of two highly respected lawyers from outside the Justice Department to handle the prosecution of Fall. The decision to name the special counsels was made by Calvin Coolidge, who had become president after Harding's death. The new president apparently decided to remove the case from the Justice Department in what turned out to be an unsuccessful effort to distance himself from the stench of his predecessor's friends, collectively known as the Harding gang.

Less than a decade after Fall's unprecedented public disgrace, the Justice Department was forced to investigate another major corruption scandal, this time the case of Martin T. Manton, a U.S. Court of Appeals judge in New York who was convicted eventually of accepting at least $400,000 in bribes from plaintiffs appearing before his court. The Justice Department, which had long ignored rumors of Manton's greedy ways, apparently was shamed into prosecuting the judge, an old-line Tammany Hall Democrat, by Tom Dewey, then an ambitious young county district attorney in Manhattan. Republican Dewey forced the Democratic Justice Department to act when he compelled the sitting judge to resign his prestigious post by threatening to prosecute him for failure to pay New York State income taxes on all the bribes he had received.[5] (It is worth noting here that about fifty years later, in much the same fashion, New York's Democratic district attorney, Robert Morgenthau, forced the Republican Justice Department to launch a serious investigation of the massive and embarrassing BCCI banking scandal.)

The next big, but still isolated, corruption case leading to the prosecution of a senior federal official—as noted in Chapter 7, on corporate crime—came in 1956 with a man named T. Lamar Caudle. Caudle, who had been the assistant attorney general in charge of the Justice Department's Tax Division, was convicted of helping a St. Louis businessman

avoid paying federal taxes in return for a bribe.⁶ The case was doubly
significant because, as in the Teapot Dome scandal, the attorney general, Democratic Party hack J. Howard McGrath, was forced to resign
for his failure to properly mind the store. As with Fall and Manton before him, however, reluctant federal prosecution of Caudle was much
more the accidental product of an unrelated political war—this time
the attack of congressional Republicans on Harry Truman's Democratic
administration—than the conversion of the Justice Department to even
a limited holy war against official corruption.⁷

The jihad would have to wait.

Despite a large number of known and suspected public corruption
problems throughout American history, the possibility of imposing
sanctions under the common law, the existence of a constitutional
mechanism for impeaching high federal officials and the passage of the
1853 bribery law, it was not until the late 1960s and early 1970s that
the federal government began to develop a systematic interest in prosecuting official corruption.

Curiously, this profound shift appears to have been another one of
those unplanned accidents of history. Even more curious, the first
stages in the revolution seem to have been executed by independent
U.S. attorneys working in different corners of the United States at the
same time that the Justice Department in Washington was drifting into
one of the most corrupt periods of its long history. The largely unrecog-
nized policy upheaval began in early 1969 when Richard Nixon appointed a substantial number of aggressive and competent U.S.
attorneys. Confronted with a variety of corruption problems in their
various districts, a handful of these freshly minted federal prosecutors
began to devise a whole new range of strategic approaches for dealing
with the persistent corruption that had been gnawing at the guts of
state and local government since the nation was formed.

Perhaps the toughest and most innovative pioneers among the new
Republican prosecutors were Frederick Lacey and his successor, Herbert J. Stern, who were the U.S. attorneys in New Jersey from 1969 to
1974. The problem was this: Although the political machines that controlled many New Jersey cities were widely known to be massively corrupt, and had been since at least the turn of the century, Congress
somehow had never gotten around to passing a law that made corruption at the state and local level a federal crime. To resolve this particular dilemma, Lacey and Stern engaged in an amazing kind of legal
legerdemain, taking a law that Congress had approved in 1946 for the
purpose of prosecuting organized crime figures and unilaterally asserting that this statute could also be applied to the elected mayor of Jersey
City and many of his colleagues.

The men convicted by Lacey and Stern as a result of their creative bending of the law undoubtedly were engaged in evil, wasteful and improper acts. But a strong argument can be made that the prosecutions were improper because the crooked politicians had in fact not violated the federal law under which they were prosecuted, but only the U.S. attorney's extremely creative and after-the-fact interpretation of that statute. The prosecutors in effect rewrote an old law to suit their own immediate needs. Despite the dubious nature of the whole process, the courts, perhaps caught up in the exciting drama of sending the old-line bosses to federal prison, eventually upheld the Lacey-Stern legal strategy. While the objective of the prosecutors appeared to have merit—the city bosses were not nice people—the courts did not seem to remember that under the Constitution, writing law is supposed to be the prerogative of the Congress.

Shortly thereafter, U.S. Attorney James Thompson, of the Northern District of Illinois, accomplished much the same kind of legal feat when he convicted Otto Kerner, a U.S. Court of Appeals judge appointed by President Johnson, of bribery. Kerner, a former Democratic governor of Illinois, was sent to prison after Thompson persuaded a jury that Kerner's acceptance of campaign contributions from a racetrack owner who was seeking a favorable state ruling violated a law originally passed by Congress a hundred years before to curb the lottery frauds that were run through the mails.

Once again, an ingenious interpretation of a law by an aggressive U.S. attorney had allowed the prosecution of a possibly corrupt state official in a way never contemplated by Congress when it was passing the statute.

The successful efforts of Lacey, Stern, Thompson and a handful of other U.S. attorneys in such states as Maryland and Oklahoma to reinterpret old laws for new purposes resulted in what appeared to be an organized federal crusade to combat state and local corruption. Given Nixon's reputation as a supremely manipulative politician, it is hardly surprising that there are Democratic students of the Justice Department who contend that the administration's selection of a group of brilliant and supremely ambitious young lawyers to be federal prosecutors was part of a broad Republican plot to undermine big-city political machines mostly controlled by Democrats.

There is no evidence to support the existence of such a clever conspiracy by President Nixon and Attorney General John Mitchell, especially when it is remembered that U.S. attorneys almost always are selected by the senior political figure in each state who belongs to the president's party. That is not to say that partisan considerations were totally banished from the decision-making process. Lacey, Stern and

Thompson, after all, were indeed Republicans and a substantial number of their targets were Democratic politicos.

The dynamic of party politics, however, operates no matter which party controls the prosecutors. Many of the U.S. attorneys appointed by Roosevelt, Truman, Kennedy and Johnson were Democratic political hacks who demonstrated massive disinterest in prosecuting the Democratic machine politicians who for many years had been so successful in producing votes for Democratic candidates.

There is obviously great irony in the fact that even as Nixon administration prosecutors were mounting the first extensive federal campaign against corrupt state and local politicians in the history of the United States, the administration itself was on the verge of collapsing under its own corruption scandals. The first major casualty, of course, was Vice President Spiro Agnew, a former Maryland governor who was forced to resign the vice presidency and plead guilty to a federal tax charge related to his routine acceptance of bribes. It should be noted that this supremely embarrassing case was the product of an aggressive investigation by a respected U.S. attorney appointed by Nixon.

Then, in rapid succession, came the Watergate disclosures, the approval by the House Judiciary Committee of legislation to impeach President Nixon and the president's decision to resign. Among the specific allegations against Nixon was the charge that he personally had sought to obstruct the prosecution of a federal criminal case by arranging the payment of cash bribes to silence dangerous witnesses. Thus it was that an administration that had pioneered an aggressive and innovative federal war on corruption within the ranks of state and local officeholders was destroyed by its own corruption at the highest levels.

THE REVOLUTION IS REGULARIZED

T he first presidential resignation in the nation's history and the abrupt elevation to the White House of an appointed vice president—a Michigan congressman named Gerald Ford—obviously were the most dramatic and visible moments of the Watergate period. These events were so sensational, in fact, that they tend to obscure the substantial procedural and structural governmental changes that grew out of them.

From almost their first day in the White House, Ford and his advisers understood that Nixon and Mitchell had done serious damage to the basic integrity of the Justice Department. They further recognized that because a certain level of public confidence in the system of justice is a vital element of representative democracy, it was absolutely essential that immediate steps be taken to convince the American people that the Justice Department was no longer for sale. As his first, and probably most important, step in reviving the department, Ford decided it was essential he appoint a new attorney general and that this person had to be very special. Unlike most former presidents, Ford could not consider appointing his personal lawyer, the former chairman of the Republican Party, or his campaign manager to this sensitive position. After an intensive search, Ford decided on Edward H. Levi, the brilliant president of the University of Chicago and the former dean of its law school. The verdict on Ford's choice was then, and is today, nearly unanimous: Edward Levi was an extraordinary choice, one of the most creative, thoughtful and least partisan attorneys general in the history of the United States.

The challenge that confronted Levi—regaining respect for the thoroughly distrusted and badly demoralized Justice Department—was a towering one. The illegal and improper actions of department officials had to be openly acknowledged and directly faced. At the same time, Congress and the public had to be shown that difficult law enforcement decisions could be made on their merits and with minimum regard to partisan politics. Finally, new policies and procedures had to be devised and put in place that would give the public confidence that the widespread misconduct of the past would be kept to an absolute minimum.

Because the Justice Department is such a large and complex organization, Levi's attempts to institutionalize reform necessarily involved many different activities. At the FBI, for example, a team of experienced agents, Justice Department lawyers and outside legal critics of the bureau were assembled to write enforcement guidelines. Although this effort may sound simple, perhaps even simpleminded, it was central to the overall goal of rehabilitating the Justice Department. The purpose of the guidelines that eventually were adopted was to provide agents with a logical and understandable method for selecting the cases they would investigate, procedures that would help the FBI focus on truly significant areas of law enforcement while avoiding improper political surveillance and harassment actions that had so seriously damaged the agency and the nation.

In the immediate post-Watergate years, the outrageous nature of some of these FBI abuses attracted a good deal of public attention both to the activities themselves and to Levi's efforts to prevent them from recurring. But several other Levi projects to institutionalize important changes in the basic operations of the Justice Department were barely noticed. In late 1975 and early 1976, for example, the attorney general acted to regularize the Justice Department's approach to official corruption by creating two special new units, the first in the department's history, with the specific mission of supervising the investigation and prosecution of government corruption and other kinds of misconduct.

Thus, while Lacey, Stern, Thompson and a handful of other U.S. attorneys had vastly strengthened federal anticorruption laws in the years just *before* Watergate, it was public revulsion to the Watergate abuses *during* the Nixon administration that led to the appointment of Levi and his decision to establish formal department units to supervise and, in some ways, to accelerate the pace of such investigations.

Under the attorney general's plan, the Public Integrity Section (PIS), one of the two new units he established, was to organize the federal response to official corruption of federal, state and local officials *outside* the Justice Department. As stated in its first annual report, the section was "responsible for coordinating enforcement of all Federal statutes dealing with bribery, conflicts of interest and miscellaneous offenses in office that are committed by officers or employees of the three branches of the federal government. In addition, the Section shares with the United States Attorneys responsibility for the Federal Government's recent prosecutive initiatives in the area of local corruption. . . ."[8]

The second unit, the Office of Professional Responsibility (OPR), was to aim its sights at a far more sensitive subject: preventing misconduct by Justice Department lawyers under the direct supervision of the attorney general. From the very beginning, and for obvious reasons, OPR has almost always played a defensive game that seemed much more interested in protecting the reputation of the attorney general than in undertaking a serious effort to minimize departmental misconduct. The words of OPR's first annual report tell it all. The office's purpose, the report explained, was "to ensure that Departmental employees continue to perform their duties in accord with the professional standards expected of the nation's principal law enforcement agency."[9] Inherent in this revealing formula was the defensive assumption that the employees then working for the department were of course innocent of all possible wrongdoing, and the only required action was to prevent any backsliding in the future. More about OPR later in this chapter.

PIS

Since its creation more than fifteen years ago, the Public Integrity Section has been extremely assertive in expanding its basically weak legal authority, in bringing cases and in seeking a maximum amount of publicity for them. It seems likely that one explanation for this unusually pugnacious character is that over the years many of its corruption cases have been less embarrassing to the political party that controlled the Justice Department than to the party that did not.

Whatever the explanation, the unit's production statistics prove that fighting corruption has been one of the fastest-growing areas of enforcement in the Justice Department. During calendar year 1970, for example, the department only indicted forty-five federal, state and local officials and eighteen businesspersons on a variety of corruption charges. By any measure, this total of sixty-three individuals charged with corruption was minuscule in comparison to the millions of government employees in a position to accept a bribe and the tens of millions of individual Americans who just might offer one.

But with the aggressive legal expansionism of Lacey and Thompson, the public dismay over the Watergate scandals, the formal establishment of the Public Integrity Section in 1975 and other factors such as the growing national concern about organized crime, federal prosecutors developed a kind of anticorruption fever. The investigation and prosecution of all kinds of government corruption became a matter of

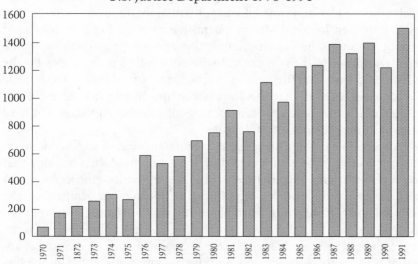

OFFICIAL CORRUPTION INDICTMENTS
U.S. Justice Department 1970–1991

The Justice Department has engaged in a steadily growing enforcement campaign against corrupt public officials. While corruption is an important problem, critics contend that the department's increasingly aggressive enforcement effort in this area could weaken the response of state and local agencies to the challenge. (ANNUAL REPORTS — PUBLIC INTEGRITY SECTION)

highest concern: from 63 individuals in 1970, to 729 in 1982 and 1,452 in 1991, the last period covered by PIS's annual reports.

Though still a small number of prosecutions in absolute terms, the twenty-three-fold growth rate is nevertheless impressive. All together, during the period from 1970 to 1991, federal prosecutors charged 16,817 government and business officials with various corruption charges, convicting 14,093 of them. The conviction rate for individuals accused of corruption—83.8 percent—was on average somewhat higher than those indicted for violating federal drug laws, embezzlement and fraud, or offenses connected with organized crime.[10]

As demonstrated throughout this book, federal investigations and prosecutions often involve partisan political considerations. This is why it should come as no surprise that in perhaps the most sensitive enforcement areas for the Public Integrity Section—policing the ethical behavior of federal judges—every one of the six judges who was indicted for corrupt acts during the years when the Justice Department was controlled by President Reagan and President Bush just happened to have been appointed by a Democratic president.

This is not to argue that any of these six Democratic judges was necessarily innocent, although one indeed was eventually acquitted by a jury and a second had his conviction overturned on appeal. However, the curious failure of Republican prosecutors to indict a single corrupt Republican judge at a time when approximately three out of four of the nation's seven hundred sitting federal judges were Republican should not be ignored. One explanation for this anomaly may be the splendid righteousness of all the men and women selected to be judges by the Grand Old Party and the unusual wickedness of the Democrats. A more likely possibility is that the Republican-appointed prosecutors of the period chose to ignore the shortcomings of Republican judges and fired away at their Democratic colleagues.

A second revealing aspect about the targets selected by the Public Integrity Section relates to where they were employed. It is obvious that corruption at the federal level would be the most embarrassing for whichever administration, Republican or Democratic, controlled the White House. It therefore is worth noting that substantially fewer than half of the 16,817 individuals indicted on corruption charges between 1970 and 1991 were employed by the federal government. Looked at another way, a substantial majority of the bad guys prosecuted by the Justice Department and its local U.S. attorneys, identified by PIS as state and local officials and "others," came from groups that represented the least political embarrassment for the man in the White House. Not only did a majority of the accused not work for the president, but because state and local governments were then predominantly under Democratic control, they represented a much bigger publicity problem for the opposition party than for Republicans.

As already noted, the Public Integrity Section was created by Attorney General Levi for good and valid reasons. Even so, however, it is remarkable how fast such units, established to supervise and coordinate a key area of enforcement, can be transformed into subtle instruments of political harassment. In an entirely different area of the Justice Department, for example, Attorney General Ramsey Clark created the Inter-Departmental Intelligence Unit to collect and coordinate information about local situations that had the potential of growing into urban riots. Only a year or so later, Attorney General John Mitchell transformed the IDIU into an integral part of the FBI's long-standing effort to undermine the legitimate political activities of blacks.

Equally disturbing, given the instinctive public appeal to all efforts aimed at throwing the rascals out, are questions that must be asked about the indirect consequences of a growing federal war against misconduct at the state and local level. Has the aggressive Justice Department effort to ferret out local official corruption actually worked in a perverse way to weaken the American government? Has it, by undermining the state and local institutions that have long fought official corruption, subverted the central constitutional concept that local government, immediately responsible to the voters, is essential to the continued freedom of the American people? And conversely, has the move to develop a single-purpose Justice Department unit to attack official corruption resulted in the creation of one more powerful, secretive and largely unaccountable arm of the Justice Department?

Stanley M. Brand, a Democratic activist and Washington lawyer who some years ago was counsel for the House of Representatives, contends that the department's systematic drive against official corruption at the local level is headed in an ominous direction: the systematic destabilization of state legislatures that happen to be controlled by another party. The government's methodical probes of the state governments of Pennsylvania, California, South Carolina and Arizona, Brand said in a 1991 letter to the general counsel of the National Conference of State Legislatures, could well culminate "in the federal government's attempt to put state legislatures into criminal conservatorship."[11]

Supporters of the Public Integrity Section mostly discount the argument that the Justice Department campaign against official corruption threatens a basic objective of the Founding Fathers: the maintenance of strong local and state governments as a bulwark against national tyranny. For knowledgeable experts like Harvard Law School professor Philip B. Heymann, an assistant attorney general in the early days of the program under President Carter, the argument for the unit is fairly simple: local prosecutors don't have the technical surveillance skills of the FBI, their jurisdictions are normally limited to a single state and they may be encumbered by political obligations that will prevent them from investigating local politicians.

Arthur Maass, also a Harvard Law School professor, scoffs at Heymann's view. He notes, for example, that local prosecutors in New York were already hard at work on a widespread corruption problem within New York City government during the mid-1980s when U.S. Attorney Rudolph Giuliani, then an undeclared candidate for mayor, won massive and free news coverage for himself by bringing his own indictments.

Maass further notes that the "newspapers of New York City, Boston and elsewhere have hardly been hesitant over the years to investigate and expose official corruption. Nor have the voters been reluctant to punish corrupt officials or district attorneys who have been complacent when faced with corruption, replacing them with candidates who promise reform and prosecution. The results of the democratic process in the states and the cities may not always be to the liking of federal prosecutors, but would they argue that their morality and judgment should be substituted for that of the voters?"[12]

Yet another problem with the federal war on corruption is that in a real way it was never fully authorized by Congress. Under our system of government, Congress usually approves general legislation granting approval of various broad programs, such as the medical research mandate imbedded in the original statute authorizing the National Institutes for Health to mount a national war on cancer. Then, on an annual basis, Congress votes approval of an appropriations bill providing funds for various specific projects. As suggested earlier, however, the Justice Department's corruption effort was very different, getting under way in the early 1970s when a handful of U.S. attorneys in New Jersey, Illinois, Oklahoma and some other states reinterpreted several old statutes in an ad hoc way to suit their new purposes. Although the executive branch's exercises in creative interpretation of the law have now been blessed by a string of supportive federal court decisions, Congress has yet to pass legislation that clearly authorizes the Justice Department to prosecute local political figures who go wrong.

The mail fraud statute, for example, was passed in 1872 to allow the prosecution of crooked lotteries operating through the U.S. mails. Over the years, Congress added provisions to the law making it a federal crime to use the mails for "any scheme or artifice to defraud or for obtaining money or property by means of false or fraudulent pretenses, representations or promises."

As mentioned by Noonan, Maass and other observers in their studies of the federal prosecution of former Illinois governor Otto Kerner, however, the logic of this particular prosecution is hard to fathom. It is not easy to see who was defrauded when a racetrack owner willingly and knowingly gave Kerner and an associate a substantial campaign contribution—somewhat more than $300,000—in hopes that when the governor was in the statehouse he would help her obtain more favorable racing dates. Why was this campaign contribution any different from the thousands of other such contributions? Who was defrauded? The federal government's creative response to these questions was that the law did not require it to show that actual money or property had been extracted from the state and its citizens in a fraudulent way. The loss that occurred when the governor acted, possibly in response to the checks mailed by the racetrack owner, was not material. Rather, the U.S. attorney contended, the loss was intangible, the "honest and faithful service" owed by the governor to the people of Illinois.

OPR

As emphasized throughout this book, the Justice Department's unsurpassed legal authority *not* to act has always been a major element of its basic power. Sometimes the *inaction* involves a broad policy matter such as the decision of a particular administration to "reward" a specific group or category of voters by *not* enforcing an inconvenient law. Other times the *inaction* is very specific, the concrete decision of a U.S. attorney *not* to indict an executive who happens to be a major campaign contributor to the senator behind the prosecutor's appointment. This usually unnoticed power to look the other way has been exercised by the attorneys general and U.S. attorneys of every administration since George Washington was president.

One target that has always enjoyed a unique immunity to Justice Department scrutiny is the Justice Department or, more precisely, the department officials who go bad. But with the creation of the Office of Professional Responsibility in 1976, hopes were raised that internal wheeling and dealing and other kinds of misconduct would be confronted. These hopes have not been realized.

The systematic failure of this tiny, extremely passive unit to confront directly the misconduct of Justice Department officials must be considered one of the most serious lapses in the department's recent history. This is because each OPR failure may well leave in place an unprincipled official who is in a position to undermine scores, perhaps even hundreds, of significant criminal and civil cases and, in some cases, even fight for questionable federal enforcement policies. The extreme reluctance of OPR to deal with internal ethical abuses, corruption and other improprieties has involved policy matters of broad public importance and specific cases where individual citizens have been wrongfully caused to suffer immense personal pain.

In 1981 and 1982, for example, Assistant U.S. Attorney Stephen Schlessinger was in charge of a federal fraud investigation of Irwin E. Margolies, a New York diamond merchant. The principal secret witness against Margolies was Lena Barbera, his accountant. According to lawyers for the Barbera family, as the case progressed, the confidential witness became concerned that if the diamond merchant discovered she was an informant he might do her harm. The lawyers claim Lena Barbera asked Schlessinger for official protection and that he refused.

On April 12, 1982, Barbera was abducted and later shot to death by a killer hired by the diamond merchant. Three CBS employees who tried to come to Barbera's assistance were also murdered. A year later, both Margolies and the killer were convicted of the cold-blooded murders.

While the two men directly responsible for the death of Barbera and the three CBS employees were thus brought to justice, a key question about the case was never resolved. How had Margolies learned that his former accountant was the principal witness against him?

According to a suit filed by William M. Kunstler and Ronald L. Kuby on behalf of Barbera's mother, the source of that awful leak was none other than the federal prosecutor in charge of the fraud investigation, Stephen Schlessinger. Kunstler and Kuby claimed that Schlessinger was further implicated in Barbera's death by his decision to turn down the request of her original lawyer—James R. Coley—for a guard.[13]

In a recent interview, Schlessinger—now an assistant U.S. attorney in Miami—flatly denied all charges. "She never requested protection, I had no special relationship with Margolies's lawyer and nothing we failed to do was actionable," he said.[14] The prosecutor further said that no improprieties were uncovered during an FBI investigation and that, as far as he knows, the matter was never examined by OPR.

At the time of the suit, however, Schlessinger was never required to defend himself in a public forum because the Justice Department persuaded a panel of the United States Court of Appeals for the Second Circuit that the specific allegations made by Barbera's family should not be explored. The court's decision was based on the legal doctrine that the actions of prosecutors are virtually immune from such examination in open court.[15]

In the Schlessinger matter, Barbera's family was denied any public accounting of the reasons behind Lena Barbera's murder as a result of the widely accepted principle that the prosecutors' task would become impossible if such suits went forward. In addition, however, the apparent failure of OPR to even examine whether the alleged actions of the prosecutor violated standards of professional conduct denied the public at large an assurance that the department was capable of policing itself.

Since the Office of Professional Responsibility was created by Attorney General Levi, this tiny but highly sensitive unit has been headed by Michael E. Shaheen, a graduate of Nashville's Vanderbilt University School of Law. Shaheen first went to work in the Justice Department's Civil Rights Division in 1973 after a three-year simultaneous stint as mayor and municipal judge in Como, Mississippi, a small town just south of the Tennessee border. In 1975, in the wake of Watergate, Levi selected this obviously gifted young lawyer to be his counsel for intelligence matters; devising statutory and administrative guidelines for the national security agencies such as the FBI, CIA and NSA was among the most difficult tasks the attorney general faced. A few months later, however, Levi selected Shaheen to be the head of OPR.[16]

Shaheen has always exhibited a strong penchant for secrecy. In his unit's first annual report, for example, the newly appointed official offered his readers an extremely limited summary description of the sanctions that had been imposed as a result of OPR's investigations. "In 1976, the Office received 30 complaints concerning prosecutorial misconduct and abuse of power. Only three complaints were found to warrant discipline," he reported.[17] Not only did the report fail to name names, it also failed to describe, even in general terms, the nature of the three situations that had been confirmed and what kind of sanctions were imposed on the malefactors.

By tradition, of course, the Justice Department is supposed to remain silent about allegations of wrongdoing until formal criminal charges have been filed. But Shaheen's selective concern for limiting public disclosure about the criminal and administrative improprieties of Justice Department officials has been obsessive, especially when it is remembered how relaxed the Justice Department has been when it came to leaking investigative information about political leaders who had the misfortune not to belong to the president's party.

Until very recently, Shaheen's devotion to what might be called the "silence-is-golden theory" of government meant that even when a department official was forced to resign because of serious misconduct, the administrative action was kept secret. Valid privacy concerns exist, but they must be balanced against other objectives, such as the importance of reassuring the public that the Justice Department is prepared to deal with official misconduct by department lawyers in a forthright way.

For many years, OPR remained a mostly unknown and largely un-criticized agency. But as misconduct complaints against Justice Depart-ment lawyers began to mount, the brickbats began to fly.

One of the most pointed attacks was launched in 1993 by James M. Ideman, a federal district judge in Los Angeles. Ideman, appointed by Pres-ident Reagan in 1984, has earned a reputation as a tough law-and-order judge not given to casual complaints about the Justice Department.

But this time he was furious. Three years before, Ideman had dis-missed a major Hollywood payola case on grounds that the federal pros-ecutor, an experienced Justice Department attorney named William S. Lynch, had knowingly failed to inform the defense attorneys that a key witness had given sworn evidence at a previous trial that one of the de-fendants had committed no crime. Such a failure was a clear violation of law. In addition to extracting testimony that "diametrically opposed" the witness's testimony, Judge Ideman also accused Lynch of attempt-ing to lull the defense with "false assurances" that the government pos-sessed no evidence that would help the accused and of engaging in "active misrepresentation to the court regarding the existence of such material."

Now the case that Ideman had dismissed three years before was back in his court as a result of a technical decision by the Court of Appeals. "I think this is a case where the government's misconduct was as seri-ous and outrageous as anything I have seen. The misconduct [of Lynch] was extremely premeditated; it was repeated over and over again over a period of weeks, even months," Ideman said. "The government, having been caught with a smoking gun . . . first denied that it had a gun, then they denied that it smoked . . . and to this day the government has not admitted their fault."[18]

What made the case even more deplorable, the judge continued, was that Lynch was an extremely experienced lawyer, "a very senior mem-ber of the Justice Department in Washington who apparently has been around the department for some 20 or 30 years."

Having thoroughly excoriated Lynch, the judge turned to the Justice Department and OPR. Noting that he had been a prosecutor and judge for thirty years, Ideman said one of the greatest disappointments of his professional life "has been the ethical standards I have seen in prosecu-tors over here on the federal side from the Department of Justice. I think Ms. Reno and others in the Department of Justice should take a very serious look at what's going on."

Ideman said he had been advised that the Justice Department had "an outfit called the Office of Professional Responsibility, whose duty it was to investigate possible misconduct by members of the department, sort of like an Internal Affairs Division of a police department. I am informed—if you can believe it—that 39 months after I dismissed the case for misconduct of Mr. Lynch the Department of Justice is still investigating [the matter]. That is very difficult for the court to believe and it certainly sounds like a whitewash to me. From the attitude displayed by the Justice Department in this case, I guess they feel that being a prosecutor means never having to say you're sorry."

One week after Judge Ideman's furious denunciation, an obviously stunned Attorney General Reno announced that from now on, with some exceptions, the Justice Department would disclose the "final disposition, including the names of attorneys investigated by OPR, of all matters in which attorneys are found to have committed knowing and intentional professional misconduct."[19]

The clock on Lynch continued to tick. On May 4, 1994, almost a full four years after Ideman's original decision to dismiss the payola case for prosecutorial misconduct, the Justice Department informed the judge that the prosecutor had been reprimanded. In a letter from Jo Ann Harris, the assistant attorney general in charge of the Criminal Division, the Justice Department acknowledged that Lynch had not provided defense lawyers information as required by law. Ms. Harris, however, contended that Lynch's violation was not intentional and that the reprimand was sufficient discipline.[20]

Continuing skepticism about the Justice Department's willingness to deal with the misconduct of its lawyers will not be dispelled by Attorney General Reno's change in the department's reporting procedures. A more fundamental question is raised by the office's tiny size.

In 1980, for example, OPR only had eight investigative attorneys on its staff, one for every 202 lawyers in the Justice Department. Given the vast discretion inherent in being a federal prosecutor, and the almost complete absence of hands-on supervision, that ratio was preposterous. Yet during the 1980s, while the total number of federal prosecutors more than doubled, Attorneys General William French Smith, Edwin Meese and Richard Thornburgh curiously decided to leave OPR's professional staff unchanged. Thus it was that by 1990, OPR's potential caseload had almost doubled and each investigative attorney was now responsible for the integrity of 386 prosecutors.

While Reno in the last few years has moved to increase OPR's professional staff, it still seems doubtful that this minuscule police force actually can achieve its twin missions of investigating misconduct among all the thousands of lawyers within the Justice Department proper and, at the same time, supervise the investigation of misconduct by similar small corruption units located within the FBI, the Drug Enforcement Agency, the Marshals Service, the Immigration and Naturalization Service and the Bureau of Prisons.

A few years ago, partly because of his doubts about the adequacy of OPR's staff, Congressman Bob Wise, Jr., the chairman of the House Government Operations Subcommittee on Justice, asked the General Accounting Office to investigate OPR. Because the GAO is an arm of Congress established to examine the performance of the executive branch of government, it was able to gain some access to the unit's records.

During its examination, the GAO found both substantive and procedural shortcomings. OPR, for example, despite a requirement in its regulations, has never analyzed the findings of its own individual investigations in a search for broader problem areas. In a second finding, the auditors said their study of a small sample of misconduct cases showed that "OPR did not pursue all available avenues of inquiry, even when little added time or effort might have been needed." Yet another problem was the lack of followup. "OPR does not regularly determine the results of investigations referred to other Justice Department units or what, if any, disciplinary actions were taken as a result of the investigations it did or the ones it supervised or monitored." Procedurally, the Justice Department unit was found to operate in an extremely informal fashion, seldom documenting its cases. "Conclusions that allegations were or were not substantiated were generally not explained," the report said.[21]

Despite these various problems, despite the GAO's indirect criticism of the attorney general's nonchalant attitude toward them, the agency's view of the OPR was not entirely negative. The GAO investigators said they had conducted an in-depth review of a sample of sixteen misconduct allegations investigated by OPR. This special study, the GAO concluded, "did not reveal that OPR had erred in its investigations or could be faulted in its judgment in any of these cases."

This positive conclusion about one aspect of OPR's performance is surely welcome. The finding, however, is far less reassuring than it appears. This is because it was based on an analysis of OPR's *completed cases*, and thus did not assess the soundness of the unit's judgments about misconduct in terms of all the allegations it had *received or reasonably could have been expected to know about.*

While analyzing OPR's performance from this wider stance is not easy, it is absolutely essential because, as noted over and over again, federal prosecutors always reject far more cases than they accept and some unknown proportion of the spurned matters almost always turn out to be of the highest consequence.

Fortunately, such research is not as difficult as it sounds. A few years ago, for example, Cathy Seddon, a member of the staff of the House Government Operations Justice Subcommittee, decided to try to measure the effectiveness of OPR in a different way. For this study, Seddon did not look at a sample of cases that OPR had completed. Instead, she focused on OPR's response to ten separate cases where federal judges had publicly accused federal prosecutors of various kinds of misconduct. Although it never could be said that federal judges are always correct, they nevertheless are trained legal practitioners who are usually selected from a pool of generally respected and respectable lawyers.

On April 13, 1990, subcommittee chairman Wise sent Attorney General Dick Thornburgh a letter listing the ten selected cases and asking him what disciplinary actions, if any, the OPR had recommended be imposed on the Justice Department lawyers accused of misconduct in open court.

For almost six months, apparently hoping the subcommittee would magically go away, Thornburgh and the Justice Department were silent. Then, on October 2, after numerous reminders of their tardiness, Bruce Navarro, the deputy assistant attorney general in the department's Office of Legislative Affairs, finally responded. "No disciplinary action has been taken in any of the ten cases," Navarro informed the subcommittee.

While it seems likely that several of the cases of misconduct described by the judges may not have merited any formal response, the failure to act on any of them is highly suspicious. Perhaps the most questionable disclosure was that OPR had not even been aware of half of them. "Five of the cases were administratively determined not to involve conduct sufficiently serious to warrant disciplinary action, and were not referred to the Department's Office of Professional Responsibility," Navarro reported. While the other five cases were sent to OPR, the Washington-based official added, "three of these were determined after further investigation not to warrant disciplinary action, and two remain open in OPR."[22]

It should be noted that even after the Justice Department mustered the courage to reply to Wise's inquiry, it sought to prevent the subcommittee from letting the public know about its questionable record by asking that a summary of the material be held in "the strictest confidence." Wise, however, noting that the request was specious because the allegations of Justice Department misconduct were already part of public court proceedings, rejected the agency's impertinence.

"The long delay, repeated findings of no misconduct, and the Department's failure to explain its disagreements with the findings of misconduct by the Courts raises serious questions regarding what the Department considers 'prosecutorial misconduct,'" the subcommittee report concluded.[23]

COVERING UP FOR THE FIRST LADY

As suggested by the specific concerns of Judge Ideman in Los Angeles and some of his colleagues in San Francisco, Chicago, Milwaukee and other cities about OPR, the subcommittee's pessimistic conclusion to confront employee misconduct was entirely warranted.

This is not surprising. It is the natural instinct of almost any officeholder, in the Justice Department or elsewhere, to minimize or suppress signs of misconduct among the people he or she supervises. Sometimes, the instinct to suppress is driven by the misguided notion that it is in the public interest to protect the institutional reputation of the agency in question. Other times the officeholders are worried primarily about their own skins.

A previously untold story of how the Justice Department refused to investigate a serious violation of law, and then how OPR refused to investigate the failure to investigate, concerns Nancy Reagan. More specifically, it involves Mrs. Reagan's taste for finery, how this led the first lady and President Reagan to violate the civil and criminal tax laws and, finally, how the department and the Office of Professional Responsibility both failed to enforce the law.

According to the persuasive documentary materials assembled by a determined citizen investigator, the Reagan case involved three kinds of malfeasance and misfeasance by the Bush administration's Justice Department. First, a series of high Justice Department officials, including former attorney general Dick Thornburgh, turned their backs on the evidence provided to them by the investigator that Mr. and Mrs. Reagan had indeed violated the criminal tax code. Second, in their successful effort to shield the former president and first lady from federal prosecution, Justice officials appear to have ignored the requirements of the Independent Counsel Act, the law passed by Congress in the wake of Watergate to prevent such coverups from ever occurring again. Third, when material about the possible tax crimes of the Reagans *and* the Justice Department's apparent coverup was brought to the attention of the Office of Professional Responsibility, it too failed to act, even though the matter was formally referred to OPR by the Justice Department's quasi-independent inspector general.

Perhaps the best point to begin this revealing and not-so-surprising story of internal corruption is October 1988. That was when *Time* magazine published a brief article which for the first time disclosed that Nancy Reagan, during her years in the White House, had accepted clothing, jewelry, shoes and accessories easily worth more than $1 million without declaring the value of the items as income to the IRS or on the financial disclosure forms required by the Ethics in Government Act.

Although White House press officials sought to confuse reporters about the matter by incorrectly insisting that the valuable designer items were gifts, that many of them had been returned and that a large number of the other objects were donated to museums, virtually all tax experts, including one former IRS commissioner, agreed that the Reagans had violated the clear mandate of law by not declaring the value of the items accepted by the first lady from the fashion world as regular income.[24] The best statement of why the items were not gifts was made in 1952 when the Supreme Court defined a gift as something that is given to another person out of a "detached and disinterested" generosity and that has no financial interest attached to it. Because the designers' chief purpose in sending Mrs. Reagan the items was to improve their sales, there is obviously no way the extremely valuable goods and services could be considered gifts.

The source of *Time*'s exclusive story was Chris Blazakis, then a thirty-five-year-old businessman turned writer with a passionate, almost obsessive, belief in the old-fashioned idea that the law should treat every one, regardless of station, the same way. Blazakis had firsthand knowledge of Mrs. Reagan's habits because he was the former vice president for marketing, advertising and public relations of Galanos Originals, one of the many designers that have acknowledged providing her with a multitude of free fashion items. On some occasions, in fact, Blazakis was personally involved in the delivery of the goodies to Washington.

While the *Time* story created a minor media stir, and infuriated the Reagans, Blazakis had a much more serious objective: He believed the case demanded the official attention of both the Justice Department and the Internal Revenue Service. On January 9, 1989, just before the end of the president's term, the New York writer sent a long detailed letter to Mr. and Mrs. Reagan, Attorney General Dick Thornburgh and IRS Commissioner Lawrence Gibbs demanding an investigation of the couple's effort "to deceive and defraud the American people."[25] Blazakis, who was working on a book about the former president and his wife, was convinced that under the law the Reagans were liable in both a civil and criminal sense. Civil, because they owed the government hundreds of thousands, perhaps millions, of dollars in back taxes, interest and penalties; criminal because when Mrs. Reagan's acceptance of the items had first become known, she actively and knowingly sought to hide the tax liability from the government. But Mrs. Reagan's chutzpah in the case was truly amazing. At the very same time she was launching an intense effort to disguise her liability under the nation's

tax laws, she continued to request and accept items from the designers,
even though her lawyers had recommended that she stop.

The immediate reaction of the Justice Department and the IRS to
Blazakis's claims could not have been more different. Within two
weeks of receiving his letter, senior IRS officials arranged a two-hour
meeting with the former fashion executive. At the end of this preliminary session, the officials told Blazakis that his allegations appeared to
be "well thought out," of "major historical significance" and therefore
could not "be dismissed."[26] Shortly thereafter, on March 27, Blazakis received a courteous thank-you note from IRS officials. It included the
news that his file on the Reagans "has been forwarded to the Los Angeles Office for further evaluation." The case was assigned to California
because the permanent residence of the Reagans was in Los Angeles.

Shortly after receiving the IRS thank-you note, Blazakis began working
with Harry Photakis, Richard Lau and several other Los Angeles–based
IRS agents to build the case against the Reagans. Virtually all of the
points of his story are documented by letters exchanged with at least a
dozen government officials, internal memorandums he obtained under
the Freedom of Information Act and transcripts of tape-recorded conversations.

The tax agency's investigation was exhaustive and greatly aided by
Blazakis's detailed knowledge of the case and the fashion world. One investigative step undertaken by the IRS at his suggestion, for example,
involved obtaining from the files of the National Archives an exact photographic record of the clothes Mrs. Reagan wore during the hundreds
of public appearances she made as first lady. The archival records were
matched with the photographs of the same items contained in the
"style books" maintained by most designers. The style books, which
Blazakis said the IRS summoned, almost always includes a photograph
or drawing of all the dresses produced each season by a given designer
and the prices they charged for them.

Although the IRS agents and Blazakis were not always in agreement
about the handling of the sensitive case, the tax investigation did not
end until sometime in 1990 or 1991 when, according to Jane Erkenbeck,
the former first lady's personal assistant, the Reagans settled their debt
with the tax agency. Although the amount of such civil settlements are
not disclosed by the IRS and the Reagans are not talking, tax analysts
for a national accounting firm told Washington reporter Jay Peterzell
that, from the available information, they estimated the total bill in
back taxes, interest and a possible negligence penalty would come to
approximately $1 million.[27]

The Justice Department's response to Blazakis's charges against Mrs.
Reagan, especially when compared with the IRS's, can only be charac-

terized as a massive stonewall. Attorney General Thornburgh did not respond at all. On July 3, 1989, six months after Blazakis had dispatched his eighteen-page letter to Thornburgh, the former fashion executive received a brief letter that bore the name of Assistant Attorney General Edward S. G. Dennis, Jr., but actually was signed by Acting Assistant Attorney General John C. Keeney.[28] Although Blazakis has two witnesses who swear he did not receive the Dennis letter until mid-summer of 1989, it was dated March 28, 1989. As the result of a taped conversation Blazakis subsequently had with a Justice Department secretary, he became convinced the letter was improperly back-dated, probably to meet a ninety-day statutory requirement to respond to all allegations of improprieties by high-level federal officials. The requirement is part of the independent counsel statute.

In any event, the Justice Department's response was largely negative. Dennis asserted that the Justice Department's Criminal Division only conducted investigations when presented with sufficient facts to suggest a criminal violation may have occurred. A criminal investigation thus was out of the question. Although Blazakis's letter to Thornburgh had said the Reagan tax matter was complex and that he would be delighted to furnish the department additional information, Dennis, unlike the officials at the IRS, made no effort to initiate an exploratory meeting. However, while the Justice Department official flatly slammed the door on a criminal investigation, he informed Blazakis that his material had been referred to the department's Tax and Civil Divisions "for their review of the materials."

This too went nowhere. In a letter dated July 28, Stuart E. Schiffer, the acting attorney general who then headed the Civil Division, weighed in with his rejection of Blazakis's request for an investigation of the Reagans. Like Dennis, Schiffer made no request for additional evidence.[29]

It was at this juncture that Blazakis first approached the OPR. In a letter to OPR head Michael E. Shaheen, the former New York executive asked the office to look into the failure of Criminal and Civil Divisions to investigate his original allegations against the former president and first lady.[30] Just like the two other Justice Department units he was complaining about, however, OPR was not receptive.

Despite a continuing stream of critical letters, the department stuck with its see-no-evil hear-no-evil position. This position changed, however, shortly after December 5, 1989. This was when the *Washington Post* published an article by Howard Kurtz that for the first time publicly disclosed the startling news that the IRS had undertaken a full-blown audit of the Reagans. This article too was based on information provided by Blazakis.

Ten days later, apparently worried that the IRS investigation disclosed by the *Post* might uncover matters that could seriously embarrass the Justice Department, Assistant Attorney General Dennis formally asked the FBI to interview Blazakis. Considering the flood of correspondence that had been flowing into the department for almost a year and Dennis's own curt rejection of Blazakis, the December 15, 1989, plea from Assistant Attorney Dennis to the FBI was both comical and shameless. "We request that Mr. Blazakis be interviewed to determine the exact nature of his allegations," Dennis wrote. "These allegations may be covered by the Independent Counsel Act, and thus require timely action."[31] The assistant attorney general did not bother explaining to the FBI his direct role in the long delay of his request.

Given the lumbering nature of the FBI and the demands of the Christmas holidays, the bureau's response was close to a lightning strike. On January 2, 1990, Special Agents Bill Ready and Tom Petrouskie interviewed Blazakis in the Federal Building in downtown Manhattan. After hearing Blazakis's story, according to a transcript of the interview obtained with a hidden but legal tape recorder, one of the agents seemed willing to accept the need for an independent counsel. "Um hmm—well, I agree with you," Ready observed after hearing Blazakis's pitch. "I'm going to report it as such and ah, like, we said, that's how it should be handled. If a determination is made"—Blazakis interrupts here with a one-word interjection, "right"—"then the best way is that an independent counsel be appointed."

As any student of law enforcement knows, while FBI Agent Ready's speculation concerning the possible appointment of a special counsel is interesting, it carried absolutely no weight with the Justice Department, still chock full of officials who were beholden to President Bush, the Republican Party and Mr. Reagan for their jobs. It therefore is totally unsurprising that no special counsel was appointed.

But Blazakis was a thoroughly idealistic man given to quoting the belief, expressed by George Washington in a 1789 letter to the first attorney general, Edmund Randolph, that the "true administration of justice is the firmest pillar of good government." So on August 12, 1990, the constantly jilted New Yorker dispatched a letter summarizing his complaints to yet another Justice Department official, this time to Inspector General Richard J. Hankinson.

Shortly thereafter, on September 18, the inspector general's office formally referred Blazakis's assorted allegations to the Office of Professional Responsibility. This time, with the semi-independent inspector general breathing down their necks, the officials in OPR could not afford to simply close their eyes.

The success of the IRS in forcing the Reagans to pay at least some of their back taxes suggests that Blazakis may have been correct in asserting they were also criminally liable. But because the statute of limitations had expired by 1990, criminal prosecution of the former president and his wife was now impossible. Disciplining Attorney General Thornburgh and the many other Justice Department officials whose inaction may have violated the Independent Counsel Act, however, was still possible. On May 22, 1992, accompanied by Washington lawyer Allen Adler and a colleague, David Farneth, Blazakis had a lengthy meeting with J. Thomas Ezell, an assistant counsel in OPR, and presented his evidence—letters and tape recordings—supporting his claim that the Justice Department had failed to initiate criminal tax charges against the Reagans and that President Bush's attorney general, Richard Thornburgh, had failed to obey the law in connection with the need for a special counsel to investigate the Reagan case.

Blazakis died in February 1993. Three months later, in response to a request under the Freedom of Information Act, the Office of Professional Responsibility refused to provide copies of all OPR documents relating to allegations that the Reagans had violated civil and criminal tax laws. The office said it was doing so under an exemption in the law that permitted withholding in cases where the release "could reasonably be expected to interfere with enforcement proceedings."[32] Although the letter suggests that the OPR investigation was still alive in the spring of 1993, it now appears that this was not the case, that the probe of the Department's handling of the Reagan case had died long before Blazakis.

MAINTAINING THE GUARD

Official corruption and official misconduct are corrosive forces that constantly eat into the basic framework of all societies. In fact, if not attended to in a diligent and timely manner, these twin forces are powerful enough to threaten the existence of even the most solidly established nation. The problem, however, is that, to an unusual extent, the organized efforts required to curb official corruption and misconduct can themselves become forces for even more corruption.

FBI sting operations, for example, are essential to uncovering certain kinds of consensual crimes. But an FBI sting to detect a crime can sometimes result in FBI agents committing a crime. Crooked state legislatures are a direct threat to representative democracy within the relevant states. But massive federal investigations of state institutions can lead to an undermining of the principle that government powers are better administered at the local level. All medium- to large-size agencies require internal affairs units to identify misconduct. But these special units, which must be answerable to the top official of each agency, can easily be perverted into informal public relations operations.

The general point here is very simple: It is frequently necessary to fight fire with fire, but it is equally important to remember that backfires can burn you just as badly as the original blaze. In a wonderful essay written about twenty-five years ago, Kenneth Culp Davis, a professor at the University of Chicago Law School, discussed the problem and then asked a series of questions.

Professor Davis observed that it was theoretically possible for the American prosecutorial system, as it functioned then and as it functions today, to operate in a just fashion. He added, however, that possibilities of such a happy result were remote, about as likely as the development of a state government where all public administrators will act "with 100 percent integrity, will never be influenced by political considerations, will never tend to favor their friends, will never take into account their own advantage or disadvantage in exercising discretionary power, will always eschew doubtful positions, will always subordinate their own social values to those adopted by the legislative body, and will make every decision on a strictly rational basis."[33]

Given this situation, Davis posed his questions. Why should any prosecutor "have discretionary power to decide not to prosecute even when the evidence of guilt is clear, perhaps partly on the basis of political influence, without ever having to state to anyone what evidence was brought to light by his investigation and without having to explain to anyone why he interprets a statute as he does or why he chooses a particular position on a difficult issue of policy?

"Why," he continued, should the discretionary power be so unconfined that, of a half dozen potential defendants he can prove guilty, he can select any one for prosecution and let the other five go, making decisions, if he chooses, on the basis of considerations extraneous to justice?

"Why should the vital decisions he makes be immune to review by other officials and immune to review by the courts, even though our legal system elsewhere generally assumes the need for checking human frailties?

"Why should he have the power to decide that one statute duly enacted by the people's representatives shall not be enforced at all, that another will be enforced, and that a third will be enforced only if, as, and when he thinks that it should be enforced in that particular case?

"Even if we assume that a prosecutor has to have the power of selective enforcement, why do we not require him to state publicly his general policies and require him to follow those policies in individual cases to protect evenhanded justice?"[34]

Good questions in 1971, when the federal prosecutive force was a fraction of its present size, a relatively small blip on the national screen. Even better questions today when the Justice Department and its investigative agencies are beginning to loom large in the life of almost every citizen.

11

The Case of
the Sleeping
Watchdogs

A few years ago, William Weld was elected governor of Massachusetts. Today he is one of a dozen or so Republican officeholders around the country who some day just might capture the Republican nomination for president and perhaps even the White House itself.

Although Weld had achieved modest political exposure during the decade following his 1970 graduation from Harvard Law School, it was his appointment as U.S. attorney for Massachusetts in 1981 that made him what the boxing world calls "a contender."

More than seventy years ago, Roscoe Pound, the astute dean of the Harvard Law School, explained why. "The position of public prosecutor is politically strategic in the highest degree," he wrote. "If the prosecutor is ambitious, he looks upon his office as a stepping stone to Congress or the Governorship. This does not mean that he must strive to carry out his tasks efficiently, but that he must carry them out conspicuously."[1]

Weld's efficiency as a federal prosecutor is hard to measure. But there is no question that the office netted him an enormous amount of television time and ink in both the local and national media, including the *New York Times*, and that this publicity was important to his election as governor in 1990.

Like many prosecutors before him—such as Tom Dewey of New York and Jim Thompson of Illinois—Weld achieved his success on the back of a massive investigation of corruption, in his case Boston corruption. With the help of a small army of federal investigators, Weld's five-year investigation, estimated to have cost federal taxpayers $15 million, is said to have led to 109 convictions out of 111 corruption cases. In many ways, it was an impressive record.[2]

In one very significant way, however, the investigation must be judged the opposite. The Boston corruption probe was a classic example of the incestuous relationship that traditionally exists between prosecutors and reporters and shows how these connections are routinely abused to advance the interests of both parties, not necessarily the interest of the public at large.

Reporters assigned to cover powerful people always have a conflict: To understand their subjects, it is necessary to gain access to them. Powerful people, however, have an understandable interest in granting access to the compliant and denying it to the skeptical. While this conflict presents problems for all reporters, it is an acute disease among reporters who cover prosecutors.

News organizations have an insatiable lust for "scoops." And prosecutors, with all their investigators and paid and unpaid informants and wiretaps and grand juries, are in a position to obtain and leak more fascinating gossip about the dark side of society than other officials in government. Can anyone be truly surprised then that the actual function of many of the reporters who cover federal and local prosecutors is to be a high-priced stenographer, if not the ventriloquist's dummy?

The reporter as a passive recipient of unsourced stories that advance the political careers of ambitious prosecutors does not comport with the news industry's image of itself. Neither does this picture of the reporter as a compliant mouthpiece fit with the Constitution's vision of the media. Implicit in the First Amendment's command that Congress may make no law abridging the freedom of the press, after all, is the notion that aggressive and skeptical reporting is essential to the mainte-

nance of freedom. When it comes to prosecutors, however, most reporters seem to have forgotten their responsibility to hold accountable
these people with so much power.

There are, of course, honorable exceptions. In January 1993, the
Washington Post ran a six-part series by Jim McGee that probed the
inner workings of the Justice Department in a critical and thoughtful
way. At about the same time, Alicia Mundy published a penetrating investigative article in *Legal Times* describing the questionable circumstances involved in Senator Charles Robb's last-minute escape from an
indictment on charges relating to an illegal tape recording of a car-
phone conversation. And in April 1994, Jim Mulvaney, a reporter with
Newsday, wrote a highly detailed article about how the FBI and the
U.S. attorney in Jackson, Mississippi, had failed to act on charges that
guards in the city's jail were systematically raping and otherwise abus-
ing young women being held in the facility.[3]

But for too many of the reporters assigned to cover the Justice Department or the U.S. attorney in their area, the regurgitation of leaks is
the bread and butter of their workday. For many years, legal critics have
complained that the flood of untested and unsourced gossip that routinely pours from the mouths of prosecutors subverts the basic concept
of a fair trial. Publication or broadcasting of the unchallenged allegations makes it almost impossible to find an impartial and open-minded
jury. This is undoubtedly true.

But the prosecutors' ability to seduce the reporters who cover them
with the latest hot gossip exacts a second penalty that has rarely been
commented upon: The reporters become so involved in satisfying their
editors with juicy tips that they seldom have time to investigate the
shortcomings of the tipsters. The subtle but widespread seduction of
media is important because, as Jim McGee, Alicia Mundy and Jim Mulvaney have shown, prosecutors probably have a greater opportunity to
act in improper, unethical and abusive ways than almost any other officials in the federal government.

CORRUPTION IN BOSTON

T he investigation of corruption in New England's largest city was
actually launched by William Weld's predecessor. But when Weld became the U.S. attorney for Massachusetts, it went into high gear. Under
tactics developed during the 1970s by federal prosecutors in New Jersey
and Illinois, assistant U.S. attorneys and scores of federal agents from

the FBI, IRS, Postal Service and other organizations began poring over thousands of financial documents looking for questionable transactions by low-level city employees.

Every so often, of course, the investigators would find evidence of wrongdoing, and the little fish would be placed under intense pressure to talk about the possibly questionable activities of their immediate bosses. Facing prison, underlings frequently choose to talk, even in those situations when their knowledge of official corruption may be limited.

Working their way up the food chain, Weld and his lieutenants were definitely after the big fish. There is no doubt that, from the very beginning, the investigators believed the ultimate target, the biggest fish in their sea, was Boston mayor Kevin White. In a telling reference to Ahab's mad obsession with the destruction of Moby Dick—the monstrous white whale that years before had taken Ahab's leg—reporters, defense attorneys and politicos in Boston began to joke about Weld's "Great White Hunt."[4] Unlike Ahab, however, the prosecutors apparently realized that there are many ways to catch a whale besides a direct attack. In the fall of 1982, for example, the *New York Times* published an article by Fox Butterfield, its Boston bureau chief, that quoted unnamed "law enforcement sources" as saying that Mayor White was then "the major target of the grand jury investigation."[5] Similar stories appeared in the *Boston Globe* and other Boston papers.

Under the lash of this and many other unsourced and unproven articles about White's alleged involvement in various corrupt schemes, the mayor began to crumble. "The leaks were hard, very hard," he recalled more than a decade later. "There was one time I went down to my place on Cape Cod by myself and wondered whether I was going to come out of the whole business alive. I realized that this was a killing and I couldn't control what was going on. I got genuinely scared."[6]

The defense lawyers, as they often do, argued that the steady stream of government leaks violated the constitutional rights of those who already had been formally accused. They further contended that the leaks breached professional rules that prohibit lawyers in federal court from making any comment on the character or reputation of a criminal defendant. In an effort to force the *Times* reporter to disclose the sources of his allegation, the lawyers subpoenaed Butterfield. Again, as almost always happens, the judge ruled that the First Amendment's guarantee of a free press meant Butterfield could remain silent.[7]

The prosecutors, of course, all denied involvement in the leaks. But during the legal sparring over the failed effort to force the reporter to talk, Weld ended up filing two affidavits about his role in the dispute. In the first one, the U.S. attorney flatly asserted that he had "not disclosed to any unauthorized person, including the media, any matter occurring before the grand jury." Eight days later, however, Weld filed the second affidavit. In this one he admitted talking to Butterfield on several occasions before the publication of his controversial article. After "considerable thought," Weld said, "I have no memory" of making any of the disclosures that Butterfield had attributed to law enforcement sources. He added that he was "quite sure that I would not have made and did not make any statement" that included improper disclosures.[8]

Which version was correct? In the first the prosecutor swore he had disclosed nothing. In the second he couldn't recall revealing the facts in Butterfield's article and he was "quite sure" he wouldn't do the wrong thing. It is almost certain that Weld's two sworn affidavits, considered together, did not amount to perjury. And even if they did, who was around to prosecute the prosecutor?

In the end, the question of whether the source for all the articles about Boston's corruption and White's involvement was Weld, or persons under Weld's supervision, did not turn out to be all that important. On May 26, 1988, White astonished political Boston by announcing he would not be a candidate for a fifth term as mayor.

"I'd be the first to admit that the leaks played a big part in my decision not to run for reelection," White remembered. "I never felt that Weld was close to me. But after four terms, the leaks on top of the investigations were just too much. I couldn't cope with them. It was a killing situation."

The final act was played out ten months later when Weld brought his multimillion-dollar corruption investigation to an end with a graceless announcement: White's lawyer, the prosecutor said, had recently been told that the former mayor was "not a target at this time."[9]

All the official whispers, all the authoritative articles, all the editorials had done the job. Without the bother of a messy trial where specific evidence would be examined by hard-nosed defense attorneys and a jury, the once-popular White was out of the way.

With the passage of the years, the former mayor now seems to have almost come to terms with the way his political life was destroyed. "The reporters, of course, were driven by two forces: their personal egos and considerations of professional advancement. Weld's lead investigator was a very young assistant U.S. attorney who became obsessed. Weld is by nature a rather cavalier person. The combination of an obsessed underling and a cavalier boss was not good for me."

ARABIAN NIGHTS

As already suggested, the seduction of reporters by chatty prosecutors and investigators has been SOP—standard operating procedure—for many years. Almost a decade before Fox Butterfield's controversial article about Kevin White, for example, the *Times* published a front-page article by Leslie Maitland about an even more extensive Justice Department political investigation with the code-name of "Abscam."

"High public officials, including a United States Senator and seven Representatives, have been subjects of a two-year undercover operation by the Federal Bureau of Investigation, according to law enforcement authorities," Maitland's article began.

During the course of the investigation, the *Times* said, the public officials were videotaped accepting hundreds of thousands of dollars in cash from undercover agents posing as businessmen and Arab sheiks.

"The results of the investigation are expected to be presented to a grand jury, according to authorities, who said the jury would be asked to bring criminal charges against some of the officials," the article continued. Specifically named as targets were eight sitting members of Congress, including Senator Harrison A. Williams, Jr., of New Jersey.[10]

This particular leak, although clearly violating department rules and the professional standards of the courts, gave every sign of being an officially approved press release. The first proof of this fact is that on the same day that the *Times* ran its front-page Abscam article, the *Philadelphia Inquirer*, *Newsday* and NBC also had it. The second proof was the finding that all the major Abscam stories were similar, closely following the structure of a confidential Justice Department memorandum that analyzed the prosecutability of the various cases. The identity of the individual who had authorized the distribution of the internal memorandum to selected reporters and arranged for its use on the same day was never determined.[11]

As in the case of the Boston investigation, federal judges denied the argument of individual Abscam targets that the massive leaks made it impossible for them to have a fair trial. The question of how the competitive need to publish unproven FBI allegations undermined the news coverage of the Justice Department was never explored.

TERRORISM IN NEW YORK

Elected officials are not the only targets of Justice Department leaks. In March 1994, for example, a federal jury convicted four men of bombing the World Trade Center. The year before, that attack had killed six people, caused hundreds of millions of dollars in damage and greatly heightened American worries about terrorism.

Most of the reporters who covered the four-month trial believe that their job—creating interesting daily stories about the struggle between the prosecutors and the defense attorneys—was made nearly impossible because most of the evidence presented to the jury had been leaked to the media long before the trial got under way.

Charles Feldman, for example, an expert reporter who covered the event for CNN, appears to have been slightly irritated by the whole process. "The proof of how well they leaked is that very little of what came out during the trial has been surprising," Feldman later observed. "I can think of only one piece of evidence—a fingerprint on a parking ticket—that we didn't know about already. And we later learned that the government didn't know about it [the parking ticket] until the trial began."[12]

Obviously, there can be no sympathy for bombers. But no matter how evil the crime or how wicked the criminals, the government's deliberate violation of important procedural rules and defendants' constitutional rights remains worrisome. The notion of a fair trial, where the government's evidence is examined by jurors who have not already made up their minds, is absolutely central to a free society.

"At the beginning, immediately after the bombing, there wasn't a single agency involved in the investigation—local, state and federal— that wasn't leaking to reporters," said one of the recipients of this illicit largess. The recipient requested anonymity because of fears of retaliation when it came to covering the next big case.

"The New York City Police Department, the FBI, the Bureau of Alcohol, Tobacco and Firearms, every one of them wanted to brag about their amazing skills and achievements," the reporter said. "I don't think the public has any idea how competitive the agencies are with each other, how much backbiting goes on, how hard each agency works to maintain its reputation. It seems to me this early leaking to reporters was more about jurisdictional disputes and agency ambitions than trying to influence the outcome of a case."

But as the trial date drew closer, the reporter believes that the motive behind the leaks underwent a definite change. "The leaking in the final weeks before the trial seems to me was very definitely designed to taint the jury pool," the writer said. "The government was afraid it might lose and they were trying to convict these people in the court of public opinion. In my view, the strategy worked. Of course, a lot was at stake. First there were the personal ambitions of individual prosecutors. In addition, it seems that the American government was trying to prove to the world at large that it could deal with terrorism. That proposition obviously was pretty dubious considering that the central figure in the case had managed to avoid arrest and escape from the country."

It should be noted that all these leaks violated the regulations of the Justice Department and, for the lawyers, Disciplinary Rule 7-107 of the American Bar Association. This rule, which has been adopted by most of the states, is part of the code of ethics that governs the behavior of all attorneys. In general, it prohibits prosecutors from commenting on pending or anticipated matters. In theory at least, serious violators can face sanctions ranging from a private reprimand to disbarment.[13]

THE GOOD OLD DAYS

The broad failure of the press to bring a healthy skepticism to the coverage of the Justice Department, U.S. attorneys and local prosecutors is not exactly a new phenomenon. Except for a brief period toward the end of the Watergate years, when Attorney General Mitchell was convicted of a variety of crimes and the FBI's systematic political operations were first uncovered, reporters have mostly been passive consumers of the very tasty official line.

Sometimes, however, reporters become more than a simple conduit for the prosecutors; they become active collaborators. Anthony Lewis, for example, is a brilliant American journalist. For the last twenty-five years, he has focused his considerable intellectual powers on writing a liberal and frequently passionate editorial column for the *New York Times*. While the columnist's interests have been global, Lewis has commented frequently on the actions and policies of the Justice Department, an agency he once covered as a beat reporter for the *Times*.

Because Lewis viewed the world in a way very different from the Reagan and Bush administrations, his Justice Department columns about the four attorneys general of the 1980–92 period—William French Smith, Edwin Meese, Richard Thornburgh and William Barr— were usually critical. Sometimes, the journalist would compare the performance of these men with one of his personal heroes: Attorney General Robert F. Kennedy.

As a columnist, of course, Lewis has every right to express his views on any subject. But an examination of the Justice Department during the Kennedy years reveals a very close relationship between Lewis and Robert Kennedy that raises many disturbing questions about the press and the prosecutor that are just as pertinent today as they were then.

In those years, Lewis was the young prize-winning reporter covering the Justice Department for what then was regarded as the single most influential newspaper in the United States—the *New York Times*.

The first few years of the 1960s were an extraordinarily busy period for Lewis as the Kennedy brothers struggled to govern a nation confronted with challenging domestic and international problems. Bitter racial tensions, perilous Cold War conditions, a troubled economy, an entrenched system of organized crime—all confronted the attorney general with complex choices of law, policy and politics.

As a natural result of Robert Kennedy's position as the second most powerful man in Washington and Lewis's employment by the *Times*, the young reporter became one of the nation's leading journalistic interpreters of the Kennedy administration. Day after day, Lewis churned out a steady stream of well-written stories, thoughtful news analyses and highly informed magazine articles. Though his coverage probed many areas, one subject of central interest to him was the one-man, one-vote issue, then heading for consideration by the Supreme Court. The pending question was deceptively simple: Did the Constitution give the federal government the power to require that the boundaries of all legislative districts be drawn so that every vote carried equal weight?

However the one-man, one-vote issue was finally decided, the political and social consequences of its resolution were hard to exaggerate. If the Supreme Court ruled that the Constitution did not empower the federal government to challenge existing political boundaries, the long-standing advantage of white voters over black, of rural voters over city and of better-off voters over poor ones would remain unchanged. If the court ruled gerrymandering unconstitutional, substantial changes in the basic fabric of American life were likely.

Lewis, however, was not content with reporting the news about this revolution in the making. He also wanted to shape it. Unbeknownst to either his readers or his editors, Lewis became intimately engaged in an organized behind-the-scenes effort to persuade the Supreme Court to rule in a way that he, the attorney general and the administration's top political advisers had all decided was best for the nation and the long-term political needs of the Kennedy family.

The story of how Lewis, an acknowledged expert on the one-man, one-vote issue, secretly fought to advance the Kennedy position was first told more than twenty years ago by Victor S. Navasky in his insightful book on Robert Kennedy and the Justice Department. While Navasky's account carefully documented the precise details of the reporter's hidden lobbying activities, the writer deliberately chose not to explore Lewis's journalistic ethics.

In one particularly questionable situation, for example, Lewis somehow obtained the galleys of an amicus curiae brief the Justice Department was about to file with the Supreme Court on one of the pending one-man, one-vote cases. The galleys of this particular brief summarized the formal legal view of Archibald Cox, the Kennedy administration's solicitor general, on how the Court should decide the case.

Lewis chose not to write a story about Cox's position, which would have shared the news contained in the confidential document with the readers of the *New York Times*. Instead, convinced that some parts of the brief were not sufficiently strong, he drove out to the home of the man who had written it, Solicitor General Cox. "I went out, feeling very nervy for doing so, and told him of my objections to those passages," Navasky quotes Lewis as recalling.[14]

When the brief was filed with the Supreme Court a short time later, some of the arguments that Lewis had felt inadequate in the original galley were in fact modified. Although it is not possible to prove that the reporter's objections were the moving force behind the changes, what is known is that Lewis's subsequent articles about the issue never acknowledged his role as a political operative and backdoor advocate.

Lewis's collaborationist practices were not limited to the one-man, one-vote issue. A few years later, while he was serving as the *Times*'s London bureau chief and Robert Kennedy had become one of New York's senators, senior officials at the paper somehow learned that Lewis had written a draft of a Kennedy speech. Tom Wicker, then the Washington bureau chief, was instructed to inform Lewis that his conduct was not acceptable and "it was not to happen again."[15]

For one given to making harsh judgments in his columns about the ethical failures of many government officials, Lewis was, in the end, quite understanding about his own deficiencies. "I have no hesitation in saying it sounds wrong," Lewis said when asked about his behind-the-scenes activity. "I think it was wrong. I can't defend it."[16]

But in fact, the columnist's defense was not long in coming. "On the other hand, I was a real expert in the area and had published a serious article about it. I am also sure that it [his direct involvement in shaping the Kennedy policy] didn't inhibit me from writing other articles critical about Robert Kennedy."

Lewis then cited an article he had written for the *Times* about a particularly questionable judicial appointment that Robert Kennedy was considering that Lewis said had caused the attorney general to throw him out of his office.

The questions go in several directions. First, given the intimate connections that existed between Lewis, Kennedy and the advisers around the young attorney general, how much credence can we give to Lewis's articles about the Kennedy Justice Department in the *Times*'s news pages during the early 1960s or its editorial pages in the 1980s? Is it ever proper for a reporter to try to influence government policy on a subject in any way other than by publicly reporting on it? Did Lewis's intense involvement in the voting issue lead him to ignore other important subjects such as Kennedy's extensive misuse of wiretapping and his possible involvement in government efforts to assassinate Castro? Finally, were the secret ties that then linked Lewis to these ambitious men an aberration or, as argued above, are they symptomatic of a pernicious disease that infects the relationships of all too many reporters and prosecutors?

These questions may be unfair. Certainly they are impossible to answer now. But the mind-set revealed by the reporter's clandestine collaborative efforts remain disturbing. Sadly, they also are not all that unusual.

Benjamin C. Bradlee became a famous man partly because when he was the managing editor of the *Washington Post* he actively supported Bob Woodward and Carl Bernstein's investigation of President Nixon's personal involvement in the Watergate scandal. The image of Bradlee as a tough and fearless editor was cemented in the popular movie *All the President's Men*. In the fall of 1962, however, Bradlee was the Washington bureau chief of *Newsweek*. He was an elegant but dirty-talking Bostonian who had been close to John Kennedy and his wife, Jacqueline, for a number of years. In May 1959, for example, Bradlee the newsman sent Kennedy the politician, then a senator, a confidential two-page memo analyzing Lyndon Johnson's chances of getting the Democratic nomination. Bradlee, after covering a Johnson event for *Newsweek*, passed on bits and pieces of intelligence and his opinion that Johnson was not an impressive figure.[17]

Several years later, with Kennedy in the White House, Bradlee asked *Newsweek*'s London bureau to obtain an excerpt from an article in the *London Observer* that had piqued the interest of the president. The courtierlike cover memo that Bradlee included with the excerpt when he dispatched it to the White House is instructive. The memo was addressed to Kennedy's secretary. "Dear Evelyn: The boss asked for the enclosed last night. Can you slip it noisily on his desk with me compliments?"[18] Bradlee's attempt at Irish dialogue—"me compliments"—was bad enough. But the reporter's reference to the president as his "boss" is worse.

Some months later, despite Bradlee's sweet talk, Kennedy became irritated with *Newsweek* because of a mildly critical comment Bradlee had made about the administration that was quoted in *Look*, another magazine of that era. Bradlee, desperate to get himself back into the good graces of the president, came up with a scheme. The Kennedy administration had become concerned about stories that several rightwing groups had published false claims that the president had been secretly married and divorced before his marriage to Jacqueline. Several mainline news organizations had investigated the allegation and decided not to report it because it was not true. But the false and politically damaging rumors continued to circulate in some parts of the country, especially the South.

"I felt *Newsweek* could be first with the story if we backed into it by writing about the hate sheets themselves in the Press section, how they were spreading the story, and who was financing them," Bradlee explained.

Bradlee approached White House press secretary Pierre Salinger with the idea, but explained he would need some "solid FBI documentation about the character of the organizations and people involved" for *Newsweek* to publish the story.

"A couple of days later, Salinger called me with the following proposition: If I agreed to show the president the finished story, and if I got my tail up to Newport where he was vacationing, he would deliver me a package of relevant FBI documents to the Newport motel and let me have them for a period not to exceed twenty-four hours. It was specifically understood that I was not to Xerox anything in the FBI files, that I was not to indicate in any way that I had been given access to FBI files and that in case of a lawsuit, I would not be given access to the files a second time."[19]

Newsweek agreed to all conditions and, after getting Kennedy's approval of the written piece, published an authoritative-sounding article outlining how the rumors had begun and the disreputable nature of those who were spreading them.[20]

Within a few weeks, having pleased "the boss," Bradlee's exile was over. But the power of the Kennedy brothers over *Newsweek*'s coverage of the White House and the Justice Department did not subside. In early 1963, for example, the magazine was planning a long cover article on Robert Kennedy. "As usual, I asked the president for help. He told me two shocking stories that I had never heard before," Bradlee wrote. One of the stories concerned an informant whom the president said had been murdered by the Teamsters after the union learned he was cooperating with the government. The second was "the recent discovery by the Justice Department of some hoodlum who reported he had been hired by the Teamsters, given a gun fitted with a silencer, and sent to Washington with what the president said were orders to kill the attorney general."

The attorney general requested Bradlee not to run the story about the murder of the Teamster informant because it might undermine his war on Jimmy Hoffa. Partly on the basis of this request and partly because Bradlee said he himself found the presidential assassination story hard to believe, the now famous journalist wrote he decided against including either of the presidential tips in the article about Robert Kennedy. "Neither story ran in *Newsweek*," he said.[21]

Bradlee's decision, while another illuminating example of his willingness to allow the president's brother to shape *Newsweek*'s coverage of the Justice Department, probably was of no historical consequence. Had Bradlee aggressively pursued the two leads given him by the president, however, it is just barely possible that the role of organized crime in American life at that time might have turned out differently.

Some years later, with President Nixon's 1974 resignation, the *Washington Post*'s hard-nosed investigation of the burglary of the Democratic National headquarters quickly became the stuff of myth. Thousands of smart young reporters dreamed that one day they could work for an editor like Ben Bradlee. Unfortunately, to the extent that the articles of Woodward and Bernstein contributed to the downfall of Nixon, the record shows that this famous investigation was very much the exception. Much closer to the national norm of leaks and cronyism was the Kennedy-era reporting by Ben Bradlee and Tony Lewis, in which journalists allowed themselves to become a part of the government's team.

The press: Some watchdog.

THE GRAND JURY

The press, of course, is not the only institution that has a widely recognized and self-proclaimed responsibility to hold the Justice Department accountable. A second such institution, at least in the minds of most Americans, is the grand jury.

The Fifth Amendment to the Constitution has long been regarded as one of the crown jewels of the American legal process, a marvelously elegant barrier against improper actions by overzealous prosecutors. The five basic principles of the amendment are well known: no person will be deprived of life, liberty or property without due process of law; no private property shall be taken for public use without just compensation; no person shall be placed in double jeopardy by being twice charged for the same offense; no person charged with a crime shall be required to be a witness against himself; and no person shall be charged with a serious crime except by the vote of a grand jury.

Obviously, however, the protections offered by the Fifth Amendment are not self-enforcing. In the real world, if protective measures are not exercised, or only exercised in a make-believe way, they are worse than meaningless because they offer the appearance but not the substance of sanctuary. Sadly, new research by TRAC overwhelmingly supports what practicing lawyers have known in an anecdotal way for many years: One of the basic safeguards promised by the Fifth Amendment is a fraud.

The particular institutional safeguard in question is the federal grand jury, a theoretically independent body of twenty-three voters whose stated mission is to make sure that when the federal government formally charges someone with committing a serious crime, the accusation is backed up by sufficient evidence. With roots going back to twelfth-century England, the grand jury was seen by the legislative authors of America's Bill of Rights as an essential device for preventing ambitious prosecutors from maliciously harassing innocent people. To this day, the grand jury remains an important fixture on the legal scene, at least in the rhetoric of many prosecutors and judges and the expectations of the public.

While experienced lawyers have long understood that federal grand juries are at best sleepy watchdogs, rarely challenging the wishes of the prosecutors, federal judges have long expressed an almost mystical faith in them. In a frequently cited 1962 decision, for example, Chief Justice Earl Warren observed that the grand jury always "has been regarded as a primary security to the innocent against hasty, malicious and oppressive persecution; it serves the invaluable function in our society of standing between the accuser and the accused" and determining "whether a charge is founded upon reason or was dictated by an intimidating power or by malice and personal ill will."[22]

Enthusiasm about the role of the grand jury has not been limited to the Supreme Court. During the last twenty years, for example, federal judges all over the country have issued scores of decisions in which they found that Justice Department lawyers had lied, cheated and taken other improper actions to win their convictions. In a good number of these cases, however, the judges did not dismiss the convictions that resulted from the tainted prosecutions, because they found the misconduct had not been sufficient to infringe upon the grand jury's ability to exercise its theoretically independent judgment. The emphasis here is on the stated belief of the courts that grand juries have a degree of independence.

While this view of the grand jury may be thrilling to many legal the-
oreticians and reassuring to the public, and obviously provides useful
cover for prosecutors, previously unexamined Justice Department data
suggest that the court's understanding of the underlying dynamics of
prosecution is way off the mark.

To an extent that even experienced criminal lawyers find surprising,
TRAC analysis of department records has discovered that federal grand
jurors may even surpass reporters in their passive acceptance of prosecutors' information. In 1991, for example, 785 federal grand juries were
convened in the United States. Altogether, these juries heard witnesses
and received information about 25,943 matters that the prosecutors argued should result in federal criminal charges. The jurors considered
these matters for a total of 61,872 hours, receiving $13.7 million in fees
and expenses for their efforts. In the end, the jurors voted against the
prosecutor in only sixteen of the matters presented to them. In other
words, the federal prosecutors appeared to have won the support of the
grand juries in more than 99.9 percent of their secret presentations.[23]

Even that one tenth of one percent may exaggerate grand jury independence. On January 12, 1993, for example, a federal grand jury in Norfolk, Virginia, overrode the formal recommendation of the Justice
Department and voted against the indictment of Senator Charles Robb
on charges connected with an illegal tape recording of Douglas Wilder.
Wilder, who was the governor of Virginia at the time of the illicit
recording of his car telephone, was a longtime political rival of Robb's.
Here was a case of a grand jury bravely going its own way.

A subsequent investigation by Alicia Mundy for the *Legal Times*,
however, discovered that appearances can be deceiving. One of Robb's
lawyers, it turned out, was Charles Ruff, a former high Justice Department official and close friend of George Terwilliger III, then the deputy
attorney general. As a result of these connections, Ruff managed to persuade Terwilliger to write a highly unusual letter to the Norfolk grand
jury reminding the members that under the law the probe was their responsibility alone, not the prosecutor's. Amazingly, Terwilliger's letter
was read to the grand jury by Deputy Assistant Attorney General Jack
Kenney, who had made a special trip from Washington for just this purpose.

"Although grand jurors can't talk about their deliberations, they had
enough experience after nineteen months, hearing numerous other
cases, to recognize it as an unusual missive," Mundy explained. "They
then voted down the two-count indictment presented by the line prosecutor and his cocounsel, refusing to charge Robb with obstruction of
justice and conspiracy to violate the wiretap laws."

THE VOICE OF REALISM?

G. Robert Blakey is an influential professor at Notre Dame Law School. During his long career, he has been a federal prosecutor, a senior staff member of the Senate Judiciary Committee and the chief counsel of a special House committee that investigated the assassinations of President Kennedy and Martin Luther King, Jr. Blakey is generally credited as being the principal author of the nation's wiretap law. On the basis of these experiences, he scoffs at the judges who have suggested that the grand jury is a significant check on prosecutorial abuse, asserting that most of them do not believe what they have written.

Informed about the finding that grand juries approve virtually every matter that is presented to them, he said what really surprised him was that the juries had gone against the prosecutors at all. "The role of the grand jury is to investigate, not to screen. Screening is only a theoretical power of the grand jury," he said. "The fact that grand juries reject so few cases is of no significance to any knowledgeable person. The idea that the grand jury protects the public is a myth."[24]

But as observed by Stuart Taylor, Jr., in one of his *Legal Times* columns, it is an extremely powerful myth that most lawyers, judges and journalists buy into, "routinely using the 'grand jury' prefix to lend a false patina of solemn, communitarian legitimacy to investigations, subpoenas, and indictments that are, in fact, essentially unilateral decisions by prosecutors."[25]

Despite the homage repeatedly paid to grand juries, lawyers have long joked that any prosecutor worth his salt could get a grand jury to indict a ham sandwich. More than twenty years ago, in an analytical article based on his years of experience as a federal prosecutor and judge in Chicago, the late William J. Campbell put it well: "Today, the grand jury is the total captive of the prosecutor, who, if he is candid, will concede that he can indict anybody, at any time, for almost anything, before any grand jury."

It wasn't just that the operations of the grand jury are so steeped in secrecy and so thoroughly controlled by the prosecutor that the institution itself "encourages abuses by permitting the prosecutor to carry on his work in complete anonymity," the judge wrote. Equally insidious, he said, was the way prosecutors use the theoretical independence of the grand jury to escape public criticism when, for one reason or another, the prosecutor decides not to bring charges in a particularly notorious case. It is not uncommon, Judge Campbell said, "for a prosecutor confronted with pressures from the news media to shift the burden for declining prosecution to the grand jury. In this way he avoids any personal accountability for the ultimate decision."[26]

Flawed as the grand jury system was in 1973, it is worse today. Contributing to its decline is a May 4, 1992, Supreme Court decision written by Justice Antonin Scalia. The Court, in a 5–4 ruling, essentially held that federal judges may never dismiss an indictment on the grounds that the prosecutor refused to provide the grand jury with evidence of the target's innocence, no matter how compelling this evidence might be.[27]

The reality is even worse than the statistical record of the grand juries suggest. The numbers show the jurors bring close to zero skepticism to their work.

What is not revealed by the data is the opposite side of the coin. Despite the rhetoric of the Supreme Court, Blakey is right: The grand jury is in fact one of the prosecutors' most powerful offensive tools. Over the years, for example, federal courts have affirmed the right of grand juries—federal prosecutors—to compel witnesses to appear, to give sworn testimony and to produce all requested documents. In addition, the courts have ruled, an accused person brought into a grand jury has no right to confront and cross examine his accusers, the grand jury is free to take hearsay evidence into account, and while a witness may step outside a grand jury room to seek legal advice, the witness has no right to be advised by an attorney while he or she is being questioned.[28] Furthermore, as just noted, a majority of the justices recently held that the assistant U.S. attorney in an Oklahoma banking case was under no obligation to inform the grand jury about evidence the government had obtained that strongly suggested that the target, businessman John H. Williams, Jr., was not guilty of the crime for which the jury eventually charged him.[29]

The reality of the grand jury in the United States today was well summarized by Stuart Taylor. "Would this license to rummage through anyone and everyone's papers on demand, without probable cause and virtually without limitation, in total secrecy and without judicial supervision, sound reasonable if rephrased to describe what is going on?" Taylor asked. "Try crossing out 'grand jury' everywhere those words appear, substituting 'the politically appointed federal prosecutor,' and read it again."

The grand jury: Some watchdog.

INVESTIGATION AND ARREST

The United States Constitution, approved at the Philadelphia convention in 1787, contained a number of general mechanisms designed to make sure that the national government did not escape the control of the American people. One of the most important such mechanisms was the establishment of a three-part federal government with each part empowered to challenge the abuses of the other. The Bill of Rights, approved by the first Congress two years later, offered more specific kinds of protections: It promised the American people freedom of speech, assembly, religion and the press, and restricted the ways the government could go about enforcing the law. With great clarity, the members of both the Constitutional Convention and the first Congress recognized that unchecked power was naturally dangerous. To varying degrees, most of these social architects had taken part in the revolution against England because of their concern about excessive powers claimed by London. In a way that has fallen out of fashion today, these early leaders openly worried that the national government they were forming could easily grow into a monster. Understanding the natural tendency of those with power to seek more of it, they constructed within the new government an elaborate system of controls.

The grand jury, of course, was just one of those controls. Wrongful prosecutions, however, have many different roots, only some of which were confronted by the Fifth Amendment. To deal with abuses that can occur in the time before the government formally charges a person with a crime, Congress approved the Fourth Amendment. The language of this fifty-four-word provision is sweeping. "The rights of the people to be secure in their persons, houses, papers, and effects, against unreasonable searches and seizures, shall not be violated," it begins. And the courts shall issue no warrants, it concludes, "but upon probable cause, supported by Oath or affirmation, and particularly describing the place to be searched, and the persons to be seized."

Precisely because the Fourth Amendment covers so much ground in so little time, however, its actual scope has been subject to constant interpretation and reinterpretation by the courts. When, for example, is a search unreasonable? What, for that matter, is a search?

One famous example of the constantly shifting official understanding of the Fourth Amendment concerns electronic surveillance. In 1928, the Supreme Court upheld the conviction of a Seattle bootlegger named Roy Olmstead, ruling that the unwarranted wiretap on the home telephone of Roy and his wife, Elsie, had not involved the kind of search protected by the Fourth Amendment because nothing tangible—only conversations—had been seized by the government. Thirty-five years later, however, in the case of a Los Angeles bookmaker named Katz, the Supreme Court reversed itself, holding that the wiretap used to collect the evidence against Katz was subject to the warrant and probable cause limitations of the amendment.[30]

In addition to being subject to constant reinterpretation, the Fourth Amendment has long had another kind of problem: the lack of a mechanism to force government agents to abide by its principles. In fact, more than a hundred years passed before the Supreme Court addressed this particular shortcoming. In a 1914 decision, a unanimous court reversed the conviction of a suspect on the ground that a federal marshal and local police officials investigating the case had made several searches and the final arrest of the suspect without obtaining the judicial warrant required by the Bill of Rights. One problem with the groundbreaking decision establishing what is now called the "exclusionary rule," however, was that it only applied to federal agents. It wasn't until 1961 that the Supreme Court decided the exclusionary rule also applied to state and local police officers.[31]

Thus, in both substantive and procedural ways, the Fourth Amendment today demands a lot more restraint from the nation's criminal investigators than it did when the amendment first became effective more than two hundred years ago. But starting about two decades ago, the Supreme Court began handing down a string of decisions that considered as a whole have cut back very definitely on the coverage of the Fourth Amendment. The effect of these decisions has been to expand the basic investigative powers of both federal agents and local police officers.

Under the Burger and Rehnquist courts, the kinds of situations in which government agents must obtain a judicial warrant before they act have slowly been reduced. Today, for example, anyone riding in a car, train or bus can be detained and searched without a warrant in a way that would have been considered constitutionally improper only three decades ago. In addition to enlarging the arena where police are authorized to act on their general suspicions, gradually reducing the reach of the exclusionary rule, the courts have also issued a number of rulings where they abandoned the traditional legal standard that required federal and local officers to have "probable cause" before they requested a warrant. Now, in many situations, the officer can obtain a warrant merely on the basis of a "reasonable suspicion."

The Fourth Amendment: Some watchdog.

REDUCING THE GUARD RAILS,
INCREASING THE SPEED LIMIT

When the schoolyard bully knocks down a smaller child, he must be challenged immediately. If the other students look away, the bully will attack again and again, and soon may succeed in terrorizing the entire class. We all know this fact of life from our direct experience as grade school students and our historical knowledge of international bullies like Adolf Hitler.

About fifty years ago, in a decision written by Justice Felix Frankfurter, the Supreme Court acknowledged this problem and held that the federal courts have "the duty of establishing and maintaining civilized standards of procedure and evidence."[32]

As a result of this important decision, working partly on the theory that federal prosecutors have a passionate desire to win their cases, federal judges around the country began to punish serious instances of misconduct by dismissing those cases where abuses occurred. Because judges, by definition, are well informed about both the ethical requirements of the law and the detailed facts of the cases that come before them, they are in an unusually good position to challenge Justice Department prosecutors when they break the law.

But the move to increase the role of federal judges in policing the behavior of prosecutors, inspired by Justice Frankfurter's 1943 decision, was to be short-lived. The gradual reduction in the court's role as a disciplinarian force can be traced to a 1973 decision where the justices reinstated a drug conviction that had been thrown out by the court of appeals because of the government's intimate involvement in the crime.

The decision was written by then-justice William Rehnquist.[33] The dismissal of the case, he wrote, "unnecessarily introduces an unmanageably subjective standard" into the legal process, while at the same time violating the separation of powers principle. The investigative conduct of the government thus should be immune from judicial supervision unless the conduct violates a specific constitutional right or is "so outrageous that due process principles would absolutely bar the government from invoking judicial processes to obtain a conviction."

Although there have been some zigs and zags in the Court's overall policy since the Rehnquist opinion, many litigators and legal scholars agree that federal judges generally have backed away from supervising prosecutors. Because of the sharp increase in the substantive powers of the prosecutors in the last few decades, in terms of the laws they enforce and the investigators they deploy, this withdrawal from the fray is doubly important.

Bennett L. Gershman, for example, is a professor at Pace University Law School in New York and a former prosecutor who has specialized in the problem of prosecutorial misconduct. He believes that the more aggressive judicial role launched by Frankfurter was a real deterrent to misconduct. But today, "prosecutors can and would be foolish to regard supervisory power [of the courts] as a serious threat to their autonomy. The doctrine [of supervisory power] has become an empty shell, liberating prosecutors from a potential check on their authority, and serving mostly as a reminder to lower federal courts not to usurp the prosecutor's prerogative."[34]

Barry Tarlow, a nationally prominent criminal lawyer, is another former prosecutor who is concerned about the court's passivity. The abandonment of responsibility by the judges, he argues, "has caused rogue prosecutors to continuously push the edge of the ethical envelope." He cites cases where prosecutors have bribed key witnesses for the prosecution; intimidated potential witnesses for the defense; repeatedly lied to defense attorneys, judges and juries; and secretly negotiated with defendants without informing their attorneys. Tarlow argues there are now "virtually no effective checks on those who disregard the rights of the accused and undermine the integrity of the criminal justice system."[35]

The lopsided batting record of federal grand juries—going along with federal prosecutors more than 99.9 percent of the time—provides concrete evidence that this ancient institution is not the corrective force envisaged by the drafters of the Fifth Amendment. Unfortunately, there is no similar way to quantify what the Supreme Court has done to the Fourth Amendment, although a strong majority of legal scholars agrees that the combined effect of the Court's recent decisions has been to weaken the oversight role of independent federal judges.

There is, however, a quantitative way to measure the impact of a special procedure created by the Supreme Court to give citizens more power to challenge the improper actions of federal agents. In a 1971 ruling, the first of its kind since the adoption of the Constitution and the Bill of Rights some two hundred years before, the Supreme Court held that federal agents who violate the constitutional rights of an individual can be personally sued for monetary damages.[36]

In the case in question, the Court said that six agents of the Federal Bureau of Narcotics were individually liable under the Fourth Amendment for conducting a warrantless search of the Brooklyn apartment of Webster Bivens, threatening his family, arresting him for alleged narcotics violations and then strip searching him at the police precinct before he was booked. In 1979, the Court expanded the Bivens-type remedy it had created to allow individuals to sue agents who had violated their Fifth Amendment rights.[37]

In subsequent decisions, however, the Court established several conditions that had to be met before a Bivens claim could be paid. One such condition was that the court should not grant damages in situations where there were other possible remedies. A second condition was that the court should not grant damages if there was a risk that such an award might interfere with the effective functioning of government.

For these and other reasons, the protections which theoretically should have flowed from the Bivens procedure, like those offered by the grand jury, are in fact a fantasy. According to a 1986 Justice Department study, for example, about 12,000 individuals brought Bivens suits alleging that federal agents had violated their constitutional rights during the fourteen-year period from the Supreme Court decision to the Justice Department report. As a result of these 12,000 suits, the department discovered, only thirty-two verdicts were rendered against the agents and, in the end, only five "individual defendants have had to pay damages."[38]

In other words, four hundredths of one percent of the Bivens suits are successful from the standpoint of the person who feels an agent has abused his rights. It can be assumed that the charges made in some Bivens suits, perhaps even many of them, are not valid. It is also clear that many are very hard to prove, partly because the individuals bringing the charges against the agents frequently have unsavory backgrounds. But when merit is found in so few cases it seems unlikely that the mechanism serves as a serious deterrent against unconstitutional actions by federal agents.*

In his famous dissent to the 1928 Supreme Court decision holding that wiretapping was not a violation of the Fourth Amendment, Justice Louis Brandeis eloquently spoke to the Bill of Rights and why it was so important that the government live by its mandates. "Decency, security and liberty alike demand that government officials shall be subjected to the same rules of conduct that are commands to the citizens. In a government of laws, existence of the government will be imperiled if it fails to observe the law scrupulously. . . . If the government becomes a law breaker, it breeds contempt for law, it invites every man to become a law unto himself; it invites anarchy."[39]

The Bivens decision: Some watchdog.

---

*Stephen A. Grant, the New York lawyer who argued the Bivens case in the Supreme Court, was not surprised when informed of the tiny proportion of successful suits. "The case was always something of an intellectual exercise," Grant said in a 1993 interview. "It was significant mostly because it ended the absolute prohibition against bringing such suits against federal agents. Jurors are skeptical about allegations made by people who often have long criminal records."

CONGRESS AT THE READY?

I n 1972, after four years' experience as a county councilman in Delaware, an amiable thirty-year-old lawyer named Joseph Biden was elected to the United States Senate. In 1977, he became a member of the Judiciary Committee. Ten years later, in 1987, Biden became the chairman of the Senate Judiciary Committee, a position he held until the Republicans took over control of the Congress in 1995.

During Biden's time as chairman, from 1987 to 1995, the Senate refused to approve the appointment of Robert Bork, the controversial scholar and judge nominated by President Reagan for the Supreme Court. Biden also headed the committee during the contentious national debate over the allegations of sexual harassment made against President Bush's equally controversial nominee, Clarence Thomas. In the end, the Senate approved Thomas's appointment.

Most of the day-to-day work of the Senate Judiciary Committee, however, does not make it onto national television. In fact, a lot of the committee's work is barely visible to anyone. One of the least publicized aspects of the committee's various official responsibilities is the way it goes about the job of judging the qualifications of the men and women nominated to be U.S. attorneys.

Given the genuine importance of this position, one of the most curious facts about the Senate Judiciary Committee is that in all of modern history, no one can remember a single public hearing when nominees to be U.S. attorneys were required to explain their law enforcement philosophy or where critics were allowed to challenge the individual's views and qualifications.

This means that a substantial number of hearings were in fact never called. During the eight years that President Reagan was in office, for example, 120 persons were nominated to the influential post of U.S. attorney. While a handful of the nominees failed to be confirmed by the Senate, not one was asked to appear in a public hearing. During President Bush's four years, the White House nominated fifty-one U.S. attorneys. Again, the Democratic-controlled committee held no hearings. It probably will not come as a surprise, then, that during the years when both the White House and the Congress were controlled by the same political party, the committee somehow failed once again to hold a single confirmation hearing for a U.S. attorney.

At first, the lack of such hearings seems a puzzle, especially after reading the part of the Constitution—Section 2, Article II—that requires the Senate to give its consent to appointment of ambassadors,

Supreme Court judges "and all other officers of the United States" nominated by the president.

In this case, however, what you read is very definitely not what you get. In a tradition that again goes back a long way, when it comes to U.S. attorneys, it actually is the Senate, and not the president, who almost always does the nominating. As stated earlier, the choice of who will be the U.S. attorney in any state is made in most cases by the senior senator of that state who belongs to the party of the president. If the state in question has failed to elect a senator of the president's party, the choice falls to the senior House member from the state of the same party. Where there is no suitable House member, the chairman of the relevant state political committee makes the selection.

Given the controlling voice of the Senate in choosing U.S. attorneys, and the ability of a federal prosecutor to shape federal enforcement within an individual district to meet the political needs of the appointing senator, it is hardly surprising that the Senate has no interest in offering anyone a public platform where its appointees might be challenged.

The largely independent position of U.S. attorneys, which has been emphasized throughout this book, is a matter of major significance. Although the Constitution and the law appear to give the president and the attorney general a clear obligation to direct the principal business of the Justice Department, the day-to-day decisions about who will and will not be prosecuted are largely in the hands of the U.S. attorneys. The point is not that the world would be a better place if the attorney general actually had the centralized enforcement power which seems to be granted by the law, but that, contrary to both the statutes and the public's understanding of them, the attorney general actually has surprisingly little direct control over the Justice Department.

This crucial fact has seldom been commented upon. Ramsey Clark, Lyndon Johnson's attorney general during the difficult period from 1967 to 1969, is one exception. The political appointment of U.S. attorneys, he wrote, "inhibits the development of career service and divides loyalties. If we believe in separation of powers, the executive branch [the Justice Department] should be independent of the legislative [Congress]. How independent will some chief prosecutors be when they have associated all their adult life with a senator, when he secured their appointment, when he approved the appointment of their assistants, when the close association between the senator and the United States Attorney will continue after administrations change and ostensible superiors in the Justice Department have retired to private life?

"The United States Attorney and the Attorney General of the United States," Clark continued, "usually start as strangers, frequently remain distant because of the burdens of their respective positions and often are divided by the different demands of national policy and local interest. Who is likely to learn first the evidence of crime with political implications—a Senator or the Attorney General? Who is likely to be influential in a case, or a grand jury investigation, or if a riot occurs and a judgment must be made as to the use of federal troops, or if civil rights or other prosecutions that are very unpopular in the district are necessary?"

Clark explained how the organizational dynamics of the Justice Department tended to give an individual U.S. attorney de facto control over the FBI agents assigned to the district. "Without the United States Attorney, there will be no prosecution, and through him there can be malicious prosecution," Clark wrote. The federal prosecutor handles "almost all federal cases developed in his district by all federal investigative agencies. He is privy to all investigative reports turned over for prosecutorial decision. Yet he is selected usually by a state or local political figure."[40]

In a 1990 law journal article, Senator Biden discussed the oversight philosophy of the Senate Judiciary Committee. When there was an attorney general working out of his own private office with no secretaries, no clerk and no salaries, he said, there was little congressional oversight. "Now, when there is an Attorney General who has close to 80,000 employees under his control and the responsibility for enforcing, honestly and vigorously, the volumes of new law that were passed since 1789, there is considerably greater oversight."

While Biden's claim may in some limited way be true, his analysis totally avoids any reference to U.S. attorneys or discussion of how individual federal prosecutors routinely bend the law to suit the needs of their patrons. It also ignores the fact that since 1980, the Senate Judiciary Committee has almost completely abandoned its previous practice of holding wide-ranging Justice Department oversight hearings on a yearly basis.

In discussing the committee's constitutional authority to confirm or not to confirm, despite his reference to the department's 80,000 employees, the chairman limited himself to the attorney general. "We are required to responsibly look into the background and get commitments from an Attorney General as to how he or she would enforce the law," he explained. "The relationship of the Attorney General to the President versus his role as the chief law enforcement officer is, also, always a subject of discussion. This is because we have had so many experiences with Democratic as well as Republican presidents who have, in fact, decided that the Attorney General's office is a political instrument to be used either as a scalpel or a bludgeon."[41]

Given the chairman's three decades of politics and the committee's record during his time as chairman, Biden's remarks surely set a new standard for either mysterious innocence or profound cynicism. Did Biden not think the Judiciary Committee also had a responsibility to inquire about how the U.S. attorneys—the individuals who actually make most of the department's daily decisions—would enforce the law? Did Biden not believe that an inquiry into the relationship between the person who was nominated to be a federal prosecutor and his or her political patron always is a subject of discussion? Did Biden not know, as asserted by Ramsey Clark and many other experts before and after him, of repeated instances where prosecutors have used the power of the law as a political scalpel or bludgeon?

The Senate Judiciary Committee: Some watchdog.

GETTING TO THE BOTTOM OF WATERGATE

One of the most highly regarded superstars of the modern Congress was an always-courteous, deeply southern country lawyer from North Carolina, Senator Sam Ervin. He became a genuine American folk hero through the intelligence and skill he brought to one of the most sensitive tasks ever taken on by a member of Congress: serving as chairman of the special committee that in 1973 investigated the Watergate scandal and the subsequent effort by President Richard Nixon and Attorney General John Mitchell to cover it up.

Ervin's unrelenting probe of an administration that managed to consume itself through a paranoid fear of its political "enemies" has been hailed as a model of responsible congressional oversight. The Senate investigation, of course, was followed by the House Judiciary Committee's vote to impeach Nixon, the president's decision to resign and the conviction of Mitchell and seventeen other Nixon aides on a variety of federal charges.

The nationally televised Watergate hearings had many dramatic moments. But certainly June 25, 1973, was one of them. This was the day that John W. Dean III, the icily contained former counsel to the president, began to testify.[42] He talked for two days, backing up his allegations with a stack of embarrassing letters, memorandums and other documents that he had obtained from White House files, including early chronologies of the Watergate activities of such infamous individuals as E. Howard Hunt and Donald Segretti, and extensive correspondence about an illegal White House plan for vast increases in the domestic intelligence activities of the FBI and other agencies.

But as Dean began to present his devastating testimony about the Nixon men, few reporters noticed that the stacks of documents the committee made public did not include everything the young lawyer had brought to the Ervin committee. Instead, at two places in the committee's inventory of the material, a note had been inserted explaining that exhibits 34-5 through 34-8 and exhibit 43 had been "submitted for identification only, not for publication, and will be retained in the files of the committee."[43]

One of the few who did wonder about the missing exhibits was a young reporter named Dan Thomasson, now the Washington bureau chief of the Scripps Howard News Service. "Jim Squires of the *Chicago Tribune*, Harry Kelley at Hearst and I noticed the gaps and immediately asked Sam Dash about them," Thomasson recalled twenty years later. Sam Dash was the committee's chief counsel and staff director.[44]

"Dash told us they involved highly sensitive matters that would do no one any good to see," Thomasson continued. "I seem to remember that we learned that Dash had stowed the memos in the committee's safe, that he would not let staff members see them at all, and that senators were permitted to read them, but not take any written notes. Dash told us the publication of the memos would serve no purpose."

The three reporters, naturally intrigued by Dash's stonewalling, decided to pool their investigative efforts. Although they were never able to unearth any of the documents, five weeks of interviewing dozens of officials and former officials produced enough information to support the publication of what at the time was a shocking series of articles about one of them.

Thomasson's first article, which ran on the Scripps Howard wire on August 15, 1973, concerned an undated five-page memo written by William C. Sullivan, a longtime former associate of FBI Director J. Edgar Hoover. The Sullivan memo that the Ervin committee had chosen to suppress, the Thomasson article said, described dozens of examples of the FBI's secret and manipulative involvement in national politics that had begun in the New Deal days of Franklin D. Roosevelt.[45]

Thomasson's article was all detail and no interpretation. This was unfortunate because the general inferences that properly could have been drawn from the specifics of the Sullivan memo were much more significant than any of the individual scandals he described.

Yes, FDR and Hoover's FBI had conspired to investigate and sometimes harass the president's political opponents. Yes, LBJ and Hoover's FBI were partners in even more numerous dirty tricks. But Sullivan's memo suggested something far worse.

The problem of an out-of-control FBI doing the White House's political bidding clearly had not begun with Richard Nixon. The systematic politicization of the FBI, in fact, appeared to have been a natural and continuing part of the Washington scene for more than three decades. The FBI's improper, often illegal, political investigations had the blessing of the nation's highest elected officials and were not the work of rogue agents or a rogue agency.

Given that the FBI and the White House had been secretly manipulating voters for many years before President Nixon was elected, driving Nixon from the White House would do little to resolve the systemic problems that for so long had threatened the basic political process of the nation. Real structural reform was required to deal with a corruption that clearly did not begin, or end, with one administration.

But the media big feet—the *New York Times*, the *Washington Post*, the television networks, the weekly newsmagazines—did not pay much attention to the investigative articles by Thomasson and his two colleagues. This was partly because Ervin and Dash were successful in keeping the Sullivan memo itself out of the hands of the press, thus forcing Thomasson, Squires, Kelley and the few reporters who followed them to base their articles on unnamed sources.

There were other reasons why the Sullivan story never went very far. One was the herd instinct of the Washington press corps. The second was the short-term political calculations of the Democratic Party then in control of Congress.

Woodward and Bernstein, the *Post*'s hard-working investigative team, had already established Nixon's culpability for Watergate—a bad person had been responsible for encouraging the officials around him to undertake a specific set of bad acts. This would remain the primary focus of most of the reporters who followed them. And although the two journalists certainly never explicitly argued the case, their investigation supported the view that Nixon and his henchmen could in no way be compared to Roosevelt, Truman, Kennedy and LBJ. This simpleminded attitude was hastily embraced by many Democrats in Congress, who naturally saw little purpose in telling the American people that Democratic presidents were often as ruthless as Nixon.

Sullivan, who had been fired from the FBI in the fall of 1971 after several private and public disagreements with Hoover, was working as a White House consultant when he wrote his memo. The request for his analysis of the bureau's past political escapades had come from John Dean, who hoped to find historical justification for the FBI abuses under Nixon's White House.[46]

Years later, much of the Sullivan memo "relative to the FBI and politics and various administrations" became public. Fred D. Thompson, the Republican counsel of the Ervin committee, published parts of it in his book on the Watergate investigation.[47] In 1993, in response to a Freedom of Information Act request, the National Archives made public a copy of the five-page, single-spaced text that Sullivan had personally pecked out on a manual typewriter. Only a few names had been deleted for personal privacy reasons.

"The FBI under Mr. Hoover always tried to develop and maintain a very close unilateral relationship with Presidents and their key Administration officials," Sullivan began. "Different Senators, Congressmen, Cabinet officers etc. were carefully and *systematically* cultivated. The cultivation included both Democrats and Republicans but it was done with such skill and finesse that each one usually thought he was alone in getting the special and helpful treatment."

Sullivan observed that the FBI's motive in undertaking the political chores was always very clear. "It goes without saying that the above relationships were based on reciprocity. It had to be a two-way street. The FBI gave out valuable information to the kinds of officeholders mentioned above in exchange for their support. At times this activity could become just a bit devious and complex. For example, President Johnson would ask the FBI for derogatory information of one type or the other on Senators in his own Democratic Party who were opposing him. This information he would give the Republican Senator [Everett M.] Dirksen who would use it with telling effect against President Johnson's opponents, etc."

The memo, personally typed by Sullivan to limit its readers to an absolute minimum, had originally been classified a top-secret document. It provided thumbnail descriptions of a dozen specific situations where the FBI had served as the political investigative arm of the White House. At the request of Franklin Roosevelt, for example, the FBI conducted background checks of those who opposed the legislative programs he was trying to push through a sometimes reluctant Congress. On the other hand, Sullivan said, both the president and Mrs. Roosevelt sometimes asked the FBI to suppress investigations of top officials who were personal friends or were important to the New Deal agenda. Most of the cases, however, involved Lyndon Johnson, Nixon's immediate predecessor in the White House. Probably the most elaborate illegal project the FBI carried out for LBJ involved the 1964 Democratic convention in Atlantic City. (The details of this particular effort are explored in Chapter 2.) Yet even LBJ's less complex requests were extremely dubious.

On November 12, 1968, Sullivan wrote, President Johnson personally requested the FBI "to check all outgoing telephone calls made by the then Vice Presidential candidate, Mr. Spiro Agnew, on the date of November 2, 1968, at the time he was in Albuquerque, New Mexico. This was done."

The FBI response, considering the fact that LBJ requested the information more than a week after the calls had been placed, was remarkably detailed. Five phone calls were made in all by the Agnew team during their Albuquerque stop, Sullivan said: three from a phone on Agnew's plane and two from a nearby pay phone. Agnew had talked to Secretary of State Dean Rusk, Johnson was told, and an Agnew staff member had made two calls, one to Cal Purdy in Texas and another to a New York sculptor named Bruce Friedel. The fourth call went to a Jim Miller, also of New York. The fifth call was to a telephone in the Nixon-Agnew Campaign Headquarters chargeable to Maurice Stans, then the finance chairman of CREEP, the Committee to Re-elect the President.

Sullivan, as already noted, wrote his memo at the request of the Nixon White House. Much earlier, according to some reports, during the period when Robert Kennedy was attorney general and Sullivan was in the FBI, the two men enjoyed a relatively good working relationship. These facts may partly explain why he wrote that "to my memory the two Administrations which used the FBI the most for political purposes were Mr. Roosevelt's and Mr. Johnson's. Complete and willing cooperation was given to both."

A few years later, however, after an extensive investigation, the Senate Intelligence Committee concluded that every administration from Roosevelt's to Nixon's had permitted, and sometimes encouraged, the FBI and other federal agencies to engage in improper political intelligence operations.

Here are two examples noted by the intelligence committee: "President Eisenhower received reports on purely political and social contacts with foreign officials by Bernard Baruch, Mrs. Eleanor Roosevelt and Supreme Court Justice William O. Douglas." A few years later, the committee found, the Kennedy brothers "had the FBI wiretap a Congressional staff member, three executive officials, a lobbyist, and a Washington law firm. Attorney General Robert Kennedy received the fruits of an FBI 'tap' on Martin Luther King, Jr., and a 'bug' on a Congressman both of which yielded information of a political nature."[48]

Obviously, it would not be fair to blame Senator Ervin or Sam Dash for the broad failure of Congress to confront directly the challenge of a lawless FBI to a free society. But surely it is possible to argue that had the two men chosen to investigate and publicize the then unknown truths of William Sullivan, Watergate could have developed into a far more effective springboard for genuine reform. While going after the Nixon White House for its various abuses was daring and difficult work, undertaking a serious investigation of the underlying political dynamics corruptly linking six administrations to the FBI would potentially have been far more significant for the nation.

The Senate Watergate Committee: Some watchdog.

THE DISTINGUISHED MEMBERS OF THE BAR

Maintaining ethical standards within a profession is always a challenge. But in recent years, faced with more and more charges of misconduct, state bar associations across the country have formalized their efforts to investigate allegations and discipline those found wanting. In 1990, for example, the annual budget for the average state bar association disciplinary unit was $1,676,362. During that same year, each of these agencies investigated an average of 1,284 misconduct complaints and found probable cause to believe that 163 of the allegations were true.[49]

Given the number of lawyers in each state, and the inherent ambiguities of the profession, few have argued that the state associations are overzealous when it comes to policing their members. It is this background which made a 1989 proposal by Attorney General Richard Thornburgh so surprising.[50] Outlined in a memorandum to federal prosecutors, the proposed ruling exempted department lawyers from a long-standing ethical rule that generally prohibits a lawyer from talking to an opponent's client without informing the opposing lawyer. The purpose of the prohibition is to prevent lawyers from using their superior skills and acumen to take advantage of people in the absence of their lawyers.

Although federal prosecutors cheered Thornburgh's memorandum, defense attorneys, law school professors, judges and other critics interpreted it as a high-handed assertion that U.S. attorneys and their assistants were free to ignore the ethical constraints of the legal profession when the attorney general decided they were inconvenient to the Justice Department's investigative efforts. Thornburgh claimed the exemption largely on grounds of the Supremacy Clause, a section of the 1789 Judiciary Act that empowered the Supreme Court to review the final opinions of the state courts.

"There is something very disquieting in what appears to be the emerging notion that attorneys for the government are to be held to a different and lower standard of ethics than other members of the bar," said Jerry E. Norton, a professor at Loyala University Law School, voicing the worries of numerous legal scholars. "The deregulation of government attorneys' ethics does not promise glory either to these attorneys, or to the government they serve."[51]

The storm of criticism halted the proposal in its tracks and Thornburgh soon left Washington to run, unsuccessfully, for the Senate. But the Justice Department's professional staff did not leave Washington.

Five years later, with Janet Reno now in charge, the department published its final version of the regulation in the Federal Register.[52]

Although it was somewhat modified, R. William Ide III, president of the American Bar Association, and other legal authorities were not mollified. "We have expressed the view—and it remains our view—that the regulation impinges impermissibly on the right to counsel. Moreover, the Department's position attempts to preempt and supersede regulation of government lawyers by state courts, state disciplinary authorities and federal courts. This approach would substitute the Attorney General's regulation of lawyers for the control and supervision that has historically been the province of the state and federal judiciary."[53]

In terms of legal authority, staffing, budget and surveillance equipment, the Justice Department has undergone almost nonstop growth for at least the last sixty years. This development makes informed oversight far more important than it ever was. But the record suggests that the key actors in this drama—vigilant reporters, independent grand jurors, fearless judges, tough-minded members of Congress and skeptical bar associations—are mostly absent from the stage.

Some watchdogs.

T he Book of Ecclesiastes tells us that to everything there is a season: a time to weep, and a time to laugh; a time to mourn, and a time to dance. Were the United States Justice Department a sentient being, the mid-1970s surely would have been a time for it to weep and mourn.

On May 2, 1972, J. Edgar Hoover died, luckily for him perhaps, considering the torrent of ugly FBI documents that were about to become public describing his direct involvement in a massive, long-lived and often lawless series of programs to suppress all kinds of political dissent.

In April 1973, L. Patrick Gray, the man Nixon had selected to succeed Hoover at the FBI, resigned his post after it was learned that he had destroyed important evidence about the Watergate scandal—two manila envelopes containing documents from Howard Hunt's safe—and then lied about this action when asked about it by the Senate Judiciary Committee.

During the same month of 1973, Mitchell's immediate successor at the Justice Department, Richard Kleindienst, resigned as attorney general after only nine months in office. In a subsequent plea agreement, Kleindienst did not contest a one-count federal misdemeanor charge relating to his failure to answer questions put to him by a Senate Committee about his role in the ITT scandal.

On New Year's Day 1975, former attorney general John Mitchell was convicted on felony charges relating to his role in the Watergate scandal. The charges involved illegal actions initiated by the Nixon administration against opponents of the Vietnam War, black militants, officials, journalists and politicians ranging from George Wallace to George McGovern. Initial planning for some of these efforts had taken place in the fifth-floor Justice Department office that Mitchell occupied while he was attorney general.

It was, without doubt, one of the worst periods in the Justice Department's history. But emerging from the appalling chaos and dishonor of the Nixon/Watergate years, like new growth from the charred earth of a forest fire, were genuinely optimistic efforts to make both the department and the FBI more open, responsive, law-abiding and effective institutions.

In early 1975, for example, Congress confirmed the appointment of Edward Levi as attorney general. A distinguished lawyer and educator with previous experience in the Justice Department, Levi was widely regarded as one of the most honorable and effective attorneys general in the history of the Justice Department.

Because of the long string of investigative abuses that had become known to the public, one of Levi's first efforts was to develop a concrete set of rules to guide FBI agents in the do's and don'ts of security investigations aimed at domestic groups. The Levi guidelines, issued in 1976, provided that "full investigations" of domestic organizations could only be initiated on the basis of specific facts that gave reason to believe the organization in question had been or was about to be involved in violent actions. The guidelines added that only when these conditions were met could the FBI plant an informant in the suspect organization. A third aspect of the Levi guidelines also established procedures under which the FBI was required to obtain the written approval of specific high-level officials in the Justice Department before it proceeded with certain kinds of sensitive investigations.

As a result of the guidelines, almost nonstop news coverage of past FBI outrages, and major organizational and staff changes within the bureau, the number of ongoing domestic security investigations went into a precipitous decline: from more than 2,000 in mid-1973 to fewer than 300 by the end of 1976. During roughly the same period, the domestic security informants on the FBI payroll dropped from 1,500 to about 600.[1]

It should not for a moment be thought that the Levi guidelines were a perfect answer to the decades of FBI abuses that had triggered their development. For one thing, because many illegal and improper activities of the past had been approved by either the attorney general or the president, cleaning up the FBI was only a partial remedy. For a second thing, parts of the guidelines were classified and thus unknowable to the American people. A third major problem was that the guidelines were laid down in an executive branch directive that was subject to modification at the stroke of the president's pen. While a handful of senior senators and congressmen sought to write the guidelines into formal law, disagreements about the details of the ground rules ultimately prevented Congress from approving the so-called FBI charter legislation. Almost inevitably this failure meant that with the election of the conservative Reagan administration only six years later, Levi's restrictions on FBI investigative practices were weakened.

With all these shortcomings, however, Levi's 1976 strictures had continuing force, partly because they demonstrated a principle of fundamental importance. Even on an extremely sensitive matter like domestic intelligence gathering, the attorney general and lawyers at the FBI were able to develop administrative procedures that allowed the FBI to go forward with one of its most important missions—investigating domestic groups suspected of terrorism—according to a set of carefully drafted rules, under the supervision of senior Justice Department officials and without the widespread abuses of the past.

THE SPECIAL COUNSEL

Attorney General Levi's success in imposing a measure of responsible management over a long out-of-control surveillance program was hardly an everyday event. On the other hand, there have been a number of similar occasions when national concerns about an obvious Justice Department failing have triggered adoption of procedures intended to alleviate the abuse.

In 1978, for example, after extended debate, Congress approved a law authorizing the appointment of a temporary special prosecutor to investigate credible allegations of wrongdoing against the president, the vice president, the director of the FBI, members of the cabinet and senior members of the White House staff.

The inspiration for the creation of the special counsel process was Watergate: For a large majority of Congress, it had proved that people appointed by a president have great difficulty investigating the president and his close associates.

There are few legal authorities who argue that either the original or the amended laws establishing the system for the appointment of what is called an independent counsel are an ideal solution. In fact, although the law has been upheld by the Supreme Court, some experts make a cogent argument that several of the powers granted the courts and the special counsel under the statutes are in fact reserved by the Constitution for the president.[2]

But during the 1977 hearings on the original law, John Harmon, an assistant attorney general for the Carter administration, argued that a special counsel was necessary because we "recognize that public perceptions and the appearance of justice are often as important as justice itself. We also recognize that in light of Watergate and its aftermath, public confidence in our system of justice must be restored. We must not only do justice, but be able to assure the public that justice has been done. It is in this spirit that I come here for the Department of Justice to support the principles underlying the special prosecutor provision."[3]

Once again, in the face of a horrendous Justice Department failure, society sought to devise an alternative method for dealing with a difficult problem. Once again, although the chosen mechanism was not perfect, a credible approach was developed to meet a widely perceived flaw in the administration of justice at the federal level.

The challenge of devising better ways to operate the Justice Department, however, is formidable. Susan Long of TRAC and Syracuse University, who has been studying the operations of large federal agencies for more than a quarter of a century, explains why. "Because there are indeed bad people in the world who are doing bad things in our society, the Justice Department has to have power," she observed. "But because it is impossible to write laws that are precisely appropriate for every situation that the Justice Department faces each day, society must grant the department's agents considerable discretion. Discretion is part of the price of government in the real world. Absolute solutions to the dilemma of discretion do not exist. While we can become obsessed with finding a perfect proposal, with creating a perfect mechanism, the very best that humans can achieve often is something that may be only satisfactory."

ALL WE WANT ARE THE FACTS

The Justice Department's development of the FBI guidelines and Congress's authorization of a procedure for the appointment of an independent counsel demonstrate how the body politic responded to several extravagantly publicized scandals. But there have been times when creative and useful Justice Department reforms have emerged from less calamitous circumstances.

More than a quarter of a century ago, for example, in a decision involving two natural gas companies, the Supreme Court ruled that an antitrust consent decree worked out by the Justice Department had failed to alleviate the very conditions that violated the antitrust laws.[4]

As a result of this and many similar problem cases, the Senate Judiciary Committee in 1973 held hearings that found that about 80 percent of the antitrust cases of the day were resolved by secret consent decrees worked out in private negotiations by the Justice Department and the offending corporate entity.

"The legislative history shows that Congress was particularly concerned that the 'excessive secrecy' of the consent decree process deprived the public of an opportunity to scrutinize and comment on the proposed decrees, thereby undermining confidence in the legal system," wrote District Court Judge Harold Greene some years later. "In addition, the legislators found that consent decrees often failed to provide appropriate relief, either because of miscalculations by the Justice Department or because of the 'great influence and economic power' wielded by the antitrust violators."[5]

To remedy these problems, Congress approved legislation imposing two changes in the consent decree process. It reduced secrecy by ordering the Justice Department to disclose the rationale and terms of proposed decrees, and required an opportunity for public comment before the decrees became final. Second, to reduce the judicial rubber-stamping of the proposals submitted to the courts by the Justice Department, it required the presiding judge to make an explicit judicial determination that the proposed decree was in the public interest.

UNCOVERING UNDERCOVER

T he search for reform in the Justice Department necessarily involves a complex weighing of values that sometimes result in inaction: proponents fail to win sufficient support to gain its implementation. But just as the adoption of controversial mechanisms like the special counsel does not mean the mechanism is without flaws, the rejection of a proposal doesn't mean it was worthless.

The failed effort of a handful of liberal members of the House of Representatives to impose outside control on one of the Justice Department's most intrusive investigative techniques—the clandestine planting of undercover agents—is an excellent example of a failure to achieve consensus.

During fiscal year 1991, the FBI opened a total of 245 major investigations in which undercover agents were used to obtain evidence in white-collar crime, organized crime, official corruption and drug cases.[6] Because short-term undercover investigations are not reported to FBI headquarters in Washington, the actual number of all such FBI operations is much larger than indicated by the official statistics.

To understand the relative importance of these undercover operations, consider the fact that during the same period the FBI asked the courts for approval to install 242 wiretaps and bugs in connection with all its criminal investigations.[7] In other words, given the fact that a substantial number of undercover operations are not centrally recorded, it appears that the sheer number of investigations involving undercover agents—sometimes armed with hidden tape recorders and other times performing before the unblinking eye of secret surveillance cameras—now considerably exceeds the number of investigations involving electronic surveillance devices.

The relative number of FBI eavesdropping and undercover operations, however, is only part of the story. In electronic eavesdropping, the government's role is passive—the collection by a hidden microphone of the target's incriminating statements. In undercover operations, on the other hand, government agents play an active role, sometimes committing illegal acts themselves to gain the confidence of the target suspects, other times forcefully encouraging suspects to engage in such acts.

In fact, as a result of these differences, secret undercover "sting" operations can be far more intrusive than secret wiretaps and bugs. It is for this reason, perhaps, that sting investigations have frequently achieved such dramatic results.

According to a 1982 Senate report on the subject, there is no question that undercover operations of the Justice Department have substantially contributed to the detection, investigation and prosecution of criminal activities, especially organized crime and consensual crimes such as narcotics trafficking and political corruption.

The committee added, however, that even with the best-motivated enforcement personnel, the technique creates a serious risk to citizens' property, privacy and civil liberties, and may compromise law enforcement itself. "These dangers assume even more importance in undercover operations managed or conducted by agents or officials whose zeal, ambition or baser motives distort their judgment about the proper role of law enforcement in a democratic society."[8]

Probably the best-remembered FBI sting was Operation Abscam, a two-year inquiry that ultimately led to the conviction of one senator and six congressmen on various corruption charges. During the course of this single operation, FBI headquarters granted approval in twenty-four instances for FBI undercover operatives, posing as representatives of an Arab-owned company, to hold videotaped meetings with specific public officials and, if certain conditions were met, to offer the officials bribes.[9]

A year and a half after the Senate published its report on the increasingly popular investigative technique, a House judiciary subcommittee weighed in with a second appraisal describing several FBI undercover operations which had failed to uncover any wrongdoing but had caused serious harm to the reputations and well-being of the targeted individuals and the institutions where they worked.

Noting that its investigation had demonstrated that the Justice Department's internal review process for the sensitive technique was seriously flawed, the subcommittee recommended that Congress approve legislation requiring the FBI to obtain a judicial warrant for its undercover investigations in the same way that it now obtains a court order before installing electronic surveillance devices.[10]

In support of its recommendation, the House subcommittee quoted a Supreme Court decision on a related matter: "[T]hose charged with investigation and prosecutorial duty should not be the sole judges of when to utilize constitutionally sensitive means in pursuing their tasks. The historical judgment, which the Fourth Amendment accepts, is that unreviewed executive discretion may yield too readily to pressures to obtain incriminating evidence and to overlook potential invasions of privacy and protected speech."[11]

The proposal, encompassing an important reduction in the independent investigative powers of the Justice Department, was opposed by Attorney General Levi. "It would be a step toward the inquisitorial system in which judges, and not members of the executive, actually control the investigation of crime," Levi declared. "This is the system used in some European countries and elsewhere, but our system of justice keeps the investigation and prosecution of crime separate from the adjudication of criminal charges."[12]

The recommendation that the FBI's use of the far more intrusive investigative technique be subject to the same judicial review process that long had been required for electronic eavesdropping was not adopted by Congress. "The Justice Department went absolutely nuts on this one," recalled Catherine Leroy, the subcommittee's director from 1980 to 1994, when asked why the proposal was dead on arrival. "But more than that, there is only a brief window of opportunity for passing controversial measures like that one. And if you don't come up with your recommendation within a year or so of the scandal that initially triggered the concern, you are dead."[13]

THE BIG PICTURE

The point implicit in Leroy's observation is valid. In a representative democracy, narrowly focused reforms—born of a specific, recent and widely perceived institutional failure—stand a chance of finding the necessary backing. More sweeping changes designed to remedy the broad administrative conflicts that cause the specific failures are far harder to achieve.

One person interested in the broadest kind of structural reform is Daniel J. Meador, an assistant attorney general from 1977 to 1979, now a professor at the University of Virginia Law School. Shortly after leaving his Washington job as the head of the office for improvements in the administration of justice, Meador organized a conference focused on "The President, the Attorney General, and the Department of Justice." The centerpiece of the conference—a discussion among fifteen former Justice Department officials and William H. Webster, then director of the FBI—was a seventy-five-page paper by Meador discussing the problems of the Justice Department and possible solutions.[14]

While several of Meador's suggestions were narrowly focused, one was almost revolutionary. The attorney general, Meador said, was afflicted by two big problems: inadequate time to deal with the work required, and inappropriate political entanglements.

The root of the difficulties, he continued, is "that nonlawyering duties distract the attorney general from his role as the government's lawyer and create a confused picture of him as a combined administrator, political adviser to the President, congressional lobbyist, grantor of funds, as well as investigator, law enforcer and advocate. These disparate functions involve him in political activity which is inappropriate for a quasi-judicial professional government lawyer."[15]

While several recent attorneys general have tried to deal with the flaws identified by Meador through modest steps such as the delegation of specific responsibilities to various assistants, these efforts have always foundered on the fact that, in the end, the attorney general was by law the responsible official.

Meador's radical answer: split the Justice Department into two fundamentally different parts. One part would be headed by a newly created secretary of justice who would take on all the nonlawyering parts of the current Justice Department, such as the administration's lobbying efforts in Congress, the Bureau of Prisons, the Immigration and Naturalization Service and the highly sensitive task of working with the president and the Senate on patronage: the selection and appointment of judges, U.S. attorneys and federal marshals.

The second part of the Justice Department would be headed by the attorney general, whose responsibilities would be limited to supervising the Criminal Division, the Civil Division, the Antitrust Division, the Environment and Natural Resources Division, the Tax Division, the Civil Rights Division, the offices of the U.S. attorneys and the FBI and the DEA.

"Freeing the attorney general of responsibility for the nonlawyering activities of the Department of Justice would create an institutional structure in which the lawyering functions would be relatively free from undesirable political and bureaucratic entanglements," Meador argued. "In addition, a restructuring of this sort would enable the attorney general to devote his time and attention to the complex and unique role of chief lawyer for the government."[16]

Any reform, big or small, requires a great deal of work. This point was emphasized in the report of the Special Prosecution Task Force that investigated Watergate. The events of Watergate, the report concluded, grew from historical roots that included the criminal abuse of power by government officials in high places, the slowly developing growth of government secrecy that remained unchallenged by Congress and most Americans and the silent, sometimes willful, judgment of some of those in power that "ethical standards are irrelevant because quick implementation of policy goals is mandatory but only achievable by social and personal injustice to others."

Assuming this analysis is correct, the report continued, then any formulation of recommendations "must begin with the simple, but basic,

observation that democracies do not survive unless elected officials do
what they are supposed to do and citizens maintain vigilance to see that
they do. Nothing can replace that kind of vigilance; and recommendations for new laws or new institutions are insignificant when compared
to the stubborn, plodding, daily work of Americans and their elected
representatives in watching over and channeling the power of the national
government, the power of concentrated wealth, the power of officially
spoken and written words, and the power of secret bureaucracies."[17]

The Watergate special prosecutor got it right.

Genuine reform is possible. Edward Levi wrote the FBI guidelines.
Congress approved legislation barring the attorney general from controlling the investigation and prosecution of high officials in his or her
own administration.

But such changes cannot be purchased on the cheap. Because the
choices are not obvious or easy, they require a critical, demanding and
informed public. And without far more attentive reporters and public
interest groups and members of Congress, this knowledge is not easy to
obtain.

The three key questions are ones of control. First, to what degree
should the president control the actions of the attorney general? Second, in a nation as large and diverse as the United States, to what degree
should the attorney general control the U.S. attorneys? Finally, given
the vast powers and repeated abuses of the FBI and the other department investigative agencies, what additional controls over their operations are required for the well-being and safety of the nation?

Author's Note

Since the earliest days of recorded history, government agencies have performed important tasks: collecting taxes, regulating rivers, building roads and making wars. With the establishment of these agencies came a need to keep track of what the individual agents were doing. At first, these records were carved in stone and scratched on damp clay, then they were written on animal skins or paper with pens and, eventually, typewriters.

In the early 1970s, public and private bureaucracies all over the world began to log the detailed work records of their agents on comput-

ers. The significance of this apparently small technical change was
large; information stored in an electronic format in a computer is substantially easier to retrieve, review and analyze than information
recorded on stone, skin or paper.

Among the many agencies in the United States that adopted the
computer for their own administrative purposes was the Justice Department. By about 1974, the department was collecting very detailed information about each of the many thousands of criminal and civil matters
that government prosecutors were considering each year. Among the
data were which investigative agency had referred the matter to the department, where within the department it was referred, what law allegedly had been violated and what happened as a result of the referral.
Was it declined or dismissed or prosecuted? In criminal matters, was
the individual found innocent or guilty? What was the fine and, in recent years, the sentence?

Despite its easy availability, the Justice Department has done almost
nothing with this amazing cornucopia of data for either administrative
or public information purposes. For many years, for example, the department has published a number of annual reports. Although some of
these reports include tabular material about the raw number of indictments, convictions and assets seized by the department and each U.S.
attorney in the previous year, the tables have little value because the
district-to-district and year-to-year information has not been provided a
context, a way of understanding its possible meanings.

At the simplest level, for example, because of the massive differences
in the population of each department district, a plain list showing the
number of drug charges brought in each area is almost incomprehensible. But when the charges are examined in terms of the population or
available staff or other such factors, a transformation occurs, numbers
become rates, and potentially important policy questions suddenly
come into focus.

Why was it, for one example, that in relation to staff, federal prosecutors in one low-crime district in 1992 brought ten times more drug
cases than federal prosecutors in another low-crime district?

The Justice Department, of course, was not the only federal agency
to computerize its records. Nor was it the only agency to largely ignore
the contributions that the collected data could make to a much improved understanding of the processes of government. Why was it, for
another example, that the IRS seizure rate on delinquent accounts in
the area around Austin, Texas, was more than ten times higher than the
seizure rates of IRS agents in the areas around Dallas and Houston?
Why, in relation to the number of operating reactors, were Nuclear Regulatory Commission (NRC) inspectors in the Northeast discovering

only one quarter of the violations that NRC inspectors were finding in the Mountain West?

It is obvious that there are valid explanations for some of the problems suggested by these questions. But it is also clear from the data that there are alternative scenarios: Poorly managed agencies are failing to achieve their stated objectives and, at the same time, violating the fundamental constitutional principle that similarly situated citizens be treated in similar ways.

Amazingly, however, twenty years after the widespread adoption of computerized record-keeping systems, there is scant evidence that either the Justice Department or any other federal enforcement or regulatory agency has done much to capitalize on the contribution these systems could make to increasing the public's understanding of government and improving its ability to treat citizens and corporations in a fair and effective manner.

This glaring deficiency in public accountability no longer need exist. One effort to combat it involves the Transactional Records Access Clearinghouse (TRAC), an organization created by Susan Long, a professor at Syracuse University, and myself in 1989. The purpose of TRAC is to systematically identify and obtain federal enforcement and regulatory information and make it available to all interested parties: public interest groups, industry, reporters, academic researchers and the government itself.

We joined forces to form TRAC because both of us—from somewhat different perspectives—had for many years been intrigued with the challenge of trying to comprehend how the large bureaucracies of the United States actually functioned. Sue is a professor of quantitative methods who, for two decades, has specialized in measuring the enforcement efforts of federal agencies such as the IRS and analyzing the extent to which these efforts induced the public to comply with federal laws and regulations. I am a reporter who, for most of my career, has focused on investigating organizations like the New York Police Department, the Atomic Energy Commission, the Internal Revenue Service and the Justice Department. Although the *New York Times* was my home from 1967 to 1968, I am now an independent writer.

The creation of TRAC's "knowledge bases" and the resulting analysis have now become physically possible for three partially related reasons. First, as already noted, beginning in the early 1970s, the Justice Department and most other government agencies began recording on their computers millions of detailed facts about the daily activities of their agents—what we call "transactional information." Second, under court interpretations of the Freedom of Information Act, federal agencies are now generally required to provide such information to requesters on computer tapes, diskettes or, more recently, CD-ROMs. Finally, because of the astonishing decline in the cost of data analysis, even small organizations and individual citizens can organize large data sets in new and revealing ways.

Shortly after World War II, the development of the electron microscope allowed scientists to actually see viruses for the first time. This ability soon led to a breakthrough in our understanding of an important form of life. The computerized analysis techniques employed by TRAC are similar to those of the electron microscope. The difference is that instead of making objects visible through magnification, the new techniques give visibility by sorting and arranging individual actions into patterns.

While it is assumed that many of the Justice Department's discretionary decisions are made for good and valid reasons, the unexamined exercise of power is always subject to abuse. Now, for the first time, members of the public can examine the overall patterns of federal law enforcement—by administration, by individual U.S. attorney, by statute— to assure themselves that the Justice Department is operating within the letter and spirit of the law.

The enforcement and staffing data that we have extracted from the Justice Department has never before been available. With analysis, the data offer an entirely new perspective about the operations of an agency that has long sought to avoid scrutiny. The challenge of obtaining this information, and then figuring out what it means, would not have been possible without the knowledge, wisdom, incredible energy and technical skills of Susan Long—my colleague, a pioneering sociologist and professor at Syracuse University's School of Management. It also would have been impossible without the encouragement and support of Syracuse University and the financial backing of the Rockefeller Family Fund, the Alida Rockefeller Charitable Trust, the Alida Messinger Fund, the New York Times Company Foundation, the Deer Creek Foundation, the Millstream Fund, the Bauman Foundation, the Fund for Constitutional Government, the J. Roderick MacArthur Foundation, the Samuel Rubin Foundation, the Philip M. Stern Family Fund, the Matz Foundation and the National Press Foundation.

CHAPTER ONE: LAW, ORDER AND POLITICS: THE WORKING OF THE UNITED STATES JUSTICE DEPARTMENT

1. Herbert Brownell, *Advising Ike: The Memoirs of Attorney General Herbert Brownell* (Lawrence: University Press of Kansas, 1993), pp. 365–82.
2. Defendant's Response to Request for Preliminary Injunction, *Dellums v. Bush*, CA No. 90-2866 (DC 1990). (Bush administration response to the motion of fifty-four members of Congress requesting District Court Judge Harold Greene to prohibit the president from starting a war with Iraq "without obtaining a declaration of war or other explicit authorization from Congress.")
3. Literally thousands of pages of documents concerning the FBI's preparation of a long series of lists of Communists and other dissidents who were to

be kept under surveillance were made public as a result of the 1975 investigation of improper activities of the intelligence agencies by the Senate Select Committee to Study Governmental Operations with Respect to Intelligence Activities. These documents, along with those describing a series of highly detailed plans for the apprehension and detention of these troublemakers, are now available in the FBI's public reading room in Washington. The documents, many of which I obtained for this book, indicate that FBI Director Hoover first began developing the watch lists and detention program as a result of a private conversation he had with President Roosevelt on August 24, 1939. Hoover transformed the World War II program into an instrument of the Cold War—first called "Security Portfolio"—a little less than ten years later, on August 2, 1948. The Senate Intelligence Committee states that FBI Director Clarence Kelley brought the program to a final close in 1976.

4. November 13, 1952, Memorandum to J. Edgar Hoover from D. M. Ladd, "Program for Apprehension and Detention of Persons Considered Potentially Dangerous to the National Defense and Public Safety of the United States," published as Exhibit 26-1, Vol. 6, Hearings on the Federal Bureau of Investigation by the Senate Select Committee to Study Governmental Operations with Respect to Intelligence Activities (Washington, D.C.: Government Printing Office, 1976), pp. 416–26.

5. November 25, 1952, Memorandum to the Director of the FBI from the Attorney General, "Program for Apprehension and Detention of Persons Considered Potentially Dangerous to the National Defense and Public Safety of the United States," Senate Intelligence Committee hearings, Vol. 6, p. 427.

6. An Interim Report of the Senate Select Committee to Study Governmental Operations with Respect to Intelligence Activities, "Alleged Assassination Plots Involving Foreign Leaders" (Washington, D.C., November 20, 1975), pp. 136 and 274–76.

7. Transcript, criminal trial of Colonel Oliver North, March 28, 1989, pp. 5747–48.

8. Deposition of William Weld, Report of the Congressional Committees Investigating the Iran-Contra Affair, Appendix B, Vol. 27, pp. 592–93.

9. Peter Kornbluh and Malcolm Byrne, eds., *The Iran-Contra Scandal: The Declassified History* (New York: New Press, 1993), p. 307.

10. Robert H. Jackson memoir, Oral History Project, Columbia University, New York, p. 715.

11. Report of Independent Counsel in Re Edwin Meese III, James C. McKay, Washington, D.C., July 5, 1988.

12. Oliver Quayle & Company, "A Survey of the Political Climate in Maryland" (Study #117, September 1963), p. 42.

13. Federal Civilian Workforce Statistics: Employment Trends as of September 1992, Office of Personnel Management (PWI 9211); Political Appointees, Number of Noncareer SES and Schedule C Employees in Federal Agencies, General Accounting Office (GGD-92-101FS, June 1992).

14. H. L. Mencken, *Notes on Democracy* (New York: Alfred A. Knopf, 1926), p. 183.

15. Robert H. Jackson, "The Federal Prosecutor," *Journal of American Judicature Society* 24 (1940):19.

16. Report, Watergate Special Prosecutor Force (Washington, D.C.: U.S. Government Printing Office, 1975), p. 138.

17. Bennett L. Gershman, "A Moral Standard for the Prosecutor's Exercise of the Charging Discretion," *Fordham Urban Law Journal*, Vol. 20, No. 3 (1993):513.

18. Daniel J. Meador, *The President, the Attorney General, and the Department of Justice* (Charlottesville: White Burkett Miller Center for Public Affairs, University of Virginia, 1980), pp. 4–6; and Homer Cummings and Carl McFarland, *Federal Justice: Chapters in the History of Justice and the Federal Executive* (New York: Macmillan Company, 1937), pp. 15–16.

19. Act of September 24, 1789, ch. 20, 1 Stat. 73.

20. Meador, pp. 26–27.

21. Eric F. Goldman, *Rendezvous with Destiny* (New York: Alfred A. Knopf, 1953), pp. 44–51; and *Food and Drug Administration Backgrounder: Current and Useful Information from the FDA* (Washington, D.C., October 1991).

22. "Crossing State Lines: Criminal Law and the Federal Government," *Congressional Quarterly*, November 21, 1992, pp. 3676–78; and "Federal Criminal Code and Rules" (St. Paul, Minn.: West Publishing Company, 1989), p. 611.

23. John T. Noonan, Jr., *Bribes: The Intellectual History of a Moral Idea* (Berkeley/Los Angeles: University of California Press, 1987), p. 589; Gregory Howard Williams, "Good Government by Prosecutorial Decree: The Use and Abuse of Mail Fraud," *Arizona Law Review*, January 1990; Sarah Lyell, "Long Island Pet Cemetery Accused of Fraud Over Cremations: The FBI Tells of Mass Burnings and Pits in the Woods," *New York Times*, June 19, 1991, p. B1; and B. Drummond Ayres, Jr., "Fertility Doctor Accused of Fraud: U.S. Indictment Says He Used Own Sperm to Inseminate at Least 7 Patients," *New York Times*, November 21, 1991.

24. As explained in the Author's Note, existing Justice Department data regarding matters referred, matters declined, cases brought, final outcome, etc., have never been systematically explored until now. The section that follows is all based on the analysis of the Transactional Records Access Clearinghouse, a research organization created in 1989 by myself and Susan Long, a professor of quantitative methods at Syracuse University's School of Management.

25. FBI, "Crime in America, 1992" (Washington, D.C.), p. 58; Centers for Disease Control and Prevention and National Institutes for Occupational Safety and Health, "Fatal Injuries to Workers in the United States: A Decade of Surveillance, 1980–89" (Washington, D.C., August 1993), p. 5; Philip J. Landrigan and Dean B. Baker, "The Recognition and Control of Occupational Disease," *Journal of the American Medical Association*, Vol. 266, No. 5 (August 7, 1991):676–80.

26. Raymond J. Michalowski, *Order, Law, and Crime: An Introduction to Criminology* (New York: Random House, 1985), p. 331.

27. Ibid., pp. 3–4; and Philip Shabecoff, "Occupational Safety and Health Administration Reports Its Investigation," *New York Times*, June 9, 1987, p 1.

28. Interview with the author, September 14, 1994, Susan Fleming, Public Affairs Office, Occupational Safety and Health Administration.

29. Justice Department enforcement statistics provided the House Judiciary Subcommittee on Crime and Criminal Justice during a May 28, 1992, hearing on federal enforcement of the Occupational Safety and Health Act of 1970.

CHAPTER TWO: BEYOND THE FRINGE

1. *United States v. Shell Oil Co.* and *State of Colorado v. United States,*
Civ. Actions No. 83-C-2379 and 83-C-2386 (D. Colo.), official transcript at 20
(June 24, 1988).
2. *United States v. Shell Oil Co.,* Civ. Action No. 83-C-2379 (D. Colo.), official transcript at 10–11 (June 30, 1988).
3. *Daigle v. Shell Oil Co.,* 972 F.2d 1527, 1531 (10th Circuit 1992).
4. *State of Colorado v. United States Department of Army,* 707 F. Supp.
1562, at 1570 (D. Colo. Feb. 24, 1989).
5. September 10, 1964, letter from C. D. DeLoach to William D. Moyers,
Vol. 6, Hearings Before the Senate Select Committee to Study Governmental
Operations with Respect to Intelligence Activities, November 18, 19, and December 2, 3, 9, 10 and 11, 1975, *Federal Bureau of Investigation,* p. 510.
6. Special Squad Memorandum, C. D. DeLoach to Mr. Mohr, August 29,
1964, Senate Intelligence Committee, pp. 495–502.
7. Special Squad Memorandum, H. N. Bassett to Mr. Callahan, January 29,
1975, Senate Intelligence Committee, pp. 503–09.
8. January 29, 1975, memo from H. N. Bassett to Mr. Callahan, Special
Squad at Democratic National Convention, Atlantic City, New Jersey,
8/22–28/64, p. 4.
9. Ibid., p. 3.
10. FBI Report, January 31, 1975, Senate Intelligence Committee, p. 539.
11. Ibid., p. 720.
12. Transcript, *An Essay on Watergate,* "Bill Moyers' Journal," October 31,
1973.
13. In an October 21, 1994, letter to the author, Moyers declined to be interviewed about the DeLoach operation "primarily because I can't trust my
memory and have wanted to be sure, if and when I wrote or spoke at all, there
would be documentary evidence to reinforce my remembrance." Along with
his refusal, however, Moyers included a densely detailed advertisement that
he personally had taken in *The New Republic,* on October 7, 1991. In this ad,
Moyers argued—as has the FBI—that the special squad was in Atlantic City
because Johnson was afraid he might be assassinated. Moyers also asserted
that not one of the FBI reports of that period cited in David Garrow's book,
The FBI and Martin Luther King, was addressed to him.
14. "Impeachment of Richard M. Nixon, President of the United States,"
Report of the House Judiciary Committee, August 20, 1974, p. 3.
15. Donald Johnson, "The Political Career of A. Mitchell Palmer," *Pennsylvania History,* Vol. 25, No. 4 (October 1958):351.
16. Stanley Coben, *A. Mitchell Palmer: Politician* (New York: Columbia
University Press, 1963), pp. 158–59.
17. Ibid., pp. 159–60.
18. Christopher N. May, *In the Name of War: Judicial Review and the War
Powers Since 1918* (Cambridge, Mass.: Harvard University Press, 1989), p.
113.
19. Ibid., p. 82.
20. Ibid., p. 119.

21. Ibid., p. 114.

22. Ibid., p. 118.

23. *United States v. L. Cohen Grocery Co.*, 255 U.S. 81 (1921).

24. Author interviews with Thomas McBride and Henry Ruth; Gerald A. Renner, "Profile of Two Modern Gangbusters: McBride and Ruth—Double Trouble," *Reading Eagle*, January 24, 1964; Maurice Carroll, "A Picture of Reading: A Reformed Pennsylvania City With Racketeers 'Waiting in the Wing,' " *New York Times*, May 15, 1967, p. 47.

25. Richard Nixon to Robert L. Meyer, December 15, 1971, Executive File G 17-12/St/A, States and Territories Appointments, Nixon Presidential Papers, National Archives and Records Administration.

26. Gene Blake and Howard Hertel, "Transcript Released in L.A. 'Mistake' Slayings," *Los Angeles Times*, May 9, 1971, p. C1.

27. Howard Hertel, "40 Wounds Found in Body of Mexican Slain by Policemen," *Los Angeles Times*, August 18, 1970, p. 3.

28. Lee Dye, "Police Kill Two Men by Mistake; Bullets Rip Near Baby's Crib," *Los Angeles Times*, July 18, 1970, p. 1.

29. Doug Shult, "Seven Policemen Charged in Killing of Mexican Pair in Raid," *Los Angeles Times*, July 22, 1920.

30. "Los Angeles: The Chief," *Newsweek*, April 26, 1971, p. 31.

31. Gene Blake, "Politics Caused Him to Resign as U.S. Attorney, Meyer Says," *Los Angeles Times*, January 19, 1972, p. 1.

32. FBI Summary, Interview of Attorney General Griffin Bell by Special Agent Thomas J. Morris, date of transcription, February 16, 1978.

33. FBI Summary, Interview of Jimmy Carter, President of the United States, by Special Agent Thomas J. Morris, date of transcription, March 29, 1978.

34. Griffin Bell with Ronald J. Ostrow, *Taking Care of the Law* (New York: William Morrow & Company, Inc., 1982), pp. 210–11.

35. FBI Summary, Interview of William B. Gray, U.S. Attorney for Vermont, by Thomas J. Morris, date of transcription, March 27, 1978.

36. Bell, pp. 182–83.

37. Application and Affidavit for Search Warrant, The Rocky Flats Plant, U.S. Department of Energy, Golden, Colorado, signed on June 5, 1989, by Jon S. Lipsky, Special Agent, FBI and Subcommittee on Investigations and Oversight, House Committee on Science, Space and Technology, *The Prosecution of Environmental Crimes at the Department of Energy's Rocky Flats Facility* (Washington, D.C., January 4, 1993), p. 10.

38. General Accounting Office, *Nuclear Safety and Health: Problems with Cleaning Up the Solar Ponds at Rocky Flats* (Washington, D.C., January 1991), p. 2.

39. *Background Information Sheet*, prepared by Bette K. Bushell for twelve members of the special grand jury investigating Rocky Flats, November 18, 1992, p. 2.

40. Bryan Abas, "The Story of the Rocky Flats Grand Jury," *Westward*, September 30–October 6, 1962, p. 1.

41. "Readings: [Grand Jury Report] The Rocky Flats Cover-Up, Continued," *Harper's Magazine*, December 1992, p. 19.

42. "DOJ Says House Rocky Flats Report 'Inaccurate, Misleading, Incom-

plete,' " *Daily Environment Report* (Washington, D.C.: Bureau of National Affairs, January 16, 1993), p. A9.

CHAPTER THREE: SEVEN BAD WAYS TO RUN AN AGENCY

1. Ramsey Clark, *Crime in America: Observations on Its Nature, Causes, Prevention and Control* (New York: Simon & Schuster, 1970), p. 192.

2. Interview with the author, April 26, 1994.

3. Interview with the author, May 5, 1994.

4. Memorandum for the Attorney General, from Anthony C. Moscato, director, Executive Office of United States Attorneys: Allocation Process for Assistant United States Attorney Positions, May 14, 1994, p. 1.

5. Homer Cummings and Carl McFarland, *Federal Justice: Chapters in the History of Justice and the Federal Executive* (New York: Macmillan Company, 1937), pp. 218–27.

6. Executive Order 11396, February 7, 1968, *Coordination by the Attorney General of Federal Law Enforcement and Crime Prevention Programs*, Title 18, Crime and Criminal Procedures, Chapt. 1—General Provisions; Federal Criminal Code and Rules (St. Paul, Minn.: West Publishing Company, 1993), pp. 378–79.

7. General Accounting Office, "U.S. Attorneys: More Accountability for Implementing Priority Programs Is Desirable" (GGD-95-150, Washington, D.C., June 23, 1995), pp. 8–9.

8. Interview with the author, July 5, 1994.

9. Interview with the author, May 20, 1993.

10. Comprehensive District Law Enforcement Plan, Northern District of Illinois, June 17, 1982, obtained under a Freedom of Information Act request, November 15, 1990.

11. Justice Department Management Division, "Government Performance and Results Act—Purpose, Summary of Major Provisions and Legislative Documents," 1993.

12. Susan B. Long, *Federal Environmental Litigation: The Processing of Criminal and Civil Environmental Matters by U.S. Attorney Offices in California During the Last Decade* (Syracuse, N.Y.: Transactional Access Records Clearinghouse, 1991).

13. Toby J. McIntosh, "Data Show Variance in Environment Cases Brought in Federal Districts in California," BNA California Environment Report, May 30, 1991, pp. C1–C5.

14. Interview with the author, July 27, 1993.

15. Interview with the author, November 14, 1994.

16. Summary and quotation drawn from Henry Mintzberg and Alexandra McHugh, "Strategy Formation in an Adhocracy," *Administrative Science Quarterly*, No. 30 (1985):160–97.

17. Interview with the author, May 5, 1994.

18. General Accounting Office, "Justice Department: Improved Management Processes Would Enhance Justice's Operation" (GGD-86-12, Washington, D.C., March 1986), pp. 20–21.

19. Harry Subin, Review of Departmental Policy on Dyer Act (18 U.S.C.

2312) Prosecutions (Justice Department Office of Criminal Justice, January 27, 1965), p. 1.

20. Ibid., p. 20.

21. Letter to the author, August 13, 1990.

22. Letter to the author from Harry I. Subin, August 13, 1990.

23. General Accounting Office, "U.S. Attorneys Do Not Prosecute Many Suspected Violators of Federal Law" (GGD-77-86, February 27, 1978), p. 15.

24. The deployment statistics cited here and in the subsequent discussion are all based on an analysis by Syracuse University's Transactional Records Access Clearinghouse. This analysis was completed in October 1993.

25. General Accounting Office, "Bank and Thrift Criminal Fraud: The Federal Commitment Could Be Broadened" (GAO/GGD-93-48, January 1993), p. 48.

26. General Accounting Office, "Greater Oversight and Uniformity Needed in U.S. Attorneys' Prosecutive Policies" (GGD-83-11, October 1982), p. 8.

27. Michael M. Phillips, "Big Cities Shortchanged on U.S. Attorneys, Study Says," *Miami Herald*, March 10, 1991, p. 10A.

28. Hearing of the House Government Operations Subcommittee on Information, Justice, Transportation, and Agriculture, October 14, 1993.

29. July 8, 1994, memorandum from Attorney General Janet Reno to all U.S. attorneys on the allocation of assistant U.S. attorney positions.

30. Memorandum to the Attorney General, June 20, 1994, from Kent Walker: Allocation of Assistant United States Attorneys, p. 4.

31. Memorandum for the Attorney General, November 7, 1994, from Kent Walker: Progress on Allocation Model, Appendix A.

32. Interview with the author, April 20, anonymity requested.

33. Complaint for Injunctive Relief and Writ of Possession, *United States v. Charles Hayes*, August 30, 1990, p. 6.

34. Transcript of recorded conversation between Ron Beckman and Charles Hayes, August 20, 1990, certified by FBI Agent Terrence Moore.

35. Declaration of James Underwood, United States Marshals Service, *United States v. Charles Hayes*, undated.

36. Deposition, *United States v. Charles Hayes*, September 6, 1990, Vol. 2, pp. 78–80.

37. *United States v. Charles Hayes*, Civ Action 90-175, U.S. District Court, Eastern District of Kentucky, Stipulation for Permanent Third Party Injunction and Order, October 29, 1990.

38. Milton J. Socolar, special assistant to the Comptroller General, testimony before the House Judiciary Committee, July 11, 1991.

39. Correspondence from Harry H. Flickinger, assistant attorney general for administration, to Kathryn Seddon, professional staff member, House Government Operations Subcommittee on Information, Justice, Transportation, and Agriculture, March 1, 1991.

40. Justice Department Office of Inspector General, "Audit Report: The Federal Bureau of Investigation's Automatic Data Processing General Controls," September 1990, p. 5.

41. Testimony of Laurie E. Ekstrand, Administration of Justice Issues, General Accounting Office, before the House Government Operations Subcommittee on Information, Justice, Transportation, Agriculture, July 23, 1993, p. 29.

42. Robert D. Hershey, Jr., "IRS Staff Cited in Snoopings: 1,300 Workers Have Been Investigated," *New York Times*, July 19, 1994, p. D1.

43. General Accounting Office, "Computer Security: DEA Is Not Adequately Protecting National Security Information" (GAO/IMTEC-92-31, February 1992).

44. John Crewdson, *The Tarnished Door: The New Immigrants and the Transformation of America* (New York: Times Books, 1983), pp. 113–14.

45. General Accounting Office, *Information Management: Immigration and Naturalization Service Lacks Ready Access to Essential Data* (IMTEC-90-75, September 1990); *Financial Management: INS Lacks Accountability and Controls Over Its Resources* (AFMD-91-20, January 1991); *Immigration Management: Strong Leadership and Management Reforms Needed to Address Serious Problems*, (GGD-91-28), *Immigration Control: The Central File Needs to Be More Accurate* (GGD-92-20, January 1992); *Border Patrol: Southwest Border Enforcement Affected by Mission Expansion and Budget* (GGD-92-66).

46. Patrick J. McDonnell and Sebastian Rottella, "When Agents Cross Over the Borderline: Charges of Wrongdoing in Border Patrol Have Forced Even Loyalists to Call for Reforms," *Los Angeles Times*, April 22, 1993, p. 1.

CHAPTER FOUR: THE NUMBERS GAME

1. Louis Freeh, December 8, 1993, National Press Club, transcript by the Federal News Service.

2. Bureau of Justice Statistics, "Criminal Victimization in the United States, 1991" (NCJ-139563, Washington, D.C., December 1992), p. 122.

3. Report from Michael Rand, Bureau of Justice Statistics, to the author, April 7, 1994.

4. Steve Cindrich, National Insurance Crime Bureau, "Vehicle Theft Down in Nation's Largest Cities," February 1994; and Paul Zajac, American Automobile Manufacturers Association, "Annual Report," March 1994.

5. Federal Bureau of Investigation, *Crime in the United States, 1992 Uniform Crime Reports* (Washington, D.C., October 1993), p. 1.

6. December 27, 1993, inquiry letter from Don Edwards, chairman of the House Judiciary Subcommittee on Civil and Constitutional Rights, to Louis Freeh and Freeh's February 24, 1994, response.

7. General Accounting Office, "Bank and Thrift Criminal Fraud: The Federal Commitment Could Be Broadened" (GGD-93-48, January 1993), p. 4.

8. Assistant Attorney General Lee Rawls to Assistant Comptroller General Richard L. Fogel, October 1, 1992, reprinted in ibid., pp. 95–113.

9. Interview with the author, March 18, 1994.

10. Interview with the author, March 16, 1994.

11. Interview with the author, March 22, 1994.

12. Interview with the author, March 24, 1994.

13. Federal Bureau of Investigation, *Crime in the United States, 1992 Uniform Crime Reports* (Washington, D.C., October 1993), p. v.

14. Interview with the author, April 11, 1994.

15. Interview with the author, April 1, 1994.

16. William M. Rokaw, James A. Mercy, and Jack C. Smith, "Comparing Death Certificate Data with FBI Crime Reporting Statistics on U.S. Homicides," *Public Health Reports*, September–October 1990.

17. Interview with the author, April 10, 1994.

18. Special 1994 analysis, Lois A. Fingerhut, Office of Analysis and Epidemiology, National Center for Health Statistics.

19. Interview with the author, May 6, 1994.

20. Philip J. Cook, "The Technology of Personal Violence," *Crime and Justice, A Review of Research*, vol. 14 (Chicago: University of Chicago Press, 1991), p. 5.

21. Ibid., p. 44.

22. Albert J. Reiss, Jr., and Jeffrey A. Roth, eds., *Understanding and Preventing Violence* (Washington, D.C.: National Academy Press, 1993), pp. 52–53.

23. "Crime Was Top TV News Story in 1993," *Media Monitor*, Center for Media and Public Affairs, Washington, D.C., January/February 1994.

24. Official FBI text, Louis Freeh speech to the American Law Institute, Washington, D.C., May 19, 1994.

25. Bureau of Justice Statistics, *Source Book of Criminal Justice Statistics* (Washington, D.C., 1993), p. 3.

26. Ibid., p. 608; and Marc Mauer, "Americans Behind Bars: One Year Later," report by The Sentencing Project, Washington, D.C., February 1992, p. 5.

27. Interview with the author, April 2, 1994.

28. "The Response to Rape," report by the Senate Judiciary Committee, Washington, D.C., May 1993.

29. FBI press release, May 1, 1994.

30. February 9, 1994, letter to President Clinton signed by twenty-eight Republican members of the House of Representatives including Newt Gingrich, Henry Hyde and Jim Sensenbreener.

CHAPTER FIVE: KEEPING TRACK OF THE AMERICAN PEOPLE: THE UNBLINKING EYE AND GIANT EAR

1. 1993 FBI Budget request to the White House Office of Management and Budget, officially classified SECRET, pp. 4–5.

2. Ibid., pp. 4–5.

3. FBI Memorandum, "Black Bag" Jobs, from W. C. Sullivan to C. D. DeLoach, July 19, 1966.

4. *Socialist Workers Party et al. v. The Attorney General of the United States*, 73 Civ 3160, pp. 95–97.

5. Kenneth C. Laudon and Kenneth L. Marr, "Productivity and the Enactment of a Macro Culture," International Conference on Information Systems, Vancouver, British Columbia, December 1994.

6. The profound involvement of the National Security Agency with the FBI is substantiated in numerous documents obtained from the NSA under the Freedom of Information Act by the Electronic Privacy Information Center. In an NSA memo entitled "Options to Address Encryption Effects on Law En-

forcement," which originally was classified as Top Secret, the author said the FBI and the NSA "had worked together to assure" that the technical standards promulgated by the federal government for encryption devices "are compatible with law enforcement requirements." Although the memo is undated, it appears to have been written in 1993.

7. Interview with the author, September 16, 1993.

8. Department of Justice Congressional Authorization and Budget Submissions, fiscal years 1988 through 1994.

9. Ibid., 4–10.

10. Ibid., 4–11.

11. Ibid.

12. Ibid., 4–17 and 18.

13. Ibid., 4–11.

14. Lucinda Franks, "To Catch a Judge: How the FBI Tracked Sol Wachtler," *The New Yorker*, December 21, 1993, p. 63.

15. Howard Blum, *Gangland: How the FBI Broke the Mob* (New York: Simon & Schuster, 1993), pp. 19–22.

16. Budget, 4–12.

17. Department of Justice, 1992 Congressional Authorization & Budget Submission, FBI Section, Vol. 2, p. 67.

18. The NSA's intense involvement in writing the proposed statute is established by twelve separate memos in which Fritz Fielding, an NSA lawyer, was sent draft versions of the legislation during the yearlong development process. The memos, dating from July 5, 1991, to June 5, 1992, were obtained on November 16, 1993, by Computer Professionals for Social Responsibility in response to a request under the Freedom of Information Act. The FBI's summary description of the legislation is drawn from an undated bureau document that accompanied the bill when it was sent to Congress.

19. Marc Rotenberg, "To Tap or Not to Tap," *Communications of the ACM*, Vol. 36, No. 3 (March 1993):36–39.

20. John Schwartz, "Industry Group Fights Wiretap Proposal," *Washington Post*, March 12, 1994, p. C1.

21. FBI Director Louis J. Freeh, speech to the National Press Club, December 8, 1993, Federal News Service Transcript, and speech to the Chicago Executive Club, February 17, 1994, Reuters News Service.

22. Budget, 4-1 and 4-2.

23. Clipper Chip Statement, Office of the White House, April 16, 1993.

24. Subcommittee on Science, House Science, Space and Technology Committee, May 11, 1993.

25. Interview with the author, April 18, 1994.

26. William Safire, "Sink the Clipper Chip," *New York Times*, February 14, 1994, p. A17.

27. Transcript of Freeh's remarks at the September 23, 1994, "Global Cryptography Conference," provided by the FBI to conference attendee A. Michael Fromkin, associate professor of law, University of Miami Law School.

28. Louis J. Freeh, FBI Director, testimony before the House Judiciary Subcommittee on Crime, March 30, 1995.

29. *Meyer v. Nebraska*, 262 U.S. 390, 401 (1923).

30. *Yniguez v. Arizonans*, 42 F. 3rd 1217 (9th Cir. 1995).

31. Based partly on a special study of the *Report on Applications for Orders*

Authorizing or Approving the Interception of Wire, Aural or Electronic Communications, an annual statistical compilation published by the Administrative Office of the U.S. Courts about eavesdropping under Title III of the Omnibus Crime Control and Safe Street Act of 1968. The study was undertaken by David Banisar, a policy analyst with Computer Professionals for Social Responsibility. The number of applications to conduct eavesdropping operations under the Foreign Intelligence Surveillance Act are reported to the Permanent Select Committee on Intelligence of the House of Representatives.

32. Department of Justice, 1991 Congressional Authorization & Budget Submission, Vol. 2, FBI Section, p. 64.

33. The Report of the Privacy Protection Study Commission, *Personal Privacy in an Information Society* (Washington, D.C., 1977), p. 7.

34. *Smith v. Maryland*, 442 U.S. 735 (1979).

35. Annual Justice Department letter reports to the chairman of the House Judiciary Committee.

36. Department of Justice, 1994 Congressional Authorization & Budget Submission, Vol. 2, DEA Section, p. 47.

37. Alecia Swasy, *Soap Opera: The Inside Story of Procter & Gamble* (New York: Times Books, 1993), pp. 295–96.

38. Ibid., pp. 297–301.

39. Gregory Millman, "How the IRS Charted a Reporter's Network of Sources," *The IRE Journal*, November–December 1992, p. 13.

40. Bari/Cherney discovery: Airtel, November 21, 1991, from senior agent-in-charge, San Francisco.

41. Bari/Cherney discovery: FBI document 174A-90788, marked confidential, p. 2.

42. Roy Neel, president of the United States Telephone Association, before the Subcommittee on Telecommunications and Finance, House Energy and Commerce Committee, September 13, 1994.

43. Sales material provided by Professor Mary J. Culnan, School of Business, Georgetown University, Washington, D.C.

44. David Burnham, *A Law Unto Itself: The IRS and the Abuse of Power* (New York: Vintage, 1989), pp. 338–341.

45. Ray Schultz, "FBI Said to Seek Compiled Lists for Use in Its Field Investigations," *DM News*, April 20, 1992, pp. 1 and 8.

46. Testimony of John Cleary, president of Donnelley Marketing Inc., before the House Government Operations Subcommittee on Information, Justice, Transportation, and Agriculture, May 14, 1992.

47. Department of Justice, 1994 Congressional Authorization & Budget Submission, Vol. 2, DEA Section, p. 47.

48. Determination and Finding by the Administrator of the Drug Enforcement Administration, Robert C. Bonner, November 11, 1991.

49. Donald P. Quinn, assistant administrator, Operational Support Division, DEA, to Russell Hayman, executive assistant, "Procurement of Phone Subscriber Database [Tape]," January 24, 1992.

50. Richard Kay to Donald P. Quinn, Price Information, Rental of Crisscross/Reverse Telephone Directories, February, 22, 1991.

51. From Operations Systems Unit, DEA, to Systems Policy Staff, Justice Department, Automated National Telephone Directory, undated.

52. Automated National Telephone Directory.

53. Department of Justice, 1993 Congressional Authorization & Budget Submission, Vol. 2, FBI Section, p. 59.

CHAPTER SIX: THE JUSTICE DEPARTMENT'S BIG, BAD, DUMB WAR ON DRUGS

1. Interview with the author, December 9, 1994. The first full account disclosing the FBI's curious role in the undermining of a small section of Dorchester was written by Kevin Cullen, one of New England's best investigative reporters, and appeared on page one of the *Boston Sunday Globe* on May 13, 1990.

2. Kevin Cullen, "Neighborhood Pays High Price for Presence of FBI Informant," *Boston Globe*, May 13, 1990, p. 1.

3. Interview with the author, December 10, 1994.

4. Interview with the author, December 10, 1994.

5. Interview with the author, December 11, 1994.

6. Interview with the author, December 1, 1994.

7. Joseph Donald McNamara, "Organizational Decision Making and Public Policy, an Analysis of Police Enforcement Strategy," Diss. John Fitzgerald School of Government, Harvard University, 1973, p. 216.

8. Ibid., p. 190.

9. Edward J. Epstein, *Agency of Fear: Opiates and Political Power in America* (New York: G.P. Putnam's Sons, 1977), p. 61.

10. Public Papers of the Presidents of the United States, Richard Nixon, 1969 (Government Printing Office, Washington, D.C., 1971), p. 515.

11. Public Papers of the Presidents of the United States, Richard Nixon, 1971 (Government Printing Office, Washington, D.C., 1972), pp. 739–49.

12. Institute for Defense Analysis, "Quantitative Analysis of the Heroin Addiction Problem" (Washington, D.C., December 1972), p. 7.

13. General Accounting Office, "Gains Made in Controlling Illegal Drugs, Yet the Drug Trade Flourishes" (Washington, D.C., October 25, 1979), p. 15.

14. Testimony of William J. Anderson, Assistant Comptroller General, before the House Government Operations Subcommittee on Information, Justice, Transportation, and Agriculture, September 9, 1986.

15. General Accounting Office, "Drug Control: U.S. International Narcotics Control Activities" (Washington, D.C., March 1988), p. 22.

16. Mark A. R. Kleiman, *Against Excess: Drug Policy for Results* (New York: Basic Books, 1992), p. 135.

17. Ibid., p. 136.

18. Max Frankel, "O.K., Call It War," *New York Times Sunday Magazine*, December 17, 1994.

19. Office of National Drug Control Policy, "National Drug Control Strategy: Reclaiming Our Communities from Drugs and Violence," February 1994, pp. 13–14.

20. Alfred Blumstein, "Making Rationality Relevant—The American Society of Criminology 1992 Presidential Address," *Criminology*, Vol. 31, No. 1 (February 1993):7.

21. Inaugural Address by George Bush, January 20, 1989, Federal News Service, Federal Information Corporation.

22. William J. Clinton, Remarks on the Swearing-In of National Drug Control Policy Director Lee Brown, July 1, 1993, Book One, Public Papers of the President of the United States, 1993 (Washington, D.C.: Government Printing Office, 1994), pp. 967–68.

23. National Drug Control Strategy, Budget Summary, the White House, pp. 184–87.

24. Bureau of Justice Statistics, "Drugs, Crime, and the Justice System" (Washington, D.C., 1992), p. 128.

25. Douglas C. McDonald and Kenneth B. Carlson, "Sentencing in the Federal Courts: Does Race Matter?" (Bureau of Justice Statistics, NCJ-145328, Washington, D.C., December 1993), p. 83.

26. Interview with the author, November 14, 1994.

27. The Comprehensive Crime Control Act of 1984 (found at 21 U.S.C. sec. 88i [a] [7]).

28. *United States of America v. One Mercedes Benz Roadster*, No. 89 C 3084, United States District Court for the Northern District of Illinois. 1991 U.S. Dist LEXIS 2757.

29. John Dillin, "When Federal Drug Laws Create Havoc for Citizens," *The Christian Science Monitor*, September 28, 1993.

30. Interview with the author, January 24, 1995.

31. Andrew Schneider and Mary Pat Flaherty, "Presumed Guilty: The Law's Victims in the War on Drugs," *Pittsburgh Press*, August 11–16, 1991.

32. U.S. Department of Justice, *Annual Report of the Department of Justice Asset Forfeiture Program, Fiscal Year 1993*, Washington, D.C., June 27, 1994.

33. Henry J. Hyde, *Forfeiting Our Property Rights: Is Your Property Safe From Seizure?* (Washington, D.C., Cato Institute, 1995), p. 10.

34. Letter, Assistant Attorney General W. Lee Rawls, to Representative John Conyers, Jr., chairman of the House Government Operations Committee, October 10, 1991.

35. Hyde, pp. 1–2.

36. Fiscal Year 1993 Report, p. 15.

37. Hyde, p. 9.

38. *Richard V. Austin v. United States of America*, Supreme Court, No. 92-6073, amicus curiae brief of the National Association of Criminal Defense Lawyers, p. 5.

39. Executive Office for U.S. Attorneys, Department of Justice, U.S. Attorney's Bulletin 214, July 15, 1989.

40. Executive Office for U.S. Attorneys, Department of Justice, U.S. Attorney's Bulletin 180, August 15, 1990.

41. *Fiscal Year 1993 Report*, p. 19.

42. Blumstein.

43. McDonald and Carlson.

44. Office of Technology Assessment, Congress of the United States, Substance Abuse and Addiction (Washington D.C., September 1994), pp. 91–94.

45. December 16, 1994, memorandum from Jan Chaiken, director of the Bureau of Justice Statistics, to Phyliss Newton, staff director, U.S. Sentencing Commission.

46. McDonald and Carlson, p. 181.

47. Ibid., p. 38.

48. Special Report to Congress: Cocaine and Federal Sentencing Policy, United States Sentencing Commission, December 1994 (Second Draft), Chapt. 6, p. 11.

49. 132 Cong. Rec 26,436 (September 26, 1988).

50. Special Report to Congress, p. 11.

51. United States Sentencing Commission, Special Report to the Congress: Cocaine and Federal Sentencing Policy, February 1995, p. 196.

52. "Reno Backs Strict Sentences for Sellers of Crack Cocaine," *The New York Times*, April 16, 1995.

53. Staff Report by the Subcommittee on Civil and Constitutional Rights, House Judiciary Committee, "Racial Disparities in Federal Death Penalty Prosecutions, 1988–1994," March 1994.

54. Blumstein, pp. 4–5.

55. Ibid., p. 5.

56. Report of the Commission to Investigate Allegations of Corruption and the City's Anti-Corruption Procedures (New York, December 26, 1972) p. 105.

57. Ibid., p. 107.

58. Ronald L. Soble, "Former DEA Agent Convicted," *Los Angeles Times*, April 17, 1991, p. 1.

59. Ronald L. Soble, "Agent Is Indicted on Theft Charges," *Los Angeles Times*, October 5, 1990, p. B1.

60. Michael Levine, "Going Bad," *Spin Magazine*, June 1991, p. 58.

61. Interview with the author, November 15, 1994.

62. Pierre Thomas, "$14.6 Billion Sought to Fight Drugs," *Washington Post*, February 8, 1995, p. A7.

63. Daniel Patrick Moynihan, "Iatrogenic Government: Social Policy and Drug Research," *The American Scholar*, Summer 1993, p. 354.

64. Kurt L. Schmoke, "Back to the Future: The Public Health System's Lead Role in Fighting Drug Abuse," *The Humanist*, September/October 1990, p. 28.

65. Moynihan, p. 360.

CHAPTER SEVEN: CORPORATE ENFORCEMENT?

1. Statements asserting the Justice Department's concern about white-collar crime abound. Benjamin R. Civiletti, President Carter's second attorney general, told the Senate Judiciary Committee on March 11, 1980, that combating white-collar and organized crime and fraud against the government were among his "high priority programs." This kind of rhetoric did not die with the election of the intensely pro-business administrations of Presidents Reagan and Bush. William French Smith, Reagan's first attorney general, told the *New York Times* on January 16, 1981, that after the problem of violent criminal behavior, white-collar crime was his top priority. Attorney General Dick Thornburgh, in an address to the Justice Department staff on October 7, 1988, said a "major push against white-collar crime" and "an unremitting effort against public corruption" were two of the five most important problems confronting department prosecutors. William Barr, President Bush's last attor-

ney general, said during his confirmation hearing before the Senate Judiciary Committee on November 12, 1991, that white-collar crime—along with drugs, violent crime and civil rights—would be on the top of his agenda during his time at the Justice Department.

2. Sutherland first presented his conception in a talk to the annual meeting of the American Sociological Society in Philadelphia on December 27, 1939. A sanitized version of his monograph, "White Collar Crime," was published ten years later by Dryden Press. Because of libel fears, the publisher had insisted that the names of the corporate offenders Sutherland had identified be deleted from the 1949 volume. In 1983, with an introduction from Gilbert Geis and Colin Goff, Yale University Press published Sutherland's original manuscript, "White Collar Crime: The Uncut Version."

3. Sutherland, p. 9.

4. Marshall B. Clinard, *Illegal Corporate Behavior* (Washington, D.C.: U.S. Justice Department, October 1979), p. 16.

5. Bureau of Justice Statistics, Justice Department, *National Crime Victimization Report, 1991*, October 29, 1992, p. 3.

6. Wallace F. Janssen, "The U.S. Food and Drug Law: How It Came, How It Works," reprint from *FDA Consumer Magazine*, Department of Health and Human Services Publication (FDA 92–1054).

7. July 28, 1992, testimony before the Senate Judiciary Committee by Janet L. Shickles, Health Financing and Policy Issues, Human Resources Division, General Accounting Office.

8. June 22, 1992, and June 10, 1993, press releases by the U.S. attorney for the Northern District of Indiana about the indictment and agreement to plead guilty of Michael Walton.

9. Interview with Daniel R. Anderson, director of Maryland's Medicaid Fraud Unit, April 22, 1993.

10. February 3, 1992, Department of Justice press release, "Barr Announces Move to Strengthen Health Care Fraud Initiatives," and accompanying report about the plan by Acting Deputy Attorney General George J. Terwilliger III.

11. General Accounting Office, "Health Insurance Fraud" (GAO/HRD-92-69, 1992), p. 14.

12. Analysis of TRAC data by the author.

13. The ponderous response of the Justice Department to the savings and loan scandals has been discussed in a number of books and congressional reports. One of the most penetrating explorations of this failure was achieved during a series of hearings undertaken by the Commerce, Consumer, and Monetary Affairs Subcommittee of the House Government Operations Committee. The subcommittee published reports on the problems in 1988 and 1990. Perhaps the most sophisticated exploration of the Justice Department's handling of the savings and loan was by the General Accounting Office, "Bank and Thrift Criminal Fraud: The Federal Commitment Could Be Broadened" (GAO/GGD-93-48, January 1993).

14. The House Judiciary Subcommittee on Crime held exhaustive hearings on the handling of the E.F. Hutton case. The subcommittee published a detailed analysis of its findings in a December 1986 report.

15. The BCCI affair is still unfolding. Beginning in July 1991, the House Judiciary Subcommittee on Crime began investigating the response of the Jus-

tice Department and other federal agencies to leads it had been receiving about the problem bank for a number of years. The subcommittee published a staff report on the matter on September 5, 1991.

16. Clinard, p. xxii.

17. Interview with the author, October 18, 1990. Stockton in recent years has been an investigator on the staff of the oversight subcommittee of the House Energy and Commerce Committee.

18. The story of Caudle's downfall was documented on the front pages of the *New York Times*, on November 17, 1951, June 15, 1956, and March 6, 1957.

19. Report of the House Committee on the Judiciary, *Impeachment of Richard M. Nixon, President of the United States* (Washington, D.C., August 20, 1974), pp. 174–76.

20. "Bush's Ruling Class," *Common Cause Magazine*, April/May/June, 1992, pp. 11–12. The article was prepared by a team of Common Cause reporters. The lead reporter on the killing of the criminal tax case against the Southern Co. was Jeffrey Denny.

21. Report of the House Judiciary Subcommittee on Antitrust, Consent Decree Program of the Department of Justice (Washington, D.C., January 1959), p. 47.

22. The story of AT&T's successful campaign to block the Justice Department's effort to force it to sell Western Electric was the subject of a lengthy investigation by the antitrust subcommittee of the House Judiciary Committee into how and why the department had entered into a number of antitrust consent decrees that were highly favorable to industry. AT&T, therefore, was one of the subcommittee's case studies. The subcommittee report, *Consent Decree Program of the Department of Justice*, was published on January 30, 1959. Herbert Brownell, still an active New York lawyer, talked about some aspects of the settlement during an interview with the author on February 20, 1992.

23. Consent decree report, pp. 52–55.

24. Ibid., pp. 66–67.

25. Ibid., p. 85.

26. Ibid., p. 97.

27. Correspondence of Attorney General Charles J. Bonaparte, Manuscript Division, Library of Congress.

28. *New York Times*, March 4, 1911, p. 1.

29. Final Report of Investigation of G.D. Searle Company, Searle Investigation Task Force, FDA, Department of Health, Education and Welfare, March 24, 1976, p. 1.

30. Ibid., p. 10.

31. Letter from Richard A. Merrill, chief counsel, Food and Drug Administration, to Samuel K. Skinner, U.S. attorney, April 7, 1976.

32. Merrill to Skinner, January 10, 1977, and undated handwritten notes taken during the February 2, 1977, conference listing all attendees.

33. Marjorie Williams, "The President's Straight Man," *Washington Post Magazine*, June 7, 1992, pp. 10–36.

34. Memo from Samuel K. Skinner to William Conlon and Fred Branding, March 8, 1977, and chronology of events prepared by the staff of Senator

Howard Metzenbaum, Democrat of Ohio, made available to the author from the office of Senator Metzenbaum.

35. Internal Justice Department memo from Charles P. Kocoras, First Assistant U.S. attorney, to Samuel K. Skinner, U.S. attorney, re the G.D. Searle Company, April 13, 1977. Copies to Bill Conlon and Fred Branding.

36. For a discussion of this issue see Hearing of the Senate Committee on Commerce, Science and Transportation of the nomination of Samuel K. Skinner to secretary of transportation, January 25, 1989, pp. 21–22.

37. Letter from U.S. Attorney Thomas P. Sullivan to Donald Kennedy, commissioner of the Food and Drug Administration, January 29, 1979.

38. Hearings of the Senate Committee on Commerce, pp. 22–23.

39. Interview of William Conlon by John P. Flannery, special counsel to Senator Howard Metzenbaum.

40. August 7, 1969, letter from President Nixon to Richard E. Berlin, president and chief executive of the Hearst Corporation; September 23, 1969, memo from President Nixon to Bob Haldeman and Peter Flanigan; Morton Mintz and Jerry S. Cohen, *America, Inc.* (New York: Dell, 1971), p. 30.

41. Morton Mintz, "Justice Department Snubbed on Papers Bill," *Washington Post*, September 26, 1969, p. A1.

42. The Failing Newspaper Act, hearing before the Subcommittee on Antitrust and Monopoly, Senate Judiciary Committee, Part 5, Excerpts from hearings before the House Antitrust Subcommittee, March 13, 14, 15 and April 9.

43. Excerpts from House hearing, p. 2516.

44. Excerpt from House hearing, p. 2457.

45. *Combating Fraud, Abuse and Misconduct in the Nation's Financial Institutions: Current Federal Efforts Are Inadequate*, Report of the House Government Operations Subcommittee on Commerce, Consumer, and Monetary Affairs, October 13, 1988, Washington, D.C., p. 34.

46. Ibid., p. 18.

47. *The U.S. Government's War Against Fraud, Abuse and Misconduct in Financial Institutions: Winning Some Battles But Losing the War*, House Subcommittee on Commerce, Consumer, and Monetary Affairs, November 15, 1990, pp. 72–73.

48. Dee Gill and Jim Zook, "Frying the Little Fish: Fraud Probes Mostly Miss Bank, Thrift Execs," *Houston Chronicle*, October 7, 1990, p. 1.

49. 1990 House report, p. 75.

50. Ibid., p. 76.

51. 1988 House report, p. 19.

52. Staff Report, Subcommittee on Oversight and Investigations, House Committee on Oversight and Investigations, "The Department of Justice Undercutting the Environmental Protection Agency's Criminal Enforcement Program," September 9, 1992, p. 8. The problems at the Puregro facility were also described in a study by the George Washington University Environmental Crimes Project released on October 19, 1992, by Representative Charles E. Schumer, chairman of the Subcommittee on Crime and Criminal Justice of the House Judiciary Committee.

53. Ibid., p. 9.

54. Ibid., pp. 11–12.

55. Ibid., p. 4.
56. January 8, 1992, letter from Ken Eikenberry, attorney general of Washington, to Attorney General William P. Barr.
57. Staff Report, p. 1.
58. Sharon LaFraniere, "Pollution Leniency Alleged," *Washington Post*, September 10, 1992, p. A1.
59. Department of Justice, "Internal Review of the Department of Justice Environmental Crimes Program," March 10, 1994, p. 60.
60. Ibid., at p. 100, n.136.
61. Subcommittee on Oversight and Investigations, House Energy and Commerce Committee, "Damaging Disarray: Organizational Breakdown and Reform in the Justice Department's Environmental Crimes Program," December 1994, p. 97.
62. 1994 staff report, p. 164.
63. Marianne Lavelle, "Environmental Vise: Law, Compliance," *National Law Journal*, August 30, 1993, p. S1.

CHAPTER EIGHT: UNCIVIL WRONGS AND CIVIL RIGHTS

1. Interview with the author, October 4, 1994.
2. Provided the author by Arrington attorney Donald V. Watkins, August 17, 1992.
3. *In Re Grand Jury Proceedings and Subpoena directed to Richard Arrington, Jr., Mayor of the City of Birmingham, Ala. v. Frank Donaldson, U.S. Attorney for the Northern District of Alabama*, Petitioners' Exhibits, Vol. 3 of 4, Section CC.
4. Ward Churchill and Jim Vander Wall, *The Cointelpro Papers: Documents from the FBI's Secret Wars Against Dissent in the United States* (Boston, South End Press, 1990), pp. 92–93. FBI airtel, dated August 25, 1967, setting forth the goals of its COINTELPRO-Black Nationalist project.
5. *Hobson v. Wilson*, 377 F.2d 1 (D.C. Cir. 1984), at 22, quoting *Hampton v. Hanrahan*, 600 F.d 600 (7th Circuit. 1979).
6. Congressional Record, Washington, D.C., March 9, 1990, p. S 2538.
7. Ibid., March 9, 1990. pp. S2533–S2546.
8. *United States v. Gordon*, 817 F.2d 1538 (11th Cir. 1987).
9. Cathy Donelson, "Perry County Black Leaders Indicted on Vote Fraud Charges," *Journal and Advertiser*, January 26, 1985, p. 1, col. 4.
10. Alvin Benn, "Marion Three Cleared of Vote Fraud Charges," *Journal and Advertiser*, July 6, 1985, p. 1, col. 4.
11. Interview with the author, August 16, 1991.
12. Hearings before the United States Senate Judiciary Committee, Nomination of Jefferson B. Sessions III to be U.S. District Judge for the Southern District of Alabama, March 13, 19, 20 and May 6, 1986, pp. 28–29.
13. Department of Justice press release, September 22, 1984, p. 1.
14. U.S. Department of Justice, Criminal Division, Public Integrity Section, "Federal Prosecution of Election Offenses," 4th Edition (Washington, D.C., October 1984).
15. March 1, 1985, memo from Richard F. Allen to Thomas J. Burke, Assis-

tant Inspector General for Investigation. Subject: Harold Guy Hunt, State Executive Director, Alabama ACS, Montgomery, Ala.—Misconduct.

16. Report of Investigation, April 25, 1985, File number At-301-182W, on Misconduct and Prohibited Political Activities of Harold Guy Hunt, p. 1A.

17. Glynn Wilson, "Hunt Says Old Memo Won't Hurt Candidacy," *The Islander* (Gulf Shores, Alabama), April 4, 1990, p. 1A.

18. The theory of how overlapping motives may influence public policy was greatly informed by discussions with Thomas Byrne Edsall, a *Washington Post* political reporter. I approached Edsall after reading the book that he and his wife, Mary D. Edsall, wrote, *Chain Reaction: The Impact of Race, Rights and Taxes on American Politics* (New York: W.W. Norton & Company, 1991).

19. Confirmation hearings, Senate Judiciary Committee, November 12, 1991.

20. Hearing, House Appropriations Subcommittee on the Departments of Commerce, Justice, and State, The Judiciary, and Related Agencies, February 26, 1992, p. 91.

21. The civil rights enforcement data are drawn from two sources; statistical reports that the FBI includes in the "Justice Department Authority & Budget Submission," a yearly series, and detailed internal administrative records obtained from the Executive Office of the U.S. Attorneys. These records, provided to TRAC on computer tapes under the Freedom of Information Act, are supposed to provide detailed information about every criminal and civil matter referred to the Justice Department from 1975 to 1994.

22. John Dunne interview with the author, October 13, 1994.

21. Many of the details of this account were drawn from a Justice Department report dated June 18, 1982, by Robert N. Kwan, an attorney in the voting section of the Civil Rights Division. Kwan's analysis focused on the reapportionment of congressional districts in the state of Louisiana during the second half of 1981. The complete report was printed in the Senate Judiciary Committee's hearings of June 4, 5 and 18, 1985, on the nomination of William Bradford Reynolds to be the associate attorney general of the United States, Serial No. J-99-29, pp. 410–40.

23. Lani Guinier, "Keeping the Faith: Black Voters in the Post-Reagan Era," *Harvard Civil Rights–Civil Liberties Law Review*, Vol. 24 (1989):409, n.70.

24. Testimony before the Senate Judiciary Committee, June 5, 1985, confirmation hearings of William Bradford Reynolds to be associate attorney general of the United States, by Lani Guinier, NAACP Legal Defense and Educational Fund, p. 385.

25. Confidential portion of Section 5 Memorandum, Robert N. Kwan, Senate Judiciary Committee hearing on the nomination of William Bradford Reynolds to be associate attorney general, June 4, 5 and 18, 1985, p. 440.

26. Senate Judiciary Committee hearings, p. 439.

27. *Major v. Treen*, 574 F. Supp. 325 (E.D. La. 1983).

28. Affidavit, Paul G. Kirk, Jr., chairman of the Democratic National Committee, October 7, 1986, p. 2.

29. Settlement Stipulation, *Democratic National Committee v. Republican National Committee*, Civ. Actions No. 86-3972, Judge Dickinson R. Debevoise, July 27, 1987.

30. Order, *Democratic National Committee v. Republican National Committee,* Judge Dickinson R. Debevoise, November 5, 1990, p. 1.

31. Carl T. Rowan, *Dream Makers, Dream Breakers: The World of Justice Thurgood Marshall* (Boston: Little, Brown, 1993), p. 132.

32. J. Eugene Marans, *The Struggle for Federal Anti-Lynching Legislation—1933–1945* (March 1962 Honors Thesis, Department of History, Harvard College, Cambridge, Mass.), p. 33.

33. John T. Elliff, *The United States Department of Justice and Individual Rights: 1937–1962* (New York: Garland Publishing Company, 1987), p 66.

34. Marans, p. 56.

35. Ibid., p. 57.

36. Letter from Homer Cummings to FDR, March 20, 1935, quoted in Marans, p. 68.

37. "Kennedy's Civil Rights Program Hit by Rockefeller," *New York Times,* March 6, 1963, p. 6.

38. "President Rejects Charge by Rockefeller on Judges," *New York Times,* March 7, 1963, p. 1.

39. Victor Navasky, *Kennedy Justice* (New York: Atheneum, 1971), p. 244.

40. Ibid., pp. 244–45.

41. Ibid., pp. 251–52.

42. Ibid., p. 48.

43. The FBI involvement in the KKK beating of the Freedom Riders was told in a series of twelve FBI documents dated April 25, 1961, to May 23, 1961—some of which were directed to Hoover's office. The documents were ordered released to the Michigan American Civil Liberties Union by Federal District Judge Noel Fox and assembled and published by Jay Peterzell, then with the Center for National Security Studies, in March 1985.

44. Franklin D. Roosevelt Library, "Survey of Racial Conditions in the United States," Federal Bureau of Investigation, September 24, 1943.

45. Ibid., p. 418.

46. Ibid., p. 423.

47. "Racial Tension and Civil Rights," March 1, 1956, an appendix, John T. Elliff, *The United States Department of Justice and Individual Rights, 1937–1962* (New York: Garland Publishing Company, 1987), pp. 792–806.

48. Ibid., p. 792.

49. Michael Isikoff and Sharon LaFraniere, "FBI Settles Black Agents' Discrimination Charges," *Washington Post,* January 27, 1993, p. A12.

50. Kenneth O'Reilly and J. Jeffrey Mayhook, "Civil Rights and the FBI," *Human Rights,* Vo. 16, No. 32, American Bar Association, Spring 1989.

51. Jim Mulvaney, "In the Deep South Rape Charges Unearth a System in Disarray," *Newsday,* April 18, 1994, p 1.

CHAPTER NINE: IN THE NAME OF NATIONAL SECURITY

1. The story of Ramon Cernuda's struggle with U.S. Attorney Dexter Lehtinen is based on interviews with the Miami businessman and art collector, federal court filings by his attorney, a court order by U.S. District Court Judge Kenneth L. Ryskamp ordering the government to return the paintings,

conversations with a number of former assistant U.S. attorneys including Dick Gregorie and David Demaio and articles by Jeff Leen of the *Miami Herald*, Dan Christensen of the *Broward Review* and Myra MacPherson of the *Washington Post*.

2. Interview with the author, April 17, 1992.

3. During my investigation of the Cernuda raid, I made numerous attempts to reach Dexter Lehtinen by telephone, leaving messages for him at both his law office in Miami and the Washington office of his wife, Representative Ileana Ros-Lehtinen. On August 9, 1993, I mailed Lehtinen a letter at his office at 801 Brickell Avenue repeating my request for an interview. There has been no response to any of these inquiries.

4. Jeff Leen, "Tyrant or Target: When They Called Him Out of Control, Dexter Lehtinen Kept Silent. When They Called Him a Wife-Beater, He Denied It Without Elaboration. Now, the Most Powerful Man in South Florida Finally Talks," *Tropic*, February 29, 1992, p. 9.

5. Myra MacPherson, "The Great Cuban Art Bust," Style Section, *Washington Post*, August 24, 1989, p. C1.

6. Interviews by the author, January 22, 1992, and April 9, 1992.

7. Gladys Nieves, "Bush Meets Miami Legislator," *El Nuevo Herald*, September 8, 1989, p. 1.

8. 720 F. Supp. 1544 (S.D.Fl 1989).

9. Interviewed by the author, May 9, 1995.

10. John C. Miller, *Crisis in Freedom: The Alien and Sedition Acts* (Boston: Atlantic–Little, Brown, 1951) p. 13.

11. Ibid., p. 88.

12. Christopher N. May, *In the Name of War: Judicial Review and the War Powers Since 1918* (Cambridge, Mass.: Harvard University Press, 1989), p. 188.

13. Michael Linfield, *Freedom Under Fire* (Boston: South End Press, 1990), p. 29.

14. Homer Cummings and Carl McFarland, *Federal Justice: Chapters in the History of Justice and the Federal Executive* (New York: Macmillan Company, 1937), p. 191.

15. Edward Bates, *The Diary of Edward Bates* (Washington, D.C., Government Printing Office, 1933), p. 483.

16. Ibid.

17. James Speed, *Opinions of the Attorney General*, Vol. 11, (Washington, D.C., Government Printing Office), p. 804.

18. Ex parte Milligan, 71 U.S. 2; 18 L. Ed. 281 (1866).

19. *United States v. Rose Pastor Stokes*, 264 Fed. 18 (8th Ci., 1920).

20. Linfield, p. 45.

21. U.S. Senate, Hearings Before a Subcommittee of the Committee of the Judiciary, *Charges of Illegal Practices of the Department of Justice*, January 19 to March 3, 1921, pp. 49–53.

22. Athan G. Theoharis and John Stuart Cox, *The Boss: J. Edgar Hoover and the Great American Inquisition* (Philadelphia: Temple University Press, 1988), p. 56.

23. Stanley Coben, *A. Mitchell Palmer: Politician* (New York: Columbia University Press, 1963), p. 227.

24. *Colyer et al. v. Skeffington, Com'r of Immigration. Katzeff et al. v. Same* (Three Cases). In Re Harbatuk et al. In Re Mack et al., 265 F. 17.

25. Report of the Attorney General (Washington, D.C., Government Printing Office, December 11, 1920) p. 172.

26. Senate Judiciary hearings, p. 582.

27. Ibid., p. 580.

28. Clark M. Clifford, *American Relations with the Soviet Union* (Washington, D.C., Top Secret, September 24, 1946), text printed as Appendix A, Arthur Krock, *Memoirs: Sixty Years on the Firing Line* (New York: Funk & Wagnalls, 1968), pp. 419–82.

29. David Caute, *The Great Fear: The Anti-Communist Purge Under Truman and Eisenhower* (New York: Touchstone, Simon & Schuster, 1979), p. 268.

30. Ibid., p. 269.

31. *Socialist Workers Party v. the Attorney General of the United States*, 73 Civ. 3160, August 25, 1986, pp. 68–69.

32. Final Report of the Senate Select Committee to Study Governmental Operations with Respect to Intelligence Activities, Book III, Supplementary Detailed Staff Reports on Intelligence Activities and the Rights of Americans (Washington, D.C., 1976), p. 3.

33. William C. Sullivan, former assistant director, Book III, p. 7.

34. Women's Liberation Movement, Internal Security—Miscellaneous, Field Office Number BA 100-25325, Bureau File Number 100-453233, May 11, 1970.

35. Book III, footnote 24, p. 8.

36. Ward Churchill and Jim Vander Wall, *The COINTELPRO Papers: Documents from the FBI's Secret Wars Against Domestic Dissent* (Boston: South End Press, 1990), pp. 139–42.

37. General Accounting Office, *International Terrorism: FBI Investigates Domestic Activities to Identify Terrorists* (GGD-90-112, Washington, D.C., September 1990), p. 16.

38. Ross Gelbspan, *Break-ins, Death Threats and the FBI: The Covert War Against the Central American Movement* (Boston: South End Press, 1991), pp. 215–16.

39. Ibid., p. 218.

40. Interview with the author, January 15, 1992.

41. June 21, 1989, letter to Senator Dennis DeConcini, Democrat of Arizona, from John E. Collingwood, FBI Inspector-in-Charge, Congressional Affairs Office.

42. Duane Webster, executive director, Association of Research Libraries, hearings before the House Subcommittee on Civil and Constitutional Rights, June 20 and July 13, 1988, on *FBI Counterintelligence Visits to Libraries*, p. 11.

43. Congressman Don Edwards, "Reordering the Priorities of the FBI in Light of the End of the Cold War," *St. John's Law Review*, Vol. 59 (Winter 1991):65.

44. White House Draft, May 2, 1995, 104 Congress, 1st Session, Antiterrorism Amendments Act of 1995.

45. Section 105 and 106, Antiterrorism Act.

46. Stephen Labaton, "Justice Department to Ease Its Standards for Targeting Groups Preaching Violence," *New York Times*, May 4, 1995, p. B14.

47. William Safire, "Beware of Proactive," *New York Times*, May 8, 1995.

CHAPTER TEN: TAKING ON THE ETHICALLY CHALLENGED

1. David Johnston, "Perot Charges Led to FBI Sting at Bush Campaign, Officials Say," *New York Times*, October 27, 1992, p. 1; "The Federal Bureau of Temptation," *New York Times*, October 28, 1992, p. A 20; FBI Director William S. Sessions, "FBI Did What It Had to in Investigation," letter to the editor, *New York Times*, October 29, 1992, p. A26.

2. John T. Noonan, *Bribes: The Intellectual History of a Moral Idea* (Berkeley: California University Press, 1984), pp. 442–43.

3. Ibid., pp. 444–45.

4. Ibid., pp. 565–67.

5. Ibid., pp. 567–69.

6. "Former Truman Aid Found Guilty in Tax Case," *New York Times*, June 15, 1956, p. 1.

7. Robert J. Donovan, *Conflict and Crisis: The Presidency of Harry S. Truman, 1949–1953* (New York: W.W. Norton, 1977), pp. 372–81.

8. Report to Congress on the Activities and Operations of the Public Integrity Section, May 1, 1979, p. 1.

9. Annual Report of the Office of Professional Responsibility, 1976, p. 1.

10. Reports to Congress on the Activities and Operations of the Public Integrity Section, 1982 through 1991, U.S. Justice Department.

11. Letter from Stanley M. Brand to John Felde, general counsel, National Conference of State Legislators, February 19, 1991.

12. Arthur Maass, "U.S. Prosecution of State and Local Officials for Political Corruption: Is the Bureaucracy Out of Control in a High Stakes Operation Involving the Constitutional System?" *Publius, The Journal of Federalism*, Vol. 17 (Summer 1987):213–14.

13. The allegations regarding the Barbera case were described in a Memorandum and Opinion Order (84 Civ. 8624) signed by district court judge Shirley Wohl Kram on February 9, 1987.

14. Interview with the author, May 10, 1995.

15. *Barbera v. Smith*, 836 F2d 96, 2nd Cir. (1987).

16. Greg Rushford, "Watching the Watchdog: Veteran Justice Department Ethics Officer Faces Questions About His Own Actions," *Legal Times*, February 5, 1990, p. 1.

17. 1976 Annual Report, Office of Professional Responsibility, p. 2.

18. *United States v. Joseph Isgro*, No. CR89-951-JMI (transcript), December 6, 1993, pp. 7–10.

19. Letter from Attorney General Janet Reno to Jim McGee, *Washington Post*, December 13, 1993.

20. Henry Weinstein and Ronald J. Ostrow, "U.S. Prosecutor Gets Reprimand in Payola Case," *Los Angeles Times*, May 4, 1994, p. B1.

21. *Employee Misconduct: Justice Should Clearly Document Investigative Actions*, General Accounting Office, February 1992 (GGD-92-31), pp. 13–24.

22. *Federal Prosecutorial Authority in a Changing Legal Environment: More Attention Required*, Report by the House Government Operations Subcommittee on Government Information, Justice, Transportation, and Agriculture, Washington, D.C., November 27, 1990, p. 24.

23. Ibid., p. 25.

24. *Time*, October 24, 1988, p. 29.

25. Courtesy of Chris Blazakis.

26. Contemporaneous notes taken by Chris Blazakis.

27. *New Republic*, February 10, 1992, p. 12, and Chris Blazakis interview with the author.

28. Letter to M. Chris Blazakis from assistant attorney general Edward S. G. Dennis, Jr., Criminal Division, signed by John C. Keeney, acting assistant attorney general, March 28, 1989.

29. Letter to M. Chris Blazakis, from Stuart E. Schiffer, acting assistant attorney general, Civil Division, July 28, 1989.

30. Letter from Chris Blazakis to Michael E. Shaheen, Jr., Office of Professional Responsibility, August 7, 1989.

31. Memo to FBI director from Edward S. G. Dennis, Jr., assistant attorney general, December 15, 1989, subsequently obtained by Chris Blazakis as the result of a request under the Freedom of Information Act.

32. Letter to the author from Richard M. Rogers, Deputy Counsel, OPR, May 27, 1993.

33. Kenneth Culp Davis, *Discretionary Justice: A Preliminary Inquiry* (Urbana: University of Illinois Press, 1971), p. 167.

34. Ibid., pp. 189–90.

CHAPTER ELEVEN: THE CASE OF THE SLEEPING WATCHDOGS

1. Roscoe Pound, *Criminal Justice in America* (1930), p. 183.

2. Philip Gardner, "The Acquittal of Theodore V. Anzalone: Seeking a Balance Between Federal Law Enforcement Priorities and Civil Liberties Concerns in the Investigation of State and Local Political Corruption," a thesis for the degree with honors of Bachelor of Arts, Harvard College 1985, p. 135. Biographical sketch, Governor William F. Weld.

3. Jim McGee, "The Appearance of Justice," *Washington Post*, six-part series, January 10 to January 15, 1993; Alicia Mundy, "Covington Partner Played Insider Game to Help Robb," *Legal Times*, February 8, 1993; Jim Mulvaney, "In the Deep South, Rape Charges Unearth a System in Disarray," *Newsday*, April 25, 1994, p. A19.

4. Gardner, p. 92.

5. Fox Butterfield, "Ex-Boston Aide Indicted on Perjury Charges," *New York Times*, September 30, 1982, p. 28.

6. Interview with the author, July 5, 1994.

7. Raymond Bonner, "U.S. Judge Quashes Subpoenas to Reveal Times News Sources," *New York Times*, December 24, 1982, p. B5.

8. John Riley, "The Last Hurrah of Kevin White, How a U.S. Attorney Affected Boston's Political Process," *National Law Journal*, June 13, 1983, p. 1.

9. Joan Vennochi and Richard J. Connolly, "White Not Target of Probe, Weld Says," *Boston Globe*, March 7, 1984, p. 1.

10. Leslie Maitland, "High Officials Are Termed Subject of a Bribery Investigation by F.B.I.," *New York Times*, February 3, 1980, p. 1.

11. Final Report, Select Senate Committee to Study Undercover Activities of Components of the Justice Department, December 15, 1983, pp. 312–13.

12. "A Trial That Has Been, Well, Something of a Trial," *The New Yorker*, March 7, 1994, p. 30.

13. Scott M. Matheson, Jr., "The Prosecutor, the Press and Free Speech, *Fordham Law Review*, April 1990, p. 5.

14. Victor Navasky, *Kennedy Justice* (New York: Atheneum, 1971), p. 317.

15. Interview with the author, April 29, 1993. Wicker's recollection was confirmed by Clifton Daniel, at one point the paper's managing editor, in an interview on May 4, 1993.

16. Interview with the author, November 8, 1993.

17. Ben Bradlee, "Memorandum for Senator John F. Kennedy," May 9, 1959, Kennedy Library.

18. Ben Bradlee to Evelyn Lincoln, February 9, 1962, Kennedy Library.

19. Benjamin C. Bradlee, *Conversations with Kennedy* (New York: Pocket Books, 1976), p. 109.

20. "The Thunderbolt: Kennedy's Divorce Exposed," *Newsweek*, September 24, 1962, p. 86.

21. Bradlee, p. 126.

22. *Wood v. Georgia*, 370 U.S. 375 (1962) 344.

23. Fiscal year 1994 Hearings, House Appropriations Subcommittee on the Departments of Commerce, Justice, and State, the Judiciary and Related Agencies, Part 4, pp. 526–27, and Fiscal Year 1991 United States Attorneys' Statistical Report, p. 17.

24. Interview with the author, December 16, 1993.

25. Stuart Taylor, Jr., "Taking Issue: Enough of the Grand Jury Charade," *Legal Times*, May 18, 1992, p. 23.

26. William J. Campbell, "Eliminate the Grand Jury," *Journal of Criminal Law and Criminology*, Vol. 64, No. 2 (June 1973):178.

27. *United States v. John H. Williams, Jr.*, 112 S.Ct. 1735 (1992).

28. Kermit L. Hall, ed., *The Oxford Companion to the Supreme Court* (New York and Oxford: Oxford University Press, 1992), pp. 344–45.

29. *United States v. John H. Williams, Jr.*, 112 S.Ct 1735 (1992).

30. *Olmstead v. United States*, 277 U.S. 438 (1928) and *Katz v. United States*, 389 U.S. 347 (1967).

31. *Weeks v. United States*, 232 U.S. 383 (1914) and *Mapp v. Ohio*, 367 U.S. 643 (1961).

32. *McNabb v. United States*, 318 U.S. 332 (1943).

33. *United States v. Russell*, 411 U.S. 423 (1973).

34. Bennett L. Gershman, "The New Prosecutors," *University of Pittsburgh Law Review*, Vol. 53, No. 2 (Winter 1992):433.

35. Barry Tarlow, "The Supervisory Power to Dismiss: An Essential Solution to the Problem of Prosecutorial Misconduct," *California Association of Criminal Justice Forum*, Vol. 20, No. 4 (1993):18.

36. *Bivens v. Six Unknown Names Agents of the Federal Bureau of Narcotics*, 403 U.S. 338 (1971).

37. Ibid. and *Davis v. Passman*, 442 U.S. 228 (1979).

38. Office of Legal Policy, U.S. Department of Justice, Truth in Criminal Justice Series, Report No. 2, Report to the Attorney General on the Search and Seizure Exclusionary Rule (1986), reprinted in *University of Michigan Journal of Law Reform*, Vol. 22, No. 573 (1989):626–27.

39. Dissent to the 1928 decision where the Supreme Court ruled 5–4 that wiretapping was not unconstitutional. *Olmstead et al. v. United States,* 277 U.S. 438, 471; 48 S. Ct. 564.

40. Ramsey Clark, *Crime in America: Observation on Its Nature, Causes, Prevention and Control* (New York: Simon & Schuster, 1970), pp. 191–92.

41. Joseph R. Biden, Jr., "Balancing Law and Politics: Senate Oversight of the Attorney General Office," *The John Marshall Law Review,* Vol. 23, No. 2 (Winter 1990):151–63.

42. Hearings before the Select Senate Committee on Presidential Campaign Activities, Book 3, 93rd Congress, First Session, June 25 and 26, 1973.

43. Ibid., pp. iii–v.

44. Interview with the author, June 5, 1992.

45. Dan Thomasson, A Scripps Howard Special Report, "Team of FBI Agents Used by President Johnson as Political Operatives at the 1964 Democratic Convention," August 15, 1973.

46. Sanford J. Ungar, *FBI: An Uncensored Look Behind the Walls* (Boston and Toronto: Atlantic–Little, Brown, 1975), pp. 305–11.

47. Fred D. Thompson, *At That Point in Time: The Inside Story of the Senate Watergate Committee* (New York: Quadrangle/New York Times Book Co., 1975), pp. 128–32.

48. Senate Select Committee to Study Governmental Operations with Respect to Intelligence Activities, Final Report: Intelligence Activities and the Rights of Americans, Book II (Washington, D.C., 1976), p. 9.

49. Mary Devlin, American Bar Association Center for Professional Responsibility, interview with the author, August 15, 1994.

50. June 8, 1989, memorandum to all Justice Department litigators, "Communication with Persons Represented by Counsel," from Attorney General Richard Thornburgh.

51. Jerry E. Norton, "Ethics and the Attorney General," *Judicature,* December/January 1991.

52. Attorney General Janet Reno, Department of Justice, Final Rule, "Communications with Represented Persons," July 30, 1994.

53. August 5, 1994, letter from R. William Ide III, president, American Bar Association, to Janet Reno, attorney general of the United States.

EPILOGUE

1. John T. Elliff, *The Reform of FBI Intelligence Operations* (Princeton, N.J.: Princeton University Press, 1979), pp. 92–93.

2. Terry Eastland, *Ethics, Politics and the Independent Counsel: Executive Power, Executive Vice 1789–1989* (Washington, D.C.: National Legal Center for the Public Interest, 1989), p. 112.

3. Ibid., pp. 57–58.

4. *Cascade Natural Gas Company v. El Paso Natural Gas Corp.,* 386 U.S. 129, 87 S.Ct. 932, 1967.

5. *United States v. American Tel. and Tel. Co.,* 552 F. Supp. 131 (1982) p. 148.

6. June 30, 1992, letter to Representative Jack Brooks, chairman of the

House Judiciary Committee from W. Lee Rawls, assistant attorney general, enclosing FBI Report on Criminal Undercover Operations (UCOs) Statistics and a summary of certain sensitive "Closed" UCOs pursuant to Public Law 101–515, Fiscal Year 1991.

7. Vol. 2, Department of Justice, 1992 Congressional Authorization & Budget Submission, FBI Section, p. 85.

8. Final Report, Select Senate Committee to Study Law Enforcement Undercover Activities of Components of the Justice Department, 1982, p. 11.

9. Ibid., p. 57.

10. "FBI Undercover Operations," A Report of the House Judiciary Subcommittee on Civil and Constitutional Rights, April 1984, p. 83.

11. *United States v. United States District Court*, 407 U.S 297,317(1972).

12. Attorney General Edward H. Levi, August 13, 1975, address before the American Bar Association.

13. Interview with the author, December 4, 1994.

14. "The President, the Attorney General and the Department of Justice," a paper by Daniel J. Meador presented at a Conference at the White Burkett Miller Center of Public Affairs, University of Virginia, January 4–5, 1980.

15. Ibid., p. 57.

16. Ibid., p. 65.

17. Report, Watergate Special Prosecution Force, 1975, pp. 134–35.

Selected Bibliography

BOOKS

Baker, Nancy V. *Conflicting Loyalties: Law and Politics in the Attorney General's Office, 1789–1990*. Lawrence: University of Kansas Press, 1992.

Bates, Edward. *The Diary of Edward Bates 1859–1866*, ed. Howard K. Beale. 1930. Reprint. New York: Da Capo Press, Inc., 1970.

Bell, Griffin B., with Ronald J. Ostrow. *Taking Care of the Law*. New York: William Morrow and Company, Inc., 1982.

Biddle, Francis. *In Brief Authority*. Garden City, N.Y.: Doubleday & Company, 1962.

Biderman, A. D. and J. P. Lynch. *Understanding Crime Incidence Statistics: Why the UCR Diverges from the NCS*. New York: Springer-Verlag, 1991.

Blank, Blance Davis. *The Not So Grand Jury*. Lanham, Md.: University Press of America, 1993.

Blum, Howard. *Gangland: How the FBI Broke the Mob*. New York: Simon & Schuster, 1993.

Bradlee, Benjamin C. *Conversations with Kennedy*. New York: Pocket Books, 1976.

Branch, Taylor. *Parting the Waters: America in the King Years 1954–63*. New York: Simon & Schuster, 1988.

Brown, Michael. *Laying Waste: The Poisoning of America by Toxic Chemicals*. New York: Pantheon Books, 1980.

Brownell, Herbert, with John P. Burke. *Advising Ike: The Memoirs of Attorney General Herbert Brownell*. Lawrence: University Press of Kansas, 1993.

Calhoun, Frederick S. *The Lawmen: United States Marshals and Their Deputies, 1789–1989*. New York: Penguin Group, 1991.

Caplan, Lincoln. *The Tenth Justice: The Solicitor General and the Rule of Law*. New York: Vintage Books, 1988.

Caute, David. *The Great Fear: The Anti-Communist Purge Under Truman and Eisenhower*. New York: Simon & Schuster, 1978.

Charnes, Alexander. *Cloak and Gavel: FBI Wiretaps, Bugs, Informers and the Supreme Court*. Urbana and Chicago: University of Illinois Press, 1992.

Choate, Pat. *Agents of Influence: How Japan's Lobbyists in the United States Manipulate America's Political and Economic System*. New York: Alfred A. Knopf, 1990.

Clark, Ramsey. *Crime in America: Observations on Its Nature, Causes, Prevention and Control*. New York: Simon & Schuster, 1970.

Clinard, Marshall B. *Illegal Corporate Behavior*. Washington, D.C.: National Institute of Law Enforcement and Criminal Justice, 1979.

Coben, Stanley. *A. Mitchell Palmer: Politician*. New York: Columbia University Press, 1963.

Cole, Wayne S. *Charles A. Lindbergh and the Battle Against American Intervention in World War II*. New York: Harcourt Brace Jovanovich, 1972.

Crewdson, John. *The Tarnished Door: The New Immigrants and the Transformation of America*. New York: Times Books, 1983.

Cummings, Homer, and Carl McFarland. *Federal Justice, Chapters in the History of Justice and the Federal Executive*. New York: Macmillan Company, 1937.

Davis, Kenneth Culp. *Discretionary Justice: A Preliminary Inquiry*. 1969. Reprint. Urbana: University of Illinois Press, 1971.

Dewey, Donald. *The Antitrust Experiment in America*. New York: Columbia University Press, 1990.

Donner, Frank J. *The Age of Surveillance*. New York: Alfred A. Knopf, 1982.

Donovan, Robert J. *Conflict and Crisis: The Presidency of Harry Truman, 1949–1953*. New York: W.W. Norton, 1977.

Drugs, Crime and the Justice System. Washington, D.C.: Bureau of Justice Statistics, U.S. Department of Justice, 1992.

Dycus, Stephen; Arthur L. Berney; William C. Banks; and Peter Raven-Hansen. *National Security Law*. Boston: Little, Brown and Company, 1990.

Eastland, Terry. *Ethics, Politics and the Independent Counsel: Executive Power, Executive Vice 1789–1989.* Washington, D.C.: National Legal Center for the Public Interest, 1989.

Edelhertz, Herbert. *Nature, Impact and Prosecution of White Collar Crime.* Washington, D.C.: National Institute of Law Enforcement and Criminal Justice, U.S. Department of Justice, May 1970.

Eisenstein, James. *Counsel for the United States.* Baltimore: The John Hopkins University Press, 1978.

Elliff, John T. *The Reform of FBI Intelligence Operations.* Princeton, N.J.: Princeton University Press, 1979.

———. *The United States Department of Justice and Individual Rights, 1937–1962.* New York: Garland Publishing Company, 1987.

Falco, Mathea. *The Making of a Drug-Free America.* New York: Times Books, 1992.

Felsenthal, Carol. *Power, Privilege and The Post: The Katherine Graham Story.* New York: G.P. Putnam's Sons, 1993.

Felt, W. Mark. *The FBI Pyramid from the Inside.* New York: G.P. Putnam's Sons, 1979.

Foerstel, Herbert N. *Surveillance in the Stacks: The FBI's Library Awareness Program.* New York: Greenwood Press, 1991.

Fox, Stephen. *Blood and Power: Organized Crime in the Twentieth Century.* New York: William Morrow and Company, 1989.

Frankfurter, Felix. *The Case of Sacco and Vanzetti.* New York: Universal Library Edition, 1962.

Friedman, Alan. *Spider's Web: The Secret History of How the White House Illegally Armed Iraq.* New York: Bantam Books, 1993.

Gelbspan, Ross. *Break-ins, Death Threats and the FBI: The Covert War Against the Central American Movement.* Boston: South End Press, 1991.

Geller, William A., and Michael S. Scott. *Deadly Force: What We Know.* Washington, D.C.: Police Executive Research Forum, 1992.

Gershman, Bennett L. *Prosecutorial Misconduct.* New York: Clark Boardman Company, Ltd., 1990.

Giglio, James N. *H.M. Daugherty and the Politics of Expediency.* Kent, Ohio: Kent State University Press, 1978.

Goldman, Eric F. *Rendezvous with Destiny.* New York: Alfred A. Knopf, 1953.

Heymann, Philip B. *The Politics of Public Management.* New Haven: Yale University Press, 1987.

Hills, Stuart L., ed. *Corporate Violence: Injury and Death for Profit.* Savage, Md.: Rowman & Littlefield Publishers, Inc., 1987.

Holinger, Paul C. *Violent Deaths: An Epidemiologic Study of Suicide, Homicide, and Accidents.* New York: The Guilford Press, 1987.

Huston, Luther A. *The Department of Justice.* New York: Frederick A. Praeger, 1967.

Hyde, Henry J. *Forfeiting Our Property Rights: Is Your Property Safe from Seizure?* Washington, D.C.: Cato Institute, 1995.

Hyneman, Charles S., and George W. Carey, eds. *A Second Federalist: Congress Creates a Government.* Columbia, S.C.: University of California Press, 1967.

Kall, Kermit L. *The Oxford Companion to the Supreme Court of the United States.* New York and Oxford: Oxford University Press, 1992.

Keller, William C. *The Liberals and J. Edgar Hoover.* Princeton, N.J.: Princeton University Press, 1989.

Kessler, Ronald. *The FBI: Inside the World's Most Powerful Law Enforcement Agency.* New York: Pocket Books, 1993.

Kleiman, Mark R. *Against Excess: Drug Policy for Results.* New York: Basic Books, 1993.

Kornbluh, Peter, and Malcolm Byrne, eds. *The Iran-Contra Scandal: The Declassified History.* New York: The New Press, 1993.

Krock, Arthur. *Memoirs: Sixty Years on the Firing Line.* New York: Funk & Wagnalls, 1968.

Kutler, Stanley I. *The Wars of Watergate: The Last Crisis of Richard Nixon.* New York: W.W. Norton, 1990.

LaFave, Wayne R., and Jerold H. Israel. *Criminal Procedure.* St. Paul, Minn.: West Publishing Company, 1992.

Lasky, Victor. *It Didn't Start with Watergate.* New York: Dial Press, 1977.

Levine, Michael. *Deep Cover: The Inside Story of How DEA Infighting, Incompetence and Subterfuge Lost Us the Biggest Battle of the Drug War.* New York: Delacorte Press, 1990.

Lukas, J. Anthony. *Nightmare: The Underside of the Nixon Years.* New York: The Viking Press, 1976.

May, Christopher N. *In the Name of War: Judicial Review and the War Powers Since 1918.* Cambridge, Mass.: Harvard University Press, 1989.

McNamara, Joseph Donald. "Organizational Decision Making and Public Policy, An Analysis of Police Drug Enforcement Strategy." Diss. Harvard University, 1973.

Meader, Daniel J. *The President, the Attorney General and the Department of Justice.* Charlottesville: University of Virginia Press, 1980.

Meese, Edwin, III. *With Reagan: The Inside Story.* Washington, D.C.: Regnery Gateway, 1992.

Michalowski, Raymond J. *Order, Law, and Crime: An Introduction to Criminology.* New York: Random House, 1985.

Miller, John C. *Crisis in Freedom: The Alien and Sedition Acts.* Boston: Atlantic–Little, Brown, 1951.

Mintz, Morton. *At Any Cost: Corporate Greed, Women, and the Dalkon Shield.* New York: Pantheon Books, 1985.

Mintz, Morton, and Jerry S. Cohen. *America, Inc.: Who Owns and Operates the United States.* New York: Dell Publishing Co., 1971.

Morris, Roger. *Richard Nixon: The Rise of an American Politician.* New York: Henry Holt and Company, 1990.

National Drug Control Strategy: Reclaiming Our Communities from Drugs and Violence. Washington, D.C.: The White House, February 1994.

National Drug Control Strategy: Budget Summary. Washington, D.C.: The White House, February 1994.

Navasky, Victor S. *Kennedy Justice.* New York: Atheneum, 1971.

Neff, James. *Mobbed Up: Jackie Presser's High-Wire Life in the Teamsters, the Mafia, and the FBI.* New York: Dell Publishing, 1989.

Pizzo, Stephen; Mary Fricker; and Paul Muolo. *Inside Job: The Looting of*

America's Savings and Loans. New York: HarperCollins Publishers, 1991.

Reagan, Nancy, with William Novak. *My Turn: The Memoirs of Nancy Reagan*. New York: Random House, 1989.

Reiman, Jeffrey H. *The Rich Get Richer and the Poor Get Prison: Idealogy, Class, and Criminal Justice*. New York: John Wiley & Sons, 1984.

Reiss, Albert J., Jr., and Jeffrey A. Roth, ed. *Understanding and Preventing Violence*. Washington, D.C.: National Academy Press (National Research Council), 1993.

Reminiscences of Herbert Brownell. Oral History Collection, Columbia University, New York.

Reminiscences of Herbert Wechsler. Oral History Collection, Columbia University, New York.

Reminiscences of Robert A. Jackson. Oral History Collection, Columbia University, New York.

Reminiscences of Thurgood Marshall. Oral History Collection, Columbia University, New York, 1977.

Report of the Special Committee on the Federal Loyalty-Security Program of the Association of the Bar of the City of New York. New York: Dodd, Mead & Company, 1956.

Robbins, Natalie. *Alien Ink: The FBI's War on Freedom of Expression*. New York: William Morrow and Company, 1992.

Rowan, Carl T. *Dream Makers, Dream Breakers: The World of Justice Thurgood Marshall*. Boston: Little, Brown and Company, 1993.

Rydell, C. Peter, and Susan S. Everingham. *Controlling Cocaine: Supply Versus Demand Program*. Santa Monica, Calif.: Rand, 1994.

Schaeffer, Ronald. *America in the Great War: The Rise of the War Welfare State*. New York: Oxford University Press, 1991.

Shannon, Elaine. *Desperados: Latin Drug Lords, U.S. Lawmen, and the War America Can't Win*. New York: Viking Penguin, 1988.

Shannon, William V. *The Heir Apparent: Robert Kennedy and the Struggle for Power*. New York: The Macmillan Company, 1967.

Smith, James Morton. *Freedom's Fetters: The Alien and Sedition Laws and American Civil Liberties*. Ithaca, N.Y.: Cornell University Press, 1956.

Smith, Jean Edward. *George Bush's War*. New York: Henry Holt, 1992.

Smith, William French. *Law & Justice in the Reagan Administration*. Stanford, Calif.: Hoover Institution Press, 1991.

Stewart, James B. *The Partners: Inside America's Most Powerful Law Firms*. New York: Simon & Schuster, 1983.

———. *The Prosecutors: Inside the Offices of the Government's Most Powerful Lawyers*. New York: Simon & Schuster, 1987.

Storey, Moorfield, and Edward W. Emerson. *Ebenezer Rockwood Hoar: A Memoir*. Boston: Houghton Mifflin Company, 1911.

Sullivan, William, with Bill Brown. *The Bureau: My Thirty Years in Hoover's FBI*. New York: W.W. Norton, 1979.

Summers, Anthony. *Official and Confidential: The Secret Life of J. Edgar Hoover*. New York: G.P. Putnam's Sons, 1993.

Sutherland, Edwin H. *White Collar Crime: The Uncut Version*. New Haven: Yale University Press, 1983.

Theoharis, Athan G. *From the Secret Files of J. Edgar Hoover*. Chicago: Ivan R. Dee, 1991.

Theoharis, Athan G., and John Stuart Cox. *The Boss: J. Edgar Hoover and the Great American Inquisition*. Philadelphia: Temple University Press, 1988.

Thompson, Fred D. *At That Point in Time: The Inside Story of the Senate Watergate Committee*. New York: Quadrangle/New York Times Book Co., 1975.

Tolchin, Martin, and Susan Tolchin. *To the Victor: Political Patronage from the Clubhouse to the White House*. New York: Random House, 1971.

Tonry, Michael. *Malign Neglect: Race, Crime and Punishment in America*. New York: Oxford University Press, 1995.

Toobin, Jeffrey. *Opening Arguments: A Young Lawyer's First Case: United States v. Oliver North*. New York: Viking, 1991.

Ungar, Sanford J. *FBI*. Boston and Toronto: Atlantic–Little, Brown, 1976.

JOURNAL ARTICLES

"A Decade of Sentencing Guidelines: Revisiting the Role of the Legislature," *Wake Forest Law Review*, Vol. 28, No. 2, Summer 1993.

"Attorney General Guidelines for FBI Investigations," John T. Elliff, *Cornell Law Review*, Vol. 69, April 1984.

"Comments and Caveats on the Wire Tapping Controversy," Richard C. Donnelly, *Yale Law Journal*, Vol. 76, No. 799, 1954.

"Constitutional Confrontations: Preserving a Prompt and Orderly Means by which Congress May Enforce Investigative Demands Against Executive Branch Officials," Stanley M. Brand and Sean Connelly, *Catholic University Law Review*, Vol. 36, Fall 1986.

"Crackdown: The Emerging 'Drug Exception' to the Bill of Rights," Steven Wisotsky, *Hastings Law Journal*, Vol. 38, July 1987.

"Early Role of the Attorney General in Our Constitutional Scheme: In the Beginning There Was Pragmatism," Susan Low Bloch, *Duke Law Journal*, Vol. 3, 1989.

"Eliminate the Grand Jury," William J. Campbell, *Journal of Criminal Law & Criminology*, Vol. 64, No. 2, June 1973.

"FBI and Dissidents: A First Amendment Analysis of Attorney General Smith's 1983 Guidelines on Domestic Security Investigations," Mitchell S. Rubin, *Arizona Law Review*, Vol. 27, 1988.

"FBI Surveillance: Past and Present," Athan G. Theoharis, *Cornell Law Journal*, Vol. 69, April 1984.

"Federal Antitrust Enforcement in the Reagan Administration: Two Cheers for the Disappearance of the Large Firm Defendant in Nonmerger Cases," William E. Kovacic, *Research in Law and Economics*, Vol. 12, 1989.

" 'Garbage In, Gospel Out': Criminal Discovery, Computer Reliability, and the Constitution," Robert Garcia, *UCLA Law Review*, Vol. 38, No. 5, 1991.

"Good and Bad Trust Dichotomy: A Short History of a Legal Idea," Eleanor M. Fox and Lawrence Sullivan, *Antitrust Bulletin*, Spring 1990.

"Good Government by Prosecutorial Decree: The Use and Abuse of Mail Fraud," Gregory Howard Williams, *Arizona Law Review*, Vol. 32, 1990.

"Industrial Resistance to Occupational Safety and Health Administration, 1971–1981," Andrew Szasz, *Social Problems, Journal for the Study of Social Problems*, Vol. 32, No. 2, December 1984.

"Justice Department and the Antitrust Laws: Law Enforcer or Regulator," Thomas E. Kauper, *Antitrust Bulletin*, Spring 1990.

"Law and the National Security Decision-Making Process in the Reagan Administration," Richard K. Willard, Symposium on Legal and Policy Issues in the Iran-Contra Affair: Intelligence Oversight in a Democracy, *Houston Journal of International Law*, Vol. 11, Fall 1988.

"Making Rationality Relevant—The American Society of Criminology 1992 Presidential Address," Alfred Blumstein, *Criminology*, Vol. 31, No. 1, 1993.

"New Seditious Libel," Judith Schenck Koffler and Bennett L. Gershman, *Cornell Law Review*, Vol. 69, April 1984.

"No Soul to Damn: No Body to Kick: An Unscandalized Inquiry into the Problem of Corporate Punishment," John C. Coffee, Jr., *Michigan Law Review*, Vol. 79, No. 3, January 1981.

"Not Thinking Like a Lawyer: The Case of Drugs in the Courts," Steven Wisotsky, *Notre Dame Journal of Law, Ethics and Public Policy*, Vol. 5, 1991.

"Political Content of Antitrust," Robert Pitofsky, *University of Pennsylvania Law Review*, Vol. 127, April 1979.

"Renaissance of Antitrust," Robert Pitofsky, 1990 Handler Lecture, Association of the Bar of the City of New York, 1990.

"Review of *The Reform of FBI Intelligence Operations*, by John T. Elliff," Morton H. Halperin, *University of Chicago Law School*, Vol. 47, Spring 1980.

"The Case for Wire Tapping," William P. Rogers, *Yale Law Journal*, Vol. 63, No. 792, 1954.

"The Political Career of A. Mitchell Palmer," Donald Johnson, *Pennsylvania History*, Vol. 25, No. 4, October 1958.

"The Public Security and Wire Tapping," Herbert Brownell, Jr., *Cornell Law Quarterly*, Vol. 39, No. 2, Winter 1956.

"The Recognition and Control of Occupational Disease," Philip J. Landrigan, M.D., M.Sc., and Dean B. Baker, M.D., M.Ph., *Journal of the American Medical Association*, Vol. 266, No. 5, August 7, 1991.

"The Wire-Tapping Problem: An Analysis and a Legislative Proposal," *Columbia Law Review*, Vol. 52, No. 2, February 1952.

"Two Models of Congressional Oversight," John T. Elliff, Symposium on Legal and Policy Issues in the Iran-Contra Affair: Intelligence Oversight in a Democracy, *Houston Journal of Internal Law*, Vol. 11, Fall 1988.

"U.S. Prosecution of State and Local Officials for Political Corruption: Is the Bureaucracy Out of Control in a High-Stakes Operation Involving the Constitutional System?" Arthur Maass, *Publius, The Journal of Federalism*, Vol. 17, 1987.

"Youth Violence, Guns and the Illicit-Drug Industry," Alfred Blumstein, H. John Heinz III School of Public Policy and Management, Carnegie-Mellon University, Working Paper Series, July 1994.

CONGRESSIONAL PUBLICATIONS

House of Representatives

Hearings, May 10, 1990, Exercise of Federal Prosecutorial Authority in a Changing Legal Environment, House Government Operations Subcommittee on Information, Justice, Transportation, and Agriculture.

Hearings, June 20 and July 13, 1988, FBI Counterintelligence Visits to Libraries, Judiciary Subcommittee on Civil and Constitutional Rights.

Hearings, February 27, 28, March 9, 22, April 5 and May 18, 1989, FBI Oversight and Authorization Request for Fiscal Year 1990, Judiciary Subcommittee on Civil and Constitutional Rights.

Hearings, February 4, March 2, April 1, 22, 29, June 2, 3, 9, July 22 and November 23, 1982, FBI Undercover Operations, Judiciary Subcommittee on Civil and Constitutional Rights.

Hearings, March 14 and 15, Federal Efforts to Combat Fraud, Abuse, and Misconduct in the Nation's S&L's and Banks and Civil Enforcement Provisions of FIRREA, Government Operations Subcommittee on Commerce, Consumer, and Monetary Affairs.

Hearings, July 30 and October 28, 1987, Securities Law Enforcement and Defense Contractors, Energy and Commerce Oversight Subcommittee and Judiciary Criminal Justice Subcommittee.

Report, Consent Decree Program of the Department of Justice, Judiciary Subcommittee on Antitrust, January 1959.

Report, FBI Undercover Operations, Judiciary Subcommittee on Civil and Constitutional Rights, April 1984.

Report, Federal Prosecutorial Authority in a Changing Legal Environment: More Attention Required, Government Operations Subcommittee on Information, Justice, Transportation, and Agriculture, November 1990.

Report, U.S. Government's War Against Fraud, Abuse and Misconduct in Financial Institutions: Winning Some Battles But Losing the War, Government Operations Subcommittee on Commerce, Consumer, and Monetary Affairs, November 1990.

United States Senate

Hearings, March 13, 1963, Failing Newspaper Act, Judiciary Subcommittee on Antitrust and Monopoly, including excerpts from the hearings on March 13, 14 and 15 and April 9, 1963, on Concentration of Ownership in News Media by the House Antitrust Subcommittee.

Hearings, March 13, 19, 20 and May 6, 1986, Nomination of Jefferson B. Sessions II of Alabama to be U.S. District Judge for the Southern District of Alabama, Judiciary Committee.

Hearings, February 2, 1988, Performance of the Reagan Administration in Nominating Women and Minorities to the Federal Bench, Judiciary Committee.

Report, Alleged Assassination Plots Involving Foreign Leaders, Select Committee to Study Governmental Operations with Respect to Intelligence Activities, 1975.

Report, Drugs, Law Enforcement and Foreign Policy, Foreign Relations Subcommittee on Terrorism, Narcotics and International Operations, December 1988.

Report, Final Report, Select Committee to Study Undercover Activities of Components of the Department of Justice, 1983.

Report, Investigation of the Assassination of President John F. Kennedy: Performance of the Intelligence Agencies, Select Committee to Study Governmental Operations with Respect to Intelligence Activities, 1976.

Joint Committees

Report, The Iran-Contra Affair, by the U.S. House of Representatives Select Committee to Investigate Covert Arms Transactions with Iran and the U.S. Senate Select Committee on Secret Military Assistance to Iran and the Nicaraguan Opposition, Washington, D.C., November 13, 1987.

GENERAL ACCOUNTING OFFICE

"Bank and Thrift Criminal Fraud: The Federal Commitment Could Be Broadened," GAO, Washington, D.C., January 1993 (GGD-93-48).

"Gains Made in Controlling Illegal Drugs, Yet Drug Trade Flourishes," GAO, Washington, D.C., October 1979 (GGD-8-4).

"Greater Oversight and Uniformity Needed in U.S. Attorneys' Prosecutive Policies," GAO, Washington, D.C., 1982 (GGD-83-11).

"Justice Department: Improved Management Processes Would Enhance Justice's Operations," GAO, Washington, D.C., March 1986 (GGD86-12).

"U.S. Attorneys Do Not Prosecute Many Suspected Violators of Federal Laws," GAO, Washington, D.C., February 27, 1978 (GGD-77-68).

OTHER MATERIAL

"Fatal Injuries to Workers in the United States, 1980–1989: A Decade of Surveillance," Centers for Disease Control, U.S. Department of Health and Human Services, August 1993.

Final Report of the Independent Counsel for Iran/Contra Matters, Lawrence E. Walsh, Washington, D.C. 1994.

Justice Department Report on Departmental Enforcement Policy of Dyer Act (Auto Theft) by Harry Subin, January 1965.

Report of Independent Counsel in Re Edwin Meese III, James C. McKay, Independent Counsel, July 5, 1988.

Results of Our Review of the Independent Counsel's Inquiry into Certain Activities of Attorney General Edwin Meese III, by Michael E. Shaheen, Jr., Counsel, Justice Department's Office of Professional Responsibility, October 28, 1988.

Special Report to Congress: Cocaine and Federal Sentencing Policy, United States Sentencing Commission, 2nd Draft, December 1994.

Technologies for Understanding and Preventing Substance Abuse and Addiction, Office of Technology Assessment, Congress of the United States, September 1994.

Watergate Special Prosecution Force Report, Washington, D.C., August 1975.

Index

health care fraud, 215–17
health and safety laws, enforcement of,
    33, 38–42
Hearst Corporation, 237, 238–39
Hellman, Martin, 146
Helms, Jesse, 196, 270
heroin, 182–83
    See also drug enforcement
Heymann, Philip B., 329–30
Hill, Eddie, 202
Hispanic Americans. *See* minority groups
Hoffman, Lance, 150
Hogue, Spencer, Jr., 255
homicide rates, 119–25
    for African Americans, 122–23
    for young men, 122–23
Hoover, J. Edgar
    anti-communism, 304–5
    and drug enforcement, 202
    efforts to enhance image of FBI, 87, 111
    and emergency detention program,
        15–16
    and General Intelligence Division, 298,
        300
    and Palmer raids, 298
    power of, 22
    racism of, 276, 277–79
    support for political use of FBI, 52
    suppression of dissent, 379
Houston, bank fraud in, 240–41
Howden, Jonathan R., 192
Howe, Louis, 273
Hughes, Tom, 175
Hunt, Harold Guy, 260–61
Hutton, E. F., 218
Hyde, Henry J., 189–90

IACP. *See* International Association of
    Chiefs of Police
Ide, R. William, III, 377
Ideman, James M., 334–35
immigration cases, prison sentences in, 37
Immigration and Naturalization Service
    (INS)
    Border Patrol, 101, 102
    budget, 30
    criticism of, 100–102
    errors in computer files, 101
    misconduct by agents, 102
    responsibilities, 100
Independent Counsel Act, 338
    See also special counsels
infant formula, 233–36
inflation, government efforts against,
    54–57
informants
    and corrupt police, 200–201
    FBI, 50, 174–75, 307–8
INS. *See* Immigration and Naturalization
    Service

Inter-Departmental Intelligence Unit
    (IDIU), 329
Internal Revenue Service (IRS)
    Arrington investigation, 252
    audit of Reagans, 340, 341, 342–43
    leaks from, 160
    misuse of information by employees,
        99–100
    politically motivated audits, 288
    tax fraud, 223
    union in, 22
    use of consumer databases, 164–65
Internal Security Act of 1950, 15–16
International Association of Chiefs of
    Police (IACP), 110–11
Iran-contra affair, 17–18
IRS. *See* Internal Revenue Service
ITT lobbying scandal, 222, 380

Jackson, Andrew, 320
Jackson, Robert H., 20, 23–24
Jefferson, Thomas, 19, 291, 292
Jenkins, Thomas, 276–77
Jenkins, Walter, 48, 50
Johns-Manville Company, 39–40
Johnson, Lyndon B., use of FBI for politi-
    cal purposes, 48–53, 305, 374–75
Jones, Willie, 188–89
journalists. *See* press
JPM Industries, Inc., 187
judges
    corrupt, 321, 328
    and grand juries, 359
    political appointments, 275
    with segregationist views, 274–75
    supervision of prosecutors, 365–67
Justice Department. *See* Department of
    Justice

Kappel, F. R., 227
Kastenmeier, Robert, 75–76
Katzenbach, Nicholas, 308
Keeney, John C., 341
Kelleher, George E., 297
Kelley, Harry, 372, 373
Kennedy, John F., 19, 273–75, 305,
    356–58, 375
Kennedy, Robert F.
    and Anthony Lewis, 353–56
    as attorney general, 19, 375
    and Castro assassination attempts, 16
    civil rights enforcement, 281
    and COINTELPROs, 308
    and federal judges, 274
    and newspaper antitrust cases, 238–39
    organized crime enforcement, 58–59,
        275, 357–58
    use of polls, 21–22
Kennedy, Roderick, 174–76
Kennedy administration